For David and Carson

Preface to the Second Edition

Welcome to the second edition of *Intercultural Communication in the Global Workplace.* We appreciate the reception of the first edition, particularly the many comments and suggestions users gave us. The second edition has benefited from the incorporation of many of these comments, and we are confident that this book presents a valuable tool in your teaching and research. Finally, we are very grateful to readers for making this book a bestseller among intercultural business communication textbooks.

Globalization and the effects of culture on human behavior are constantly in the news today. The New Economy is active across national and ethnic boundaries in ways we did not begin to anticipate a mere five years ago. Dramatic changes in technology, such as the growth of the Internet and the adoption around the planet of satellite and cellular telephony, make international communication even more commonplace today. Businesses need intercultural communication skills even more than they did when this book was first written. The second edition of *Intercultural Communication in the Global Workplace* has updated discussions of knowledge management, globalization, and technology in business communication today.

What else is new? This second edition also addresses an issue that is ever more present in the increased volume of intercultural interactions today: ethics. Readers will find a new discussion in Chapter 7 of ethical issues across cultures. The discussion of world religions in Chapter 3 has been expanded also. In Chapter 1, brief summaries of intercultural theory help focus the approach of this book, which is understanding cultures through values orientations.

We have added more short cases. Readers will see introductory vignettes to each chapter to illustrate the issues covered in the chapter. Chapter summaries are in bullet outlines, to give succinct overviews of the chapters' contents. New illustrations and examples have been added, often drawn from cultures not mentioned in the first edition. Specific sample communications have been added to Chapters 5 and 10. Finally, the entire book has been improved with more discussions.

Users of the first edition will also notice a difference in appearance of this edition: The text that illustrates chapter key points is printed against a screened background for more emphasis. Key words have been boldfaced and a few new exhibits have been added.

These changes reflect our commitment to offer an accessible source for readers looking for a conceptual basis with practical applications to help readers develop intercultural communication awareness, knowledge, and skills. Books on international business mention the need for intercultural communication skills but tend to emphasize functional areas—

finance, marketing, and management—and to eschew skills development. Training programs tend to favor do's and taboos of international interaction—don't cross your legs and be sure to accept that cup of tea—without an underlying conceptual basis that enables people to interact effectively when they are outside the scripted list of rules. In spite of the numbers of businesspeople who need intercultural business communication skills, few sources exist for a systematic development of competence. This book fills this void.

As in the first edition, this second edition of *Intercultural Communication in the Global Workplace* provides examples of the implications of cultural values for business communication. We explore the relationships among the cultural environment of the firm, the structure of the firm, and appropriate ways to communicate within and from/to firms. Throughout the discussions about specific communication tasks, we concentrate on the underlying cultural reasons for behavior. We confidently believe that this approach, as we asserted in the first edition, will help the reader develop an ability to work successfully within an environment of cultural diversity, both at home and abroad.

We have continued to strive to avoid specific cultural viewpoints in this book, but have come to realize since the first edition that total cultural neutrality is not possible. Nor is it ultimately desirable; every human has some cultural filters through which she or he views the world. Nevertheless, the framework we develop here applies to all readers regardless of their own native cultures. This book is for anyone from anywhere around the globe who wants to develop and improve intercultural business communication skills. Intercultural business communication is an exciting field, and we are proud to be able to contribute to a broader understanding of it.

Acknowledgements

Intercultural Communication in the Global Workplace is the result of many years of work. While this book is based to a great extent on our professional research and our personal experiences, we also want to acknowledge the suggestions and advice we have received from our families, friends, clients, colleagues, and students. We are particularly indebted to the users of the first edition for giving us valuable feedback. Many people were generous in sharing information with us, and we are grateful for their support.

We give special thanks to the reviewers who carefully read the first edition and offered their insights and suggestions.

Gina Poncini—University of Lugano, Italy
Martha Blalock—University of Wisconsin–Madison
Zhu Yunxia—UNITEC Institute of Technology, New Zealand
Janet Heyneman—University of Rochester
Allyson D. Adrian—Georgetown University
Deborah Valentine—Emory University

Last, but not least, we thank the people at Irwin: Craig Beytien for supporting the second edition; Andy Winston the sponsoring editor, Sara Strand, the editorial coordinator, and Craig Leonard, the project manager. Their work and support made this edition possible.

About the Authors

Linda Beamer is a full professor in the Department of Marketing at California State University, Los Angeles, where in addition to marketing courses she teaches business communication, intercultural communication, diversity in the workplace, and courses in high-performance management and international business in the MBA core.

She has taught and consulted in Britain, Canada, the Middle East, China, Argentina, Hong Kong, and New Zealand In addition, she and her husband spend as much time as possible in their house in central Mexico.

Her BA is from the College of Wooster, in Ohio (with one year in Scotland at Edinburgh University), and her MA and PhD are from the University of Toronto. The latter led to dual US–Canadian citizenship. Her research, resulting in about two dozen publications, has focused primarily on the effect of culture on communication, with special interest in Chinese communication issues. She serves on the Editorial Board of the *Business Communication Quarterly,* and is Associate Editor of the *Journal of Business Communication.* She served as chair of the Intercultural Committee of the Association for Business Communication for three years and as a member of the Board of Directors for five years. She was voted a Fellow of the International Academy of Intercultural Research at its inception, and is a member of the International Communication Association and the Association for International Business.

Beamer is the recipient of two two-year grants from the Department of Education's program for Business and International Education, as well as a research grant from the C.R. Anderson Foundation. She was honored to receive the outstanding publication award (1995) from the Association for Business Communication, and a three-year Adjunct Professor appointment at UNITEC, Auckland, New Zealand.

Iris I. Varner is a professor in the Department of Management and Quantitative Methods, College of Business at Illinois State University, where she teaches the cultural environment of international business, international management, and managerial communication both at the undergraduate and graduate level. Her PhD, MBA, and MA are from the University of Oklahoma. She has the Staatsexamen and Assessorenexamen from the Albert-Ludwigs-Universität, Freiburg, Germany.

Varner has extensive international experience. She grew up in former East Germany, studied in Germany, France, Great Britain, the United States, and Taiwan. She has given seminars and lectures around the globe, including New Zealand, Russia, France, Belgium, Japan, and Germany, and has spent time in many other countries.

Varner is the author of numerous articles in the area of intercultural managerial communication. She is the author of *Contemporary Business Report Writing,* published by the

Dryden Press, and has presented her research at regional, national, and international conventions. She has been honored with the Outstanding Membership Award and the Meada Gibbs Outstanding Teaching Award of the Association for Business Communication. She was named a Caterpillar Scholar and a State Farm Fellow by Illinois State University.

Varner is president of the Association for Business Communication, where she has been a member since 1976. She was chair of the Ethics Committee and an active member of the International Committee. She is a member of the Academy of Management and the Academy for Human Resource Development. She serves as a reviewer for a number of scholarly publications and consults for a variety of national and international firms.

The Need for Intercultural Business Communication Competence

What does culture have to do with business? Many business majors and practitioners immersed in questions of financial forecasting, market studies, and management models have turned aside from the question of culture and how it affects business. Unlike the hard data from measurable issues, culture is soft and slippery; you can't really grasp culture in your two hands and understand what you've got.

But more and more organizations are finding themselves involved in communication across cultures, between cultures, among cultures—because they are doing business in foreign countries, perhaps, or because they are sourcing from another country, seeking financing from another country, or have an increasingly multicultural workforce.

In the United States, for example, the percentages of Latinos from Mexico and Central and South America and Asians from Southeast Asia, China, India, and Pakistan, are growing. In Europe, the composition of the population is changing as more and more people immigrate from Africa, Asia, and the Middle East. In the Middle East, many workers come from India, the Philippines, and Southeast Asia.

As a result of these migrations, people from diverse backgrounds and different languages are working side by side in many countries. Intercultural communication at work is not the goal of some distant future; it is a real need here and now, and this book addresses that need.

Business communication *is* intercultural communication. In order to communicate with another culture, you have to come to terms with it somehow. You need to understand it. This book offers an approach to unfamiliar cultures that makes understanding easier and consequently makes business communication with them more effective. This book is based on the idea that intercultural business communication skills can be learned.

At its lowest level, business communication with unfamiliar cultures means simply finding a translator for conducting discussions in a foreign language. However, as more and more corporations are finding out, communication is about meanings and not just words.

In order to understand the significance of a message from someone, you need to understand the way that person looks at the world, and the values that weigh heavily in that person's cultural backpack. You need to understand the meanings that are not put into words, the importance of the words that are used, and the way the message is organized and transmitted. You also need to know what to expect when that other person engages in a particular communication behavior such as making a decision known, or negotiating a sales agreement, or writing a legal document such as a contract. And you'd be wise to know something about the organization that person works in and how its structure affects communication.

In applying intercultural communication skills to practical business concerns, this book makes an important contribution. Most books about doing business with people from other cultures come from one of two areas: intercultural communication and its near relative intercultural training, or international business. Intercultural communication is grounded in a body of theory, but has little application to business communication. Intercultural training draws from psychology and related fields and specializes in preparing people for sojourns in foreign countries for development work, such as for the Peace Corps for instance, for studying abroad, or for working for an employer in an expatriate posting. This particular training also has little application to business communication.

Books on international business, on the other hand, concentrate on business functions such as finance, management, marketing, shipping and insurance, and accounting. They tend to ignore the importance of the all-encompassing communication tasks and the skills necessary to complete them successfully. They also tend to ignore the different priorities in other cultures that affect the act of communication and its outcomes.

This book connects business communication and understanding of cultural priorities with actual business practices. Of course, business practices themselves, as this book points out, are culturally based.

In combining intercultural communication skills with business, this book helps you become a successful communicator in culturally diverse environments both at home and abroad. As more and more firms are finding out, effective intercultural communication is crucial for success, domestically and internationally.

INTERCULTURAL BUSINESS COMMUNICATION COMPETENCE AND GROWING DOMESTIC DIVERSITY

All over the world nations are trying to come to terms with the growing diversity of their populations. Reactions range from acceptance to mere tolerance to rejection. As migrations of workers and of refugees have increased globally, some countries are trying to control diversity by establishing strict guidelines for immigration from other countries. Other countries are attempting to develop government policies concerning the rights of immigrants to preserve their own cultures in adopted homelands. Canada is an example of a country where federal and provincial governments have Ministers of Multiculturalism to protect the cultural "mosaic" pattern that immigrants bring to Canada.

The United States historically afforded a home to more people of diverse cultures than any other country. But even in the United States, with its ideals of equality and tolerance, the advantages and disadvantages of acknowledging diversity are hotly debated. Recently some social critics in the United States have voiced opposition to measures that preserve immigrants' cultural differences. They say the insistence on diversity actually *separates* Americans from one another by forcing them to focus on what differentiates them. Some authors argue that the "melting pot" that describes American culture depends upon the fusing of all other cultural identities into one. They claim that efforts to preserve immigrant cultures actually divide immigrants into categories, instead of treating them all as one "American" group. They suggest this is contrary to the American ideal of offering equal American-ness to everybody. Furthermore, they warn that multiculturalism may threaten the very characteristic that is so American: the union of one from many.

Today in the United States, a longstanding tradition of tolerance coexists side by side with an aversion to difference. Uniformity (for people of all cultures) is easier to deal with than diversity. Diversity is difficult. Often the impulse to deny cultural differences comes from an embarrassment at focusing on difference, since frequently to be different in the United States is to be excluded. It isn't polite to point out that someone looks different, talks differently, wears different clothes, or eats different food. So, many times out of a concern to avoid making someone feel uncomfortable, difference is played down.

This attitude may be motivated by a sincere desire for equal behavior toward people, regardless of their ethnic or cultural background, under the all-encompassing umbrella of the ideal of equality. After all, most people who call themselves "American" have ancestors who were immigrants. Today many still have a strong desire to include newcomers in a friendly and tolerant national embrace and to affirm the high priority of equality in American culture.

But the truth is that people from different cultures really are different. That's a great strength of the human race and a potential source of delight and wonderment as much as of fear and suspicion—the choice is ours. People of different cultures begin with different databases, we use different operating environments, we run different software and process information differently—we may even have different goals. To pretend we're all alike underneath is wrong and can lead to ineffectual communication, or worse.

While the debate is growing about how much to focus on cultural diversity, in fact cultural diversity is the reality. Businesses must deal with it. Individuals within organizations must also come to terms with diversity. *The way to deal with diversity is not to deny it or ignore it, but to learn about differences so they don't impair communication and successful business transactions.*

The description of the United States as a "melting pot" is neither an accurate description of the reality nor an ideal that many of the more recent immigrants embrace. Even the European immigrants of a previous century did not totally "melt"; they created a new culture with distinct differences based on cultural heritage. As the new immigrants arrive, the United States culture becomes a "spicy stew." The potatoes stay potatoes, the carrots stay carrots, the onions stay onions, but all take on certain characteristics of each others' flavors. This blending creates a unique combination that gains from each ingredient. The United States' value of tolerance allows immigrants the freedom to keep their own identities while becoming part of a new culture. It is an ideal, but it is also achievable; in fact, it already exists to a degree in some communities in the United States.

Cultural differences don't prevent us from working with each other or communicating with each other or having productive business transactions. Indeed, we *must* learn to work with each other. The future of any organization depends on it. The reality is that businesses will increasingly be spicy stews of cultures, and so increasingly will the whole globe they inhabit. This fact is one reason why we must all acknowledge diversity and accept it. Another reason is that immigrants can add enormously to a society's—or an organization's—culture.

The biggest gain from accepting cultural differences is that cultural diversity enriches each one of us. People around the world and throughout history have developed a stunning variety of social systems and hierarchies of values. As a member of the human race, you can claim your rightful part-ownership of this richness, and you can celebrate the fertility of the human imagination along with its diverse products.

The essential ingredient for a successful cultural stew is skill in intercultural communication. Companies like Hewlett-Packard in the United States have discovered the value of intercultural communication skills and the increased productivity they bring, and they have instituted diversity programs to train employees. They understand that the first step in effective intercultural communication is acceptance of diversity. This means we examine our own values and the values of others, look at the implications of these values for business, determine where the differences lie, and see how we can best overcome the differences and work together.

CHANGES IN COMMUNICATION TECHNOLOGY AND POLITICAL STRUCTURES

The 20th century nurtured an unprecedented change in communication technology. International communication that only a few decades ago took days, if not weeks, now takes seconds. With E-mail, faxes, telephones, and the Web we can contact our international partners at a moment's notice. If we want a more personal exchange, teleconferencing can bring the other person right into our office. And if we want a true face-to-face discussion, jets can take us anywhere within hours. The variety of channels of communication is amazing. The choice of which channel to use in a particular situation is itself influenced by cultural priorities and values.

The changes in technology have facilitated the exchange of ideas, but they also have magnified the possibilities for cultural blunders. It is so easy to assume that the person on the other end of the line communicates just as we do. After all, he or she uses the same technology and maybe even the same business terminology.

In addition to changes in technology, there have been massive political and economic changes in recent years that affect business communication internationally. Countries that once were part of the Soviet Block now struggle to define and realize national goals; China is adopting Western practices and experimenting with a market economy. Small industrialized countries resent being bullied by the big ones. Non-Western countries are becoming more assertive and protective of their cultural values and behaviors and do not quietly accept Western business practices any longer.

These new voices are increasingly powerful. Not long ago an elite of industrialized countries could more or less dictate economic practices. This is changing. Today those first-world countries must take into consideration the cultural values and practices of these new players.

As a result, understanding other cultures is more important than ever. If we consider that people from the same economic, political, and cultural background have problems communicating effectively, we can appreciate the difficulties and challenges that people from diverse cultures face when trying to communicate. Misunderstandings will always be a part of intercultural communication. One of the goals of this book is to minimize misunderstandings through an awareness of the priorities and expectations of business partners.

INTERNATIONAL BUSINESS AND CORPORATE RESPONSES

Many firms around the world have expanded internationally over the past decade. Yet until recently, the implications of intercultural communication skills for globalization were seldom addressed. Managers talked about the need for faster and more efficient communication, as if speed guaranteed effective communication. They paid lip service to the need for good cross-cultural communication, but staffing decisions were typically based on technical knowledge rather than good cross-cultural communication skills.

With growing competition and increasing globalization, that attitude is beginning to change. International experience is becoming more important for making it to the top of the corporate ladder, but it will undoubtedly be more universally valued in the future.

Consider the "world car" Ford produces in Europe and sells in 52 countries worldwide. An international team designed the car, the "Mondeo." The engines come to Kansas City from Cleveland, Ohio; Chihuahua, Mexico; and Cologne, Germany. Seats are made in the United States and the moon roof is made in Canada. Air-conditioning is made in Charleville, France, and the catalytic converter comes from Brussels, Belgium. Throughout the Ford Motor Company, intercultural business communication takes place constantly to get the job done. Engines and other components come to the Genk, Belgium plant from Britain, Germany, France, Holland, Sweden, Spain, Michigan, Indiana, and Ohio. Ford uses a global sourcing procedure for choosing suppliers of the thousands of smaller parts, through an intense international competition.

Ford produced the global "Mondeo" in order to meet global competition. For the same reason Volvo, the national pride of Sweden, and Renault, a French firm owned largely by the government of France, combined forces to form the sixth largest automobile company in the world. Ford is now a part-owner of Volvo, as well as Mazda from Japan, and Jaguar and Aston Martin from Great Britain. Daimler-Benz, a German firm that produced top quality cars for decades, merged with Chrysler from the United States. The new company, DaimlerChrysler, recently added a share of Mitsubishi from Japan and Hyundai from Korea to the ownership mix.

The trend toward a global business environment is not restricted to the big industrialized countries such as the United States, Germany, Japan, France, Canada, and Great Britain. Nor is it restricted to large cities or, in the United States, the industrial centers on the East and West coasts. It involves geographic locations that just a few years ago were considered to be wholly engaged in domestic business. Many small towns in the landlocked states of Mexico, for example, are involved in international business today.

Local firms may export or import, they may be owned by foreign firms, or foreign firms may establish subsidiaries. People who never dreamed of going into international business may work side by side with recent immigrants from different cultures. The salesperson in a small business in a small town in any one of a hundred countries may have to answer inquiries from around the globe. The salesperson won't have time to think about how to deal with a foreigner. She or he must be ready to communicate on the spot.

THE FOUNDATION FOR INTERCULTURAL BUSINESS COMMUNICATION

The first step in effective intercultural communication is the understanding and acceptance of differences. That does not mean we have to agree with another culture's viewpoint, or that we have to adopt another culture's values. It does mean we and they examine our and their priorities and determine how we all can best work together, being different.

In the process, we will realize that a person entering another culture will always have to adapt to a number of cultural conditions. That doesn't mean turning one's back on one's own culture or denying its priorities. Rather, it means learning what motivates others and how other cultural priorities inform the behavior, attitudes, and values of business colleagues. This approach means adding to one's own culture, not subtracting from it. For example, a businessperson from New Zealand going to Japan must adapt to many Japanese practices, just as a Japanese businessperson going to New Zealand must adapt to a variety of New Zealand practices.

In attempting to understand another culture's perspective, we will be further ahead if we take off our own cultural blinders and develop sensitivity in the way we speak and behave. That is not always easy. We are all culturally based and culturally biased.

For example, people in the United States refer to themselves as "Americans." They often say that they live in "America." Most Europeans use the same terminology. Germans, for example, refer to the country of the United States as *die Staaten* (the States), or as *USA,* but they always refer to the people as *Amerikaner* (Americans). The French call the people of the United States *les americains* (Americans); they refer to the country as *les Etats Unis* (the United States) or *l'Amerique* (America). The Japanese refer to people from the United States as *america-jin.* But this is not precisely accurate; it is an example of cultural bias. People from Central America and South America call themselves *American* too. They call people from the United States *Yanquis* (Yankees).

As residents of the United States, accustomed to using the word *American* to refer to people of the United States, we have struggled with the terminology in the writing of this book. We have attempted to distinguish between other Americans and those of the United States. But no exclusive term exists for the people of the United States—such as *Statesians*—comparable to *Mexicans* or *Canadians.* We use *the United States* when referring to the country, and often use the phrase *people of the United States* and *United States businesspeople* to refer to the people. But occasionally, when we feel the context is clearly the United States, we also use the term *Americans* to denote the people.

ORGANIZATION OF THIS BOOK

This book has three major parts:

1. An understanding of culture and how to know unfamiliar cultures for business, and culture's impact on communication.
2. The application of intercultural communication skills to specific business communication tasks.
3. The implications of intercultural business communication for the domestic multicultural/international/global firm.

PART ONE   This section begins with an introduction to culture followed by the first steps in developing intercultural communication skills and a look at the way culture affects communication. Then Chapter 2 examines the issue of language in communication with an unfamiliar culture and discusses the important role of the interpreter. Chapters 3 and 4 present a structure for understanding the dimensions of an unfamiliar culture through posing specific questions in five different categories. These questions cover the priorities or values of any culture that are important for business. Examples show how these priorities affect business transactions.

PART TWO   This section examines how culture affects business communication. Chapter 5 discusses the influences of cultural values and language patterns on the organization of business messages. Chapter 6 looks at the role of nonverbal communication across cultures. Chapter 7 discusses what happens when people from different cultures encounter one another in specific social contexts that have different meanings for each party, and touches upon ethics across culture. Chapter 8 examines the impact of cultural priorities on information gathering, decision making and problem solving—all activities that involve certain communication tasks. Chapter 9 concludes this section on the application of intercultural communication skills to business negotiations across cultures.

PART THREE   Chapter 10 explores the legal environment and the communication implications for the international/global manager. Chapter 11 ties intercultural business communication practices to the organization and structure of the international/global firm. A broad variety of examples illustrates the impact of structure on communication. The last chapter discusses the relationship among cultural awareness, the position of the communicator in the firm and the firm's degree of international involvement, and choice of communication channel. Who should communicate with whom? What are the appropriate channels? What is the appropriate level of cultural understanding? In short, how can the communication be carried out most effectively?

In connecting intercultural communication theory and international business concerns, this book presents a unique approach. It probes the reasons for cultural priorities and behavior and identifies the major applications in intercultural business communication tasks. In this process it establishes a framework that will help readers ask the right questions and identify cultural issues so they can communicate effectively in new cultural settings.

This book is based on many years of experience, living and working in a variety of cultures, and of research. As other scholars in this field have pointed out, this is not an exact science. The many examples make the book particularly valuable for anyone who wants to be an effective player in international business.

NOTES

Raymond Cohen. *Negotiating Across Cultures,* (Washington, DC: United States Institute of Peace, 1991).

Paul Gonzales. "Driven to Think Globally," *The Los Angeles Times,* "The Great Trade War" supplement, Tuesday, May 18, 1993.

Martha Groves. "Hewlett-Packard Co. Discovers Diversity is Good for Business," *The Los Angeles Times,* "Workplace Diversity" supplement, May 17, 1993.

Contents in Brief

Contents

CHAPTER ONE

Culture and Communication

Donald Hastings had been chairman of Lincoln Electric, a leading manufacturer of arc-welding products, for only 24 minutes on the July day in 1992 when he learned the company was suffering huge losses in Europe. The losses meant the company might not be able to pay U.S. employees their expected annual bonus. Since the bonus system was a key component of the manufacturer's success, with bonuses making up about half the U.S. employees' annual salary, this was a much greater threat than simply a disappointing performance by the company. For the first time in its 75-year history, it looked like Lincoln would have to report a consolidated loss.

Lincoln Electric, based in Cleveland, Ohio, had expanded hugely in the late 1980s, spending about $325 million to acquire foreign companies. But according to Hastings, lack of knowledge about either the cultures of the acquired companies or the cultures of the countries they operated in was a critical factor in the company's financial nosedive. For example, the bonus system was not an incentive to European workers, who were hostile to the idea of competing with co-workers for their annual pay. Instead they follow pay scales that are the result of contract negotiations by labor leaders who represent workers and reach agreements with management. The idea that individual workers might exceed or fall below the agreed amount of income depending on individual performance was unacceptable to European workers.

Lincoln Electric also learned that products not made in a European country would not easily be able to penetrate that country's market because of a cultural loyalty to domestically produced goods.

A third problem was that executives of Lincoln's recently acquired European companies only wanted to deal with Lincoln's top executives, not with lower-level people sent over from Ohio. This status issue arises from the cultural characteristic of hierarchy in German culture.

Another cultural issue is that workers in Germany, France, and other European countries typically have a month of vacation in the summer, so production gears down during this slow time.

A fifth problem was that nobody in the executive jobs at Lincoln had had international experience or had lived abroad—the chief financial officer (CFO) didn't even have a passport, and a last-minute panic occurred to get one for him before a trip he urgently needed to make to Europe. It finally became clear to Hastings that he could not hope to bring Lincoln back to profitability without moving to Europe himself, where he could be at hand to deal with problems immediately while learning what he and the other executives needed to know about culture.

The story of how Lincoln Electric rallied and finally achieved success is a drama about the enormous efforts by the U.S. workers who had been fully informed of the bleeding in Europe. It is also a cautionary tale of how the chairman and executives painfully learned the lessons of culture they needed to know to operate overseas.[1]

Failure in business activities abroad can be fatal to a company, as the Lincoln Electric experience almost demonstrated. Mistakes can be unconscious as well as unintentional. A whole body of literature has appeared that documents cultural blunders in international business efforts. The list of errors is very long. Along with the errors are lists of do's and taboos for businesspeople. These are *caveats* against those potentially fatal *faux pas*—as if remembering not to cross your legs in Thailand and not to refuse a cup of coffee in Saudi Arabia is all you need to know in order to close a deal. But lists can't cover everything, and this proliferation of print does not tell you *why* you shouldn't cross your legs or say no to the coffee. And unless you understand the why, you will sooner or later trip up and fall on your face. The blunders-and-bloops literature is full of instances in which the fall really was fatal and the deal came apart. It is always because someone didn't understand the *why* rather than the what of culture.

Front-stage culture is what people in contact with one another find easiest to observe and react to. It involves culturally identifiable actions such as shaking hands or bowing or kissing upon meeting. At the front of the stage, interactants can respond to cultural cues and modify their own behavior, creating a transactional culture between them. In this transactional culture, which may be transitory and last only as long as the interactants are involved in communication, the participants can form behaviors and act upon attitudes that are shaped primarily by the interaction. The context of the interaction becomes more important for molding actions than the individuals' own cultural backgrounds.

When interactants are sensitive to another culture and knowledgeable about it, they adjust their behavior. The amount of adjusted behavior that occurs in their co-created transactional culture depends upon their level of sophistication with the other culture. For instance, a Canadian businessman may bow to a Japanese businessman, although the Canadian would not bow to a fellow countryman. A Taiwanese businesswoman with experience of Brazilian culture may kiss the cheek of a Brazilian businessman on first meeting, but would not kiss the cheek of a Taiwanese man or woman. These people have adjusted their native cultural behavior and have learned to act as if members of the other culture. Their counterparts may also exhibit adjusted behavior: The Japanese may offer his hand for a handshake and the Brazilian may keep a distance in deference to Taiwanese custom.

Individuals' own cultural backgrounds give rise to the back-stage cultural behaviors. These are not so easily observed by others as are the front-stage behaviors, but they underlie what others do see. The back-stage behaviors are usually unconscious; the actors are not aware they are behaving in a culturally driven way. Usually people think their own back-stage behavior is simply normal. Back-stage behaviors include the way people make decisions, respond to deadlines, accomplish tasks, rank events by importance, and conceptualize knowledge. If you understand the *why* of culture, you can explain back-stage behavior.

The *why* is the essence of a people's culture. Everything you may know and can say about a culture leads back to that: answers to why people believe as they do, act as they do, and give importance to things as they do. If you understand why people value some things, then you can make good guesses about why they value other things. If you understand why they behave a certain way, you can interpret other behavior with a degree of accuracy. Once you have an insight into what people think is important and how they behave, you can do business with them. You know what makes them the way they are.

Culture: the Operating Environment or Windows of the Mind

Geert Hofstede, author of research in intercultural communication and organizational practices, refers to culture as "the software of the mind." But we want to take that computer analogy further and say that culture is *the operating environment* that enables software programs to run. Culture is like DOS or Unix or Windows: It is what enables us to process information in various specific applications. We find the metaphor of *windows* very appealing to describe culture: Culture is a mental set of windows through which all of life is viewed. It varies from individual to individual within a society, but it shares important characteristics with members of a society. How the windows differ from society to society and how an outsider can learn to recognize what is essentially transparent to the individual member of a culture are the subject of this book.

The rest of this chapter is divided into three sections: Understanding Culture, Responses to Other Cultures, and Culture and Communication.

UNDERSTANDING CULTURE

There are hundreds of definitions of *culture*. It is difficult to define because it is a large and inclusive concept. "Everything you need to know in life to get along in a society" is not as useful a definition, however, as one that focuses on what culture's characteristics are. Culture involves learned and shared behaviors, norms, values, and material objects. It also encompasses what humans create to express values, attitudes, and norms. A culture is not usually discussed by the members who share it. Edward Hall, a key researcher into cultures, wrote

> Culture [is] those deep, common, unstated experiences which members of a given culture share, which they communicate without knowing, and which form the backdrop against which all other events are judged.[2]

Culture is like the water fish swim in—a reality that is taken for granted, rarely examined. It is in the air we breathe and as necessary to our understanding of who we are as air is to our physical life. Culture is the property of a community of people, not simply a characteristic of individuals. Societies are programmed by culture and that programming comes from similar life experiences and similar interpretations of what those experiences mean. If culture is mental programming, it is also a mental map of reality.[3] It tells us from early childhood what matters, what to prefer, what to avoid, and what to do. Culture also tells us what ought to be.[4] It gives us assumptions about the ideal beyond what individuals may experience. It helps us in setting priorities. It establishes codes for behavior and provides justification and legitimization for this behavior. From among the many definitions of culture, here is the definition this book will use:

> **Culture** is the coherent, learned, shared view of a group of people about life's concerns that ranks what is important, furnishes attitudes about what things are appropriate, and dictates behavior.

This definition deserves a closer examination. First, it contains three characteristics of culture; then it outlines three things culture does.

Culture Is Coherent

Each culture, past or present, is coherent and complete within itself—an entire view of the universe. The pioneer researcher into the study of cultures, Edward Tylor, said in 1871 that culture is

> the outward expression of a unifying and consistent vision brought by a particular community to its confrontation with such core issues as the origins of the cosmos, the harsh unpredictability of the natural environment, the nature of society and humankind's place in the order of things.[5]

That different groups of human beings at different times in history could develop different visions is both a cause for wonder, and as we shall see, a cause of misunderstanding. The incredible richness of the variety of cultures fascinates historians, anthropologists, travelers, and nearly everybody. It makes all our lives richer to glimpse and even claim a bit of this treasure of human achievement.

Regardless of how peculiar a fragment of a culture seems, when it is placed within the whole tapestry of the culture, it makes sense. Consider a hypothetical case. A boat full of south-coast Chinese decide to set sail for San Francisco, known as "Old Gold Mountain" in China for a century and a half. It is a place where immigrants can acquire gold, if not by mining it then by working for it. Somewhere along the way they are blown off course by a storm, and they actually reach landfall off the coast of Mexico. It is the last week of October, and they wearily go ashore to the nearest town to see where they are. But to their horror and dismay, in every store window and every home are images of skeletons, skulls, and graves. In China, death is not to be mentioned even by homonym (words that merely sound like words associated with death are avoided), let alone broadcast by images everywhere. However, *El Dia de Los Muertos,* the Day of the Dead, is a fiesta with deep meaning for Mexican families. It emphasizes family ties that reach beyond the grave, as departed family members are remembered and consciously brought to join the living family members through a celebration. (In fact, the Chinese traditionally hold a celebration with a similar objective, called *Qing Ming,* on the fifth day of the fourth month, or April 5.) If the Chinese understood *why* the Mexicans display skulls and skeletons everywhere, they could respect the Mexicans' attitudes toward death symbols. But if all they have is the culture fragment—a bit of behavior—they will probably regard it as bizarre, unnatural, and odious.

The completeness of cultures also means members looking out from their own seamless view of the universe probably do not see anything lacking in their "unifying and consistent vision." Why do I need to know another culture? How can I see the possibility of something existing where I have always seen nothing? How can I know what I don't know? The response to these questions first recognizes that culture determines business practices. Business practices are not neutral or value-free. Neither are business communication practices. You need to understand the cultural values you transmit when you interact with someone from another culture, as well as the other person's cultural values. You also need to recognize the likelihood that there will be gaps in comprehension—holes instead of connections—in your interaction.

Understanding another culture is a legitimate concern of businesses. More than that, it is essential. Those who make the effort to understand another culture gain knowledge about how to behave in that culture. Or put it another way: If you know what people value and understand their attitudes, you won't unintentionally do something that offends and diminishes your chances for business success. An author speaking about the need for businesspeople to know about another's viewpoint says, "relatively few people understand that mastering appropriate behavior takes precedence over mastering the language."[6]

Culture Is Learned

Culture is not something we are born with, but rather it is *learned*. This is *not* to say people can talk objectively about their own culture. Much of what is learned about one's own culture is stored in mental categories that are recalled only when they are challenged by something different. We all have to be taught our culture. The process begins immediately after birth—even earlier, according to some.

If culture is learned, then it is also *learnable*. That means nobody has to remain for a lifetime locked inside only one culture. If you want to understand other cultures, you can learn them—not just learn about them, but actually get inside them and act according to what is expected in them. Many people have learned more than one culture and move comfortably within them. When circumstances dictate, they make the transition from one culture to another easily. Businesses don't have to accept failure in another culture simply because no representative of the organization grew up in that culture.

This book is about how to learn other cultures. We believe it is not only possible to do so, but interesting and rewarding.

Culture Is the View of a Group of People

A culture is shared by a society. Members of the society agree about the meanings of things and about the *why*. Along with everyone from whom they have learned their culture—older family members, teachers, spiritual leaders, peers, and representatives of legal, political, and educational institutions—they have interpreted life experiences in ways that validate their own culture's views. Therefore, since they have little doubt about that validity, they all share the view that their interpretations are correct. They agree about what the important things are that truly merit respect.

Members of a society probably agree without having to say so that something is necessary and important. Groups are motivated by common views, and these views are a dynamic force in enabling groups to achieve societal goals—protecting economic resources from unscrupulous outsiders, for example.

People in a given culture share symbols of that culture. The most obvious set of symbols is language. Much more will be said about the role of language (Chapter 2) and communication (later in this chapter). Cultures also share visual symbols. Company logos, icons, religious images, and national flags are examples of visual symbols.

A story is told of the Sultan of Brunei, one of the world's wealthiest men, who was shopping in a department store in Manhattan. When he made a purchase, he was asked for identification. However, he carried no identification. "I'm the Sultan of Brunei," he stated. The salesperson insisted he needed to show identification. A quick-thinking aide darted forward, put his hand in his pocket, and pulled out a bill in the currency of Brunei. All the money in Brunei has the Sultan's picture on it.

Now we'll look at what culture does.

Culture Ranks What Is Important

What is of paramount importance to one group may be virtually meaningless to another. For instance, consider the amassing of wealth. In one Pacific Island culture, the Gururumba of New Guinea, a rich man is required to expend all his carefully amassed fortune—in this case, pigs—in the lavish entertainment of the members of his society. To be able to entertain this way is the real meaning of wealth because it means the giver is owed and therefore has great prestige. But explain that to a businessperson in the United States or Hong Kong or Italy who has spent his or her life amassing wealth! Usually in these cultures resources are to be husbanded and increased, not depleted in one big blow-out. To be sure, businesspeople in these cultures often make generous charitable and philanthropic donations, but their cultures teach them to treat wealth with care and make it grow. Cultures rank what is important. In other words, cultures teach values or priorities.

The term *values* crops up frequently in books about intercultural business. So does the term *attitude*. What is the difference? In distinguishing between attitudes and values, one writer explains that **values**

> provide us with standards of competence and of morality, guiding or determining attitudes, behavior, judgments, comparisons of self and others, rationalizations and justifications, exhortative attempts to influence others, impression management and self-presentations. Thus defined, values are moreover fewer in number than attitudes, are conceptions that transcend specific attitude objects and situations, are determinants of attitudes as well as behavior, are dynamically closer to needs, and are more central to that core of the person that we identify as the self.[7]

Values underlie attitudes. They also shape beliefs. They enable us to **evaluate** what matters to us or to apply standards to our attitudes and beliefs. Values are what people go to war over or conduct business by. In order to communicate about business in another culture, it is necessary to understand the values that operate in that business culture.

Because values tell us how to weigh the worth of something, they indicate a relative hierarchy. We can talk about values as cultural priorities. Within a culture, values may be of greater or lesser importance. For example, a culture may put a high priority on honesty and a low priority on making a minimal effort. Priorities vary from culture to culture: Progress reports about the delivery of a component from a joint-venture may be of great value to a Dutch firm doing business with Japan, but may be of little value to a Japanese firm awaiting delivery of a component from Holland.

Cultures enable people to find answers to their recurring questions:

- Who are we?
- Where did we come from?
- What is the meaning of our being here, on this particular whirling planet, at this time, within this ecosystem?
- How does the meaning of life reveal itself?
- How should we organize so we can get along?
- How can we know our spiritual dimension?
- What does the *best* life include?

The variety of responses to these questions can astonish and enrich us all. We all can recognize and make a claim to some elements of all cultures because we understand the fundamental need that is behind them.

In business contexts, the motivations of employees, partners, superiors, contractees, social associates, and members-at-large of a society spring from cultural values, or in other words, what people think is important. In order to understand how to do business with members of another culture, it is necessary to understand what motivates them. No list of do's and taboos tells you that. But where to begin? What do you need to know to cover all necessary bases in order to do business?

Chapters 3 and 4 present a strategy for learning about another culture. The strategy can be applied to any culture. It involves asking certain questions about a culture—and continuing to ask them without being content that the whole answer has ever been received. You will constantly be building your knowledge structures about cultures. The questions are in five general areas:

1. How do people in this culture think and know?
2. What do they consider achievement?
3. What is the relation of members of this culture to time and spiritual issues?
4. How do they see the individual self in relation to the rest of the culture?
5. How is their society organized?

These categories and subquestions within them can give enough information for a learner of the culture to become fluent in that culture. When you understand the priorities people have, you can predict with some confidence how they probably will respond to a specific situation.

Culture Furnishes Attitudes

An **attitude** is learned, and it is a tendency to respond the same way to the same object or situation or idea. Attitudes are feelings about things, based on values. Attitudes can change, although change can be difficult. You can have an attitude toward eating raw fish, for example, that is positive and is based on the belief that expert preparation of *sushi* and *sashimi* by Japanese chefs results in culinary delicacies. Or you may have an attitude that is negative, based on the belief that raw fish can contain parasites that cause unpleasant consequences in the human digestive system. You can even hold both attitudes at the same time. If you do, then probably you **value** both fine eating experiences and physical health.

Attitudes are based on beliefs as well as values. **Beliefs** are convictions or certainties based on subjective and often personal ideas rather than on proof or fact. **Belief systems** or religions are powerful sources of values and attitudes in cultures. We will look at religions in more detail in Chapter 3.

Attitudes vary according to how important something is reckoned to be (value). In Mexican culture, a death of an aunt is an event that business associates are expected to view as significant to the family members; a boss is expected to have an understanding attitude toward an employee who is not able to get a report done by a deadline because of the funeral and family needs. In Britain, the attitude toward a business associate's loss of an aunt is that this is a private affair, regrettable and perhaps very sad, but something that should not affect work to a great extent. In fact, for a businessperson, handling the situation well means keeping it from having an impact on work. Reports should come in on time if possible.

Culture Dictates How to Behave

To continue the example of the previous discussion, a brief expression of sympathy by one businessperson to a bereaved work associate at their next meeting is appropriate British behavior. If the association is longstanding, perhaps a card is sent. In Mexico, on the other hand, much more than an expression of sympathy is appropriate behavior. Business associates may attend the funeral, send flowers, offer services such as transporting family members, and visit the family home to show respect.

Behavior comes directly from the attitudes about how significant something is—how it is valued. Values drive actions. Business is a composite of actions. So we're back at the point made earlier: Cultural priorities motivate business behavior.

In business, cultural differences usually make themselves known first by behavior, which is related to attitudes and which springs from priorities (values) in the culture.

Take the case of an overdue report in the following scenario. A Japanese employee in Tokyo whose report is not ready by the deadline goes to his superior and explains that problems at home with his wife have driven him to drinking more than he should and going home very late after the employees' evenings out. The result is a raging hangover that makes him unable to concentrate on writing the report. For the Japanese worker, neither the excessive drinking nor the domestic problem is a source of shame, and his expectation is that the superior's attitude will be acceptance and a paternalistic concern for the employee's plight. The superior's behavior is probably to counsel the employee and to inquire into the domestic situation in subsequent weeks.[8]

When this scenario is presented to businesspeople in the United States, they typically say that an employee who explained that he had failed to complete a report because of a hangover from excessive drinking (whether or not it was to escape domestic problems) would probably incur double condemnation, at least in the mind of the superior. He would be criticized for drinking too much and also for not completing the report on time. Generally speaking, in the United States the superior's behavior would be to tell the employee to get hold of himself and get some help or else expect the unpleasant consequences that follow from failure to perform one's work. The employee in the United States may be no less debilitated by a hangover than his Japanese counterpart, but he will offer some other reason for not being able to get the report done: He may call in saying he's ill.

Behaviors by the employee and the superior in Japan and the United States are different; attitudes about the role of the superior are different; attitudes by the superiors toward the employees' situation are different. All these differences can be traced to the root difference: The cultural priority placed on submitting a report on time is different. In Japan, the passed deadline may not be as significant as the maintenance of the relationship between employee and superior, and that relationship is a kind of paternalism or patron-client relationship. In the United States, an employee's performing work on schedule is significant as an indicator that the employee is responsible, shares the organization's goals for achievement, and puts the organization's goals for performance above personal matters. Of course, individuals and individual organizations will not all share these generalized characteristics, either in Japan or in the United States. But when this scenario is presented to Japanese and American groups, they respond with these generalizations.

RESPONSES TO OTHER CULTURES

When members of different cultures find themselves face to face, a number of responses are possible. History shows that a common response is to clash and to struggle for the dominance of one set of values over another. This is what happened in the early history of the United States.

Immigration has tremendously increased the population of the United States within the past 400 years, after initially reducing the native population dramatically. The United States, of course, is primarily a nation of immigrants from other cultures. The history of the past 400 years is the history of the values of certain cultures dominating the values of other cultures.

Priorities in the Native cultures of the United States included (and traditionally still include today) some things the European immigrants did not value, and vice-versa. For example, immigrants wanted to own land; Natives thought the idea absurd that humans, with their short life span and feeble strength, would try to *own* land.

Members of Native cultures found significance in knowing their place in the scheme of things in the natural world, their relationship to other living creatures, and their ancient origins. Native Americans looked back over immeasurable time to the source of their existence in animal ancestors who were endowed with significant spiritual characteristics.

The European immigrants were trying to break with history and start something new and brave. The models the founding fathers consciously emulated were classical Greek and Roman governors. The Europeans believed God and reason were on their side, and they had a post-Renaissance view that human beings were enabled by their will to accomplish whatever they wanted. They saw no animal origins behind the superb apex of creation they believed humankind to be. The Native Americans were assumed to be less than human, although some Europeans thought they were redeemable through education into the European view. Nevertheless, immigrants to the western United States in the 19th century were rewarded in cash for the scalps of Native Americans.

Behavior of the two groups was also very different. The immigrants were loud when the natives were silent; they were aggressive when natives were passive.

The immigrants bought and sold slaves that were not considered quite human. The slave owners would have been astounded by the notion that the slaves possessed their own view—from their own cultural windows—of a whole and complete vision of the meaning of life. The slave owners had no appreciation for the complex, rich, old cultures that had flourished in West Africa for centuries. The slave owners thought they were offering the slaves an opportunity to become "civilized" by their exposure to European culture.

Until the mid-20th century, the greatest number of immigrants to the United States came from Europe. Since the change in immigration law in 1968, the largest number of immigrants has been from Asia. They speak languages that are unrelated to European languages; they write in systems Europeans cannot decipher; they clearly have world views that have been developed without reference to the West. It is sometimes a shock to the sensibility of United States residents to realize that far from aspiring to assimilate the culture of the dominant European immigrants, these immigrants do not want to assimilate and thereby lose their own cultures.

The Challenges of Diversity

Diversity is a fact, and it is not going to go away. Not all cultures in the world are going to become like yours. Most people in the world actually think others ought to try to imitate and adopt their culture. This is true, no matter who "we" and "they" are. Pakistanis who work in the oil-rich emirates of the Middle East, Poles who work in Germany, Peruvians in Canada—whoever they are, people tend to believe their view of the universe, as shared by many others and verified by their experiences, is familiar and normal and *home.* Especially when confronted with another view of the universe, humankind takes refuge in the comfort of the familiar.

Somehow we need to learn, in Hall's words, to "accept the fact that there are many roads to truth and no culture has a corner on the path or is better equipped than others to search for it."[9] We can start with Hofstede's advice: "The principle of surviving in a multicultural world is that one does not need to think, feel and act in the same way in order to agree on practical issues and to cooperate."[10] We can agree to be different and to allow for diversity. We can celebrate our own culture in terms of how it is or is not like another, and celebrate other cultures because they are different or similar. The more we know about other cultures the more we will know about our own. Then we can begin to explain why people from different cultures behave the way they do in business situations. Their behavior *will* differ, even if their workplace is in the same culture.

Diversity Abroad

Often intercultural business communication is regarded as something necessary only for international business. But we want to emphasize that many cultures are represented within the borders of one nation: This is true of all countries that already have, or are rapidly developing, a high degree of technological expertise. In fact all large city centers, from Delhi to Detroit, from Caracas to Canton, are peopled by members of cultures from all over the world.

As materials, capital, expertise, and organizations migrate, so also the workforce of every major center in the world is increasingly made up of migrants. Markets, labor, and money are all global. Correspondingly, intercultural communication skills are extremely important for businesspeople looking for markets, suppliers, associates, partners, subsidiaries, or joint venture companies in foreign countries. Today's successful businesspeople must be able to communicate interculturally both at home and abroad.

Business travelers are often characterized as unaware of—and unconcerned about—priorities in other cultures and the behaviors they generate. They are supposedly interested only in profits. They say, "It works at home, so it will work anywhere," or "I know how to sell/manufacture/manage anywhere," or "My product is the best, so I don't have to worry about the culture." Donald Hastings, Chairman Emeritus of Lincoln Electric, attributed many of the company's mistakes abroad (see the opening of this chapter) to an executive attitude that since they were successful in the United States they must certainly succeed in other countries. But these characterizations may not be accurate. Most businesspeople want to act appropriately and avoid offending their counterparts in foreign countries. Most businesspeople want to know the buttons to push that motivate people in other cultures, if only for the sake of making a sale. But those who are genuinely concerned about how to learn what matters in another culture have few guides, beyond lists of "do's and don'ts." As we have suggested, such lists are never complete. One researcher suggests that McDonald's success—it has more outlets worldwide than in the United States, and a new McDonald's opens somewhere every 17 hours—is because they practice a localized approach. McDonald's succeeds because it offers what local people want.[11] That means being sensitive to the cultural needs of the immediate market.

Some businesspeople turn to lists of do's and taboos for help, such as this one governing nonverbal communication:

- Never refuse the offer of coffee from a businessman in Kuwait.
- Be very careful not to cross your legs so that the sole of your foot points to someone in Thailand.
- Only remove your jacket and work in shirtsleeves in Japan when your Japanese colleagues do so first.
- Never help yourself to food when you are the guest of honor at a banquet in China.
- Do not become irritated if you find yourself waiting half an hour or more for an appointment with a businessperson from Venezuela.
- Use business courtesies in India, such as shaking hands when introduced, except when females are involved.
- Do not discuss politics in Nigeria.
- Do not offer your host gifts for his wife or children when doing business in Saudi Arabia.
- Plan to spend about two hours on lunch in France.

The do's and taboos lists are usually accurate, but their helpfulness is limited. One-sentence advice on behavior is like seeing a snapshot from a movie. It is accurate, but without the context of the movie's story line, character development, or even the specific episode, the snapshot's significance may not be understandable. Lists of do's and taboos can't explain *why* you should or should not behave in a particular way in a particular place. Lists can't possibly be comprehensive. And even if a business traveler were armed with a very long list, who can consult a list for every nuance in every different country? It's no wonder that businesspeople may seem to discard tips on do's and taboos in favor of simply being themselves and acting the same way abroad that they would at home. And yet most businesspeople know that business as usual—doing what they do at home—can be counterproductive when doing business abroad.

To be effective in a foreign business setting, you need to know certain things, but not necessarily everything, about that culture's priorities, its members' attitudes, and how they think people should behave. With the right set of questions, you can learn what you need to know about how people of another culture think. Then you can draw parallels from how people think to how they probably expect you to act. For example, if you know people in a particular culture have great respect for age and seniority, you can infer they will appreciate your standing up when an older representative from their company comes into a meeting room. Because cultures are coherent and made of elements knit together in a fabric, understanding *why* enables you to understand the specific *what* of behavior.

For example, consider some of the list of do's and don'ts above in the light of these explanations. Hospitality is highly valued in Kuwait, and refusing the offer of coffee offends that value. In Buddhist Thailand, the sole of the foot is the furthest part of the anatomy from heaven and the least sacred. To show the bottom of the foot to someone is to show disrespect. Similarly, it shouldn't surprise you to know that Thais consider touching a person's head to be disrespectful, since the head is sacred. In Japan, where standing out and being different threatens social harmony, matters of form—such as clothing—are dominated by consensus. In China, a host can lose face if the guest appears to be hungry, since it is the host's role to offer even more than the guest can eat. Therefore, "cleaning your plate" is not a good idea. Time in Latin American cultures is flexible; it can be stretched to allow things to be attended to properly.

Once you begin to build a picture of a culture's priorities, you can draw fairly accurate deductions about what kind of behavior will be offensive and what behavior will be pleasing. Chapters 3 and 4 discuss what questions to ask in order to have an understanding of a culture that will enable you to do business effectively.

CULTURE SHOCK   One of the inevitable experiences of immersion in a new and unfamiliar culture is culture shock. It happens to everybody. It's important to know that culture shock and its symptoms are normal and to be expected in cross-cultural immersion experiences.

The term *culture shock* is not quite accurate because it refers to a range of responses that take place over time. It isn't a single jolt. Culture shock is the sense of dislocation along with the problems, psychological and even physical, that result from the stress of trying to make the hundreds of adjustments necessary for living in a foreign culture.

The first stage of experiencing a new culture is usually **euphoria.** Everything about the exciting new adventure is wonderful. This stage generally lasts no longer than two weeks, and some people skip it altogether. Travelers sometimes go home before they have progressed to the next stage.

The second stage is usually a downturn as **disillusionment** and **frustration** arise. This is usually the stage people refer to when they use the term *culture shock.* It is a sense of dislocation that results from finding out that inadequacies exist in your understanding, your mental road map, for navigating in this new culture. You don't know what you don't know. Finding out what you don't know is exhausting, even when it is also exciting. Inevitably there are disappointments, in yourself and in others; inevitably you make mistakes. When the adjustment to a new culture means an upward change in status, people feel good about the new culture longer. When the adjustment means a downward change in status, people feel unhappy more quickly.

Most sojourners experience psychological symptoms of culture shock. Some people find themselves becoming depressed. They may experience long periods of homesickness. Some are very lonely, and they may be involved in relationships that they wouldn't form if they were in their own culture. Nearly all sojourners and temporary residents in a new culture experience dissatisfaction with the way things are. Things that formerly seemed acceptable become irritations. Sojourners can become aggressive and exhibit unpleasant behavior that they would not use at home. They may get angry easily and express hostility and suspicion towards members of their host culture. Frequently culture shock shows itself when sojourners believe native members of the culture are trying to take advantage of them—to overcharge them, for example—because they are foreign.

Physical symptoms of distress also can result from this stage of culture shock. They include aches and pains in limbs, headaches, chronic fatigue and lack of energy, loss of appetite, inability to get a good night's sleep, stomach upsets, and frequent colds or flu. This stage can last longer than the first euphoric stage—perhaps months.

The third stage is **adjustment.** As the expatriate sees both sides and learns more about how the other culture works, he or she is able to cooperate more effectively with members of the host culture. Some successes may occur, and solutions may be found for the problems that seemed so unreasonable and intractable in stage two. At this stage business can probably be conducted successfully.

The fourth stage, **integration,** occurs when the expatriate becomes fluent enough in the other culture to move easily within it and not be thrown by the different attitudes, beliefs, and values and by the behaviors they generate. Often linguistic fluency accompanies this stage. At this stage the expatriate is able to identify with the host culture. Businesses whose employee achieves integration in another culture may feel at some risk. They may worry that their employee, who is now so at home in another culture, does not totally represent them any more.

Most people who work in another culture, regardless of the length of the stay, experience all four stages of culture shock. Furthermore, the longer one stays, the more cycles one goes through; the fourth stage, in which one feels comfortable in the new culture, leads to another euphoric stage, followed by frustration and disappointment, followed by adjustment, and so on.

You can reduce the symptoms of culture shock if you are prepared to deal with it:

- Before you leave home, think about what you'll miss most and try to make some arrangements to keep it in your life. Take books, music, and personal possessions that are important to you.
- Think about what you can do to pass holidays and special days that you usually spend with family and friends.
- Make plans to keep in touch with special people and to have funds for an occasional phone call or package. E-mail is widespread and a convenient way to feel you are in touch. In some countries it is expensive, so you may need to make some arrangements before you go for ensuring a reliable connection.
- If you can get people to write on a regular basis, you'll find you appreciate their news very much. For example, family members or people you work with could take turns, each writing a message by E-mail or snail mail once a week.
- You can also feel closer to home if you can find people in the new environment who are from your own culture. But beware of the tendency to develop an "us" and "them" attitude toward the host culture; foreigners can encourage each other to adopt hostile views of the natives that make it harder to deal with culture shock, not easier.
- It helps to have someone to talk to who will listen sympathetically—preferably someone from the host culture. You may be able to be the listener, too; look around and see who is a foreigner in your midst.
- It also helps to know that culture shock does pass. The downward pattern of depression and loneliness eventually gives way to an upward swing of optimism and connection with the new culture. As the date of departure for home draws near, most sojourners feel positive about the new culture they have experienced, and positive about themselves.

REVERSE CULTURE SHOCK   A similar adjustment period and its accompanying symptoms usually occur when a sojourner returns home. This is often called reverse culture shock. It takes people by surprise who don't realize it is normal. After all, it's somewhat ironic—the sojourner has been longing to return to the old, familiar culture of home. But once home, the sojourner finds many things to criticize and often asks why the old culture can't be more like the one so recently encountered. Friends and family typically find the traveler impatient with things that never used to cause complaint. Sojourners' most frequent complaint is that nobody wants to hear about the wonderful new experiences they've had.

Expatriates also find that people at home have had new experiences to which they must adjust. Things have changed at the company where the sojourner works, and people have been promoted, achieved successes, retired, left for another employer, and so forth. The sojourner is something of an outsider and may have a new job to get used to as well as new contacts to make. Returnees feel they have been laboring in the foreign fields for the sake of the corporation, usually at some (nonmonetary) cost and personal sacrifice, but upon return they often feel they are not valued. Some companies provide mentors and training programs to ease reentry.

The Question of Change in Cultures

Much is written about the constant change cultures undergo. Agents of change, it is said, include global companies like Pepsi or Sony or DaimlerChrysler. It is true that popular taste changes; fads come and go, especially in the marketplace, which is driven by changing tastes. Popular culture, which comprises the products of the culture that are widely consumed—for example, music, food, hairstyles, clothing, recreational activities and their equipment, styles of cars, furnishings—does constantly change. But back-stage culture, the values, attitudes, and behaviors that have been learned from birth, change very little and very, very slowly.

Sometimes the shifting emphasis of existing values in a culture is mistaken for cultural change. As if a spotlight first illuminates one and then fades while another is illuminated on the stage, so circumstances—geopolitical, economic, even spiritual—spotlight some values as others recede. All cultures include values that can be in opposition. In the United States, the value of independence is sometimes in conflict with the equally held value of respect for personal property. In Singapore, the value of belonging to a group is sometimes at odds with the value of asserting one's position to accomplish a task. But these values are in the culture all the time. Certain situations bring out one or another value.

In Hong Kong, South Korea, and Taiwan, going out for fast food has become an accustomed social pastime for teenagers and for seniors. Students from Korea visiting Taiwan were delighted when, after eating the food of Taiwan for a week, they were allowed to go to one of "their" restaurants—a McDonald's! They are no less Korean because they eat fast food that originated in the United States. Sufferers from migraine headaches in Argentina who consult acupuncturists are no less Argentine for seeking a Chinese traditional treatment. These are instances of popular taste.

More significant change in social organization occurs with economic change. In China, a country that has always practiced behaviors associated with the Confucian value of filial piety, economic change is making a shift in family structure. Rather than a son bringing his wife to his parents' home, married couples are increasingly living on their own. This change has come about because young people can afford housing of their own, and their parents can also afford to house themselves. It isn't clear, however, that this change in housing means filial piety is no longer valued in China. Filial piety—the duty children have to look after aging parents and to put their wishes before the children's own—may simply take other forms than living with the parents.

A study of many generations' values will be necessary to demonstrate that cultures actually change, in China or anywhere else, and that the change is more than proceeding and receding emphases on values that exist within the culture. In the short term, the older members of a culture always deplore the way young members seem to be abandoning the traditional values. When those children are parents and grandparents themselves, the cultural values they were taught as youths often reassert themselves.

Technology is called an agent of cultural change, and its role deserves some discussion. Technology is the way humans relate to their environment. For example, technology has altered the way space and time affect human communication; cell phones and E-mail have reduced both time and space constraints to almost nothing. Microchips are making smart machines possible in a wide range of applications. The constraints of the human body and the physical environment are disappearing, and activities that were not possible except by great effort and expense are now occurring with ease. Activities as different as online shopping and online academic research are changing the marketplace and the university. Medical innovations include the possibility of surgically embedded microchips in humans who are physically unable to do some things. But this marvelous technology does not change the cultural imprint on the individual member of a culture. Individuals still carry the map of their cultures in their minds and hearts, whatever technological innovations they implement.

E-mail messages, for example, appear to favor a direct communication style that is informal. However, members of formal cultures that prefer indirect communication still practice that behavior in E-mail messages. They still begin messages with attention to the relationship they have with the reader, and they may mention family or some shared past experience. They will use courteous language if that is their cultural behavior. In cultures where politeness matters in correspondence, E-mails will exhibit a greater level of politeness than the E-mails of cultures where politeness is not as important as getting to the point.

Cultures appear to remain unchanged at deep levels and only change on the surface. This is front-stage behavior, where popular culture thrives.

Nor are all cultures becoming alike. Evidence does not suggest that one global culture will one day dominate the planet. A glance at the events in recent years in former Yugoslavia shows how far ethnic groups are willing to go to defend their culture. French Canadians who wanted to defend their culture nearly succeeded in separating from the rest of Canada in 1995 when a national referendum on the question failed by less than half of 1 percent. As societies achieve more economic stability, defending their cultures seems to increase in importance, not decrease. In spite of an increasingly global technology, and in spite of the availability of the same consumer goods in many countries, and even in spite of changing tastes and fads that sweep from continent to continent, the deep values of cultures remain unchanged.

Typical Reactions to Unfamiliar Cultures

The most common response to diversity is to choose somehow not to accommodate it. Human reaction is to reject difference. We insist on sameness and require people to conform to us. Or we deny difference, choosing not to see it even when it is there.

It is more comfortable to believe your own culture is all you'll ever need to know than to embark upon a riskier openness. And it is *much* more comfortable to believe your own culture can't be improved upon, and everyone who encounters it will inevitably be drawn to adapt to it and leave behind whatever inferior view preceded it. It's more comfortable, but in spite of historical evidence that some cultures dominate others when they come into contact, it is unrealistic to assume one's own will be the culture of choice for members of another culture.

ASSUMPTIONS OF SUPERIORITY   A universal response to differences in cultures is: "Of course they're different, but we're better." What this does is minimize difference by making it unimportant compared to one's own culture. Most cultures assume their own values and practices are superior to those of the rest of the world. English-speaking cultures encode this assumption of superiority by using words such as *backward* and *primitive,* when actually those evaluations are one cultural view, seen through specific cultural windows, not an absolute assessment. A village in Bangladesh that lacks most of the technology taken for granted in the workplaces of other parts of the world—telephones, electricity, automobiles, airplanes—may have a more sophisticated conflict-resolution process than the technologically advanced cultures of the world. So who is "backward"?

ETHNOCENTRISM

> The Germans live in Germany, the Romans live in Rome,
> the Turkeys live in Turkey, but the English live at home.[12]

Businesspeople can generally depend on this: Members of other cultures, deep down in their heart of hearts, are convinced their own culture is the *right* one. People everywhere tend to assume their own culture is right and normal, and to assess all other cultures by how closely they resemble their own. Most people, especially those with little experience of other cultures, believe their own culture (ethnicity) is at the center of human experience—hence "ethnocentrism." The further from our own another culture is, the more it seems to belong on the fringe, to be peripheral and not of primary importance. Conversely, the closer another culture is to our own, the truer it seems to be. Along with the preference for cultures that are similar to our own is the view that difference is dangerous. Difference may even be wrong.

For this reason, ethnocentrism can lead to complacency. We may not make an effort to look further than our own culture, and we may see little importance in understanding other cultures. In other words, ethnocentrism leads to assuming one's own culture is superior to all others—the assumption of superiority. Business organizations that have proven they can succeed in one culture often adopt an ethnocentric position: We know how to make it work for us at home, so we can make it work for us anywhere. After all, learning another culture takes time, effort, and resources. It's much easier for an organization to operate from an ethnocentric position. But unfortunately it can be much costlier.

ASSUMPTIONS OF UNIVERSALITY   One of the comments you often hear from travelers to foreign countries is, "They may talk (dress, eat, etc.) differently, but underneath they're just like us." But this is profoundly mistaken and potentially dangerous romanticism. People underneath are *not* alike. People begin with different operating environments and run different software. People have different databases and process information differently. As a result, they arrive at different results. As we saw earlier, culture is the whole view of the universe from which people assess the meaning of life and their appropriate response to it.

To assume you know how someone else is thinking based on how you see things is called *projected cognitive similarity.* It occurs when you think you know someone else's perceptions, judgments, attitudes, and values because you assume they are like your own. This can lead to disrupted communication and even conflict. After all, people may have different goals. Even when people may agree on goals—say, for example, the corporate goals of an organization—they may expect to reach those goals by different methods.

Business is multicultural; business is worldwide No organization can afford to go along believing that members of different cultures are all seeking to conform to one culture, or that one day differences will cease to exist. Therefore, the key for business is *to find ways for people who think differently to work together.*

The Importance of Self-Knowledge

The best response for business across cultures is openness to what may be learned about another culture and drawn from it in order to communicate more effectively with its members. The same openness needs to be applied to one's self and one's own culture.

> Know thyself; know thine enemies:
> One hundred battles; one hundred victories.
>
> SunTzu, *Chinese martial philosopher*

"Know thyself" is advice handed down from ancient philosophers of many cultures. In order to understand the other person you have to understand yourself. This isn't as easy to do as it may seem at first; most of what makes up a culture is absorbed unconsciously in the growing-up process of socialization. How do we get at it? How do we distinguish what we take for granted as universal human experience from what is culturally determined? We need to be able to examine the operating environment of the mind that enables us to run various mental programs. The transparent nature of the culture windows is the basic difficulty in coming to terms with one's own culture. The more deeply embedded cultural values and attitudes are, the less conscious they are and the harder they are to examine. Or as Hall says in describing a man in a foreign environment, "The more that lies behind his actions . . . , the less he can tell you."[13]

For example, take an accountant. She operates with mental processes and parameters that she learned through accounting courses and through practice—they constitute her mental software about accounting. But she uses a set of values and ideas about how to act that are not only part of the accountancy software in her mind, but also part of the larger operating environment of unconsciously held values, attitudes, and behaviors from her society. It's easier for her to look at what makes up her view of accounting than what makes up her view of life.

Most people assume that what they take for granted as *natural* is what everyone on this planet also considers natural. Most people only discover when they come into contact with something different that the ideas they hold as absolute truths are actually culture-based positions. It can be a disorienting experience, like encountering people who seriously tell you that two and two make five-and-one-quarter, or that the world will end precisely on June 29, 2021. When basic assumptions about life are challenged, one typical response is to find the other culture's assumptions irrational. They seem to be crazy. Rationality is, of course, culturally defined.

What is "normal" business attire? In Indonesia, a businessman wears a loose cotton shirt over pants. A male proprietor of a small firm might not wear pants at all, but a skirt-like wrap. In Saudi Arabia a businessman wears a long robe over his trousers and shirt. In Japan, a businessman wears a dark suit with a white shirt. In each of these countries, expectations are that a serious, responsible businessman in that culture will dress like that.

Businessmen from the United States often dress informally, in sweaters and slacks, or in short-sleeved shirts without jackets. When they are in very warm countries they may wear shorts for leisure. This attire can be acceptable in certain situations, but it can also appear disrespectful toward the other culture's attitudes.

Recently a United States automobile parts manufacturer was shown on television trying to make a sale to some Japanese automobile firms. He was dressed in a boldly patterned cardigan sweater; his hosts were all in dark suits and white shirts. The camera caught one of the host party, a woman, repeatedly looking at his sweater with something like alarm in her eyes, and looking away again. The sweater could indeed have been a factor in his reported failure to get a single sale.

The salesman in this episode was acting according to ideas about dress that seemed appropriate to him, from his cultural windows. He may have considered the informality of his dress as signaling a willingness to put aside rigid rules of behavior and be friendly. He may have been cold and enjoyed the warmth of a large sweater. He may have spent the previous 20 hours on a plane and, without a chance to change his clothes, may have gone straight to the trade show, because, to him, being there was more important than being dressed a certain way.

If a salesman's priority is to fulfill the expectations of his company in sending him to a Japanese trade show, he will be less concerned with his appearance and more concerned with being successful. His employer wants him to promote the company's products and to make contacts. He has a mental image of what a good employee does in foreign trade shows. We all behave according to representations in our minds.

MENTAL REPRESENTATIONS   One way of understanding our own culture, as well as another, is to use mental categories to represent groups. These are often called "stereotypes." These mental representations are not necessarily bad. In fact, they can be very useful tools. But some distinction is necessary between stereotype and prototype.

The term *stereotype* comes from printing, when type set in one frame identically reproduced that type in another frame: stereo type. The limitation of stereotypes, however, as illustrated by the historical origin of pieces of type set in a frame for printing, is that they are fixed and rigid. We use the term *prototype* to mean mental representations based on general characteristics that are not fixed and rigid, but rather are open to new definitions. When confronted with something unfamiliar or complex, people categorize data in order to make sense out if it. If you know nothing about the market for frozen french fries, for example, but you suddenly have an urgent need to know, you begin with organizing the topic into categories: producers, their market shares, commercial users (by size, by type), retail market segments, prices, potato suppliers, and so forth. The same categorizing occurs when you encounter a new culture. If we couldn't make generalizations and put similar items into categories, we couldn't make any sense of an unfamiliar subject.

Mental representations change with the induction of new experience. They are dynamic and can be altered to form new mental categories as more data comes in. Everyone has a large data bank of mental representations. In order to understand yourself you need to be aware of your own data bank and its categories. Then when you encounter an actual culture, you can understand how your mental prototype is being transformed by reality. You can be open to new awareness and have a dynamic experience of the transformation of your mental categories.

Even incomplete, sketchy prototypes based on objective observation usually have some truth in them. That's why they can be useful. "Latin American businesspeople talk about their families, often before getting down to business"; "Japanese negotiators use silence a lot more than Europeans."

Generalizations that express an *evaluation* of members of a culture are prejudices—*pre-judgments:* "Chinese always give you a fish-eye look; they don't feel any emotion"; "Irish have hot tempers and get angry easily; they can be really difficult to deal with." In other words, it's when we begin drawing evaluative conclusions from the mental representations that we may be in trouble. It may be one's experience that Chinese do not readily show emotion, but that doesn't equal *coldness,* which is an evaluation. It is judging Chinese character, not simply observing behavior. It may be one's experience that Irish easily find words to express emotion. But *hot-tempered* is a judgment one assigns based on one's culture. Prejudice, or prejudging before all the facts are known, is leaping to an evaluative conclusion without gathering information about the culture and the context.

BIAS   Everyone has biases and many are readily acknowledged. You may have a bias towards tough disciplinary measures for dealing with those who break the rules, or a bias toward a work environment where the superior is approachable and low-key, or a bias toward a four-day work week. A bias for something is really nothing more than preference. Many biases are recalled from long-term memory only when forced by an external challenge.

For example, in studies done of job interviews, results show interviewers are biased toward interviewees who appear to come from their same cultural background—who have an accent that indicates membership in the same ethnic group, for example. When other factors remain constant, the accent is the factor that determines which candidate gets the job from which interviewer.[14] In this case the bias has an easily understandable basis; we prefer what is known and familiar because it poses little threat.

We need to be aware of our biases. We need to be open to the discovery within of unrecognized biases that can exert an influence on how we understand another culture.

DISCRIMINATION AND PREJUDICE   When biases are *acted upon,* the actor is showing discrimination and prejudice. Discrimination is the act of sifting out and selecting according to bias toward something or someone. We say someone has "discriminating taste" as a compliment because that person is able to sift carefully through a mass of items and identify the best. To be undiscriminating is to lack judgment and to be unable to discern the best from the second-best or the inferior. In the United States discrimination became a widely used term for racism. People identified other people as better or worse than the rest based solely upon their perceived racial membership, and the term *discriminate against* began to be used. This changed the meaning: "to discriminate" with "against" came to mean "to sift through and select out the unacceptable."

Prejudice is an evaluative opinion that is based on emotion or some other irrational basis, but not on facts. It may be held in spite of the facts. A prejudice is usually negative, and because it is not grounded in fact, it can be called an irrational bias. Prejudice is often accompanied by or based upon suspicion, fear, hate, or contempt. Just as business communicators need to be aware of stereotype and bias, we also need to be aware of prejudices and consciously avoid acting upon them.

Racism is one form of prejudice. Sexism is another. Ageism is prejudice in favor of younger rather than older individuals. *Homophobia* is the term usually used to mean prejudice against homosexuals, although the word really means a phobia or irrational fear of same-sex eroticism. Prejudices can affect intercultural business. Not only are they often unrecognized by the people that have them, but also, in foreign surroundings, people's prejudices can come to the forefront. People who would not allow themselves to express prejudice in their own culture may nevertheless do so in an unfamiliar culture. This is a well-documented expression of culture shock, as discussed earlier.

An interesting experiment was conducted to identify the presence of prejudice. E.S. Bogardus asked people to rate on a scale from 1 to 8 how favorably they felt toward groups of people according to their national identity.[15] The most favorable, number 1, indicated a willingness to have a daughter or son marry someone of that group; an 8 meant not being willing to allow someone of that group into the country, let alone into one's home. The interesting thing was that the list of more than 60 nations—Italians, Czechs, Moroccans, Nigerians, Thais, and Turks, for example—included three fictitious ones: Danireans, Pireneans, and Wallonians. Bogardus found that the people who were more unwilling to admit members of other nations into close relationships were unwilling to admit the unknown nations' members also. And conversely, tolerance toward many nations included tolerance toward the three unknown and nonexistent nations. This finding implies that intolerant people are intolerant across the board, while tolerant people are tolerant even of unknown nationalities.

COMMUNICATION AND CULTURE

Communication systems such as language and nonverbal communication are products of culture. They are also tools intricately bound up in the processes of culture itself: Language is related to thought processes and to mental learning processes. Linguists like Whorf, Sapir, and Hayakawa have connected how we know something and how we think about something with language. So interconnected are communication and culture that some scholars have been led to use them interchangeably: "culture is communication" and "communication is culture."[16] Yet language is the tool we most often use to describe culture, which suggests they are indeed separate phenomena. Language is clearly inadequate

Edward Hall,
" Beyond Culture "

to help us understand culture, especially our own. Language puts limits on expressing certain qualities or concepts with a single word. Language can also limit the order in which we present thoughts. When language is turned back upon itself and communication is the object of its inquiry as well as the means, then at least understanding communication can help us to understand culture.

High-Context and Low-Context Cultures

One tool for examining the culture windows is the approach to cultures described by Edward Hall, distinguishing among cultures on the basis of the role of context in communication.[17] High-context cultures rely on the context, either the actual physical environment of communication or an internalized social context or both, to convey a large part or even all of the message's meaning. In cultures in which context is implicitly referred to in communication, the messages themselves can be elliptical, indirect, and allusive. In cultures in which context is not assumed to be understood, messages are explicit, direct, and completely encoded in words. This describes low-context cultures, in which the meaning is trusted almost entirely to words.

Hall drew a continuum reaching from the extreme of low-context cultures to the opposite extreme of high-context cultures, and plotted national cultures along the continuum. He identified German Swiss as a very low-context culture, in which messages are spelled out fully, clearly, and precisely. He identified Japan as a high-context culture, where messages are multilevel and implicit. He put the United States on the low-context side of middle.

High-context cultures, in which the context of the message is well understood by both sender and receiver, use the context to communicate the message.

A very distinguished 75-year old Chinese scholar and statesman was being honored by a university in the eastern United States. He and his wife had just made the 21-hour flight from Beijing, and they were met at the airport by some friends who exclaimed, "You must be very tired!" His response was *keyi*, "It's possible" or "It's OK." Of course he was tired! He was an old man who had sat on airplanes or in airports for 24 hours straight. But the context—the meeting in an airport at night, the fact of his long journey, his age, his slightly glazed eyes—communicated the obvious. It was unnecessary to put it into words.

Yet it is not hard for a Western imagination to suppose the situation in reverse. A traveler to Beijing gets off the plane after 24 hours of continuous travel and, in response to the same comment, "You must be tired!" replies, "Tired! I've never been so tired in my life! I've been sitting on planes or in waiting rooms for 24 hours and wondered if my legs would work again! My eyes are so gritty with sleep they feel like the Gobi desert was in that plane!" and so forth.

Members of low-context cultures put their thoughts into words. They tend to think if thoughts are not in words, then the thoughts will not be understood correctly or completely. When messages are in explicit words, the other side can act upon them. But high-context cultures have less tendency to trust words to communicate. They rely on context to help clarify and complete the message.

A Turkish male graduate student in the United States lived in a residence hall where he shared a room with an American. One day his roommate went into the bathroom and completely shaved his head. The Turkish student easily discovered this fact when he himself visited the bathroom and saw the hair everywhere. He returned to his room and said to his roommate, "You've shaved your head." The American replied, "Yeah, I did."

The Turkish student waited a little, then said, "I discovered you'd shaved your head when I went into the bathroom and saw the hair." "Yeah," the American confirmed. The Turk was at a loss. He believed he had communicated in the strongest possible language his wish that the American would clean up the mess he'd made in the bathroom. But no such meaning was attributed to his words by his roommate. Later he discussed the surprising episode with Turkish friends who told him, "Listen, with Americans you actually have to say 'Clean up the bathroom'!" The Turkish student believed his message had been very clear. He was relying on the context of the communication for the message to be understood: Hair was recently and widely scattered all over the bathroom, and his roommate now had no hair.

Perception and Communication

Communication is the perception of verbal (worded) and nonverbal (without words) behaviors and the assignment of meaning to them. Communication takes place whether the sending of signals is intentional or unintentional. It even takes place when the verbal or nonverbal behavior is unconscious, as long as it is observed and meaning is assigned to it. When a receiver of signals perceives those signals, decides to pay attention to them as meaningful, categorizes them according to categories in his or her mind, and finally assigns meaning to them, communication has occurred. Communication is a process that can falter at any one of these steps when it takes place between members who share values, attitudes, experiences, behavioral expectations, and even a history together. When communicators come from different cultures, however, not only the meanings, but also the mental categories are very different.

We all develop categories in order to make sense of life. Your experience reading this book belongs in certain activity categories. The way you dress, eat, and get to work every day is behavior that belongs to certain categories. All the value priorities that underlie your behavior also belong to certain categories. These categories are learned from the culture around you. You learned to understand the world according to these categories.

Signals can be either verbal or nonverbal or a combination of both. Imagine a glance from someone, accompanied by a noise in his or her throat. When you encounter something unfamiliar, you have several choices. You can assume it is nothing. It fits no category known to you, and means nothing. At this point, you have perceived a signal but have chosen not to attend to it. Or you can assume it is simply a variant of something familiar that is already in a mental category. It may seem the noise in the throat is a prelude to speech that will be directed at you, since the person is looking at you. In this case, you have categorized it and assigned meaning to it, but both may be wrong. The glance may in fact be past you to someone or something else, and the noise in the throat may actually be words in a language you don't understand. Another option is that you can choose to perceive the signals as unfamiliar and therefore not to be matched with existing mental categories; thus you reject them or keep them waiting until you can relate them to something already familiar. It's hard to keep the uncategorized and unmeaningful in your mind for very long,

EXHIBIT 1–1   Perception Model of Communication

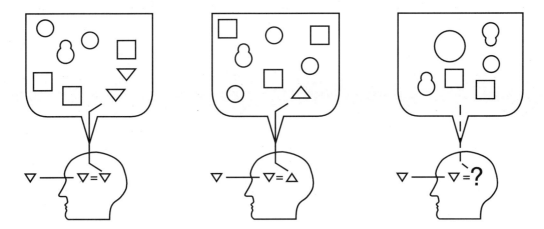

unless you have learned to do so. Finally, you have the option of altering your mental category to accommodate the new information and assigning a new meaning. This is how categories are constantly being revised and increased, as shown in Exhibit 1–1.

Meaning is assigned to verbal and nonverbal behavior based on one's accumulated experience and understanding—one's mental data bank. We attribute meaning on the basis of what has been meaningful to us in past experiences. People from cultures that are similar will have a similar store of past experiences and knowledge in their data banks, and that usually leads to attribution of meanings that are close. If we share common experiences and values with others, it is easier to interpret the meaning behind their behaviors accurately. However, when we don't share common experiences, there is a greater chance we will assign an incorrect meaning to the signals. When people from different cultures communicate, the data bank categories are not all the same, the operating environment—the culture window—is not exactly the same, and the meanings assigned to signals are not all the same. This can happen with verbal (worded, written and oral) communication. In fact, people feel most uncomfortable when they understand the words someone is using, but don't understand what those words mean to the user. It also describes what happens with nonverbal communication, which is much broader in scope with greater possibilities of misunderstanding.

In order to have good communication with another culture, you need to understand meanings in that culture. This is because good communication means good relationships, and "Good relationships mean increased productivity and profits. Bad communication leads to conflict, inefficiency, and loss."[18] It is true for communicators who share one culture as well as for communicators from different cultures.

A Schemata Model for Intercultural Communication

The mental categories we create in order to make sense out of the world can be called *schemata*. Among the schemata are those that categorize what we know about cultures other than our own. If you are asked to summon up what you know about a culture, say the dominant culture of Ethiopia, you may not have much data in your schema—indeed, you may even have to create a new schema because this is the first time you've thought about Ethiopia.

If you know this Ethiopia is a country in Africa, you may make certain additions to your schema, which may or may not be accurate. Does it help to know that over 100 different ethnic groups find a home in this country?

Here is some more information. The dominant culture is Amharic, which is also the official language. Ethiopia is one of the oldest countries in the world. The capital is Addis Ababa. Businessmen typically wear a white robe (*shamma*) over their shirts and trousers, and may stand closer to people in conversation than Europeans do. Bureaucracy flourishes; a strong chief or leader dominates business organizations. Families are strong units and family members may be business partners. People tend to make distinctions based on social and economic position. Business encounters are formal; hospitality is highly valued. Businesspeople are not afraid to stand up for their individual rights, but at the same time they also show sensitivity to the rights of others. They have the ability to endure adversity with patience. Age is respected.

About 45 percent of the population are Muslim, while another 40 percent of the population are Ethiopian Orthodox Christians. Formerly the highest levels of society were mostly Christian, but, since the political upheavals in Ethiopia in recent years, Muslims as well as Christians occupy all levels. Women often own small businesses, and, unlike some other Muslim cultures, the Muslim women of Ethiopia do not wear a veil or *chador*. Ethiopians are Semitic people (like Jews and Arabs). Coffee is a major export product.

We can model our expanding knowledge of another culture and how we communicate with it.[19] The following diagram (Exhibit 1–2) shows your culture as Culture A, Ethiopian culture as Culture B, and your projection or schema about Ethiopian culture as B¹. The diagram shows that your understanding of Culture B is really the projection, or schema, you have put together about Ethiopia.

EXHIBIT 1–2 Communication Is with Schemata, Not Actual Culture

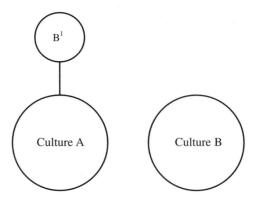

EXHIBIT 1–3   Communicators Send and Receive Messages through Schemata

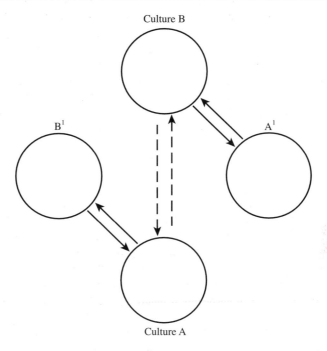

Culture B

B¹

A¹

Culture A

If you imagine yourself traveling to Ethiopia for business, you now may be able to make further projections, based on the categories in your schema, of what you would expect to find. What food will you be offered by your business contacts there? What will be unlikely to be offered? Would it be acceptable for you to refuse refreshment? You will observe Ethiopians eating with their fingers. Why? What will you do? If the businesspeople you spend time with all represent one company, what else may they have in common?

Whatever you know about Ethiopia, based on these few facts and questions or on your prior knowledge, unless you are Ethiopian, your mental schema will not quite accurately reflect the reality that is Ethiopian culture. Furthermore, if you attempt to communicate with Ethiopian counterparts for business purposes, you will probably be communicating with your mental projection of Ethiopian culture. Exhibit 1–3 describes this process.

When you communicate, you are sending messages to B^1, the schema of Ethiopian culture. When you receive messages from a member of that culture, they arrive after being filtered through B^1.

The more you learn about Ethiopia, the more you can revise and adjust your mental projection of B^1, and the closer it can come to the reality (B) that is Ethiopian culture. Exhibit 1–4 shows this process as a result of induction, or the accommodation of new data by alteration of the schema. The more you understand of another culture, the closer your schema will be to the reality that is the other culture, and the better your communication will be. You will have fewer misunderstandings of the kind that arise when messages are assigned different meanings and different categories.

EXHIBIT 1–4   Schema Modified and Coming Closer to Actual Culture

---

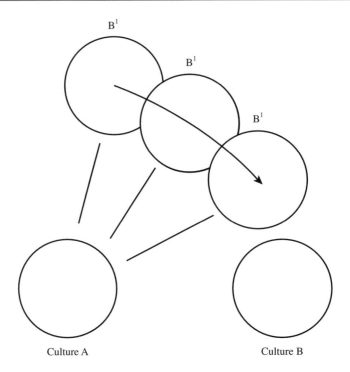

Culture A   Culture B

Multilevel Messages

When communication depends heavily upon the context of the communication act and messages tend to be understood through the context rather than the words, as in high-context cultures, then the message sender can play around with the relationship between meaning and words. Language that encodes the message can differ from the real meaning. Of course, this can happen in low-context cultures also. Encoders can play with language; the result is puns and double-meaning jokes. Sometimes the additional meaning is unintentional. Messages that fit this description are operating on more than one level at once: the encoded message of the words, the apparent but implied message, the real message, and so forth. These messages are not separable from the context that also communicates the message. The context and the language together create messages that communicate on more levels than just the words. In English, if a speaker responds to a question with "yes" in a drawn-out, downward, skeptical tone, while looking away and frowning, the message may really be, "This probably will not be possible."

Here is an example of how messages operate on more than one level and misunderstanding results.

A female neurologist from Beijing was working on a research project in a Toronto hospital. She shared a small office with a young Canadian male from a large family, who loved peanut butter. He was so fond of peanut butter, he kept a jar in the office. One day he came into the office and exclaimed, "Who took my peanut butter?" (This was not clearly encoded even though his Canadian culture is lower-context than higher-context. He really meant, "Where is my peanut butter? I can't find it.") But the Chinese woman immediately felt accused. After all, there were only two of them in the office.

She was deeply distressed, but true to her learned cultural behavior of never showing anger in public, she said nothing. Later that day she was working in a room where a physiotherapist was treating a patient who suffered paralysis of his legs and arms from a motorcycle accident. The physiotherapist moved one of the patient's legs in a way that caused him pain.

"Ouch!" he cried.

"Oh, I didn't do that," said the physiotherapist. "It was that doctor over there," and she pointed to the Chinese woman.

"How could she have done it since she's on the other side of the room?" the patient pointed out.

"Ah, she has three hands," the physiotherapist replied.

At these words the Chinese doctor became even more upset. She was so disturbed she behaved in a way uncharacteristic of her culture. She waited until the patient had gone, and then said to the physiotherapist, "I'm very upset by what you said." The physiotherapist was taken aback. What had she said? "You said I had three hands," the doctor finally choked. "You think I took the peanut butter."

What was going on in this exchange? The physiotherapist was making a joke that operated on two levels when she said the doctor had "three hands." She wasn't serious, of course, and expected the patient to be amused at her fanciful explanation for his pain: that the doctor on the other side of the room could have reached an imaginary third hand out to touch him.

The Chinese woman came from a culture where the question "Who did this?" means someone is to blame. Her culture furthermore prohibits direct accusation unless a person has been targeted for shame. Shame is a terrible ordeal since it means punishment for not being a cooperative member of the group. And finally, in Chinese a "three-handed person" is slang for a thief.

The physiotherapist didn't know that, nor did she know anything about a missing jar of peanut butter. But because the Chinese woman spoke out loud and put her distress into words, the whole episode was resolved. The therapist explained to the doctor that she only said "three hands" because it was so obvious the doctor was not responsible for causing the pain to the patient.

Playing around with the gap between the coded message and the real meaning involves context; many instances are not transferable to written language because they depend upon nonverbal behavior. For example, when a co-worker responds to the question, "How was your weekend with your in-laws?" with eyes rolled upward and a monotone vocal delivery, the worded message "Great" takes on a meaning that is the opposite of the word's usual meaning.

Multilevel messages do occur in lower-context cultures, but these cultures tend to trust the message mostly to words and to equate ambiguity with increased risk of miscommunication. (The Chinese neurologist knew that Canadians usually encode messages in words when the subject is serious.) Higher-context cultures view word-level-only messages as unsophisticated, childish, and rude. They prefer conventions of communication—allusion to classical texts, parables and proverbs, understatement, and antiphrasis (saying something in terms of what it is not)—that can lead to misunderstanding by communicators who are not versed in these conventions.

Take that last convention, antiphraxis, for instance. In Thailand, Japan, China, and other Asian cultures it is polite to describe one's abilities in self-deprecating terms. "I have some small experience in that" may be the way a world-famous mathematician describes a life's work. In North America, however, the words are taken at face value and the context is ignored—it is not probed; it is not the subject of further inquiry.

The methods of communicating are only part of the situation, of course. There are also varying concerns about what belongs to the communication context and what is appropriate to be communicated rather than withheld. Should an Indonesian trainee in the United States voice concerns about a possible insult to his host university if he also takes a course in another institution? Or is this better left unsaid? Should an Indian job applicant in Australia with considerable experience put forward past achievements? Or is that unacceptably self-important? These questions arise in communication situations in any given culture; they are magnified when communication occurs across cultures. Then the significance of what contextual elements belong in the encoded message is unclear.

A Dutch businessperson in Indonesia might get into trouble when simply asking for clarification in the following way: "You said yesterday you understood the importance of having this phase of the project completed by the deadline. Now are you saying you can't meet the deadline after all? Or don't you understand the situation?" The businessperson's Indonesian counterpart would likely perceive these questions as a deliberate attempt to humiliate.

Pattern Recognition

Another key factor in communication is related to the way people process information. In other words, communication is affected by the way people think, their processes of cognition. Culture—the operating environment of the mind—determines how people think.

One of the keys to understanding cognition is the mind's ability to recognize patterns and its dependency upon patterns to organize information into schemata. The rules for sentence structure of each language form a complex pattern that orders spoken or written thought. Other patterns that structure cognition include relationships of mutual interdependence (a spring season implies an autumn), relationships of cause and effect ("if . . . then"), relationships of division and addition (parts that add up to the whole), patterns of antithesis (opposites), patterns of deduction and induction, and patterns of saying something in terms of what it is not. These are just a few patterns of cognition, not an exhaustive list.

The last, "describing something in terms of what it is not," is awkward to express in English, because English-speaking cultures do not often use it. Descriptions by English speakers who write about this Asian thought pattern often use the term *negative space*. This is the space that is not foreground. Look at the bare branches of a tree, for example. If you then look at the spaces between the branches, you'll begin to understand the negative space concept. When you look at a mountain range, the peaks in the foreground seem to have other peaks beyond them, and perhaps more beyond those. But what lies between the mountains? That is a metaphysical question that has interested many Asian thinkers, and contemplating the unknown space between what is known is a way of looking at something that is merely implied.

SUMMARY

This chapter began with a glimpse at why intercultural business communication matters to organizations: Communicators who understand *why* people think and behave the way they do can prevent miscommunication more often.

Second, the chapter has defined culture as

- *Coherent.*
- *Learned.*
- *Shared.*

Culture performs three functions:

- *Culture ranks what is important.*
- *Culture furnishes attitudes.*
- *Culture dictates behavior.*

Next the chapter considers how we respond to foreign and unfamiliar cultures in the following ways:

- *The challenge of diversity* (diversity is not a future but rather a present reality).
- *Diversity abroad, including culture shock and reverse culture shock.*
- *The question of change in cultures.* Cultures appear to change very little on a deep level, although popular culture and popular taste do change.
- *Typical reactions to unfamiliar cultures.* These include assumptions of superiority, ethnocentrism, and assumptions of universality.
- *The importance of self-knowledge.* Self-knowledge is critical for understanding other cultures and communicating successfully with them. This means recognizing the mental representations each of us uses to understand and generalize, facing bias in ourselves, and acknowledging discrimination and prejudice as behaviors that can affect intercultural business interactions adversely. *Self Knowledge exercise) Then mini-case, Dyads)*

Finally, the chapter has looked at the relationship between culture and communication. The main points include the following: *a Time I Was Exposed to a Different Culture*

- *High-context and low-context cultures.*
- *Perception and communication.*
- *Schemata Model for Intercultural Communication.*
- *Multilevel messages.*
- *Pattern recognition.*

Learning about culture and about communication across cultures will be discussed in more detail throughout the book. The most obvious issue for communication across cultures, of course, is language. That is the subject of the next chapter.

NOTES

1. Donald F. Hastings, "Lincoln Electric's Harsh Lessons from International Expansion," *Harvard Business Review* 77, no. 3 (May–June 1999), pp. 163–175.
2. Edward T. Hall, *The Hidden Dimension*, (New York: Anchor Press/Doubleday, 1966).
3. Norma Carr-Ruffino, *Managing Diversity*, (Needham Heights, MA: Simon & Schuster, 1998).
4. Richard Mead, *International Management,* 2nd ed., (Malden, MA: Blackwell, 1998), p. 8.
5. Raymond Cohen, *Negotiating Across Cultures*, (Washington, DC: United States Institute of Peace, 1991), p. 8, paraphrasing Tylor's *Primitive Culture*.
6. Hendrick Serrie, "Cross-Cultural Interaction: Some General Considerations for Innocents Abroad." In *Anthropology and International Business*, Studies in Third World Societies no. 28, Hendrick Serrie, ed. (Williamsburg, VA: Department of Anthropology, College of William and Mary, 1986), p. 55.
7. George A. Borden, *Cultural Orientation: An Approach to Understanding Intercultural Communication*, (Englewood Cliffs, NJ: Prentice-Hall, 1991) p. 98, quoting M. Rokeach, "Value Theory and Communication Research: Review and Commentary." In D. Nimmo, ed., *Communication Yearbook 3* (New Brunswick, NJ: Transaction Books for the Intercultural Communication Association, 1979), p. 10.
8. Hiroko Sakomura and Sue Winski, unpublished case from Transform Corporation, Tokyo, in an unpublished paper, SIETAR International Congress, Denver, 1988.
9. Edward Hall, *Beyond Culture*, (New York: Anchor Press Doubleday, 1976), p. 7.
10. Geert Hofstede, *Cultures and Organizations: Software of the Mind*, (London: McGraw-Hill, 1991), p. 237.
11. James L. Watson, "China's Big Mac Attack," *Foreign Affairs*, May–June 2000, pp. 120–134.
12. J. H. Goring, 1909 nursery rhyme, quoted in Hofstede, *Cultures and Organizations*, p. 235.
13. Hall, *Beyond Culture*, p. 116.
14. Larry Copeland and Larry Griggs, *Going International* video. New York: Random House, 1985.
15. Survey instrument reproduced in a paper by D.A. Goings, Stephen F. Austin State University, Nacagdoches, TX.
16. Edward Hall, *The Silent Language*, (New York: Anchor Press Doubleday, 1959); Larry A. Samovar, Richard E. Porter, and Nemi C. Jain, *Understanding Intercultural Communication*, (Belmont, CA: Wadsworth, 1981).
17. Hall, *Beyond Culture*, pp. 85–128.
18. Richard Mead, *Cross-Cultural Management Communication*, (New York: John Wiley & Sons, 1990), pp. 2–3.
19. Linda Beamer, "A Schemata Model for Intercultural Communication and Case Study: The Emperor and the Envoy," *Journal of Business Communication* 32 (April 1995), pp. 141–161.

CHAPTER TWO

The Role of Language in Intercultural Business Communication

The Language Barrier and Its Consequences: Real and Perceived

Robert Breckenridge from the United States is meeting Klaus Hartmann from Germany. They are meeting for the first time, and they are going to discuss opportunities for cooperation between their two firms. Robert Breckenridge is 32; Klaus Hartmann, 55. Robert is excited about the opportunities and wants to come across as friendly and outgoing. He speaks German but has not dealt with Germans before, and Mr. Hartmann has not done business on an international level either. This is Mr. Hartmann's first trip to the United States; his English is limited.

As Mr. Hartmann walks into Robert Breckenridge's office, he is greeted with, "Hallo, wie geht's? Ich bin Robert Breckenridge, aber alle nennen mich Bob. Ich freue mich, Sie zu treffen und bin sicher, Klaus, daß wir gut zusammen arbeiten werden." (Hi, how're you doing. I'm Robert Breckenridge, but everybody calls me Bob. I'm excited to meet you, Klaus, and I'm sure we'll be able to work together well.) He offers his visitor a chair. Robert is comfortable and relaxes as they discuss the future. He puts his feet up on the table and puts another piece of chewing gum in his mouth. "This is going to be easy; doing business with someone from another country is not going to be bad at all," he thinks. "In fact, we'll come to an agreement pretty fast here." Mr. Hartmann seems to go along with his proposal. Robert is, therefore, very surprised when Mr. Hartmann informs him some time later that he is no longer interested in the deal. What happened?

The Relationship between Language and Culture

In the above example, Robert Breckenridge spoke grammatically correct German, but he failed culturally. Mr. Hartmann, who is rather formal by United States standards, resents being called by his first name and resents the familiarity of the greeting. But he resents even more that Mr. Breckenridge put his feet on the table and chewed gum while talking. "How can one do serious business with someone like that?" he thinks.

As the example shows, culture and language are intertwined and are shaping each other. It is impossible to separate the two. Language is not neutral codes and grammatical rules. Each time we select words, form sentences, and send a message, either oral or written, we also make cultural choices. We all agree that language helps in communicating with people from different backgrounds. However, we may be less aware that cultural literacy is necessary in order to understand the language being used. If we select language without being aware of the cultural implications, we may at best not communicate well and at worst send the wrong message.

In our own environment we are aware of the implications of the choices. For example, if an American says, "How are you?" other Americans register the phrase as *Hello*, the equivalent of *Guten Tag*, *Bonjour*, or *Ohio Gozayimasu,* rather than the literal meaning. A foreigner in the United States, who knows some English but is not familiar with the culture and usage of English, may attribute a very different meaning to the phrase and interpret it much more literally. Klaus Hartmann, for example, may

1. Consider the phrase as too personal and think that it is none of Robert's business how he is.
2. Think that Robert literally means what he says and proceed to answer the question.
3. Consider Robert insincere because it becomes obvious that Robert is not really interested in the answer.

The point is that words in themselves do not carry the meaning. The meaning comes out of the context, the cultural usage. For example, a German who has lived in the United States for many years will take on, often unknowingly, many American behavioral patterns. She may be more outgoing and enthusiastic, less formal, more optimistic. When she goes back to Germany, she speaks German but increasingly with an American frame of reference. At social functions, she will introduce herself by first and last name rather than by last name and professional title. "Ingrid Zerbe, erfreut Sie kennenzulernen" (Ingrid Zerbe, pleased to meet you) rather than "Dr. Zerbe, erfreut Sie kennenzulernen." The Germans are at a loss; they don't know how to address her. They could say "Frau Zerbe," but if she has a professional title that would not be correct. In any case, nobody cares about her first name anyway. Ingrid Zerbe, on the other hand, finds those Germans getting stiffer all the time; with every visit they are becoming more reserved. It is getting more difficult to establish a connection and feel comfortable.

Language as a Reflection of the Environment

Language reflects the environment in which we live. We label things that are around us. For example, in the Amazon area snow is not part of the environment; therefore, people in the region do not have a word for snow. It simply does not exist. In areas where it snows occasionally, people have a word for snow, but it may just be one word without any differentiations. Most Americans, for example, use terms such as *snow, powder snow, sleet, slush, blizzard, ice.* That's the extent of most people's snow vocabulary. People who live in an environment where it snows during most months of the year may have a much more differentiated terminology for snow.[1] If you go to a pub in the north of Germany and order wine, you may ask for "ein Glas Weißwein bitte" (a glass of white wine, please). You may specify *Moselwein* or *Rheinwein*, but that's it. The north of Germany is beer country, and the knowledge of wine is much more limited. In Baden, the southwest of Germany, on the other hand, any waiter would just stare at you if you asked for a glass of white wine. Here you would specify the type of wine, the vineyard, and the year. Wine is important in the region, and you are expected to know about wine.

The environment will influence the development of technology, products, and the appropriate vocabulary. For example, cultures in tropical climates will not develop heating systems and, as a result, will not have any of the accompanying vocabulary, just as people in cold climates have no need for air conditioning.

Language as a Reflection of Values

In addition to the environment, language also reflects cultural values. Hall, for example, points out that the Navajos do not have a word for *late*.[2] Time, he tells us, does not play a role in Navajo life. There is a time to do everything, a natural time rather than the artificial clock time that industrial countries use. As a result, the Navajos do not have the differentiated vocabulary connected with time and clocks that Americans have. Time and the passing of time are things one can't control; therefore, one should not worry about wasting time and setting schedules. In Mandarin Chinese, one word (*qing*) represents various hues of blue and green. What might be called *green* in English will be called *qing*, and what could be called *blue* in English is also called *qing*. It isn't that Chinese speakers cannot distinguish the difference in hues; they simply use one word for a range of hues.

One of the problems in dealing with people from other cultures is that we translate concepts from a foreign language and culture with words that fit our priorities. For example, businesspeople in the United States typically are frustrated with the *mañana* mentality of Spanish-speaking countries: "They said tomorrow, but they did not mean it." For Americans *tomorrow* means midnight to midnight, a very precise time period. To Mexicans, on the other hand, *mañana* means in the future, soon. A Mexican businessman speaking with an American may use the word *tomorrow* but may not be aware of or may not intend the precise meaning of the word. This vague terminology is not precise enough for American emphasis on efficiency. The difficulties over the word *mañana* are at least as much an American problem as a Mexican problem. Dictionaries do not help because they typically pretend that there are exact word equivalencies that have the same meanings. In order to communicate concepts effectively, cultural knowledge is as important as linguistic knowledge.

The Chinese, for example, do not have a word for *communication*, as in the term *business communication*. They use *letter exchange* or *transportation traffic* but not *communication*. The Chinese also do not have a concept of privacy; as a result, there is no corresponding word in the Chinese language. Typically *privacy* is translated *reclusiveness*, which brings up very different connotations in English than the word *privacy*. The word *privacy* has a positive connotation for people in the United States. They think of the privacy of their homes, the right to privacy, the right to private property. The word *reclusiveness*, on the other hand, indicates that a person withdraws from society, is a loner, or does not fit in. In the U.S. context, a reclusive person is considered somewhat strange. In China a reclusive person is much more negatively viewed.

The Meaning of Words

Sometimes different cultures use identical words that have rather different meanings. The results can be humorous, annoying, or costly depending on the circumstances. Let us look at several examples.

An American university and its French partner discussed the possibilities of exchanges for students, professors, and administrators. Both sides agreed that would be a good idea. The French negotiator spoke pretty good English, at first glance very good English; the American spoke good French. In the discussion they used both French and English. In both languages they used the identical word *administration* when they talked about exchanges between the two institutions. The surprise came later. For the American, *administration* in the university context meant department chair, dean, provost. For the French, *administration* meant upper-level clerical staff. What the American considered to be an administrator, the French considered faculty.

The word *manager* is used worldwide, but it has different levels of importance and meaning in different cultures. The same is true for the title *director*. Many Japanese, for example, have the title *director* on their business card. In the American context, a director is a person of some importance and power. In Japan, the title may not carry the same level of authority. It may take some time to determine what titles mean and where the person stands in the hierarchy. The term *director* could be a loan word from English to translate the position for use on a business card; the word is the same, but the meaning may be slightly different. The term could also reflect cross-cultural differences in organizational structure. The word *director* may be the closest translation of a job title that does not exist in the U.S. corporate structure. Likewise, the words *office worker* or *staff* are often used for the general administrative workers in a Japanese work group, which tends to have less defined job categories than its U.S. equivalent. An understanding of the specific title would require a more detailed explanation of the job and its fit in the organizational structure.

In the United States documents are often notarized. This is not a complex process. One simply goes to a notary public and gets the stamp and signature. Sometimes one pays a fee; sometimes the service is free. The German term, *notarielle Beglaubigung,* often translated as *notarized,* means something quite different. In this case one would go to a *Notar,* a lawyer. The Notar would prepare the document or, at a minimum, sign the document. This service is much more expensive. The meaning of the United States concept *notarized* is better reflected in the German term *Beglaubigung,* something any official person can do. The confusing part is the word *notarized* in the American expression. A notary public is not a *Notar*. The same confusion arises in Mexico where a *Notario* is a lawyer with special privileges to perform certain functions that require special qualifications.

Both the French and the Americans use the word *force majeure*, but the phrase carries very different meanings. Literally the term means superior or irresistible force. In U.S. legal language, the term refers generally to forces of nature or possibly war. The implications are that the terms of a contract may be changed because the risk was not allocated in either the expressed or implied terms of the contract.

In European law the term has a broader meaning. It also includes changes in economic conditions or other circumstances that were not reasonably anticipated when the contract was drawn up. The implication is that when Americans make agreements with Europeans that include discussions of unforeseen circumstances and use the term *force majeure,* they need to clarify what they mean and spell out what that term covers.

Changes in Language

As anyone who has been abroad for any length of time can attest, language lives; it changes over time. Words and phrases that are commonly being used at one time may be discontinued or their meaning may change over time. For example, the word *gay* means happy, light-hearted. In recent decades, however, the word has taken on the meaning *homosexual.* As a result, English speakers in countries like New Zealand, Canada, Australia, the United Kingdom, and the United States don't use the word in its original meaning any more, and young speakers of English may not even be familiar with the traditional meaning. In other cases, the words may take on additional meanings, and one must understand the context in order to understand the meaning. An example is the word *hardware,* which used to refer to tools and materials used in repairing and building houses. Today the word also refers to computers and components that can be added to a computer, such as a printer or an extra drive.

Foreigners and U.S. citizens who have lived outside the United States for some time may not be familiar with subtle changes in language usage. Twenty years ago words such as *businessman, chairman, salesman, airline stewardess,* and *fireman* were regularly used. Today, with more women in the workforce and with growing awareness of the way gender and power can be linked to communicate value, the use of gender-neutral terms, such as *businesspeople, chairperson* or *chair, sales clerk, flight attendant,* and *firefighter* is common. The old terminology is seen as too restrictive.

Countries such as France and Iceland try to keep their language pure. The French *Academie Française* polices the language and ensures that businesses use pure French. But even here the language changes. The officials may frown on *Franglais,* but people in France eat a *sandwich,* go on a trip for *le weekend,* and go on *le jogging,* all pronounced in the French manner with the accent on the last syllable. To use English is "chic," and somehow the English terms just seem to be more precise and descriptive. French Canadians make the Academie Française really nervous when they use *char* for car, and many other English words in their French. French Canadians do not feel compelled to follow the rules of the Academie Française.

The example of Canadian French illustrates that a language, if spoken in different parts of the globe, will ultimately develop differently. The Academie Francaise may insist on certain rules, but other French-speaking groups may make their own rules and consider their French just as correct. The same is true for the development of English. What is standard and correct English? Former British colonies such as India and Nigeria increasingly insist that their English is just as correct as Oxford English. The result is the emergence of different "Englishes" used in different parts of the world. Attention recently has focused on "Singlish"—the English of Singapore that incorporates Malay and the Hokkien dialect of Chinese as well as English words, and follows a syntax like other pidgin Englishes. Here are three examples of Singlish:

- Eh, this road so narrow, how you going to tombalik your big fat Mare-see-deese? You going to do 100-point turn or what? Sekali tombalik into the lang-kau your father kill you then you know!
  (Oh, this road is so narrow, how are you going to turn around your big fat Mercedes? Are you going to do a 100-point turn, or what? Wait until you turn it into the roadside ditch. Your father will be furious!)
- Eh, Katong sopping sehnta got the "Sah-Leh" you know. Some up to hap-pride ah! (Hey, the Katong Shopping Center has a sale, some [items] are up to half-price off!)
- Aiyah, you want to chit in your exam tomolloh, har? You tink you can lite the ansir on the table? Cher catch you, lppl (lam pa pak lan) man! (Oh no, you want to cheat on your exam tomorrow? You think you can write the answer on the desk? Teacher will catch you, and it [your plan] will backfire!)[3]

Many countries adopt English terms specifically in business and related areas. Some words are simply taken over without changes. For example, the Germans frequently use the word *shop* instead of the German word *Geschäft* or *Laden; ticket* instead of *Fahrkarte; standard* instead of *Norm.* They use the words *computer* and *software,* but they do not use the word *calculator,* retaining the German word *Taschenrechner.* The difficulty is that the outsider cannot be sure whether they will use German or American terminology. An increasing number of Germans are concerned about the use of English in everyday German and advocate the use of German whenever possible. The newly formed Verein Deutsche Sprache, for example, has requested replacing English computer terminology with German terms, and there are some changes. For example, a few years ago Germans would use "download material" and "shut down the computer." Today they say "runterladen" and "runterfahren."

In some cases people use foreign words, but adapt them to their own language both in grammatical usage and pronunciation. For example, the Japanese have changed the word *salaryman* to *sarariman, homerun* to *homurunu, headhunter* to *heddo hantaa,* and the German word *Arbeit* to *arubaito,* meaning a part-time job. After some time, the words are considered Japanese because they have been integrated into the Japanese language and culture. In German, for example, the word *stress* has been integrated. Thirty years ago nobody used the word. Today everyone uses it. The pronunciation is German and when used as a verb is given German grammatical form. A German says, "Ich bin gestreßt," I am stressed. The word has become part of the language.

Acronyms

Acronyms pose special problems because they are based on a particular language. The same institution may carry a different acronym in different languages. For example, MITI, the Japanese Ministry of International Trade and Investment, is referred to as MITI by the Germans but then spelled out as *Ministerium für Industrie und Außenhandel.* The UN stands for United Nations, but the Germans transcribe UN as *Vereinte Nationen.* The former East Germany was called Deutsche Demokratische Republik, DDR. The English translated the term but also changed the acronym to German Democratic Republic, GDR. Germans would not have immediately recognized that GDR and DDR stood for the same thing.

Implications of the Language Barrier

As the previous examples show, communication across cultures and languages is difficult and full of hurdles and pitfalls. Even if two people from different cultures can speak a common language, they may misinterpret the cultural signals. The result is confusion and misunderstanding. Many people have difficulty identifying the root of the problem. For example, American students often complain that they can't understand their foreign professors. In some cases the professors may actually have a poor command of the English language; however, in most cases the problem is not the language itself but different intonation patterns and different cultural signals. English-speaking students listen to their instructors with certain expectations. For example, if the instructor's voice drops to a low pitch, the students take that as a signal of a rhetorical topic boundary—"I'm finished with this idea,"—whereas the instructor may actually mean no such thing. Students adjust their interpretation of the lecture according to those intonation signals, thereby misconstruing the instructor's intent. A professor who comes from a culture where the professor is almighty and never challenged, Korea or India, for example, may send signals to that effect to his students. If the students are not aware of the cultural issues, they will in all likelihood identify the problem as a language problem rather than a cultural problem.

In this context the phrase, *I don't understand you,* can mean any of the following:

1. I don't understand the words you use.
2. My interpretation of what you say raises a flag and makes me wonder if this is actually what you want to say.
3. In my perception, your words and nonverbal behavior do not complement each other, and I am puzzled.

SELECTION OF THE RIGHT LANGUAGE

In other parts of the book we discuss the importance of cultural literacy in more detail. Here let us concentrate on linguistic literacy. The United States may be the only country in the world where businesspeople involved in international business do not unanimously advocate fluency in a foreign language. In the rest of the world it is accepted that, of course, one has to learn a foreign language if one wants to be engaged in international business. The arguments Americans use to excuse their failure to learn other languages are legion. The following are examples that are used frequently:

1. Everyone speaks English.
2. You never know where you will wind up, so you may be learning the wrong language; therefore, it is better to wait until you know what language you will need.
3. A good manager is a good manager everywhere (meaning that language is not important).
4. I have been successful without learning a foreign language (implying that learning a language is a waste of time).
5. You can always hire a translator.
6. You will probably not be good enough to negotiate in the foreign language anyway; therefore, don't waste your time.

Misguided research tends to exacerbate the problem. A recent survey, for example, determined that Canadian and U.S. managers of international firms by an overwhelming margin did not think that a foreign language was very important in doing business abroad. The conclusion of the study was that language indeed is not that crucial. What the survey did not address was the problem with the approach. Monolingual managers, and the subjects in the survey were monolingual, are probably less likely to advocate fluency in a foreign language than bi- or trilingual managers. The survey also did not include managers whose native language was not English. The survey furthermore did not examine the implications of monolingualism in a competitive environment.

Linguistic Considerations

If you have decided to study a foreign language, the next question is which one? Given the number of languages on the globe, this decision is not easy and will be influenced by many factors. Experts don't agree on exactly how many languages are spoken in the world; the figure is somewhere between 3,000 and 6,000. Estimates are that within the next 100 years half of these languages will disappear and with them some of the diversity of cultures. Since no one language can express all forms of human thought and ideas, this reduction would make all humanity poorer.[4] One problem is a definition of what constitutes a language. An additional factor is the distinction between language and dialect.

At what point does a person speak a different language from ours, and at what point does that person speak a dialect, or variation of our language? To a German from the north who speaks *Plattdeutsch,* the dialects called *Swabian* or *Bavarian* from the south are in many ways unintelligible and, therefore, foreign languages. Officially, however, all three are dialects of German. The Japanese, even though they like to tell us that they are a homogeneous culture, have dialects. People from Honshu speak differently than people from Kyushu. The political, economic, and entertainment centers of Japan are in Tokyo, which is located on Honshu. As a result, the speech of people from Honshu carries more clout and people from Honshu tend to look down on the dialect of the people from Kyushu.

India is the prime example of linguistic diversity with about 600 languages, of which 14 major languages are spoken by about 90 percent of the population. This diversity causes problems both domestically and internationally. The 14 languages belong to two distinct language families. Languages in the north are Indo-European; in the south, Dravidian. In order to facilitate communication in the country, India recognizes three official languages, Hindi, English, and the local language (for local affairs). Of course, the number of people who actually speak English fluently is small and restricted to the educated upper middle class. Among that group, many people speak English even at home. They use the local language for communication with servants. Indians who live abroad find that in most cases the common language among Indians is English.

China also has a number of different languages, the two dominant ones being Mandarin and Cantonese. Mandarin is spoken by about two-thirds of the population, and the political power center, Beijing, is Mandarin speaking. The south and Hong Kong, which are more open to outside influences, speak Cantonese although Mandarin is the official language everywhere. Mandarin and Cantonese speakers do not understand each other when they communicate orally, but they have no problems when they communicate in writing.

A businessperson learning Chinese should be aware of the implications of choosing either Mandarin or Cantonese. People who speak Mandarin tend to look down on people who speak Cantonese and vice versa. The Cantonese think northerners are barbarians, and northerners feel superior to the Cantonese speakers. This is a clear sign of regional and linguistic snobbery. Since Hong Kong has become part of China, the official language has changed from Cantonese to Mandarin. It will be interesting to see how this move will affect linguistic and cultural sensitivities.

Business Considerations

After weighing linguistic aspects, you must also consider business aspects in deciding which language to learn. Partially your decision will depend on whether you are the buyer or the seller of a product. Many businesspeople argue that one needs to speak the language of the customer. If you want to sell a product, it is in your interest to adapt and learn. However, other economic considerations will influence your decision also. For example, if you are the only manufacturer of a product that is in high demand, you may be able to sell and be very successful without speaking the language of your customer, at least in the short run. However, if you look ahead, you may find that even under these favorable circumstances it is in your long-term interest to adapt to the customer.

After World War II U.S. businesses dominated the international markets. The production facilities of most other industrial countries lay in ruins. As a result, products made in the United States were in high demand. In the short run this was very beneficial for American firms. Unfortunately, the Americans did not look at the long range. They acted as if this situation would continue forever and their products would remain in demand not because they were the only products around but because they were somehow superior. The United States has paid dearly for the unwillingness to adapt and for the shortsightedness and arrogance of its businesspeople. For example, Caterpillar Tractor did not consider Komatsu as a serious competitor until after Komatsu had established itself in international markets.

If businesses in the United States want to expand their international markets, their people must learn the languages of the potential markets. The Japanese are learning English, the Koreans are learning English, yet very few English are studying Korean or Japanese. The typical argument is that these languages are just too difficult to master. The Japanese have contributed to the sentiment by insisting that their language is very special and outsiders can never penetrate and master it. In reality, Japanese is not impossible to learn if people are determined. The point is that the Japanese have decided that they can learn English whereas the Americans have decided that Japanese is mysterious and alien and not worth the effort. This attitude helps explain why so many Japanese people study English while comparatively few Americans study Japanese.

The language you choose will depend on your goals and purposes. If your native language is not English, you may want to study English because English is the lingua franca of international business. In fact, in many countries, English is the most frequently taught foreign language; often it is required in school. If you live in an English-speaking country and if you come from a family that considers its ethnic roots as very important, you may study that language and decide to do business with that country. For example, if your family is from Iran, you may decide to study Farsi and do business with Iran. You may find that culturally you have some background already and are therefore at an advantage. If it is your life's dream to do business in Brazil, then you should study Portuguese and then look for a job in Brazil or with a firm that does business with Brazil.

If you don't have a particular reason to study a particular language, you might want to decide based on political and economic importance in the world and the importance of the language in the business relations with your country. A number of people might argue that, if your native language is English, you should choose German or Japanese because these two countries are very strong economically. Others would add Spanish (particularly because of the North American Free Trade Agreement), French, and Chinese. Others might argue that Russian is a good choice, or Arabic because of the oil interests. You need to think of your goals and then choose the appropriate language. There is no right language, but there also is no wrong language if you have good reasons.

What if you study French, and then you are sent to Japan? This is a realistic possibility. Many U.S. companies still argue that they cannot send someone to a country just because the person is familiar with the culture and language of that country. One major multinational corporation (MNC) actually argued the point and insisted that business decisions had to carry the most weight rather than language and cultural facility. It is interesting to note that this company has had major problems abroad over the past decade and is facing increasing international competition. It seems strange to think that linguistic and cultural ability are not considered aspects of a business decision.

If you have mastered one foreign language, the second foreign language is easier. So even if you have the "wrong" language, you may find it takes less time to gain facility in the second. In many cases, foreign businesspeople react negatively to the fact that the American speaks *no* foreign language rather than the ***wrong*** language. If the Japanese find out that you only have a few words in Japanese but are fluent in English, Spanish, and French, they may be less critical. While ideally you would speak Japanese, at least you speak other languages—you have worked at languages and gone through the effort. The sentence, "I'm sorry, I do not speak Japanese, but I do speak French and Spanish," can work very well to show that you are not the typical monolingual American.

Political Considerations

If you already work for a firm, your decision as to which language to study will be influenced by where your company does business. The political environment of international locations will also play a role. If you will be involved with the government to quite an extent and if all that communication must be in the native language, you may find it necessary to become at least functional in that language, meaning that you can communicate both orally and in writing although you may not have mastered the grammar and fine points of the language. The private sector might be more forgiving than the public sector when it comes to speaking the language. Being able to speak the language also carries symbolic value. If you do business with a firm in Quebec, you may get through on English, but your linguistic insensitivity could have serious negative consequences.

Appropriate Level of Fluency

Ideally you speak several languages fluently; that is, like the natives of the host country, you speak, write, understand, and think in the foreign language. That's the ideal; most people fall short of that goal. We use all sorts of phrases to describe the level of fluency. Typical labels are native, near-native, fluent, functional, and conversational. The labels are not very precise, and many speakers have a tendency to overstate their language proficiency. A Midwestern law firm in the United States claims that all of its partners are "fluent" in at least two foreign languages. Given the typical American attitude towards studying foreign languages, one may wonder what definition of *fluency* the firm uses.

While linguistic fluency is undoubtedly important and a great advantage when doing business with people from other cultures, it is not the only criterion. Equally important, as pointed out previously, is cultural fluency. A person who speaks some Spanish but is knowledgeable about the culture of Mexico will be more successful in doing business in Mexico than the person who speaks Spanish fluently but does not know anything about the culture of Mexico. Cultural learning must accompany language learning. Some argue that by learning a foreign language you are automatically exposed to the culture. That is not necessarily true. All too many language courses in the United States, Japan, Thailand, Russia, and many other countries are taught by teachers who have never been to the country or were only there for a short period of time, and possibly quite some time ago. Furthermore, the emphasis in many language classes is on the mastering of grammar and spelling rather than on understanding the underlying culture. Students studying the Japanese language may learn very little about Japan and the Japanese.

If you plan to live in the foreign country for an extended time period, your need to speak the language is greater than if you are there just for a few days. If you want to make that country a major center for your foreign manufacturing, your linguistic needs are greater than if you want to export a product that is in high demand (also see Chapter 10).

If you want to understand why people act the way they do, if you want to get a feel for their way of thinking to be better at negotiating, you need a higher level of fluency than if you have decided always to use an interpreter. If you rely on an interpreter, however, you should also be aware of the limitations you impose upon your business opportunities.

For most people it is easier to comprehend than to speak a foreign language. Listed below are a few possible reasons for this phenomenon:

- People are intimidated; therefore, they do not try.
- People are worried about using the wrong verb forms and tenses.
- People may be trying to translate a sentence from their own language word for word into the foreign language and realize that this process is not very effective. As a result, they get discouraged.
- People think too long about what they want to say so that they don't participate in the conversation. By the time they have formulated what they want to say, the conversation has moved on.
- People are worried about being judged negatively and about losing face.

Our level of comprehension is influenced by the speed with which the speaker goes through points, by the pronunciation, by the pauses in the conversation, and by colloquialisms and idioms. Speech patterns are affected by a variety of factors, among them ethnic background, geographic differences, and gender. For example, recent research studies have pointed out that men and women have very different speech patterns that greatly influence the perception of communication and the success of communication. Men tend to interrupt a speaker more frequently than women do. Men are more direct, whereas women are more indirect and ambiguous in what they say. If people who are native speakers of the same language have different communication styles based on different communication principles, we can understand that the problems are compounded when the speakers come from different cultures.

Perceptions of fluency are also influenced by nonverbal communication. Nonverbal communication plays a major role in all countries; however, the nonverbal is more pronounced in high-context cultures than in low-context cultures. If we are from a low-context background, we may not be consciously aware of the nonverbal—we may think that the meaning comes out of the spoken word. How much the nonverbal influences our comprehension, specifically if we speak in a foreign language, becomes obvious when we communicate in a foreign language on the telephone. The ring of the telephone in a foreign country can strike terror in the hearts of even courageous people. Even people who are fairly fluent may have problems on the telephone. All of a sudden they speak in isolation without nonverbal clues and nonverbal feedback. For example, they cannot see a facial expression signaling approval or doubt. The nonverbal aspects definitely help us in the comprehension process (also see Chapter 6).

THE COMPANY LANGUAGE

Choosing a Company Language

As companies expand their international dealings, the number of languages the employees have to deal with increases also. A domestic Korean company does not have to worry about different languages. As the company expands, the picture changes. When the firm establishes subsidiaries in Thailand and Taiwan, the company deals in three linguistic markets, Korean, Mandarin, and Thai. In which language should employees communicate with each other? The answer is to some extent influenced by staffing patterns (for a more detailed discussion of the influence of staffing on communication, refer to Chapter 11). If the Korean firm uses **ethnocentric staffing**, filling all managerial positions with Korean personnel in all three locations, all communications with headquarters and among the managers from the three subsidiaries can be in Korean. In ethnocentric staffing, all managers in all subsidiaries are from the home country, and the interface between the language of the home country and the host countries occurs somewhere in the subsidiaries. The Korean managers either must learn the local language or depend on translators to communicate with the local workforce.

Today, ethnocentric staffing is considered insensitive, exploitative, and outdated. Many firms, therefore, are using **polycentric staffing** patterns. In polycentric staffing, all managers in all subsidiaries come from the respective subsidiary country. That means the same Korean firm would hire only Taiwanese people for its subsidiary in Taiwan and only Thais for its subsidiary in Thailand. Polycentric staffing is based on the argument that local managers will be better able to communicate in the specific environment. The linguistic interface—the contact between the language of headquarters and the language of the subsidiary—occurs in the communication between headquarters and the subsidiary. In ethnocentric staffing, on the other hand, this contact of different languages occurs within the subsidiary. Polycentric staffing also makes the communication between subsidiaries more difficult. In which language, for example, do the Thais and the Taiwanese communicate with each other?

The communication problem is even more pronounced in **geocentric staffing**. In geocentric staffing, the best person is chosen for a job regardless of linguistic, cultural, and national background. In the above scenario, the company may have Taiwanese, Thais, and Koreans working at headquarters in Korea. Geocentric staffing brings people from diverse linguistic and cultural backgrounds into the same office where they must work side by side. Exhibit 2–1 summarizes the characteristics of the various staffing patterns.

As a result of geographic expansion and changes in staffing, more and more companies have designated an official company language. That means all communication in a company will be conducted in the company language. That sounds easy enough; in practice it is somewhat more complex. A firm that is headquartered in Japan and does business in the United States, France, Germany, Holland, Saudi Arabia, Mexico, Brazil, South Africa, and Nigeria may decide that the company language is Japanese. It is unlikely that all of the employees in the various subsidiaries speak Japanese. The speaking of Japanese could hardly be made a condition of employment. In this case the company language refers to communication among managers from a certain level up. In the case of Japanese, given how few non-Japanese people actually speak Japanese, the firm would need a good number of Japanese managers at each subsidiary who would communicate with headquarters.

The firm does not have to choose the language of the home country where headquarters are located as its company language. It could decide that the language of the home country is not spoken by many people around the globe and therefore a more widely spoken language is a better choice. For example, Philips, a Dutch firm, has chosen English as its company language. Komatsu from Japan has set the goal that all employees, even in the Japanese home office, should communicate in English, and the firm provides the appropriate language lessons. Samsung from Korea also has started obligatory English language lessons for all its employees. This clearly is a recognition of the importance of English in international business. Indeed, English has become the lingua franca of international business. One typical example is the language of aviation. Pilots and flight controllers around the world are expected to communicate in English. For years French pilots resisted the use of English in French airspace, but then Air France ordered all its pilots to use only English

---

EXHIBIT 2–1   Staffing Patterns

	Headquarters Managers	*Subsidiary Managers*
Ethnocentric staffing	Home country	Home country
Polycentric staffing	Home country	Home country
Geocentric staffing	Best person regardless of country	Best person regardless of country

when talking to air-traffic controllers at Charles de Gaulle. It seems that safety considerations favor the change from French to English. Modern technology, the Internet, E-commerce, E-mail, and teleconferencing have greatly contributed to the international use of English. What U.S. businesspeople must keep in mind, however, is that ***all*** of these businesspeople are fluent in at least one other language besides English, namely their respective native language, and many of them in at least one additional language. A Korean businessperson fluent in English can do business in both Korean and English; an American businessperson fluent only in English can do business only in English. The Korean market will be more difficult to enter for Americans under these circumstances.

Traditionally, the choice of the official company language was the language of the home country. That seems to be changing, as the above examples indicate. If two firms from different countries do business and the language of neither is widely spoken, they face a different dilemma. They each may have their company language but that does not necessarily help in this case. To illustrate, let us assume a firm from Poland does business with a firm from Japan. The two firms have at least three options for communicating with each other, assuming the Poles do not speak Japanese and the Japanese do not speak Polish:

1. They can use a Polish-Japanese interpreter; however, the number of Polish-Japanese interpreters is probably quite limited.
2. They can use two interpreters: one a Polish-English interpreter, one a Japanese-English interpreter.
3. Both companies may have declared English as the company language; therefore, managers could directly negotiate in English.

Even if both sides speak English, they still face hurdles. For example, do they speak the same English, or does the Polish firm speak British English while the Japanese firm speaks American English? Furthermore, the English the Polish managers speak will have some Polish characteristics, and the English the Japanese managers speak will have some Japanese characteristics. Typically, the cultural references, thought, and language patterns of each side will influence their communication in English. They may have different preferences for organizing material and providing detail. [5]

No matter what the company language is, any international firm experiences the need to adjust to the differences between the company language and the local language(s) of foreign subsidiaries, partners, clients, and suppliers. With a company language that applies to all managers, the interface between languages typically takes place between management and local employees below the managerial level. A U.S. firm that uses English as the company language cannot expect that all of its employees in Venezuela speak English. Employees below the managerial level will probably speak Spanish. Therefore, translation will be necessary where the two languages come together.

A company language facilitates communication among subsidiaries and between headquarters and subsidiaries; it can, however, also give headquarters a wrong sense of security if headquarters personnel think everyone in the company is fluent in the company language. As many reports attest, businesspeople from English-speaking cultures have difficulties understanding the complications and consequences of limited English.

The following case illustrates some of the issues that arise even if a firm has a company language.

A U.S. firm with a subsidiary in Tokyo used English as the company language. The subsidiary had one American employee who spoke some Japanese but was not fluent. He did not read or write Japanese. The president and the two vice presidents spoke native Japanese. The president spoke very good German and on the surface good English. The vice president for finance also spoke German and some English, but his English was much more limited. The vice president for sales had very limited English. The marketing manager was Japanese with a B.A. from a university in the United States. His English was very good but getting rusty. The rest of the employees generally spoke a little English, such as tourist phrases, but not enough to carry on a conversation or do business in English.

Nobody at headquarters spoke Japanese. In this situation, all communication between headquarters and other subsidiaries occurred in English. Headquarters relied on the company language and assumed that communication was no problem. The reality was rather more complicated. In the Japanese subsidiary, for example, the American employee received all incoming memos from headquarters. He would read many of them and often respond to inquiries and, if asked, help the Japanese managers with their communications with headquarters. In effect, he was an interpreter in the communication between the subsidiary and headquarters. But he had not been sent to Tokyo for that purpose. He had a specific job to do; he was the operations manager and in charge of computerizing the subsidiary. The interpretation took place "on the side."

Headquarters sent lengthy financial memos on a weekly basis to the vice president for finance, whose English was limited. The memos were not adapted to a foreign speaker of English. Headquarters assumed that the vice president for finance read all the material; however, when the correspondence between headquarters and the subsidiary was examined, it became obvious that headquarters had to ask repeatedly for information a second and third time before the vice president for finance actually responded. Initially, the vice president was reluctant to discuss the situation, but after some time he admitted he was overwhelmed by the sheer volume of the correspondence. He did not read the original memos because it took too much time and because he got frustrated with all the details. He worked under the assumption that if someone *really* needed information from him, they would get back to him with specifics. He would have preferred a clear and concise summary of major points adapted to his level of English but what he got was lengthy memos written by native English speakers for native English speakers, and he was worried about losing face if he explained the problem. The vice president developed his own way of coping with the situation, a solution that was costly and time consuming.

The vice president for international operations at headquarters in the United States, when first asked about his communication with Japan by one of the authors, said there were no problems. "The Japanese speak English, so there is no language hurdle." Only after lengthy discussions did he admit that he was concerned about his interaction with Japan. He felt that the Japanese president of the subsidiary spoke "social" English but that he had a limited grasp of English when it came to business concepts and business discussions. The president of the Japanese subsidiary pretended to understand, and on the surface there were no problems, but the vice president at headquarters became increasingly frustrated with the communication process. He somehow just did not seem to get through. As a result, communication between headquarters and the subsidiary, although smooth on the surface, was complicated, often redundant, and ineffective.

Using Additional Foreign Language Expertise

How can you use your foreign language expertise if the company language is English? The purpose of the company language is to ensure that everyone in the company can understand everyone else; therefore, the use of foreign languages may be discouraged or at least limited. This comes back to the assumption that in an English-speaking firm, native English speakers do not need a foreign language since everything is written in English and all negotiations within the firm take place in English. As a result, a Japanese subsidiary of a firm headquartered in an English-speaking country may not hire the best person, but the person with the best English.

Patricia, who is French but speaks fluent English, Spanish, and Dutch, works for an American firm in the United States that does business in many countries, one of them France. The company language is English. She sends a copy of all the memos she prepares to the European subsidiaries to her boss and, if necessary, to other managers. When she corresponds with Arnaud Marchais, who is French and speaks limited English, she must write in English because that is the company language and because the managers at headquarters she sends copies to speak either no French or only limited French. It looks as if her language expertise is being wasted.

Patricia has found a way around the dilemma though. In some cases, she writes a memo to Arnaud Marchais in French and then sends a copy of the original plus an English translation to the people who need a copy. This, of course, takes extra time, and some managers at headquarters may still resent the use of French and may be suspicious of secret dealings.

Patricia can use her foreign language expertise more extensively when she talks to Arnaud on the phone or when she visits the subsidiary in France. Arnaud appreciates the fact that he can contact Patricia and explain to her in French about a particular problem and get an answer he can understand. Patricia's ability to communicate with Arnaud in the French language and culture has improved business considerably, and Arnaud feels understood and appreciated.

In both the examples, the Japanese and the French, the company language, although the official language, may not be sufficient for clear and effective communication. An official company language will simplify communication within an international firm, but to assume that the declaration of an official language will eliminate all communication problems, even within the firm, is absurd. Monolingual companies of native speakers have many communication problems; no wonder that people from different backgrounds speaking the same company language have communications problems. Intercultural communication goes beyond the mastery of a foreign language.

THE ROLE OF THE INTERPRETER

To overcome the communication problems in international business created by the multitude of languages spoken around the globe, businesses hire interpreters or translators. Many people use the two terms interchangeably; however, there is a difference. Strictly speaking, a translator translates a message verbatim; the interpreter also translates but, as the word implies, also interprets the message in cultural terms. An interpreter not only translates an idiom but provides the equivalent idiom in the target language. The question that arises is how far the interpreter can go in the cultural adaptation. For example, it is generally considered acceptable to translate *bonjour* with *hello*, but it is not acceptable to translate a very casual greeting with a very formal one just because the listener comes from a formal culture.

The interpreter facilitates mutual understanding and comprehension. She is a conduit and does not enter the discussion on her own behalf. In successful interpretation the

EXHIBIT 2–2   Communicating through an Interpreter

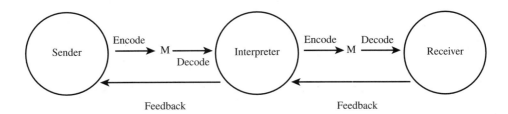

intended message gets across at first try. This sounds easy enough, but there are numerous hurdles and problems. Let us look at the process as illustrated in Exhibit 2–2.

The interpreter must decode what the speaker says and then encode the message for the listener. Businesspeople who are new to international business often assume that the interpreter understands all the signals that are being sent and decodes them appropriately as intended. This requires that the interpreter is both linguistically and culturally fluent in both languages and cultures. The interpreter must pick up both the verbal and nonverbal signs of all people in the discussion.

The Importance of Choosing a Good Interpreter

Interpreters should be chosen with great care. Native speaking ability does not automatically make a person a skilled and effective interpreter. For example, a U.S. transportation company asked a woman from Germany to translate several business letters relating to trucks. The problem was that the woman did not know the terms relating to trucking in either German or English. She was well educated but had no idea what a *Sattelschlepper* was in German and, therefore, could not translate the term correctly as *semi-truck*. When she pointed that out to the American who made the request that she translate, he was puzzled. His response was, "If you speak German, then you can translate this well enough. We just want to know what the letter says." Actually, however, the interpreter must be fluent in the language of the field in which she translates. A poet may be able to interpret for Japanese and English speakers in the field of literature but be at a loss when asked to interpret in business.

Interpreting is hard work. People study for many years to become effective interpreters. Many businesspeople who don't speak a foreign language are under the assumption that a native speaker can easily and effectively act as an interpreter. They are totally unaware of the work involved in the process. As a result, many businesspeople hire foreign students or native speakers of the foreign language who live in the United States as interpreters for their companies. The results may be costly, embarrassing, and amusing.

Ricks, for example, relates that in one case a student from Indonesia who was not familiar with computer terminology translated *software* with *underwear*.[6]

Hiring people who claim to be fluent in the target language when they are not can also be a problem. The Economic Development Committee of a county in Illinois was interested in attracting foreign businesses to the area. One of the target countries was Germany. The committee developed a brochure in English and then had it translated into German. The brochure looked good but had a number of language mistakes, although no major problems. In the process of preparing the brochure, the names of two members of the council had been omitted. The committee went ahead and prepared a brief statement explaining the omission and providing the names. This statement was translated and attached to all brochures. The translation of the supplement was a total disaster. It was almost unintelligible even if the reader knew both English and German. The committee would have done better to leave the names off rather than to send the "correction." Reading the supplement just confirmed all the prejudices Germans have about the low language ability and superficiality of Americans. The disastrous translation also showed that the committee was not very thorough and careful in checking the credentials of the translator.

Interpreters, then, must be chosen with the greatest care. The following guidelines will help you in making a good choice and getting an interpreter whose work you can use.

The Effective Use of an Interpreter—Some Guidelines

Hire Your Own Interpreter.   It is amazing how many businesspeople who are usually very careful about business matters rely on the foreign business partner to supply the interpreter. You definitely need to hire your own interpreter. Most embassies or commercial sections of an embassy have lists of translation and interpretation services that you might contact if you don't know anybody. Language institutes such as Berlitz, the Alliance Française, and the Goetheinstitut may also be able to help in finding an interpreter.

Why do you need your own interpreter? You need an interpreter who understands your side and who is loyal to you.

Midori Ito, a Japanese woman who regularly interprets for Japanese and U.S. businesses, emphasizes this particular point. She explains that in most cases she is hired and paid by the Japanese side and is asked to translate both for the Japanese and the Americans. Let us assume the Americans are preparing an answer to a question by the Japanese. They discuss the point among themselves before they finalize the answer. Mrs. Ito says that the Japanese negotiators regularly ask her for a translation or at least a summary of the discussion preceding the official response. The Americans don't know that, and they, in turn, hardly ever ask for that information on the Japanese side. The translator, on her part, does not volunteer that information. Her argument is that the Japanese pay her; they ask and the Americans don't. Her loyalty is to the Japanese side, not to the American side. Clearly, the Americans are at a disadvantage in this situation.

Whenever Possible, Meet with the Interpreter Beforehand.   You need to feel comfortable with the interpreter and develop a level of trust. Unless you can use the same interpreter each time you do business in Cairo, Taipei, or Seoul, you need to establish some common ground. This meeting will also assure you of the interpreter's competency in your language even though you may not be able to check the competency in the target language.

Hire Qualified Professionals.   Don't ask a colleague from another department to translate for you unless it is that person's job to translate for others. If you do use a colleague, you need to set the ground rules very carefully. Do you want translation only, or do you want input from the colleague? If you want input, then the colleague has to separate carefully his or her own comments from what the other side says.

Check the Technical Expertise of the Interpreter.   Even if you hire the interpreter via a reputable agency, you need to check the technical background of the interpreter. Has she translated in your field before? How much experience does she have? Has she kept up in the field? You may want to check references from past employers. As pointed out above, the technical expertise in your field is very important to ensure correct translations.

Inform the Interpreter of Your Business Plan and Objectives.   If the interpreter understands the overall objectives and the purpose of the meeting, she will be more effective than if she comes into the session uninformed and is asked to translate phrase by phrase. If the interpreter understands the overall goal, she will be able to interpret nuances better and see otherwise isolated statements in the overall context. It is easier to translate in context.

Treat the Interpreter as a Professional.   Even though you inform the interpreter of the objectives and provide necessary background information and details, the interpreter is not a member of the negotiation team. She is hired as an outside professional with specific expertise. To ask the interpreter to enter in the actual decision-making process and to ask the interpreter for business advice is wrong. It is neither fair to the interpreter nor to your business. Your relationship to the interpreter is professional and should be kept at arm's length.

Provide Breaks.   Interpreting is hard work. It is both mentally and physically exhausting. If you want good work from the interpreter, you must provide the right environment. Regular breaks for the interpreter are essential even if you feel you can still continue.

Speak Clearly.   Even if the interpreter is fluent in your language, you must speak clearly and at a reasonable pace. You should be particularly careful if you speak a dialect. The interpreter may have difficulty understanding you and following your reasoning. Dialects can be difficult for speakers of the same language; with foreign speakers the problems are compounded. Your interpreter must feel comfortable asking you to repeat something if she does not understand you the first time. The following example illustrates the difficulties that can arise between two speakers of the same language when one speaks a dialect.

A German MBA student at a university in the United States had an internship with a major German multinational. The student came originally from the north of Germany, from the area around Dortmund, and had been in the United States for four years. Her English was excellent. The German firm was located in the south of Germany near Stuttgart where people speak the local dialect, Swabian. This area is referred to as the German "Silicon Valley," the name used for the area in California where many high-tech computer companies have their headquarters.

Since the area around Stuttgart had been rather prosperous in the last few years, the natives were proud of their dialect and some even argued that the economic success was proof that the language, usually belittled by people from the north, was superior.

The intern had a hard time communicating with her co-workers in German. She spoke German, her manager and supervisor spoke German, but she typically would have to ask them to repeat what they said. Even after they repeated their messages in what they considered to be standard German, she sometimes didn't understand. Pronunciation and word choice were still affected by their dialect. A foreign interpreter who learned standard German would face the same problem. International managers need to remember to enunciate as clearly as possible. They don't want to waste time by needlessly repeating information.

Concentrate on the Business Partner, not on the Interpreter. Many businesspeople look at the interpreter as they speak and neglect the business partner. In order to get every bit of nonverbal information you can, you must concentrate on the other side and watch them as you speak. This is even more important if the other side has some knowledge of your language. Maybe they don't speak your language fluently, but they may speak some and follow the general trend of what you say as you give your message to your interpreter. In that case you want to be able to read their reaction to what you say as early as possible. Also, you want them to understand your nonverbal communication; therefore, you need to speak to the audience and not the interpreter.

When the interpreter translates your message, again you must watch the other side for all the nonverbal signals. In some cultures the nonverbal signals may be obvious; in others, such as Japanese culture, you will have to concentrate and watch more closely. With practice you will be able to decipher the nonverbal reactions more accurately and use the information in your responses and questions. If, for example, the other side acts surprised at what you say, you may want to find out the reasons. You may want to ask about the expectations in more detail.

As the people on the other side discuss your response, again watch closely. You need to ask the interpreter for the specifics of the discussion.

Also watch the other side as the interpreter translates into your language. They will watch for your reaction. In some cases you may want to ask the interpreter for word-for-word responses and also for the cultural translation of the response.

Find Out the Role of the Interpreter on the Other Side. The other side may have a professional interpreter or use an employee from the company. Maybe the person even is a regular member of the negotiation team. If at all possible, you should find out the status of the interpreter.

A number of businesspeople from the United States, not speaking the language of the partner and not knowing the status of the interpreter, talk to the interpreter. After all, the interpreter speaks English and seems to know what is going on. They feel comfortable with that person. Only too late may they find out that they have just spent time with an outsider or subordinate and neglected the person or persons in charge.

Check the Work of the Interpreter. You may argue that the reason you have an interpreter is because you can't speak the language and, therefore, you cannot check the accuracy of the translation. Still, you can do a lot to ensure accuracy. In all written materials you need to check the accuracy of names, dates, and numbers. An interpreter who realizes that you check will be more careful in her work. As numbers can be difficult to translate and as misunderstandings can easily occur, you should always write out numbers, just to be on the safe side. In Chinese, for example, where 10,000 is a unit of measurement, people should always give the number of zeros in the number. Chinese frequently mis-translate as *millions* numbers that are hundreds of thousands. A similar problem occurs between English and German. The Germans use the following sequence: thousand, hundred thousand, million, milliarde, billion. English jumps from million to billion. When the Americans say that the flood damage in the United States in 1993 was $15 billion ($15,000,000,000), in German the same figure would be $15 *milliarden.* If the translator uses the word *billion* in the German context, the damage would be greatly overstated. Even within the English-speaking world *billion* does not mean the same quantity. In British English, 1,000,000,000 is a thousand million; the British billion is a million million, or a trillion in the United States (1,000,000,000,000).

COMMUNICATION WITH NON-NATIVE SPEAKERS

In many situations you may not be fluent in the other language but an interpreter may not be available, and you must deal with the non-native speaker who is not fluent in your language directly. The success of the communication will depend to a great extent upon how well you adapt to that person. Talking loudly and repeating everything does not necessarily improve the communication. If the other side does not understand you at your regular pitch and volume of speech, that person will not understand you any better if you scream. If the other side is not familiar with baseball, they will not understand your statement, "This time we are going to be successful; all the bases are loaded and our heavy hitter is stepping up to the plate," and no amount of repeating will change that. Communicating with non-native speakers in any language takes skill and experience. The following points may help you to be more successful.

Effective Face-to-Face Communication

Enunciate.   You must speak clearly so that the person understands the words you use. Contractions are difficult because they blur over individual words.

Speak Slowly.   Native speakers in any language seem to speak fast; at least that is the perception of the non-native speaker. Slowing down helps the non-native speaker to comprehend what you say. You must adjust your speed to the level of the other side. The non-verbal clues your partner sends will help you to adjust. If the other person looks puzzled or often has to ask you to repeat something, you may be speaking too fast. In that case you should repeat your idea slowly and, if that still does not work, repeat it again using different words.

An Australian who has studied some Arabic wants to show what he has learned. He will appreciate it if his partner from Egypt will slow down and give him a chance to both understand and speak.

Avoid Slang and Colloquialisms.   Unless the speaker has lived in your country for some time, you should avoid slang and colloquial expressions. Slang changes; therefore, the other side may not be familiar with the latest terms. For example, a person who speaks English fluently but has not had any contact with the United States over the past few years may not know what a student means when saying *Get a Life* or *awesome.* An executive

idiomatic expressions

who studied German years ago will not have any idea what *Ich hab keinen Bock*, the adolescent expression for *I'm not interested* or *I don't care,* means. The French-Canadians say *J'ai mon voyage* (I have my trip) when an English speaker might say *That's the last straw.* They say *Ce n'est pas un cadeaux* (it is no gift) when something is not going well; English speakers might say *It's no joke.* In France these French-Canadian idioms would sound odd and be unclear.

Foreign language instruction in most countries emphasizes the correct and formal rather than the colloquial language. Also, in very formal cultures, slang may be offensive and signal a lack of respect. Curse words may also signal disrespect. While in formal American English cursing is not acceptable, many businesspeople use terms that at one time were considered swear words. *Damn,* as in "I know damn well he is going to be at the meeting," is one of those words. Unless you know the other side very well, avoid any language that could be offensive.

Be Careful about Jokes. Humor does not translate well. What one culture considers funny another may consider not funny, crude, or rude. In addition, humor loses much in translation. Johnny Carson found that out when his show was aired in Great Britain. His jokes were rooted in American culture and often were based on current events. The British were not familiar with the events and did not share the American sense of humor, and the show was canceled after only a short time. In order to appreciate jokes, the listener must share cultural references with the speaker. In the absence of that common experience, jokes lose their funniness.

Humor, in many cases, is based on puns and word plays. Those seldom translate into another language. If a lengthy explanation is required, the situation is usually not considered funny anymore. You may have heard of the speaker who delivered his speech through a translator to his foreign audience. His audience laughed at the appropriate places. What the speaker did not know was that the interpreter supplied his own jokes or asked the audience to laugh because the speaker just told a joke and it would be impolite not to laugh. Just imagine this situation if the speaker is addressing an audience of people from 10 different countries who all have their own simultaneous translators. Jokes would be a nightmare in this environment.

Be Sincere. While goodwill and sincerity alone do not get the message across, they help in creating a positive atmosphere. When both sides are sincere and each side recognizes that, then both will try harder to communicate verbally. Genuine sincerity can help overcome obstacles. If businesspeople from two countries sit down to negotiate a deal, one can reasonably assume that both sides are sincere and genuinely interested. One can also assume that they respect each other and don't intend to insult each other. If something sounds strange or even insulting, chances are that the speaker used the wrong words and didn't mean any harm. If both sides assume goodwill, many hurdles can be overcome.

Be Culturally Sensitive. The more you know about the culture of the other side, the easier it will be to speak with a foreigner who speaks only a little of your language. For example, a person doing business in Japan will be more successful if he knows the basics of social behavior and etiquette. Even though he speaks no Japanese and the Japanese counterpart only speaks some English, they can communicate if both sides are culturally sensitive. The non-Japanese businessperson who is formal, uses last names, is nonaggressive, and listens carefully may succeed. The Japanese businessperson who is more outgoing and verbal than he normally would be when dealing with someone from a more assertive culture may be more successful also.

Cultural mistakes sometimes drown out the verbal message. That is true in both international business and in domestic firms that employ people from a variety of ethnic and cultural backgrounds. Maria Lopez from Peru has worked for several months as a supervisor in the United States. She speaks some English. She comes from a very traditional and formal background and is used to being addressed with her last name by nonfamily. As her fellow-supervisor, you think she does good work and you want to compliment her. You are outgoing and friendly and say to her "Maria, you are doing good work." She may be so offended about your using her first name that the rest of the message may be lost.

You may argue that if Maria Lopez wants to get ahead in an American company, she must adapt to American cultural norms. However, you need to ask yourself what your goal is. Is it to Americanize Maria or to build an effective work team? If you want the effective team, then you need to consider the values of your employees. Ideally, you would provide training for your non-native speakers in American language and culture, and for your American employees at least in the culture of their foreign co-workers.

Keep a Sense of Humor.   Perhaps this should be the guiding rule for communicating in any foreign language. You must be able to laugh at your own mistakes and not be offended by honest mistakes from the other side.

Effective Written Communication

To avoid any confusion on the other side, you must carefully proofread all written communications for spelling, punctuation, and grammar. Errors that may not pose a problem for native speakers can be serious hurdles to understanding for the non-native speaker. The following guidelines will help you to be more effective in your written communication.

Use Plenty of White Space.   The non-native speaker may need space for comments and translations. Provide that space to facilitate understanding and communication.

Use Correct Titles and Spellings of Names.   Accuracy in the spelling of names will show that you care, that you are sincere and of goodwill. Most people get annoyed at the misspelling of their names, so be doubly careful in that area. Ask if necessary.

Understand Patterns of Organization.   With our limited language ability, we are better able to follow information if all the other "noise" (any type of distraction) is eliminated. One source of noise is organization. People from different cultures organize information differently. People from East Asian cultures organize material based on relationships of elements rather than the linear progression typical of Western thinking. Both groups are convinced that their arguments are logically developed and presented. There are also differences, however, within each camp. Canadians, for example, like to have recommendations at the beginning of a report. The rest of the report provides a rationale and necessary background. The emphasis is on the practical use of information. The Germans, on the other hand, prefer a chronological arrangement and presentation. They give the background first; the recommendation comes at the end. The French, much more than the Germans and the Canadians, delight in the linguistically elegant presentation of the argument. The presentation is of importance for its own sake in addition to the practical considerations.

If the German knows that the Canadian prefers to have the recommendations first, he may decide to arrange his information that way. Since the organization corresponds with his expectations, the Canadian will be able to concentrate on the actual message and not lose patience with the "slower" German presentation (also see Chapter 5). Both the Germans and the Canadians may want to watch more carefully for style and presentation of the argument when communicating with the French.

The French, Germans, and Canadians, however, are puzzled by the relation-building arrangement of the Japanese presentation. While rapport is considered important, neither the French, nor the Germans, nor the Canadians consider the building of rapport as an integral part of the presentation. The logical argument is what sells, rather than the establishment of relationships (see Chapter 5).

Use Headings.   Headings, important in all business writing, are particularly important when communicating with non-native speakers. They will help the person understand the organization and your line of reasoning.

Be Careful with Numbers.   You always need to check the accuracy of numbers and be familiar with the conventions of writing numbers. $5,350.48 becomes $5.350,48 in most European languages. The comma and the decimal point are reversed, and often the punctuation to set off thousands is not used at all. Confusion in the punctuation of numbers creates confusion in the meaning. To be safe, you may want to write out crucial numbers.

Be Careful with Dates.   Dates can become important when two firms disagree on contract conditions, delivery dates, and meeting dates. Different cultures have different ways of writing dates as the following example illustrates:

American usage: May 6, 20xx or 05/6/20xx

German usage: 6. Mai 20xx or 6. 5. 20xx

Increasing international usage: 20xx May, 6 or 20xx, 05, 06

To avoid confusion, you should always write out the name of the month.

Avoid Abbreviations.   Abbreviations hinder the process of comprehension. They may be convenient for the writer, but they are difficult for the reader. The same goes for acronyms, as pointed out earlier. A reader who does not know that ASAP means as soon as possible will have to pause and think before going on. The abbreviation interrupts the flow of thought. A businessperson from Manila who speaks German may not know that the abbreviation *betr.:* stands for *betreffs* and means *subject.*

Follow the Conventions of Written Communication.   You should study the conventions of your counterpart's culture. For example, business letters follow different formats in different countries. In international firms, subsidiaries around the globe may use the same format. A letter from a Nigerian subsidiary in France probably uses a French format; Japanese employees of a German firm probably use the German format.

Although business letters from different countries all provide information on the sender, the receiver, and the date of the letter, the placement of this information can vary widely. If you cannot read the language of the sender or if you do not know the placement of the parts, you may get confused. Following are some examples of letters from different cultures. Obviously, within a country variations in style and format exist. The letters presented here are simply samples of formats. The cultural influences on organization of business letters are discussed in more detail in Chapter 5. The format of letters is also influenced by channel choice. For example, some writers do not follow the conventions for letters when they transmit them by fax. The letters from Iran and Hong Kong (see Exhibit 2–6 and 2–7) do not provide an inside address.

In most cases, business letters are written on letterhead stationery providing information on address, telephone, and fax numbers. German letters also provide the company's bank numbers.

United States Business Letters.   In the United States, a business letter has the following parts (Exhibit 2–3): letterhead/return address, date, inside address (address of the receiver), salutation, body of the letter, complimentary close, and signature block with typed name of sender below the handwritten signature. After that comes information on enclosures, initials of the typist, and names of people who receive a copy of the letter. Increasingly American business letters are blocked; that means paragraphs and all parts of the letter are flush with the left margin. Business letters are always single spaced.

German Business Letters.   The German format is quite different. Most company stationery has a line for annotations. In the example in Exhibit 2–4 this line lists (left to right) the initials of the recipient, the subject of the letter, a filing number for the recipient, the telephone extension of the writer, and the date. Sometimes this line gives the initials of the secretary and the sender. The important difference is that this information comes before the salutation, whereas in the United States most of that information comes at the end if it is provided at all.

The name of the company appears below the complimentary close. Traditionally, German letters are signed, but the name of the sender is not typed. In the example, it is impossible to decipher the name of the writer. If Frau Boehmer, who received the letter in Exhibit 2–4, wants to send a reply, she must send it to the department rather than to a particular individual. In contrast to practice in the United States, the German style emphasizes the company rather than the identity of the individual sender. The writer is an agent of the firm. Frequently German business letters are signed by two people. [7]

French Business Letters.   French letters (see Exhibit 2–5) typically use indented style; blocked style is rarely used. The date can follow or precede the inside address, which appears on the right-hand side. As in German letters, the zip code precedes the name of the city, and the name of the city is set off by a double space. The format of the address is governed by postal regulations.

French business letters always have a subject line. Initials and reference numbers, if they are given at all, appear after the inside address before the subject line and salutation.

In French business letters the complimentary close may be followed by the signature of the writer and the typed name or just the typed name.[8]

Iranian Business Letter.   The letter in Exhibit 2–6 is from Iran. Unless you can read Farsi, you will not be able to read anything in the letter, not even the date, name of sender, or name of company. The letter is written from right to left. The English translation appears in the Western style, left to right. In the upper right-hand corner of the original appears the reference number of the letter by which it is filed. Below that number comes the date, October 2, 1360. The date is based on the Islamic calendar, which starts in 632 A.D. of the Western calendar. The signature at the bottom comes after the typed name of the sender and the company.

EXHIBIT 2–3   United States Format for Business Letters

COMMUNICATION CONSULTANTS INTERNATIONAL

3829 Willow Road
Normal, Illinois 61761
Tel: (309) 452-1111
Fax: (309) 452-2222

February 29, 20xx

Mr. Abraham Monroe
Director of Marketing
Leisure Wheels, Inc.
501 Grant Street
Kansas City, MO 64141

Dear Mr. Monroe:

Thank you for the background information on marketing training at Leisure Wheels, Inc. This material will be very helpful in preparing training sessions that will meet the particular needs of your people.

At your request, the two-day seminar will pay special attention to intercultural communication issues to enhance the skills of the marketing team as Leisure Wheels, Inc., expands internationally. The attached seminar schedule reflects the changes we discussed on the phone yesterday.

For the seminar I will need the following equipment:

- overhead projector
- flip chart
- video equipment
- slide projector

Communication Consultants, Inc. appreciates the opportunity to provide the training for your employees. I look forward to being in Kansas City on March 20 and 21, 20xx.

Sincerely,

Maxwell Hamill
IV

EXHIBIT 2–4   German Business Letter

Bayer AG

Personalabteilung
Auszubildende

5090 Leverkusen, Bayerwerk
Telefon: (02 14) 30-1 (Vermittlung)
Telex: 85 103-0 by d
Telefax; (02 14) 3066328 und 3066411
Telegramme: Bayerpersonal Leverkusen
Konten: Postgirokonto Köln 37 82-501
Landeszentralbank Leverkusen 37
508001

Frau
Christina Boehmer
401 Walker Hall

USA-Normal, Illinois 61761

Ihre Zeichen	Ihre Nachricht	Bewerber-Nr.	Telefon-Durchwahl	Leverkusen
			(0214) 30	
		nk	81477	29.09.00

Sehr geehrte Frau Boehmer,
Sie haben sich bei uns um ein Praktikum beworben.
Leider können wir Ihre Bewerbung nicht berücksichtigen, da im angegebenen
Zeitraum alle Praktikantenplätze in der von Ihnen benötigten Fachrichtung bereits
vergeben sind.
Wir bedauern, Ihnen diesen Bescheid geben zu müssen und senden Ihnen Ihre
Bewerbungsunterlagen zurück.
Mit freundlichen Grüßen
BAYER AG

Anlage

(continued)

Chinese Business Letter from Hong Kong.   The letter from Hong Kong in Exhibit 2–7
is written by hand, although new computer programs now enable Chinese to key in words.
The letter is written from left to right although traditionally Chinese is written from right
to left and top to bottom. In this letter the date appears last after the signature. Since
the letterhead is in English, a non-Chinese reader can read the name and address of the
company.

EXHIBIT 2–4 German Business Letter (translation)

Very honored Mrs. Boehmer,

You have applied for an internship.

Unfortunately, we cannot consider your application because during the time you requested all internship slots have already been filled.

We regret to have to give you this decision and send back your application materials.

With best wishes

BAYER AG

Encl.

THE IMPACT OF TECHNOLOGY ON ORAL AND WRITTEN COMMUNICATION

The technological revolution during the last decade has had a tremendous impact on intercultural communication practices. We will address the influence of technology throughout the book.

As telephone service has improved around the world and as prices have dropped, more and more businesses use the telephone for discussions that would have required formal letters or a personal visit in the past. The immediacy of the contact has advantages and disadvantages. In the past, Cheetan Shah from India could take some time and contemplate the business relationship with Mario Escalante from Chile. He might think about the relationship for several days, discuss it with some business colleagues, and ultimately send a letter to Mario Escalante. Today, it is very likely that Cheetan Shah gets on the phone to discuss the issues at hand. That means Mario Escalante must react immediately; it also means both sides are directly confronted with language issues.

Teleconferencing is used by more and more businesses in an effort to cut down on travel costs. People can have a virtual meeting and be in the "same room." They can see each other and get all the verbal and nonverbal feedback that allows. For this medium to be successful, participants should get training. Even if everyone participating speaks the same language, a teleconference may be intimidating, particularly for people from more quiet and reserved cultures. An Italian manager, for example, might come across as domineering, whereas a manager from Vietnam might appear to the Italian as uninterested. In addition, bringing people together from 10 different locations around the globe may present a logistical problem, and time differences and holiday schedules may make a global teleconference challenging.

E-mail has become a channel of choice for communication. It is fast and unrestricted by different time zones. However, the immediacy also can present some problems. E-mail

EXHIBIT 2–5 French Business Letter

ETABLISSEMENT MAZET

15, rue de Verdun
44000 Nantes

Tél.: 605 90 22   TELEX 340722
Adresse Télegraphique EDUREX   CCP PARIS 23650
                                                        Banque Société Générale

IRAF COMMUNICATION
23, avenue Gaston

33100 BORDEAUX

Nantes, le 26 mars 20xx

Réf. JL
Objet: LAKISRA ESAL

A l'attention de Messieurs Frédéric et Michel Ruselary

Messieurs,
    Faisant suite à nos divers entretiens, je vous confirme, par la présente, que je détiens actuellement 50% des parts de la LAKISRA ESAL dont le siège est situé à Paris, 78 rue de Richelieu et dont le gérant est Monsieur Attregab.

    Je m'engage irrévocablement par la présente à vous en céder le nombre correspondant à 50% des parts totales de la dite LAKISRA ESAL.

    Cette opération sera réalisée dans les meilleurs délais, et selon des modalités conformes aux pratiques professionelles. En particulier, la valeur de cession des dites parts sera établie en fonction de la situation comptable de la LAKISRA ESAL au jour de la cession.

    Par ailleurs, je vous confirme que le capital de cette société est en majeure partie constitué par l'apport du scénario du projet du film "Hotel Godin" dont je suis l'auteur intégral et exclusif.

    Dans l'attente, veuillez recevoir, Messieurs, nos meilleures salutations.

Jaques Lagose

(continued)

EXHIBIT 2–5   French Business Letter (translation)

Gentlemen,

To follow up on our many meetings, I am confirming to you by this letter that I am actually holding 50 percent of the shares of LAKISRA ESAL whose headquarters is located in Paris, 78 rue de Richelieu, and of which the general manager is Mr. Attregab.

I am engaging myself irrevocably by this letter to transfer over to you the amount corresponding to 50 percent of the total shares of said LAKISRA ESAL.

This operation will be carried out without delay, and according to modalities that conform to professional practices. In particular, the value of the transfer of said shares will be established within the accounting regulations of LAKISRA ESAL for the day of the transfer.

Herewith I am confirming to you that the assets of this corporation for the greater part consist of the revenues of the script of the film project "Godin Hotel" of which I am the main and only author.

In the meantime, please receive, gentlemen, our best salutations.

Jaques Lagose

---

lends itself to an informal and personal writing style that may turn off someone who comes from a more formal cultural background. As the nonverbal feedback is missing, the sender of the message does not get any signals that would help to gauge the level of tone and salutation and complimentary close. E-mail seems to invite a more chatty approach; it feels more like talking, and as a result, the writer may use an informal approach where a more formal one would be more appropriate.

Compatibility of technology may also play a role in the success of communication. Lynn Robertson sent an E-mail with an attachment to Brian Eldridge in Moldova. She wanted to make sure that the format of her message was kept. The E-mail message itself was a short cover note. The problem was that Brian had a hard time opening the attachment. Even worse, once the technical issue of downloading had been overcome, it turned out that the downloading process took almost 45 minutes. In a country where telephone lines are not reliable and the cost of the use of the Internet is based on the length of the connection, this became a very expensive message.

Some Guidelines for Communicating with Businesspeople from Different Cultures

Every language has its own unique speech patterns, idioms, and metaphors that are difficult to translate. The dictionary, as pointed out previously, does not always help. For

EXHIBIT 2–6 Iranian Business Letter

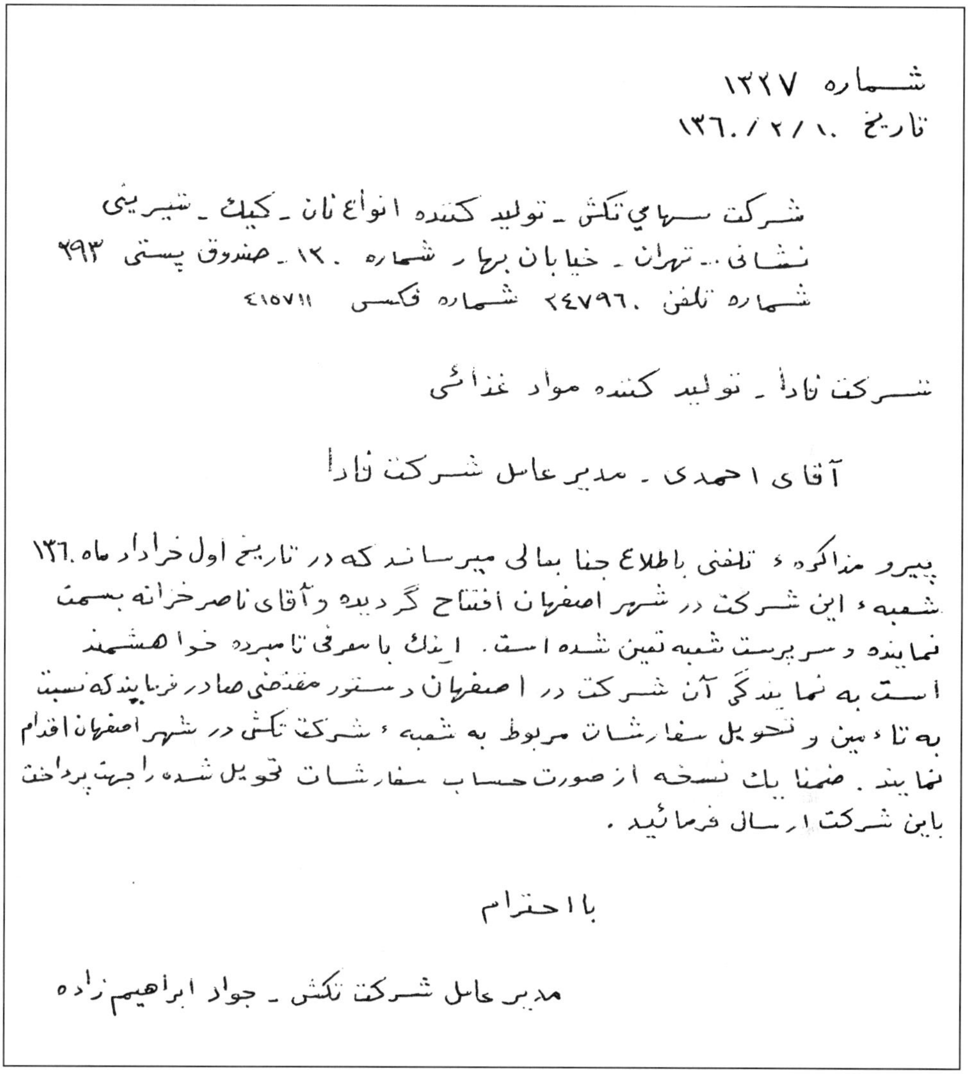

شماره ۱۲۲۷
تاریخ ۱۳۶۰/۲/۱۰

شرکت سهامی تکش ـ تولید کننده انواع نان ـ کیک ـ شیرینی
نشانی ـ تهران ـ خیابان برج ـ شماره ۱۲۰ ـ صندوق پستی ۲۹۳
شماره تلفن ۲۴۷۹۶۰ شماره فکس ۴۱۵۷۱۱

شرکت نادا ـ تولید کننده مواد غذائی

آقای احمدی ـ مدیر عامل شرکت نادا

پیرو مذاکرهء تلفنی باطلاع جنابعالی میرساند که در تاریخ اول خرداد ماه ۱۳۶۰
شعبهء این شرکت در شهر اصفهان افتتاح گردیده و آقای ناصر خزانه بسمت
نماینده و سرپرست شعبه تعیین شده است . اینک با معرفی نامبرده خواهشمند
است به نمایندگی آن شرکت در اصفهان دستور مقتضی صادر فرمایند که نسبت
به تأمین و تحویل سفارشات مربوط به شعبهء شرکت تکش در شهر اصفهان اقدام
نمایند . ضمناً یک نسخه از صورت حساب سفارشات تحویل شده را جهت پرداخت
باین شرکت ارسال فرمائید .

با احترام

مدیر عامل شرکت تکش ـ جواد ابراهیم زاده

(continued)

example, businesspeople from the United States use many words and idioms from the military and from sports. Businesses have strategies, they go on the offensive, they plan the attack, they dig in, they have price wars, they destroy the enemy (the competition), they rally the troops, they are on the offensive or defensive, they have intelligence gathering systems, and so on. Most Americans use this terminology without being aware of its militaristic origin. To people from a more reserved and peaceful culture, businesspeople from the United States may come across as very combative and aggressive. Thus U.S. businesspeople may want to tone down the fight symbols and choose a more cooperative approach in their language.

EXHIBIT 2–6   Iranian Business Letter (translation)

No. 1327
Date: 10/2/1360

           Takesh Corporation—Producer of Various Breads, Cakes, and Pastries
           Address—Tehran-Bahar Street No. 120-mailbox # 293
           Telephone 247960   Fax 415711

Fada Corporation—Food Supplier
    Mr. Ahmadi—President of Fada Corporation

Since our previous telephone conversation, I have to inform you that as of date March 1st 1360 Takesh Corporation opened a new branch at the city of Esfahan and Mr. Nasar Kaha has been placed as the branch manager. With the introduction of the new branch, you can order your pastry supplies directly from Esfahan. In addition, please send a copy of your receipt indicating that you have paid for the pastries back to our home office in Tehran.

           Sincerely
           President of Takesh Corporation—Jawadeh Ebrahimzade

---

Sports also have provided U.S. businesspeople with countless metaphors. Again, most businesspeople use the terminology without being aware of the consequences. Baseball and football are important sports in the United States, and both men and women have integrated sports terminology into their business vocabulary. They assume that everyone understands what it means, even though in many cases they themselves do not know or care much about sports. Some typical phrases are listed below:

The bases are loaded.

He hit a home run.

He got to first base.

Send him down to the minors.

He struck out.

He is out in left field.

He has a good batting average.

We want a level playing field.

All the bases are covered.

Monday-morning quarterbacking.

Third down, nine to go.

Touchdown.

EXHIBIT 2–7   Letter from Hong Kong

EFI-TECH INTERNATIONAL
ROOM 1200
16 CHATER ROAD
HONG KONG
Tel: 63124   Fax: 64144

李文山先生：

　　您好，我們雖然不相認識，但我曾通過萬年塑膠廠的何廠長介紹，對貴公司產品很感興趣，何廠長自上月到貴廠參觀後，事後感觸很深，特別是對您們所用的科技以及產品的質素，更是讚不絕口。

　　本公司是經營出入口生意，已有廿多年經驗，產品多從內地入口，再轉消到世界各地，尤以美國為主，從何廠長口中得知貴公司最近有意找出口商把產品轉消到美國，我相信本公司有絕對的能力和經驗給您提供服務。

　　所以，我希望李先生能在百忙之中，安排一個時間讓本人親自與您介紹本公司，我十分希望能早日收到您的回音。

祝　商安

　　　　　　　　　　　　　　　　　　張元欽敬上

　　　　　　　　　　　　　　　　　　1994 - 4 - 20

(continued)

EXHIBIT 2–7   Letter from Hong Kong (translation)

Dear Mr. Lee:

How do you do? Even though we have never met before, I have heard a lot about your company from Mr. Ho, the plant manager of Men-Nan Manufacturing Company. Mr. Ho visited your factory last month, and he is impressed by the kind of technology you use in your factory, and the high quality of your product.

We have twenty years of experience in the importing and exporting business. Most of the merchandise comes from Mainland China, and then is resold to the United States. According to Mr. Ho, your company is looking for an exporter to help expand the U.S. market for your products. We truly believe that our company has the ability and experience to serve your needs.

I hope that we can arrange to meet sometime in the future. I am looking forward to introducing our company to you.

Wishing you prosperity in business,

Truly,

Yuen-Yam Cheung
General Manager

20th April, 1993

Unless people from other cultures are familiar with baseball and football as played in the United States, they will not understand the above phrases, no matter how good their English is. A professor of English business communication in Belgium, for example, had read Lee Iacocca, former president of the former United States–based Chrysler Corporation. However, he admitted that he did not understand much of the terminology. Lee Iacocca used U.S. sports terminology, and the Belgian, not familiar with baseball and football, had a hard time understanding the meaning. He found reading the book a frustrating experience.

A dictionary, unless it is a specialized dictionary of sports or colloquial expressions, will not help in all cases. For example, *Langenscheidt New College German Dictionary* translates *home run* with: *Baseball: Lauf um sämtliche Male auf einen Schlag* (run around all bases with one hit).[9] This means absolutely nothing to a German who does not understand baseball. The German would not understand the meaning of a home run in baseball, let alone the meaning the term takes on in business. *The New Cassel's French Dictionary* does not even list the word *home run*. As with military terminology, the American-English speaker must avoid sports terminology when speaking to non-native speakers of English.

If you know some characteristics of a foreign language, even if you don't speak it fluently, you may be better able to adapt your English to speakers of the other language. Many English words have either a Germanic or French/Latin root. You can communicate better with a native speaker of French who has limited English if you choose English words based on French or Latin. The French person will find it easier to understand *descend* than *going down*, *ascend* than *going up*. The German, on the other hand, will understand you better if you say *going down* rather than *descending, going up* rather than *ascending* because these words are closer to German.

You must, however, be careful that you don't use words that appear similar but have very different meanings. You may know that the word *gift* is also used in German and decide to use it when talking with a German. In that case, you need to know that *gift* in German means *poison*. The word is exactly the same, but the meaning is radically different. A gift shop in northern Michigan whose owner was trying to give the establishment an ethnic flavor is called the *German Gifthaus,* literally the *German House of Poisoning,* hardly what the owners intended to communicate.

Clearly, the more you know about another culture and language, the easier it will be for you to communicate. For any country you do business in you need to learn at least the basic phrases for greeting, asking directions, making an apology, and showing appreciation. This does not make you fluent, but it can show your sincerity, especially if you improve your language proficiency over time.

Communication with a Multicultural Workforce

Since World War II, the world has seen unprecedented migration of people. The United States has an increasing number of immigrants from India, Pakistan, Arabic countries, Mexico, China, and Southeast Asia. European countries have recently had to cope with an influx of people from Russia, Poland, Turkey, Bosnia, Algeria, and Vietnam. Many of the people come in hopes of a better economic future. Even Japan, which prides itself on a homogeneous population, faces a growing foreign workforce, though very small by American and European standards. And oil-rich Arabic countries employ a number of foreigners from the Philippines, India, Pakistan, and Indonesia.

As a result, businesses in all industrial countries are confronted with an increasingly diverse workforce, and business must deal with the issues of diverse languages and cultures on an everyday basis. Intercultural communication is an important topic not just for international business but for domestic business as well. The question is what businesses need to do to build a team with common goals, not always an easy task. The old attitude that immigrants should adapt to the culture of the host country and learn the language may be unrealistic. Some immigrant groups cling to their native language; others don't want to give up their culture. They may perceive a materialistic obsession in industrial countries and resent it even though they may come to an industrial country to improve their economic situation.

A business that manufactures high-precision instruments must make sure that all employees understand the importance of accuracy and tolerances. The business must see to it that all non-native speakers understand instructions clearly and follow them. Social issues aside, it is in the best interest of the business to educate the foreign workforce in the goals of the business. For the process of education to be successful, managers need to understand the backgrounds of the workforce.

If the workforce has a mixed cultural and linguistic background, then this business must see to it that people from different backgrounds get along with each other. Management should provide intercultural training to all employees from the top down to facilitate the work towards a common goal. Companies may have to prepare instructions and policies in the major languages spoken by the employees and establish groups and teams that help overcome cultural hurdles. This process takes time and resources. It is important that all employees receive training, not just the ones from the "foreign" culture.

While one can argue that it is the responsibility of the immigrants to adapt both culturally and linguistically, one must look at the broader context and the nature of the business. A business might very well decide that adaptation to the immigrants' culture pays off.

A woman from China who sells insurance in central Illinois has developed the Asian community as her major clientele. She has been extremely successful with that group and ascribes her success to the cultural and linguistic adaptation of American insurance practices to the values of the Asian clientele. She has business cards and brochures printed in Japanese, Chinese, and Korean, her major client groups. She wants to sell insurance; therefore, she works very hard at pleasing her clientele. This saleswoman has adapted to the culture of the United States in many ways; she is assertive and outgoing, and she has a good grasp of the concept of profit. She also knows, given her own background, that she must be more indirect and willing to enter into long-term relationships with her clients that in many cases go beyond a typical American business relationship. A number of her clients ask her to give marital advice for children, act as a go-between in marriage arrangements and help with other personal matters.

The insurance saleswoman in the above example could argue that the people she deals with are in the United States and should, therefore, adapt to American practices; however, with that attitude she would not reach her customers who are from East Asian countries. As a result, she would severely restrict her business success. Her ability to communicate in a foreign language and at the same time to understand the cultural background of her clientele makes her successful.

SUMMARY

In this chapter we have examined some of the major issues related to the use of language in intercultural business communication. The focus has been on five issues.

The language barrier and its consequences, real and perceived:

- Language and culture are intertwined and shape each other.
- Our environment influences our language and the development of linguistic concepts.
- Language reflects our priorities and values.
- Different cultures may give different meanings to identical or similar words.

- Language changes over time.
- Acronyms present special challenges in communicating.
- The language barrier makes intercultural communication more difficult.

Selection of the right language:
When selecting a language for intercultural communication, managers need to be aware of

- Linguistic considerations. Out of the thousands of languages around the globe, which one would be most appropriate?
- Business considerations. Are you the buyer or seller? Which language do your partners speak? What are the implications of the role of English as the lingua franca of business?
- Political considerations. Governments frequently regulate which language is acceptable for official use with the government.
- Appropriate level of fluency. In order to be effective, linguistic fluency must go along with cultural fluency.

The company language:

- Choosing a company language. Many companies use one official language for their worldwide operations.
- Using additional foreign language expertise. Even if a company selects an official company language, not everyone in the firm will be fluent in this language. Expertise in the local language will still be an asset.

The role of the interpreter:

- The importance of choosing a good interpreter. A good interpreter has linguistic, cultural, and technical fluency.
- The effective use of an interpreter. You need to prepare the interpreter before a session, provide breaks, and determine what role the interpreter should play in any discussions.

Communication with non-native speakers:

- Effective face-to-face communication. You must speak clearly and be able to read the nonverbal and cultural signal your partner sends.
- Effective written communication. Knowledge of different business formats, organizational patterns, and conventions will help in becoming more effective.
- The impact of technology on oral and written communication. The development of communication technology, such as E-mail and teleconferencing, has changed the communication patterns in international business by allowing instant messaging.
- Guidelines for communicating with businesspeople from different cultures. People from other cultures, even if they speak your language, may not be familiar with metaphors and idioms that are frequently used in your culture and can, therefore, present a communication barrier.
- Communication with a multicultural workforce. Intercultural communication has become an important issue not just for international businesses but also for domestic businesses.

NOTES

1. Richard Mead, *Cross-Cultural Management Communication,* (New York: John Wiley & Sons, 1990).
2. Edward T. Hall, *The Silent Language,* (New York: Doubleday and Co., 1959).
3. http://www.geocities.com/SiliconValley/Heights/4766/shumor.html
4. "Death Sentence," *The Guardian.* October 25, 1999.
5. Janet Frank, "Miscommunication across Cultures: The Case of Marketing in Indian English," *World Englishes* 7 (1), 1988, pp. 25–36.
6. David Ricks, *Big Business Blunders: Mistakes in Multinational Marketing,* (Homewood, IL: Dow Jones-Irwin, 1983).
7. Iris Varner, "Cultural Aspects of German and American Business Letters," *The Journal of Language for International Business, III* (1), 1988, pp. 1–11.
8. Iris Varner, "A Comparison of American and French Business Correspondence," *The Journal of Business Communication* 25 (4), 1988, pp. 5–16.
9. *New College German Dictionary, German-English, English-German,* (Berlin: Langenscheidt, 1973).

CHAPTER THREE

Getting to Know Another Culture

Juan Marin is meeting with Lei Peng about a business deal. Marin wants to open a Chinese restaurant in Mexico City and is working out a joint-venture agreement with Lei, who has a number of successful restaurants already in Hong Kong and California. But Marin is discovering a number of things that surprise him about his would-be partner as they negotiate the details, meeting face-to-face at last in Los Angeles, California.

Lei has just mentioned that Juan should construct a fish tank in the entrance to his restaurant. "Why?" asks Juan. "We're not just serving fish, apart from a few dishes. But people will see the fish and think it's a fish restaurant."

"You need fish," Lei asserts. "You need that because it means good profit!" He explains that the phrase "to have fish" (*you yu*) sounds like the phrase "to have profit after expenses" and for that reason Juan must have a fish tank. Juan is amazed that the Chinese man thinks he should go to the expense of constructing a large fish tank at the front door of his restaurant simply on the basis of the sound of the word for *fish*.

Juan can't help noticing the gold Rolex watch Lei wears and his well-cut jacket because these things are indicators to Juan of good taste and style. While he and Lei continue their discussion, Juan notices that several times people interrupt to bring him a telephone, or to provide tea, or to ask for answers to quick questions. Juan doesn't really mind; he understands that these are signs of how important and busy Lei is.

Juan is a little hungry, though, since it's three o'clock in the afternoon and time for his large meal of the day. Lei seems unaware of the hour, and although someone provides tea for them there is no mention of dinner. He thinks he'd better clarify the hours the restaurant will operate in Mexico. Lei simply says, "No problem. The Chinese staff I'll get for you will work whenever you tell them." Juan wonders about that. What if a relative needs some help at home? After all, he had arrived at their meeting just before 2 P.M. although he had meant to come at 1 P.M. as agreed. But Juan's son had asked his father to bring a special video game back from the United States, and the traffic between the store and the meeting was heavy, so Juan was nearly an hour late. Lei's face didn't show any emotion, so Juan can't tell if he was angry. Family matters always take priority, as the Chinese must agree. But maybe the Chinese restaurant isn't such a good idea for his family business interests. How will he explain the fish tank?

For his part, Lei Peng is surprised at Juan Marin's behavior in person. How serious is he about this restaurant venture? He was an hour late for their first meeting! And although it's the middle of the afternoon, he keeps suggesting they go out for a meal to a nice Mexican restaurant he knows. As if Lei weren't an owner of restaurants in Los Angeles! How odd his associate is. Is it a good idea to open a restaurant in Mexico City?

Understanding another culture is an ongoing experience that can last a lifetime. However, sometimes businesspeople have only a short time to prepare to do business in another country. How can a brief amount of time best be spent to yield the greatest understanding?

ASKING QUESTIONS

The approach of this book is to identify certain questions to ask about cultures to gain the most useful level of understanding. It is derived from work done in the early 1960s by Kluckhorn and Strodtbeck[1] and further developed by the more recent interculturalists Condon and Yousef.[2] The answers to these questions help businesspeople understand why their foreign counterparts think, believe, and act as they do. The questions don't cover every aspect of life lived in another culture. For example, behavior related to bringing up children is not included since it seldom impinges upon business. Courtship and marriage customs, kinship systems, types of music and dance, and many other aspects of life lie outside the world of business. We are interested in how culture affects business, so we will focus on questions that pertain to the world of work.

Business cultures exist wholly within the larger culture of a society. Nothing occurs in the business culture that does not occur in the general society of which it is a part. But business cultures do not include everything from the general culture; they select out what is useful for conducting business transactions. David and Terpstra, in their book *The Cultural Environment of International Business,* give an example from India.[3] Two forms of paternalistic leadership exist in India: one that is benevolent and one that is autocratic. Indian business culture typically uses only the autocratic form of leadership. So for business purposes, one needs to know what the business culture includes, not everything in the general culture.

Theories about Understanding an Unfamiliar Culture

As background to our approach, which focuses on cultural dimensions that reflect values in a culture, it may be useful to know something about scholarship in the field of intercultural research. Perhaps the most significant study was conducted by Geert Hofstede, a Dutch interculturalist who did a study involving 116,000 respondents to a questionnaire distributed in 40 countries.[4] The first survey round was in 1968 and the second in 1972. The participants in the study were all managers for IBM (that, of course, raises questions about reliability and validity as discussed in Chapter 8). The research identified four dimensions on which country cultures differ:

- Individualism versus collectivism.
- Power distance.
- Uncertainty avoidance versus uncertainty tolerance.
- Masculinity versus femininity.

Of these, the first is the most widely researched. Individualistic cultures are those that emphasize individual achievements and rights, including the individual's right to make decisions for himself or herself; collectivistic cultures emphasize the group's achievements and rights, including the group's right to make decisions for the individual. Power distance is the degree to which less-powerful members of an organization will tolerate unequal distribution of power, say between manager and employees. Uncertainty avoidance is the tendency to arrange things in a way that minimizes unforeseen consequences; tolerance to uncertainty results in behavior that is less concerned with unforeseen consequences. Masculinity, according to Hofstede, is a way to characterize cultures that value assertiveness, competitiveness, and material success, whereas femininity characterizes cultural preferences for collaboration, nurturing, and harmony. Hofstede's work is cited often by international business and intercultural communication scholars. Later, Michael Bond, a Canadian working and living in Hong Kong, developed a way to assess cultural values based on a survey instrument written by Asian, not Western, minds. This resulted in a fifth cultural dimension reported by Bond and Hofstede as long-term orientation.[5] It includes values that can be called "future-looking" such as perseverance, thrift, observing a hierarchy of status in relationships, and having a sense of shame. Short-term orientation, looking more to the past, includes protecting your "face," respecting tradition, maintaining personal steadiness, and reciprocating favors and gifts.

Another Dutch interculturalist, Fons Trompenaars, developed seven cultural dimensions.[6] They include universalism versus particularism, individualism versus collectivism (Hofstede's influence), neutral versus emotional, specific versus diffuse, and achievement versus ascription. To these he added attitudes toward time and the environment. Meanwhile, other scholars were developing cultural values by which to compare cultures. Andre Laurent looked at European managers and came up with four parameters for understanding how culture affects relationships of power: perception of organizations as political systems, authority systems, role formulation systems, and hierarchical relationship systems.[7]

These brief descriptions of well-known studies indicate that there are many ways to approach understanding a culture. We synthesize these studies into the following five categories of questions that focus on values in a culture. These questions allow you to compare cultures by assessing the answers for different cultures. Questions about a culture that need to be asked for business fall into these five categories:

- Thinking and Knowing.
- Doing and Achieving.
- Our Place in the Universe.
- The Self.
- The Organization of Society.

The first three categories are discussed in this chapter; the last two in Chapter 4. These categories cover the **cultural priorities** that motivate people to behave in certain ways. *Priority* is a useful term because it implies relative importance along a sliding scale. Our questions ask about relative values: For example, does a culture value youth more or does it value age more? Does it look upon change as more positive or negative? Are results more important than relationships, or are relationships more important than results?

Where Can Information about Cultures Be Found?

Anyone can ask the questions that follow, but of whom? The obvious place to start is to ask people who are members of the culture you want to understand. A logical source is someone who comes from a background similar to yours (in terms of economics, education, family) or who has had similar experiences or holds the same kind of job. You can gain insight this way, since people can identify to some degree the value orientations of their own culture. For instance, if someone asked *you* whether members of your culture learn by probing and questioning or by mastering and memorizing a given body of knowledge, you would probably give an answer that would concur with others in your culture (or others who study your culture).

But some of the questions are not easy for people to discuss because they have never considered them. For instance, most people don't know whether they think in a linear pattern or in a cluster pattern. Members of a culture are not necessarily the best authorities on that culture.

That may surprise you. But culture is embedded deep in the unconscious part of our minds. As Edward Hall pointed out in *Beyond Culture,* the closer something is to seeming true, the less aware we probably are of its cultural origin.[8] People's own culture seems normal to them; it seems just the way things are. One way of asking questions is to notice that another culture goes about something differently from the way you expect. People tend to evaluate everything they see and experience on the basis of their own background, and then act on their evaluations accordingly. This is called the *self-reference criterion.*[9] Those who understand their own self-reference criterion and who are open to making adjustments in their evaluations are likely to become more aware of their own cultures while they are also learning about other cultures.

Another good source may be someone who has spent considerable time in that culture, but is not a native member of it. Someone who has lived in the other culture has had exposure to the differences between his or her own culture and the culture you want to understand. You may be able to learn from a non-native about cultural priorities that a native of that culture simply takes for granted.

But asking questions is a general approach that includes inquiring into a culture's priorities by finding out what is important to its members, and it is more than simply asking questions of people. For example, you can inquire by reading fiction written by authors of the culture you want to understand. By reading how and why characters act and interact, you will learn something about what is important to that culture, what its priorities are. For example, you can learn how Japanese culture views public expression of emotion, the relative status of older people compared with younger people, the importance of not causing someone to lose face, and the difference between outward, public action and private opinion by reading modern short stories in translation. You can also watch Japanese movies and see what people's behavior—their nonverbal communication—looks like and how they sound when they speak the Japanese language.

Another way to pursue your inquiries is to find out what people of a culture say about themselves. Countries publish nonfiction books in translation describing their institutions, history, beliefs, practices, and goals for the future. Even travel guides contain some insights.

Cultures also define themselves less directly in communications that are nevertheless revealing. For example, television commercials offer insights into cultural priorities—not so much in the products they advertise as in the values implied by the appeals the commercials make to the viewers. Whereas peer group membership (doing the "in thing") is the central appeal in certain breakfast cereal advertisements to young married couples in the United States, family membership is the central appeal in advertisements for the same product in Mexico.

In China in the mid-1980s, most television commercials advertised industrial products such as seats for mini-vans, not retail products. The appeal was to the Chinese value of membership in work units. Since nearly all Chinese belonged to work units, the commercials reinforced their attitude that the correct way for China to approach economic reforms was through work units. The work unit bought advertising time on television as much to promote the image of the economic unit that produced the goods as to reach buyers.

A Japanese television commercial from the same period offers a contrast.

One particular television commercial [for a Lexus] shows the car being driven down a country lane; it stops, and a woman in a *kimono* and a man in a suit emerge. As they walk around the car, the camera shows a close-up shot of a green leaf that had fallen on the windshield. There are drops of moisture on the leaf and the window; birds are heard in the background. The man and the woman walk up to a potter who is looking at a recently fired bowl. Silence. The potter throws the bowl to the ground; it breaks. The couple get back in the car and drive away.[10]

The message is that only perfection is good enough for the master craftsman (the product's slogan in English is "the pursuit of perfection"). It is communicated in the Japanese ad without words. (Chapter 5 discusses the cultural priority of words—high or low priority—in communication.)

Print ads also reflect cultural values. One Southeast Asian country has advertised its airlines for years by showing attractive young women attentively serving male customers. In North America and Europe, this approach has offended many who see in it the evaluation of women as objects of sexual interest whose role is to attend to the physical comforts of men. To members of Islamic cultures, the Asian women of the commercials display an availability to strange men that devout Muslim women are taught to reject.

Other sources of information about cultures are studies by anthropologists who research cultures in the field, going to live among the members of the culture they want to understand. They are trained to observe and report their observations. As a result, their accounts are more objective and less anecdotal than those of other visitors. But even the casual, anecdotal tales of travelers can often add to your understanding.

Are Generalizations Productive or Perilous?

Before launching into the cultural priorities, a brief rationale about generalizing is necessary. The following discussions about cultural priorities generalize out of necessity. It can be useful to learn that *in general* members of a culture view something a certain way. But it is also true that in any culture individuals have their own priorities that may deviate from the general culture. So each specific case you encounter has to be the subject of fresh inquiry and fresh testing of the validity of the priority you expect in order to avoid fixed, inflexible mental categories. *Individual episodes can always be found to contradict generalizations about a culture.*

For example, several years ago one of the authors invited a young nurse, recently arrived for a work-study year from Beijing, home for dinner. Since her hosts knew the Chinese have a strong orientation toward form and politeness in social situations, they expected to have to urge the young woman repeatedly to help herself to the dinner dishes. In China, refusal of proffered food is polite and further refusal is even more polite. However, the young woman's first words as she came through the door were, "Oh I'm so hungry; I hope you don't mind if I eat a lot!" Contrary to the cultural generalization, she didn't hesitate at all to help herself and didn't need to be urged. This specific instance was completely contrary to the cultural generalization. But generalizations are not therefore meaningless. It could be useful to know that generally in China—as in Jordan, for example—a guest will twice refuse food out of politeness.

In addition to individual differences, there are also cultural paradoxes. Cultures are seldom a strict either-or in every instance, for all people. For example, Americans are individualistic but the group is important as well. Americans join groups very easily, and the local Welcome Wagon is just one example of making people feel comfortable in the group. The young woman from Beijing may have been paying her hosts the compliment of treating them like family, in which formal politeness is not appropriate and can make family members feel they are being treated as strangers.

General insights you form about a culture from asking about cultural priorities will always need to be revised and reexamined in specific contexts. Key factors include how much previous knowledge the others have about your culture, how much time both parties have spent in each other's cultural environment, and what the dominant influences of prior encounters were. Former soldiers from various nations and both sides in the conflicts in Vietnam during the 1960s and 1970s who want to do business together today will have to consider how much they really know about each other and what their war experiences can tell them about former enemies or former allies that is useful for business.

The pursuit of answers to the questions about cultural priorities is an ongoing process. You can continue to learn about other cultures and your own for as long as you continue to pose questions. The cultural priorities this chapter discusses are all related to business communication, but they do not include all the ways to view cultures. The five categories of questions are just the first step to get you started in cross-cultural communication fluency.

Finally, each of the questions to pose of a culture should be thought of as a continuum, with the first characteristic at one pole, and the other at the opposite pole. You can position the culture you are considering at any point between the two poles where it seems appropriate, given your level of knowledge of that culture. So if you are asked to locate United States culture somewhere between the two poles suggested in the question "Are results important or are relationships important?" where would you put it? Right in the middle? Slightly toward the results end? Strongly towards the results end? Draw upon your own experience and understanding to answer. This is the way to consider each question in the five categories.

CATEGORY 1: THINKING AND KNOWING

Does Knowing Come from Concepts or Experience?

How do people know things? The answers vary from culture to culture. Some people know because they have experienced for themselves what a thing means. Few of us would argue that knowing how to bargain prices for cold-rolled steel is acquired by anything other than experience. On the other hand, since few of us have done it, we know *about* doing it from reading about bargaining and the market and past prices. Our information is secondhand, but in English-speaking cultures most people accept the validity (if still second best) of knowledge that is acquired from a reliable source—books, training programs on bargaining—rather than from first-hand experience (see Chapter 8 for a more detailed discussion).

In some cultures, however, first-hand experience alone legitimately constitutes what is known. All else is hearsay. This is particularly true in cultures that have no written language, but it can also be identified in cultures that emphasize personal vision. The vision of the individual prophet or priest or shaman constitutes knowledge that is undoubted by the visionary himself or herself. Followers often also believe that the visionary knows what they themselves cannot know. Reading or hearing about a vision is not the same as experiencing it. Visionaries play powerful roles and enjoy high status in many cultures that are trading partners with the West. Some members of cultures that honor visionaries have made their homes in the United States, Canada, Britain, and the rest of Europe (all of which have had their own share of visionaries). Corporations cannot assume all their employees, associates, partners, and subsidiaries share the same definition of *to know*.

Knowing by intuition is another kind of experience. In some cultures where Daoism, Buddhism, and Hinduism are dominant religions, knowledge of the true nature of things comes from meditation, which isn't quite the same thing as intuition. Buddha taught that each person has truth within; meditation is a way to reach that inner knowing and to allow it to be recognized. Accordingly, Buddhists believe that knowledge gained from study or listening isn't as valuable as knowledge that comes from meditation. Only by emptying the mind of sensory stimuli and concerns and finally of thought can one experience true understanding.

The notion of *knowledge* in European cultures often calls to mind a traditional body of abstract concepts, philosophies, and arguments reaching back to the classical works of Greece and Rome. Knowledge sometimes seems rather solemn, dusty, and remote. Perhaps that is the reason we have a number of other terms for *know: grasp, comprehend, understand, ken, perceive.* There are even more terms for a person who knows, or who is *in the know: smart, knowledgeable, savvy, perceptive, clever, astute.* Another key term is *learned.* This leads to the next question we can ask of a culture.

Does Knowing Come from Asking Questions or Mastering Received Wisdom?

What does it mean to learn? Cultures have a variety of answers. People learn how to learn when they are very young, first at home before they go to school, and then later at school. Those early learning patterns are followed with little change throughout our lives. In North America, learning is a process that involves asking questions. This book is by two United States residents of northern-European descent. In the culture from which we write, asking questions opens the door to understanding. Therefore, the process we present for learning about cultures is specifically one that involves asking questions.

In the United States, from kindergarten through graduate seminars, students who ask questions are rewarded. They bask in their teachers' approval and often receive higher grades than their unquestioning peers. Teachers tend to find question-askers intelligent. In commerce, industry, and medicine, legends are told about heroes who asked, "What if we do it this way?" and "Why not?" Stephen Wozniak and Steve Jobs, the computer whiz kids who began their company in a garage, asked why computers couldn't be fun to use by someone who had no technical background, and they thereby created the Apple Computer Corporation. The hero in your own organization, whoever he or she may be, asked a question and by the light of that question went forward to illuminate previously unlit territory. Many leaders in United States businesses have proclaimed a belief, with a fervor the 18th-century Age of Enlightenment would have approved, in the candlepower of question asking. They believe that when they have answers to questions, they know.

Physicists are busy trying to identify the ultimate minute particle of creation. It has been elusive and the search has been intense, but some physicists believe that they will be able to find evidence it exists: a single basic building block, a "God-particle" used to fashion everything in the known universe.[11] The Western tradition of learning since ancient Greece (and perhaps they learned it from Arab scholars) has followed this process to knowledge: dissect, deconstruct, and atomize until you identify the smallest component and can relate each building block to each other building block. Then you have mastered the understanding of something. Then you know it.

In many cultures, knowing does not involve laying something open and examining its components minutely. Quite the opposite. Knowing involves seeing the connections and links between something and everything else. Knowing something means being able to fit it into the universal scheme of things. A prominent Chinese scientist once described the difference between Western and Chinese approaches to knowing. He used the disease AIDS as an example, and pointed out that in the West medical researchers were diligently trying to isolate the virus that causes the disease. But in China, researchers were trying to find ways to strengthen the body's immune system. One method looks at the most elemental unit of the disease while the other looks at its place in the whole context of what the disease does.

The point here for business communication is that Chinese businesspeople, along with members of other Asian cultures, tend to look at the links between things and the relationships that give things meaning by providing a context. Western businesspeople, however, tend to consider issues in isolation. For example, a Westerner trying to establish joint-venture guidelines in China may look at professional credentials only in relation to hiring personnel. The Chinese look at credentials, but also at the character of employees, their seniority, their past service, perhaps their family members' service, and certainly at who the candidates' contacts are—a large tissue of interrelated factors that form a context for hiring and wages.

In many cultures of Asia, Latin America, and southern Europe, learning does not come from asking questions. Learning means receiving and taking in what is given by teachers. Some teachers may speak through written texts. Teachers *know;* their role is to pass knowledge on to learners so they will know too. In China, Japan, Thailand, Hong Kong, Vietnam, Cambodia, and Indonesia—among other places—the teacher in the classroom is an unassailable authority. The textbook and the teacher do not disagree. What they deliver to the student is true knowledge and is not to be doubted. Although sometimes students ask questions for clarification, students do not question the authenticity or reliability of the knowledge they are given. Their role is to master it. Frequently that means committing it to memory to be able to reconstruct it when called upon to do so, as in an exam. Reproducing exactly what was delivered is the best possible demonstration a student can give of really having learned.

Culture defines what it means to know and to learn. This basic fact is important for any organization that plans to—or already does—operate with personnel from many cultures. Most organizations have training programs for employees and expect their workers to continue to learn new things as technology and the organization's needs change. The need to learn is unavoidable when an organization engages a multicultural workforce or engages in global activities for the first time.

Does Knowledge Have Limits?

What can be known? Are some things unknowable? In Western Christian cultures, following a separation between sacred and secular that began hundreds of years ago, spiritual truths are generally held to be knowable through faith: If you believe, then you can know. Even where scientific inquiry and faith intersect, science's findings have little effect on the beliefs of the faithful. Scientific analyses of the Shroud of Turin, which some Christians believe bears the print of Christ's body, have had little effect on belief or unbelief.[12] Attempts to explain the Star of Bethlehem, which Biblical accounts say shone at the birth of Christ, by astronomical computer programs run backward in time, have similarly had little effect on belief. For Christians in this cultural tradition, *knowing* in spiritual terms involves a different approach from *knowing* in material terms.

Other cultures find this approach to knowing very strange and schizophrenic; for them there is no separation between sacred and secular. For many Hindus in India, for example, all human undertakings and all episodes of nature—in fact, all things—are embraced by the spiritual. Believers visit temples daily, sometimes three or four times a day. Businesspeople obtain blessings for ventures, and new work premises are blessed before they are occupied. No separation is made between material life and spiritual life; all life is seamlessly part of the real, unseen but felt realm of the divine. All of life is sacred. Any foreign organization that wishes to do business in India will need to accept this view of knowing.

Some things are too ineffable—too sacred and inexpressible—to be known by any means. The ineffable may be delineated to a greater extent by the persons who are assigned that role—priests, shamans, wise women—than by ordinary businesspeople. When this is true in cultures where such knowledge is valued, these people enjoy a high status.

In What Patterns Do People Think?

How people know is closely related to how people think. Thinking patterns also vary from culture to culture. Patterns in the mind map a person's life experiences. (And the opposite is also true: Experiences verify patterns of the mind.) The map affects how a person frames communication about life.

Patterns are processes learned from birth; they are culturally determined. We suppose all normal human babies are capable of any of the thought patterns ever used in the whole history of human existence, but babies learn to pattern thinking after the patterns their world shows them. If they are fortunate enough to have more than one culture in their socialization process, they will learn more patterns than their monocultural counterparts. It is remarkable to watch someone moving from one culture into another and to discern the difference in an individual's patterns of thought that the cultural change brings.

Perhaps the most typical pattern of thinking for members of Western cultures is cause-and-effect. To speak of *reasons* in English is to speak of causes, of reasons why. In fact, a *reasonable* person is one who sees relationships of cause and effect between things. *Why* questions in Western cultures inevitably invoke explanations of causes: Why has the market share shrunk for widgets in Malaysia? Why are productivity figures up for March? Why is the chief accountant not at work today? (Because Widgets, Inc., our competitor, launched a marketing campaign last month. Because the new equipment was running without problems in March. Because her husband is in surgery.)

Cause-and-effect thinking is linear. We could draw a straight line from cause to effect, with an arrowhead at the results end. Many sentences in English employ this pattern. Consider that last one: The subject is *sentences,* and it has some descriptors around it (*many, in English*); *employ* is what the sentences do; *this pattern* is the outcome, or the result of the activity of the verb.

Westerners think that cause-and-effect patterns are logical, and that *logical* means cause-and-effect, the pattern Westerners call Aristotelian syllogism. So deeply embedded is this notion that it is assumed to be universal. But as experts in intercultural understanding warn, it isn't:

> The syllogistic reasoning of Aristotle . . . is not a universal phenomenon; it has been a part of the Anglo-European tradition for such a long time that speakers of English tend to assume that it is a natural phenomenon of the human mind, rather than an invention of the human mind.[13]

What a blow Western business minds suffer when they discover *logical* means something very different to non-Western people! For example, Chinese often use a pattern of logic that contrasts elements: An A must have a B, hot implies cold, and so forth. When this pattern of thinking is communicated, the form that results is parallelism by contrasts, or a sequence of antitheses, which nevertheless are not mutually exclusive.

The Chinese *yin-yang* symbol used in many Asian countries and displayed on the Korean flag [see Exhibit 3–1] expresses the way opposites contain something of each other. *Yin* is negative, cold, downward and inward, dark, and night; it is also feminine. *Yang* is positive, hot, upward and outward, light, and day; it is also masculine. The *yin* and *yang* interact. Where one grows, the other contracts, but they make a whole. Neither can exist without the other.

Furthermore, each has an element of the other within it. As the *yin* grows larger, so does the *yang* element within it, and vice-versa.

Yin and *yang* can offer a perspective for understanding the technological growth and development in Asia.[14] Urban development, telecommunications, and fast transportation systems bring people into contact; this is a *yang* aspect of technology. Family structure is threatened by urban growth as people leave their villages and migrate to urban centers; this is a *yin* aspect of development and technology.

EXHIBIT 3–1   Yin-Yang Symbol

The key in Chinese patterns of thinking is linkage. Links are always being sought to show the wholeness of life, even when that whole embraces contrast. The importance of the fish tank to Lei Peng in the opening episode shows a linkage of ideas because of the sounds of the words that represent those ideas: fish and profit. Events are likened to other larger events that occurred in past times. Businesses in China use this linkage pattern in negotiations. For example, a meeting between negotiating sides is related to momentous encounters between nations in distant historical accounts. This kind of historical reference often figures in the early, informal stages of negotiation, specifically in the toast a Chinese host makes to foreign guests.[15] It often sails past Western guests, who do not recognize in a historical reference any substantive link to the business at hand. The unity of human experience with the whole of life is the fundamental philosophical basis for the thinking patterns that can be identified in Chinese business communication.

Roderick McLeod describes Chinese patterns of thinking in *China Inc: How to Do Business with the Chinese:*

> I believe that the subject of patterns of thinking, explored in all its daunting depths and complexities, holds a promise of a "quantum leap" in cross-cultural understanding and communication.[16]

Europeans prefer thought patterns that categorize. This discussion about patterns of thinking has presented cause-and-effect on the one extreme, and linkage on the other. That is, opposites are identified. But that is itself a pattern generated by culture. In Russia, thinking patterns embrace contradictions rather than oppose them. Extremes and contradictions delight Russians, who do not seek to reconcile them but to see them exist together in a pattern.[17]

CATEGORY 2: DOING AND ACHIEVING

Is Doing Important or Is Being Important?

The existential view of some cultures is to value the present moment and to celebrate being. This is hard for the activity oriented to understand. It looks like shirking. One worker expressed an existential view by saying that he regards work as a blessing; you work hard at whatever your work is. But you don't continue to set yourself new challenges or imagine new activity beyond the blessing you have been given.

On the other hand, to the celebrators of existence, a great deal of activity in *doing* cultures looks pointless. Where are people going in such a hurry? What have they left behind? What is the meaning of so much activity? *Being* cultures value stillness, collectedness, serenity. Many visitors to Western cultures are amazed by the pace of life, especially in cities—so many activities crammed into a short time, requiring so much speed to fit them all in. Such crowded agendas seem to leave little room for simply being.

According to Condon and Yousef, Clifford Clarke (as Foreign Student Advisor at Stanford) first observed the correlation between cultures where activity is valued—almost for its own sake, at times—and where silence is of little value.[18] Members of *doing* cultures view silence as a waste, when "nothing is doing." On the other hand, members of cultures that value *being* also often value silence. In silence the present moment can best be appreciated and experienced. A businessperson in Japan, who is unaware of the importance silence has in that culture, may rush to fill silence with words. Silence is discussed in more detail in Chapters 6 and 9.

Obviously, great potential for conflict exists when co-workers have opposing views about doing versus being. The potential is increased when neither side understands that the other side may feel sure of the rightness of its view. The most obvious arena for conflict is in negotiations. Both sides have goals for the outcome, but low-context cultures—which emphasize results—generate more concretely framed goals. Negotiators from high-context cultures have expectations for the outcomes that are less specific and more relationship oriented.

Are Tasks Done Sequentially or Simultaneously?

Even when many cultures value activity, they may regard *doing* differently. In some cultures sequential performance of tasks is considered normal behavior, whereas in others simultaneous performance is normal.

A Canadian sales representative from British Columbia to Venezuela goes to the office of a shipping office to arrange for the ongoing shipment of an order in transit from Quebec to another country. She is on time for her appointment, but she has to wait while the shipping agent serves a number of customers who are already in the office. When the Canadian's turn finally comes, she explains what she needs and the agent begins filling out the documentation for the shipment and discussing prices. At the same time the agent takes a phone call, responds to a question from a co-worker about schedules, and directs the faxing of a message about something else—in effect working on three other projects besides the Canadian's. This is efficient activity within the Venezuelan agent's culture.

To the Canadian, however, this is unfocused activity that is not nearly as efficient as it could be—particularly from her point of view—if the agent simply were to deal exclusively with her during her scheduled appointment.

In Canada, businesspeople typically write appointments and activities into the day's agenda every day. They then work sequentially through this agenda until they have completed each task or the day is over.

People may have personal styles and preferences for getting the work done; that is, within a sequential-task culture individuals may prefer a flexibility that allows them to do more than one thing at a time. (They may be called "disorganized" by others in the sequential-task culture.) In general, however, workers in sequential-task cultures know at the start of the day what they will do during the segments of the day: morning, lunch hour, afternoon, and divisions thereof. When unexpected tasks arise, others that had been scheduled are rescheduled. The essence of *time management* is organizing and sequencing tasks—a notion that seems peculiar in other cultures.

In contrast, although the simultaneous-task performer knows in general what the tasks in a given day will be, the day has a fluidity that allows for more and less important tasks that take more or less time. A businessperson in this culture assumes many tasks will be attacked simultaneously. (The question of time and how it is valued will be discussed in detail in a later section of this chapter, under the heading "Our Place in the Universe.")

Simultaneity is extremely useful when people and the relationships between people are valued highly: You can spend all the time you want or need with a person when you are at the same time giving some attention to other (valued) persons. This leads to the next question to pose of a culture concerning doing and achieving.

Do Results or Relationships Take Priority?

Results-cultures regard ends as more significant than the means used to achieve those ends. The United States is where Management By Objectives (MBO) had its origin, which isn't surprising when you consider the dominance of cause-and-effect thinking in U.S. culture. The basis of MBO is that you identify your goals and then work out a strategy to achieve them. Along the way you measure how close you have come. That's how you know you are making progress.

Goals-oriented societies place a very high value on making progress, which naturally leads to methods by which to measure progress. Measurements that seem logical to Americans may not seem so logical to others, however. The French (among others) often marvel at the American penchant for statistics and measurements of qualities they consider intangible. ("How satisfied are you with your present superior: 10 percent? 25 percent, 50 percent, 75 percent, 90 percent?" "On a score from one to five, how well do you think you are performing in your job?")

The emphasis on measurement has led to an enormous preoccupation by business with figures of productivity and cost, which has led in turn to the high status and power accorded accountants. MBO has fallen from its former high favor in recent years. Nevertheless, continuous measurement as a way to assure quality has been successfully promoted by William Deming in the United States and much more successfully in Japan, although with less emphasis on measurements.

Not all cultures feel the need to identify goals and work toward them. Management By Objectives hasn't exported very well. One reason is that the goals that matter to many people of other cultures include nurturing close relationships with co-workers. So even if a proposed sale falls through, the relationship may have been strengthened by the contact made in the effort to close it.

In countries where power is concentrated at the top levels of organizations and is wielded according to personal favor, a healthy and strong relationship with the powerful one is a primary goal of every endeavor. This is particularly evident in formerly and presently communist countries. Having good access to the party secretary, or a member in good standing of the party, was a conduit to effecting desired outcomes. The immediate goal for a floor supervisor in a textile factory in former–Soviet Georgia may have been a new apartment, but the ongoing goal of every interaction was to nurture a good relationship with the party secretary of the factory.

Relationships are the basis for much of the business conducted in Asia. Where relationships are so highly valued, business is only done with people who have entered into a relationship with you and whose organization has connections to your organization. In fact, in the high-context cultures of Asia, business is preferably transacted face to face.

In China, every work unit has a travel allocation from the State in its budget so that representatives can travel and meet with suppliers, buyers, associates, and related organizations (reporting to the same ministry in Beijing). Similarly, many work units have hotels on the premises to receive visitors from within and outside China. Business correspondence is minimal; business is transacted face to face. Relationship building is the key activity.

When there is a strong relationship, specific outcomes can be worked out. Contracts can be written and signed because relationships exist that will ensure their performance. The ends flow from the means. No wonder relationship-oriented cultures value the means to an end more than the end itself. Furthermore, if success eludes you this time, you can always try again if the relationship is intact.

Finally, people don't necessarily agree about what signifies an achievement. You may assume that all businesspeople equate achievement with profit, but that assumption would not always be correct. Furthermore, even when people agree that making money is their goal, they may have very different ideas what it means to have money—what it is worth.

For instance, in Hong Kong wealth is important because it can buy an elite car, a spacious apartment in a desirable area, servants, memberships in private clubs, travel, exclusive brands of liquor, clothing, personal entertainment equipment—and banquets for friends, although the banquet may not be number one priority.

But consider what money means in a place where private ownership of cars and homes is rare, where travel requires permission of the employer and government in addition to money, where private clubs do not formally exist and where employing private servants was formerly called class exploitation. What is the meaning of wealth in such a place?

When a group of graduate students in Shanghai were asked in 1985 to describe *wealth,* they all agreed it meant having money in your own pocket; they also agreed that, "If you have 10,000 yuan in your pocket, you're rich because you can buy the best banquet for all your friends!" Today, with higher wages and high inflation in China, and with the large salaries paid by joint-venture and foreign-owned firms, those same people may indeed be buying banquets along with homes, cars, and consumer goods. Consumerism is rampant in China today, driven in large part by the willingness and ability of parents to spend money on their child. By the year 2025, when there will be more people over 60 in China than the population of the United States in 2000 (275 million), consumer patterns will no doubt change focus and they may also increase in volume.[19]

This dimension of results versus relationships corresponds in part to Hofstede's dimension of individualism versus collectivism. Individualist cultures are performance oriented, and they emphasize personal achievement, winning the competition. Collectivist cultures are relationship oriented, and they emphasize supportive networks and collaboration.

Is Uncertainty Avoided or Tolerated?

Uncertainty exists in all cultures and, Hofstede points out, in all organizations as well. Some people react to uncertainty with greater levels of anxiety than others, and what Hofstede showed is that some *cultures* react with greater anxiety than others.

Two members of an organization who come from different cultures but who have to work together—say a production manager and a supervisor—who do not agree about whether to avoid or tolerate uncertainty may have a hard time understanding each other. If the person from the avoiding culture wants more guidelines about how to deal with uncertainty, and if that person is a subordinate, the resulting relationship with the boss may suffer from distrust and diminished respect for the superior who does not share the inclination toward more guidelines. The uncertainty-avoider may not understand that a different attitude toward uncertainty lies behind what appears to be simply an irresponsible approach by the superior who is supposed to be responsible. The uncertainty-tolerator, the boss, may identify the subordinate as anxious for no good reason—simply a worrier—rather than someone with a different attitude toward uncertainty.

Uncertainty is not the same thing as risk. Risk involves a specific potential loss, but anxiety does not involve a specifically identifiable loss. Risk in business is an everyday fact; risk in business that involves multicultural and multinational contact is even more inevitable. The risk may be social ostracization or economic loss or a legal liability. Businesses must consider risks in all business transactions. Businesspeople from various cultures approach risk differently, but all organizations want to minimize risk.

Is Luck an Essential Factor or an Irrelevance?

Luck is one way of dealing with one's anxiety about the unknown. Cultures vary in the importance they attach to the power of an unseen Power over events. Is luck (fortune, fate) responsible for success? Or is success the responsibility of the human engineers of it? Not surprisingly, in cultures that think in cause-and-effect patterns and that value results, *planning*—not luck—is the key to success. Westerners are fond of sayings that present this view: "We are the architects of our own destiny."

Planning appears to equal control. If you plan carefully and omit no detail, you may ensure the outcome. Control is calculating the variables so nothing unexpected can intervene between cause (means) and effect (ends). Attending carefully to the details resembles an orientation toward rules, as discussed below—they are both attempts to shape outcomes by controlling variables.

As anyone who has carefully laid plans knows, however, the unexpected has a way of ambushing you. Even some Westerners think Western rationalism, which is our heritage from Aristotle through Voltaire to modern technocrats, has traveled too far from human experience. The discounting of fate and the belief in human planning and engineering seem foolish to some Western thinkers.

These thinkers point out that, increasingly, many environmental concerns and ethical dilemmas are exposed as products of technology; pollution and waste, euthanasia, and genetic engineering, to name just a few, seem to have little to do with Nature. Instead of freeing us from outdated procedures and enabling us to participate fully in life, as the mid-century defenders of technology promised, technology scares us with its nuclear power, sophisticated telecommunications, and gigantic data banks that know intimate details about us. As one pundit paraphrased Churchill, "Never before in the course of human history have so many known so little about so much."

Western cultures, which have tended to discount the role of fate since the Enlightenment of the 18th century, nevertheless number millions of horoscope readers. This perhaps is because in spite of technology and planning and control mechanisms, life frequently persists in not being orderly. People whose cultures acknowledge the role of luck in human affairs view the attempt at control by planning as merely illusory and pointless activity—the gyrations of water spiders.

Hong Kong may be the place where practices to ensure good luck and avoid bad luck are most often observed. For example, a business office desk may display a jade carving of a stylized bat (the flying rodent); the word for bat sounds like the word for prosperity, and the jade carving is a conscious invocation of luck that brings prosperity. (Luck means material wealth to the pragmatic Hong Kongese.) Fortune-tellers abound, and businesses consult them about making business decisions.

Feng shui (literally "wind water") is the ancient practice of geomancy—aligning sites and buildings in harmony with the earth's energy forces so locations will be propitious. Its expert interpreters are typically called in when buildings are oriented on construction sites. Owners of restaurants, hotels, and retail businesses also call in the *feng shui* experts when business slumps. Their recommendations often include repositioning the manager's desk or hanging mirrors to deflect the flow of disharmonious influences into the building or partially screening the entrance to prevent money from running out the door.

Some numbers are lucky in Hong Kong, such as eight (which sounds like the word for prosperity), seven, and three. The government raises extra money by auctioning off auspicious-number license plates, and in recent years one man paid $5 million HK ($641,000 US) for lucky number eight. By contrast, number four is unlucky since it is pronounced like the word for death. Hotels and office buildings do not have a number four, and observers say subway passengers are reluctant to pass through gate 44, even during rush hour. Phone numbers and street addresses with four in them are also regarded as unlucky by many.

In Taiwan, the Ghost month (the seventh in the lunar calendar) is traditionally not a time of good luck for making any important decision such as a new business venture. Rather than risk a business loss, some people figure that they might as well wait until the (lucky) eighth month to make decisions. After all, although it might be superstitious nonsense, you never know. Fate is unpredictable.

Filipino fatalism is summed up in the phrase *bahala na,* which in Tagalog roughly means, "accept what comes and bear it with hope and patience"—success in a business venture may well be attributed to fate rather than effort.[20] In Thailand, *mai pen rai* means, "Never mind; it's fate and you are not responsible." In Chinese, *mei guanxi* has a similar meaning. It literally translates as "no connection," and suggests the addressee isn't responsible for the inexplicable whims of fate.

In India, fate is widely credited for events. Fate is preordained and can be known by studying the stars and procession of the planets. Many companies in India have their own astrologers who practice the 5,000-year old *jyotish* or astrology. Businesses consult with astrologers when recruiting new employees to ascertain whether or not they are lucky. After all, if employees have no luck as individuals, how can they be lucky for the organization?

Wearing specific precious and semiprecious stones can counteract the planetary influence and mediate fate somewhat; many Indians wear specific stones for the purpose of just such intervention.[21] In Turkey, business people often wear a blue-bead amulet for good luck and more specifically for warding off the bad luck of the evil eye.

In Mexico, the unexpected working of fate is well known. A supplier might promise delivery on Thursday, for example, knowing all the indications are that Thursday will not be possible because he has already promised a full agenda of other orders for Thursday. But the supplier might consider that perhaps one of the previously scheduled orders will cancel, or perhaps the driver of the delivery truck won't come to work that day making all deliveries impossible, or perhaps it will rain too heavily for delivery, or perhaps the company placing the new order will change it, which could reasonably alter the delivery day. A student may sigh over a failed exam, "It was my destiny, I guess."

In the United States, observances to ward off bad luck also affect business. Office buildings frequently do not have a 13th floor, for example, and airplanes have no aisle numbered 13. Then there are the pyramid letters that supposedly bring good luck to the person who doesn't break the chain (throw the letter away) and bad luck to the scoffer who fails to send the letter on to more people. While few executives admit to playing along, nevertheless their names often crop up on the lists of senders of the chain letters, with comments about not needing any more bad luck.[22] Many people of various cultural backgrounds have become interested in *feng shui.*

The popularity of *feng shui* from the United Kingdom to New Zealand is obvious from the number of newspaper column inches devoted to it. Experts and gurus tell radio and television audiences how to position their homes, businesses, and furniture within buildings in order to increase prosperity and avoid calamity.

A Chinese-American owned business in California was poised to purchase a property adjacent to it when the property came up for sale, and had an investor willing to pay the $1.2 million price in 1998. However, when a *feng shui* master expressed strong negative opinions about the purchase, the company did not complete it. Instead, an Armenian businessman bought the land. Within 18 months the value had soared to $3 million, and the hapless Chinese-American business owners were deeply chagrined. They needed the property but now lacked the funds to buy it.

It's not hard to recognize that an attitude of, "Oh well, might as well play safe . . . you never know," in the United States can be an earnest belief in another culture. In cultures where luck is acknowledged to play a role in business, people that discount luck may not only insult the luck-seekers, but also can risk being thought negligent in not paying enough attention to what is viewed as a legitimate business concern.

Are Rules to Be Followed or Bent?

This cultural dimension is closely related to uncertainty-avoidance or uncertainty-tolerance, and to luck. Having rules and following them, and making sure others follow them too, is a way of diminishing anxiety about the uncertain. However, whether rules are followed or not also has to do with what is important in a society: neat, predictable behavior or meeting human needs. In all societies conflicts arise between what the rules state ought to be done, and what will be convenient or helpful to individuals.

For example, take the simple act of crossing the street. In strongly rules-adhering societies, pedestrians may not cross anywhere they like. They must use crosswalks that are marked; they must wait until a signal indicates they may walk (perhaps a white-lit figure walking, a traffic sign used throughout the world). When the signal changes to a blinking red hand, they must hurry to finish crossing, and must not begin to cross at this point. When the red hand is unblinking, they must remain on the side of the street. In London the corners of some intersections have railings so pedestrians cannot cross exactly at the corner but must use a designated crosswalk some feet away. In Canadian cities, pedestrians are ticketed for jaywalking. But in rules-bending societies—China is one—people cross whenever they perceive a break in motor (or bicycle) traffic, wherever it is convenient to them to cross. Although they have been told the rule is to cross at a designated crosswalk only when the signal indicates they may, they cross where it suits them. (In China this is *not* the case when traffic police are present.) Rules-oriented cultures are puzzled by this seemingly cavalier attitude towards safety. In the United States, for example, the Occupational Safety and Health Administration—OSHA—would get after the company for not cracking down on the behavior in the following example.

In the Beijing airport an amazing sight greets the visitor. Check-in takes place at portable booths; airline personnel come to a booth with a sign that declares it is open, about one hour before departure. Once passengers have all been checked in, the airline employee takes down the sign and may move the booth to a less prominent position. Behind the booths is the luggage belt. It is about a meter high, fairly wide, and always moving. Behind the belt are offices for the airlines personnel. Clearly many people use these rooms.

There is much coming and going, laughter, cups of tea being carried in and out, and so forth. When employees wish to leave the office area and come out to speak to passengers on the other side of the luggage belt and the booths, they climb up onto the belt and straddle it to jump down on the other side! They could go around the belt, but that would take them perhaps 10 meters out of their way. No doubt they have been cautioned about the physical danger of crossing directly over the moving belt, but expediency wins over rules.

CATEGORY 3: OUR PLACE IN THE UNIVERSE

This category of cultural priorities rather grandly proposes to encompass the big things cultures deal with: the questions every society has to answer. Why are we here? What is the significance of life? Where did we come from? What do we go to after this life?

The ways cultures answer these questions determine many of the beliefs and attitudes that we can identify with a particular culture, and they motivate the behavior that we identify as belonging to a particular culture.

Religion is a belief system that informs attitudes and behavior of members of a culture—even of those that do not actively practice the religion. But when you are learning about an unfamiliar culture, studying the religion(s) is a lengthy and demanding undertaking. It's like studying Russian so you can read the street signs—a worthwhile endeavor but not the first thing you need to begin doing business in Russia. Religions or belief systems come from cultural values and also contribute to cultural values. You can benefit from understanding the world's belief systems, but you can benefit for purposes of business by understanding the cultural priorities of your business contacts.

Do Humans Dominate Nature or Does Nature Dominate Humans?

Nature is the natural environment and natural phenomena that envelop human endeavor. At one extreme, humans view nature as an inexhaustible resource. The assumption is—or at any rate, was—that the land was there to sustain life, especially human life. The Book of Genesis in the Bible proclaims that after God made man

> God said, "Behold, I have given you every plant yielding seed which is upon the face of all the earth, and every tree with seed in its fruit; you shall have them for food. And to every beast of the earth, and to every bird of the air, and to everything that creeps upon the earth, everything that has the breath of life, I have given every green plant for food." And it was so.[23]

However, archeologists show that ancient cultures, for example those around the Mediterranean and Aegean seas, cultivated land for crops in ways that ultimately exhausted the soil and deforestation caused its erosion. Nevertheless, the assumption that the earth and all that flourishes in it is for use as a God-given right has persisted into this century. Only in this generation, and particularly in the past two decades, has the argument for environmental protection seriously been put forward as public policy, even though the concept of stewardship of the created universe is present in Genesis. Simultaneously, the assumption that the earth is an inexhaustible source of sustenance is part of the Judeo-Christian tradition and of Islam.

In religions such as Hinduism, Daoism, and Buddhism as well as earlier animistic religions that endow certain trees and rocks and rivers with spirits, nature plays a different role. But what role? Japanese culture, which reflects the value orientations of Buddhism more than other religions, views nature as a source of aesthetic appreciation. Nature is observed, contemplated, and meditated upon just like a painting or object of sculptural art, and it is shaped into art in forms such as *bonsai*. Wilderness—unadulterated nature—has virtually no role in modern Japan. For example, boatloads of Japanese citizens organized protests against a dam in the Nagara river, but not to protect the ecology of the river. Rather, it was to protest the intrusion of a large concrete structure in the carefully cultivated scenery. (It was also to protest the impact on the fishing industry that the dam would have, since it would prevent trout from spawning.) However, Japan has pledged the largest amount of money of any nation for environmental protection worldwide.

In India, some Hindu sects such as the Bishois do not allow the cutting down of any trees or the slaughter of animals. This is extreme reverence for Nature, which has precedence over human activities. On the other hand, piety does not always mean protection of the environment in that country. The pollution of India's rivers has been an enormous problem for the environmental protection ministry. Pollution is a particularly tricky problem when the sacred Ganges, with its freight of untreated waste and the ashes and remains of cremated people from funeral pyres, is the issue.

The Daoists in traditional China held that the Way, the *dao,* meant becoming one with nature and its life energy. Chinese gardens represent mountains, streams, and caves, all places where spirits dwell and sources of meditative serenity that allow escape from the pressures of the world. Nature dominates human activity in that view. But in modern China traditional gardens are state owned and constantly crowded with Chinese visitors who litter. Devotion to the spirits of nature has been publicly denounced. The government has allocated little money for protection of the environment or cleanup of pollution, which is considerable. Nature is dominated by human activity today.

Among cultures whose priority is dominating nature, technology is often invoked. Technology is concerned with the relationship of people to their natural environment.[24] All cultures develop tools for survival in their immediate surroundings. Very old and very new cultures share this human endeavor; creating tools is something all cultures have always done and will always do. It has been called a particularly human activity; certainly only humans create tools from pondering imaginatively upon other tools.

Members of cultures with advanced tool-making capability often assume their culture is superior to others with less-advanced technology. This is not a basis on which to assess a whole culture; it is only one priority. Present-day technology is not necessarily the most sophisticated ever known; some processes used by ancient civilizations, like mummifying corpses in the Egypt of the pharaohs or glazing pottery in the China of the Song dynasty, cannot be reproduced exactly today. Technology, the relationship of a people to their natural environment, is often tempered and influenced by other cultural priorities.

A challenge to the view that technology can dominate nature lies in the *butterfly theory,* which suggests that a butterfly moving its wings on one branch in one place can ultimately be a factor in whether a hurricane blows in another place. Whether the hypothesis can be demonstrated satisfactorily or not, the fragility of the world's ecosystem is of greater concern than ever before. Scientists warn about holes developing in the ozone layer and about global warming. Governments and businesses worldwide—not just in countries that possess the most technology—are addressing that concern with policies to protect the environment. But even though space photography, sophisticated measurements of contamination, and other sources of information change our scientific understanding, the cultural priorities about nature as dominable or indomitable change slowly.

Another attitude that can have an impact is found where nature, such as certain mountains or rivers, is endowed with spiritual life. Human activity appears to the believers to be too insignificant to have a lasting impact on transcendental nature.

Thus most nations have a plurality of complex attitudes from different value orientations in their culture toward nature. That means businesses have to contend with complex attitudes toward nature, too. A foreign firm may identify an ideal site for a joint-venture manufacturing plant on a river. But the site may be revered by local citizens as a spot of natural beauty or spiritual significance. Who wins—the sacred or the secular—will depend on the priorities of the culture. That brings us to the next question to ask of a culture.

Are Divine Powers or Humans at the Center of Events?

Who controls outcomes of activity? Of business? Of life and death? In many cultures today deities exist in a sphere of influence that is apart from the secular world.

Businesspeople you know may pray regularly to a God whom they revere but make their business decisions based on factors that appear not to be divinely inspired. Devout individuals may indeed act upon private divine guidance, but they probably will not publicly explain their actions that way. This is generally the case in societies that follow a stated policy of separation of public affairs and private belief. Religious spokespersons in these cultures are respected but not relied upon for decisions. Questions of ethics may be referred to them, but the decisions rest with others whose responsibility it is to make the decision: organizations' CEOs, union presidents, newspaper publishers, directors of government programs, and so forth. Even among societies where human activity is considered accountable for outcomes, such as the United States, Great Britain, Canada, Poland, Hungary, Austria, and Greece—to name a few—public reference to a deity in carrying on human activity varies greatly. Canadians, for example, are bemused by the frequency with which leaders in the United States refer to God.

Some cultures see little or no separation between secular and sacred life. All human activity, including business, comes within the all-embracing circle of the divine. A deity is at the center of every occurrence. In Madras, India, a businessman goes to the temple several times a day and has his company truck blessed each morning before work begins. In

Bangkok, Thailand, a businesswoman offers food to Buddhist monks early in the morning before opening up her shop, and she may stop at one of the street shrines later in the day to pray. In Ankara, Turkey, the day begins with prayers to Allah, and prayers follow at intervals throughout the day in response to the muezzin's call. India, Thailand, and Turkey are all secular states and guarantee freedom of religion for all, but the practices of the faith of the majority have an impact on all affairs.

Of course, some nations of the world historically have been theocracies—their governments followed the principles and regulations of a religion in order to conduct their activities. A modern example of a theocracy is Iran. The tendency to see divine power at the center of human endeavor is widespread. Let's examine some of the major world religions.

Hinduism is one of the world's oldest religions. It includes the idea of the world as a great system of hierarchies, with the purest at the top. Living things are reborn in cycle after cycle of death and rebirth until they at last reach *nirvana,* a state of eternal peace and bliss. In hierarchies of people, called *castes,* the purest are the *Brahmin* priests. They are not necessarily also the most powerful, which can confuse businesspeople from Western cultures. Each caste carries its own *dharma* or duties, and members of each caste are encoded with aptitudes for certain work.[25] People traditionally are expected to live according to the expectations of their caste. This has had an effect on ambition and social mobility. Furthermore, it means individuals have specific careers in which they enjoy mobility and others that are closed to them. The caste system has been declared illegal as a basis for hiring and promoting, but its priorities still exist in Indian culture.

Hinduism has a dynamism that is the result of its embracing both many ancient beliefs and rituals and, at the same time, newer religions such as Buddhism. This means Hinduism has remarkable diversity. Hindus in western India do not worship the same god or observe the same holy days as Hindus in eastern India. While most Hindus venerate cows and do not eat beef because souls can be incarnated as animals as well as humans, the Tantric (mystical) tradition is an exception. Basic beliefs in one part of the country are rejected in another. Hinduism has been called the most accommodating of religions; it has also been charged with resisting change.

For many Hindus, the belief system is a way of life more than a religion. But educated Indians are likely to separate work and the rest of life, often as a result of Western influence. The foreign businessperson will need to learn what people's beliefs are in the specific area of India. Gentle questioning will reveal how willing an Indian is to speak about religious issues and the impact of caste upon professional life.

Buddhism began in India in the sixth century B.C. with the teachings of prince Siddhartha Gautama. He led a sheltered life of wealth and luxury until one day he met a beggar, an old man, and one who was dead. His eyes were opened to the harshness of life, and he left his home to ponder the meaning of suffering. He became enlightened after meditating under a sacred *boda* tree and subsequently taught what he had understood.

The Buddha's Four Noble Truths are as follows:

- To exist is to suffer.
- Suffering is caused by desire, which is never satisfied completely.
- Suffering stops when desire ceases.
- The Noble Eightfold Path is the way to end desire and thus suffering.

From the view of Western, action-oriented thinking, Buddhism is a passive resistance to suffering. Desire and ambition are positive in many Western cultures, not the cause of suffering.

Buddhism's Eightfold Path outlines ethical behavior that avoids evil and violence and contemplates the transitoriness of the body. Meditation is the complete concentration of the mind on a single thought to achieve freedom from desire and finally freedom from sensation.

Buddhism was originally a reformation movement within Hinduism. It interprets one of the ideas of Hinduism, *karma,* to mean the inevitable result of behavior in an ethical cause-and-effect sequence. Good deeds will generate good karma; bad deeds, bad karma. The good or bad karma is not only the results one experiences in this life, but in subsequent lives as well. Gautama taught that the end of the cycle of rebirths is *nibbana,* similar to the Hindu nirvana, except that it is a state of nothingness beyond creation. Individuals merge themselves with it in a final nonbeing that is ultimately the end of suffering.

Buddhism has two great branches, Theravada and Mahayana. Theravada ("teaching of the elders") Buddhism is based on scripture, and believers do not also practice any other religion mixed in with Buddhism. It tends to be found primarily in South and Southeast Asia. Countries that practice Theravada Buddhism include Sri Lanka, Cambodia, Thailand, Laos, Burma, and Vietnam. The Mahayana Buddhists are generally found in East Asia. *Mahayana* means "the greater vehicle," meaning Gautama intended his teachings to include other ways as well, and Mahayana Buddhists observe other religions along with Buddhism. Mahayana Buddhism is practiced in China, Nepal, Mongolia, Korea, and Japan. In China, Buddhist priests often share their temples with Daoist priests. In Korea, Buddhism and Confucianism are practiced together. In Japan, Zen Buddhism and Shintoism are practiced together. In Taiwan, Buddhism includes observances from Daoism, Confucianism, and Animism.

In some Buddhist cultures, such as Thailand's Theravada Buddhism, strict observances impact upon business life. Men become monks for some period of their lives, usually before entering the workforce. Women must never come in physical contact with monks or their robes, but daily offer rice and other food to gain merit. The monks may be influential in decisions that affect local businesses, such as labor and wages, locations for new businesses, and markets. Theravada Buddhism emphasizes learning not to desire things, and this can be contrary to the goals of a market economy. Yet many countries with Buddhist followers—Thailand, Taiwan, Japan, and South Korea—were economic dynamos in the early 1990s.

Hinduism and Buddhism are both polytheistic religions—more than one god is worshipped—although the emphasis on specific deities varies from one geographic region to another. In contrast, three other major world religions are monotheistic: Worshippers pray to only one god.

Judaism is the religion of the Jews. It began before 1200 B.C. and is the basis or context for the development of both Christianity and Islam, which followed. The Christian Bible contains the 39 "books" or separate writings, called the Old Testament, that make up Judaism's sacred scripture. Most of these 39 books were written originally in Hebrew. The first five books together are called the Torah. Another important document is the Talmud, made up of the Mishna (which deals with the legal component of the Jewish oral tradition) and the Gemara or commentary by Jewish scholars over centuries upon the Mishna. Both written texts and oral tradition are the basis of the practice of Judaism. Practice means following the rules and holy laws.

Most Jews share certain beliefs. Among these are belief in

- One God.
- God's concern for humans.
- The concern that one person should show for another.
- The *covenant,* an agreement between God and the people of Israel expressed through God's laws for the proper use of the universe.
- The world to come or the Messiah or the Messianic Age.

Jews who participate in religious observances also share

- Jewish practices.
- Jewish holy days and the Jewish calendar.

Finally, those who in any way identify themselves as Jews share the long chain of tradition that is the history of the Jewish people.

Judaism as it is found in the United States today is divided into four modern religious movements represented by synagogue membership: Orthodox, Reform, Conservative, and Reconstructionist. These four movements are also represented in other countries in the world, although perhaps in different proportions than in the United States. A small percentage of Jews identify with more or less extremist, right-wing, cult-like movements (such as Hasidism) that had their origins in 18th-century Europe. A large percentage of Jews worldwide identify themselves as Jewish though they belong to no movement—some of these do join synagogues from time to time, but others prefer to remain "secular" for ideological reasons. Mixed among both secular and synagogue-based Jews are others who center their Jewish identity on Zionism, the movement to create and sustain a Jewish homeland in Israel.

No matter what beliefs a Jew subscribes to, there is a sense of solidarity among Jews born of the recognition that they share a common history, heritage, language, and culture. They also feel themselves to be a community. The Talmud expressed its recognition of this commonality in a positive statement, "All Jews are responsible one for another." This captures the Jewish value called *Klal Yisrael,* the "Community of Israel."

Christianity is the faith of the majority of the world's population, but Christians are divided into several major branches: Catholicism, Protestantism, and Orthodoxism had an estimated 2 billion adherents in the year 2000.[26] Roman Catholics are the largest body. They emphasize the authority of the Roman Catholic Church in a centralized, hierarchical system. Jesus, the Son of God as well as Son of Man, born of a woman, Mary, is held to be the advocate for the individual with God. Apart from this advocacy (or that of his mother), and observation of the sacraments of the Church, there is no salvation. Priests carry out the sacraments. Protestants differ from Catholics in that they hold Jesus alone is the mediator by grace, and individuals have direct and personal access to Jesus.

Christians believe in one God. Believers claim Jesus was God incarnate in an historical person who was an itinerant teacher in Judea, Samaria, and Galilee (present-day Israel). He spoke about God as Father, and of himself as the Son of God. Jesus was born during the Roman occupation of the area and was put to death by the Roman powers with the cooperation of the local governor and religious leaders. His death was not the end, however; after three days in a tomb, according to Biblical accounts, Jesus appeared and walked among people who knew him before being taken up into heaven. He claimed to have eternal life, and furthermore to offer eternal life to believers. The resurrection of Jesus is what Christians celebrate at Easter, the holiest event of the Christian year. Christianity is based on the teachings of Jesus and of interpreters of his teachings.

The Catholic church, centered in Rome, historically had large economic interests but discouraged its priests from involvement in business. Individuals in religious orders usually renounce personal economic and business endeavors. The Protestant Reformation emphasized the lack of distinction between religious and secular life, and thus the way was opened for the merging of the pursuit of financial goals with spiritual goals.

The concept of predestination, prominent in some Protestant sects, is that the elect or chosen individuals are the ones who receive the gift of grace. Some historians see the linkage of material prosperity to the elect as a visible sign of God's blessing, as the linkage that made the development of capitalism possible and even pious. Wealth came to be seen as a sign of God's approval and blessing. If God's approval rested upon you, you worked hard and became wealthy. Wealth wasn't to be spent on self-indulgence, however. Along with the notion of gaining riches went the notion of not spending it, but rather saving and investing it—in other words, creating capital. Capitalism grew in this environment.

Islam is the religion of about as many people as Hinduism and Buddhism combined.[27] Muslims live in 30 countries and Islam is the dominant religion in 19. Islam began in 622 A.D. when Mohammed withdrew from Mecca to Medina; that withdrawal is called the *hegira.* Islam then spread rapidly through military conquest for 200 years. Part of its appeal, besides the imperative of the sword, was and is its undiscriminating and equal embrace of members of all races. It is the fastest growing religion in the United States.

Islam means "to submit" and *Muslim* means "submitting" or "obeying." A believer submits to the word of God as transmitted through the prophet, Mohammed, in the book of the *Koran.* The *Koran* is in Arabic. As mentioned in Chapter 5, this makes Arabic a holy language of the word of God. In Muslim countries, perhaps the most common phrase is *Inshallah,* meaning "the will of God be done." A fundamental belief in Islam is that everything, good or bad, proceeds from the will of God. Islam is a way of life that affects every aspect of daily life, through the *Sharia* or law of Islam. Iran, Libya, and the Taliban in Afghanistan follow the Sharia as the law of the land. Its punishments sound medieval: amputating the hands of thieves, stoning unvirtuous women. They nevertheless are effective.

The Five Pillars of Islam are

- *Shahadah,* the profession of the faith. This is summed up in the creed, "There is no god but God, and Mohammed is his prophet."
- *Salah,* worship. Islam requires prayer five times a day. Worshippers face Mecca, the holy city, and pray in Arabic. The most important prayer time is noon on Friday, when males are required to attend the mosque.
- *Zakat,* almsgiving. Mohammed was himself an orphan and Muslims are urged to give generously to the poor.

- *Sawm,* fasting. Fasting from sunrise to sunset is required during the month of *Ramadan,* the ninth month of the calendar.
- *Haj,* pilgrimage. Every adult who can afford it is required to visit Mecca. Pilgrimage occurs during the 12th month of the Muslim calendar.

Some precepts of Islam are contrary to Western business practices, giving Islamic countries no little difficulty in sorting out behavior that is within Islamic principles but also in keeping with good intercultural business. For example, Muslims are not supposed to charge or pay interest on loans. By receiving a guaranteed interest, an individual gets a reward without working for it. A return on the deposit is only acceptable if the individual either works for the return or is at risk, for example, if the individual's account goes down by a proportionate amount when the bank loses money. This way of thinking has given rise to Islamic banking, and banks that practice it cannot compete effectively for customers who want to earn interest on deposits. Since the will of Allah is omnipotent, Muslims who carry insurance policies risk being accused of lack of devotion or even defiance of Allah's will. Foreigners with contracts to develop or build in Mecca and Medina face the difficulty of not being allowed to enter these holy cities unless they are Muslim.

Muslim governments may not support welfare programs in times of economic recession, since *Zakat* requires believers to give charity. In Western countries, Muslims' daily prayer may be at odds with business schedules. Fasting during *Ramadan* can affect productivity.

Just as Buddhism and Christianity both have two great branches, so does Islam: Sunni and Shia. Their difference concerns the rightful heir to Mohammed's power. Sunnis—who won a majority of followers—claimed Mohammed's disciples should be his successors, while Shiites claimed a nephew should be. Shiites are dominant in Iran and eastern Iraq and are a powerful minority in other countries, which produces conflict because they tend toward reviving fundamental principles of Islam and against compromising Islam with modern cultures.

The role of religion in people's lives is something businesspeople need to know about. Most cultures have some procedure for young people to learn about their family's religion. Children in Catholic homes have their first communion at about seven years of age. Protestant children of mainline denominations are accepted as members into a church as teenagers (in some Protestant churches adult members are received upon baptism). Jewish offspring have bar mitzvahs and bat mitzvahs at the age of religious responsibility, usually 13. In Thailand, every male is expected to spend some time, usually six months to two years, as a Buddhist monk after completing his education and before getting married and establishing a family.

One way religion affects people's lives is in the special days of observance or celebration. Business travelers need to be aware of religious holidays in other cultures. Friday is Muslims' holy day; Saturday is the Jewish Sabbath. Sunday, the holy day of Christians, may mean that stores and places of business are closed. Ramadan, the ninth month of the Islamic year, is a month of fasting from sunrise to sunset—not the time to invite a business colleague to lunch.

The new year begins for Buddhists on the first new moon of the lunar year, any time from late January to mid-February, and usually involves several days' closure of businesses. (But Thailand, the most Buddhist nation in the world, also celebrates new year in

April.) In China, the Buddhist lunar new year has been replaced by Spring Festival, which takes place at the same time, the first new moon of the first month of the lunar calendar. Obviously, a business traveler to another country needs to find out when that nation's holidays are and when people will be available to meet in order to plan an effective visit.

Businesspeople also need to be very careful not to make assumptions based on stereotypes about other religions. Whether welcoming a new employee or investigating the possibility of a business operation abroad, you will want to keep your mind open and your inquiries gentle. Learn what you need to know in order to do business together.

How Is Time Understood, Measured, and Kept?

Another value orientation to do with *big* questions concerns a culture's view of time. Traditional cultures think of time as cyclical. The rhythms of nature and the cosmos dictate this view: Day yields to night, which in turn yields to day again; rain follows dry periods that come after rain; the time to plant leads to the time to nurture, then the time to harvest and the time plants die. Everything follows a pattern of birth, life, death, and renewal, even in daily activity after which the weary body sleeps and wakes again refreshed. Within the cyclical framework, events that occur take as long as they take; their time is dictated by their own essential nature. This view is common among agrarian cultures whose members are closely attuned to rhythms of cultivation. The corn will be ripe when it has finished ripening, in its own time. It is also persistent in cultures that value human interaction and relationships.

Monastic life of the so-called Dark Ages is often credited with developing a notion of time as modern European and North American cultures know it. The monks needed to regulate their prayers as a community. If everyone woke up late one day and earlier the next, the community's prayer life would be undisciplined and their other activities would be erratic. So monasteries began ringing bells to maintain a scheduled, ordered life. An idea took shape: to measure something abstract, intangible, and defined however you wanted to define it, called *time*. Time could be given an identity and then segmented into component parts. Monks gave the segments names, like *none* (noon, the fifth canonical hour and midafternoon prayer) and *compline* (the seventh and last of the canonical hours and evening prayer).

European monks weren't the only ones to try to measure time; Mayan priests had been doing it in Mexico, Guatemala, and Belize for a thousand years. Measuring instruments became more precise as navigational needs grew in Europe and as astronomy developed. By the 18th century, the instruments to measure time and the movement of planets seemed able to reveal the secrets of the clockwork universe. And time became a commodity.

"Time is money." "Save time." "Spend time." "Use time wisely; don't waste time." "Make time." "Take your time." These are some of the phrases we commonly use that underscore the value of time as something to be bought and sold. Employees sell their time to an organization and they are paid for their time. Lawyers and consultants of all stripes bill clients for their time. In a later discussion about what is private and what is public, we talk about doing something on the company's time versus doing it on one's "free" time. Telecommuting employees who work at home using a computer modem say "my time is my own," suggesting that they "own" their work schedules and can work when they please, not only when the organization's doors are open to the public. The opposite is an employee whose hours are "owned" by the organization.

What does it mean to be "on time"? The definition of punctuality varies from culture to culture. The cultural priority of time has close links to another cultural priority: relationships versus results. Where people are important and the nurturing of relationships matters, the time necessary for nurturing activities is flexible.

You may have an appointment in Puerto Rico for 10:30 in the morning; you may be the second appointment on the other person's agenda; and you can still be waiting at 11:30. Everybody is so important that no meeting can be rushed for the sake of a schedule imposed arbitrarily. In China, traffic snarls often delay people from arriving on time at meetings and although an apology is expected, lateness is not an insult. Both Puerto Rico and China have strong orientations toward building relationships in order to do business effectively.

In results-oriented cultures, adherence to schedules is much more important. In Israel, for example, promptness is a basic courtesy as well as an indication of seriousness about work. In Russia, time is not related to cost or profits, and punctuality—being "on time"—is an alien concept: "Russians are notoriously not on time, and they think nothing of arriving long after the appointed hour, which is not considered as being late."[28]

What does effective use of time mean? As we discussed earlier, results-oriented cultures tend also to use a cause-and-effect pattern to understand something and to use planning to control uncertainty. These cultures also have a linear view of time; after all, a cause-and-effect sequence unfolds in time from the generation of something to its results. People who view time as a highway progressing from the past into the future also tend to believe the past is background and preparation for the present. They think the present in turn will be the basis for the future. Time is used effectively when goals can be accomplished speedily. This is very different from people who see cyclical patterns that repeat themselves.

People who view time as linear and as divisible into chunks that have a market value measure time in relatively short periods: minutes, hours, days. In cultures where time is expansive, measurements are in weeks and months, such as in Russia where patience has a high priority.

Time can be monochronic—one-dimensional time—or polychronic—multidimensional time.[29] Monochronic time is linear. People are expected to arrive at work on time and work for a certain number of hours at certain activities. Then after resting for an appointed period, they are expected to resume work activities. In some monochronic organizations, being even a few minutes off schedule is not acceptable.

In polychronic cultures, time is an open-ended resource not to be constrained. Context sets the pace and rhythm, not the clock. Events take as long as they need to take; communication does not have to conclude according to the clock, and the clock does not require closure of the business at hand. The idea of monochronic or polychronic time can be related to a previously examined cultural dimension: whether tasks are done serially or sequentially.

Is Change Positive or Negative?

The culture of the United States thinks of change as desirable and positive. At the nation's founding, *new* was thought to be better than the old. In advertising slogans today, new means *better* products and services. Change means moving forward in linear time toward ever more desirable achievements. The business culture of the United States puts a high priority on the accomplishment of goals, accumulation of wealth, efficient use of time to do so, and a positivism that claims tomorrow will be better than today just as today is better than yesterday. When change has a high priority, members of a culture express optimism about the future.

Traditionally agrarian cultures typically view change in the opposite way. Since people who live on the land cannot move away and take their work with them, they tend to develop stable, static communities. They see the cycles of planting and harvest, rain and sun, day and night at very close view. They also think of change as negative. It means some disruption to the established patterns of life. They believe yesterday was better than today, and tomorrow will be worse than today. Products that call themselves *new* are not to be trusted.

Pessimism appears in the way Russians view change, for example. Russians expect things to be bad in the present and worse in the future, and in part this posture enables Russians to face change and uncertainty stoically. There is justification for pessimism. After all, historically the "best and brightest have traditionally been banished. In Old Russia independent thinkers were exiled to Siberia . . . Stalin's purges of the 1930s further decimated the intelligentsia, and today many of Russia's best are being lost through immigration."[30] Endurance is one of Russian culture's top priorities.

Clearly the priority about change has a close connection with an earlier one, uncertainty avoidance. Change always involves uncertainty about what will result, and cultures that view change negatively are also typically keen to avoid uncertainty. The old ways are best—the familiar is trustworthy even when it is known to have faults. Yesterday is often endowed with a golden glow and thought of as superior to today. This view holds that the past may one day come again if things stabilize, and we may return to the old ways. Cyclical views of time are consistent with antichange cultures.

Cultures that are conscious of their long histories cannot easily understand severing connections to the past or wanting to do so. Businesspeople from younger cultures such as the United States are often impatient with other cultures that cling to old ways. They operate with cause-and-effect logic and see that in order to accomplish a particular goal (an orientation they value highly) new ways (or products or procedures) are helpful. They cannot understand why others balk at adopting something new.

Is Death the End of Life or Part of Life?

The final priority we'll consider in this chapter for posing questions of a culture is about final things. Some cultures view death as the end of life, a quenching of the light. People in these cultures dread death. Some cultures view death as another phase in life, a necessary step in the pattern of life. People in these cultures accept death.

Hindus believe in reincarnation, and in India's burning ghats, bodies are cremated and sent on their journey towards another birth. People are reincarnated over and over in a cycle that can't be numbered. Your status in life is the result of how you lived a former life, and your present life will affect the next. When a loved one dies the loss is mourned just as it would be in Copenhagen or Cairo, but the mourners know the soul will be born again. In Russia, death is familiar; in a contradictory approach it is fought and welcomed. A former American Foreign Service officer quotes a modern Russian poet's response to his question about what Americans should know to understand Russians better:

In our cold winter each opening of the door
is a repetition of dying. Russians do not
fear death because every day is a struggle.
It is a pity to die, and a pity not to die.[31]

Mark Davydov

Death is not such an enemy as it is in the West.

In Holland, the enemy Death is sometimes embraced by appointment since doctors may legally assist terminally ill patients in dying. This enables them to die with dignity rather than dying by pieces. There is a relationship with this death-by-appointment and control over the unknown; uncertainty avoidance and a preference for planning and doing correlate with this approach to death.

Many cultures have religious beliefs that teach death is the only way to join the gods or God. In Islam, life after death is freedom from obstacles to enjoyment of God's gifts. A Muslim's heaven is experienced through the senses. A Christian also looks forward to heaven after death, to joy and an absence of pain, but the Christian heaven is less clearly defined than the Islamic heaven. Attitudes toward dying vary widely among members of Christian cultures, as they do among members of Islamic cultures.

Funerals mean different things in different cultures also. In Nigeria, funerals are very important. Unless you are dying yourself, you are expected to attend. It is thought that the deceased will reward you for your presence.

Funerals are dreaded in Asian cultures, where even the suggestion of death or funerals is rude. That's why you should never give a clock or watch to a Taiwanese as a gift (a reminder of the inevitable end of one's life span) or a bell (rung in funeral ceremonies) or white flowers (white is the color of mourning). You must even avoid using the word *death*. In Japan, it is intolerably rude to stick your chopsticks straight up in a bowl: they resemble the incense burned at funerals. In mainland China, lavish funerals were discouraged by the communists. But in recent years they have once again been mounted, to the dismay of the political leaders. Funeral objects made of paper, such as televisions, cars, and money, are burned to accompany the deceased into the world of the dead. Expensive tombs have been created, some for living people who have not yet been able to use them. In Hong Kong recently, many people were upset when clairvoyants charged that ghosts of dead children had appeared on TV commercials. Reminders of death are impolite at best, and unlucky at worst.

Businesspeople need to be aware of the cultural priority put on death and the observances that attend it. Chapter 1 gave several examples of different expectations work colleagues may have toward a co-worker who has lost a family member. Expectations for how the mourning friends and relatives will act differ from culture to culture.

In many cultures mourners wear a black armband or black clothing to signal to others that they are grieving the loss of someone and should be treated with respect. The color of mourning in China, however, traditionally is white, as it is in India. (Brides in these cultures traditionally wear red.) Mourning is signaled with a white armband or rosette in some countries.

Special observances besides the funeral service may include a wake or special feast where mourners come together to solidify new social relationships without the departed one. This is true in such divergent cultures as Catholic Ireland, with its wakes, and

Buddhist Taiwan. These two different cultures share characteristics common to high-context cultures, however, where the meaning of the individual is derived from the network of relationships into which an individual life is woven. The next chapter deals with cultural priorities concerning relationships. Chapter 4 discusses the two remaining categories of questions you can ask to learn what you need to know about a culture. It is about the self, and the self in relation to others.

SUMMARY

This chapter introduces the approach of asking questions in order to understand cultures. Asking questions involves

- *Where information can be found.* People from a culture or people who have lived in it are good sources, as are novels or other publications by authors from the culture. Even advertisements contain clues to cultural values.
- *Generalizations as both productive and perilous.* Categorizing information is how we make sense of the world, but we need to keep our generalizations flexible enough to accommodate new information.

The first category of questions is Thinking and Knowing, which covers these dimensions:

- *Does knowing come from concepts or from experience?* Some people truly know something only when experience has taught them; without experience they merely know *about* something. For others, knowing comes from conceptual understanding.
- *Does knowing come from asking questions or mastering received wisdom?* In many cultures the acknowledged authority gives knowledge, and one knows when one has mastered what the textbook or teacher says. In other cultures, going beyond what one has been given is how one truly knows something.
- *Does knowledge have limits?* In some cultures, not everything is knowable. Other cultures have the idea that everything can be known, if the key is found.
- *In what patterns do people think?* Western cultures primarily use a cause-and-effect pattern of thinking. Other cultures use other patterns. The balance of complementary opposites, as illustrated in the *yin-yang* symbol, is one example.

The second category of questions covers Doing and Achieving—how people understand their actions at work.

- *Which is more important, doing or being?*
- *Are tasks done sequentially or simultaneously?* Some cultures view one who works efficiently as one who accomplishes several things at once. Other cultures value a one-thing-at-a-time approach as the most efficient.
- *Which matters more, relationships or results?* Relationship-oriented cultures tend to be collectivistic. The relationships that connect people in networks are more significant than whatever tasks the people accomplish. Results-oriented cultures value outcomes of actions, especially measurable outcomes, as what matters at work and in life.
- *Is uncertainty tolerated or avoided?* People who are uncomfortable with uncertainty tend to stay with their employer and follow established procedures at work. People who

are able to tolerate uncertainty with lower levels of anxiety may attempt new things in their professional lives.

- *Is luck essential for success or is it irrelevant?* Luck or fate or destiny plays a large part in some cultures, where people recognize that their role in achieving success has less effect than forces outside themselves. In other cultures, outcomes are not left to luck but are considered to be largely controllable by human effort.
- *Should rules be observed or can they be bent?* Where relationships are primary and power distances are great, the rules may be bent to serve those more important values. Where results matter, rules are viewed as important in order to facilitate results.

The last category in this chapter is Our Place in the Universe. This section deals with the "big" questions cultures answer.

- *Do humans dominate nature or does nature dominate humans?*
- *Are divine powers or humans at the center of events?* Belief in divine beings underlies the values, behaviors, and attitudes of many people of different cultures. Two major polytheistic religions are Hinduism and Buddhism. Three other major world religions— Judaism, Christianity, and Islam—share roots and a belief in one deity.
- *How is time understood?* Cultures differ in attitudes toward time and how it should be observed. Some view time as cyclical while others view it as an unrolling continuous line. Some cultures treasure time as a commodity while others use it as the medium in which activities take place.
- *Is change good or bad?* "New" may not be positively received in traditional cultures. "Old" may not be approved in cultures that embrace change.
- *Is death the end of life or a part of life?* How death is viewed and how that view impacts business varies from culture to culture.

The last two categories of questions to pose of an unfamiliar culture follow in Chapter 4: The Self and Social Organization.

NOTES

1. Florence Kluckholn and Fred Strodtbeck, *Variations in Value Orientations,* (Evanston, IL: Row, Peterson, 1961).
2. John C. Condon and Fathi Yousef, *An Introduction to Intercultural Communication,* (New York: Macmillan, 1974).
3. Vern Terpstra and Kenneth David, *The Cultural Environment of International Business*, 3rd ed. (Cincinnatti: South-Western, 1991), p. 13.
4. Geert Hofstede, *Culture's Consequences,* abridged ed., (Beverly Hills: Sage, 1984).
5. Geert Hofstede, *Cultures and Organizations,* (New York: McGraw-Hill, 1991).
6. Fons Trompenaars, *Riding the Waves of Culture,* (Burr Ridge, IL: Irwin, 1994).
7. Andre Laurent, "The Cultural Diversity of Western Conceptions of Management," *International Studies of Management and Organization* 13, no. 1–2 (1983), pp. 75–96.
8. Edward Hall, *Beyond Culture,* (New York: Anchor Press Doubleday, 1976).
9. Iris Varner, "The Theoretical Foundation for Intercultural Business Communication," *Journal of Business Communication* 37, no. 1 (2000), pp. 39–57.

10. Shiela Ramsay, "To Hear One and Understand Ten: Nonverbal Behavior in Japan." In *Intercultural Communication: A Reader,* 4th ed., Larry A. Samovar and Richard E. Porter, eds. (Belmont, CA: Wadsworth, 1985), p. 311.

11. See Leon Lederman and Dick Teresi, *The God Particle: If the Universe is the Answer, What Is the Question?* (New York: Houghton-Mifflin, 1993).

12. http://home.fireplug.net/~rshand/reflections/messiah/shroud.html

13. Robert B. Kaplan, "Writing in a Multilingual/Multicultural Context: What's Contrastive About Contrastive Rhetoric?" *The Writing Instructor* 10, no.7 (1990), p. 10.

14. Colin E. Tweddell and Linda Amy Kimball, *Introduction to the Peoples and Cultures of Asia,* (Englewood Cliffs, NJ: Prentice-Hall, 1985), pp. 319–320.

15. Linda Beamer, "Toasts: Rhetoric and Ritual in Business Negotiation in Confucian Cultures," *Business Forum,* Winter 1994, pp. 22–25.

16. Roderick McLeod, *China Inc.: Doing Business With the Chinese,* (New York: Bantam, 1988), p. 72.

17. Yale Richmond, *From Nyet to Da: Understanding the Russians,* (Yarmouth, ME: Intercultural Press, 1992), p. 45.

18. Condon and Yousef, *Intercultural Communication,* p. 137.

19. James L. Watson, "China's Big Mac Attack," *Foreign Affairs,* May–June 2000, pp. 130–134.

20. *Culturgrams,* vol II (Provo, UT: Brigham Young University, 1984).

21. Margaret Lyons, "Australia: Jyotek Sets up Local Office," *Business Review Weekly* 21 (June 1991), p. 46.

22. Mike Clowes, "Superstition Extends Yet to Top Levels," *Pensions & Investments* 15 (April 1991), p. 14.

23. Genesis 1:29–30, revised version.

24. Terpstra and David, *The Cultural Environment,* p. 136.

25. Ibid, p. 83.

26. "The Southern Cross," *Economist,* ("The New Christendom" section), December 24, 1988, p. 61.

27. The following discussion is adapted from Terpstra & David, *The Cultural Environment,* pp. 89–94.

28. Richmond, *From Nyet to Da,* p. 122.

29. Edward Hall, *The Silent Language,* (New York: Doubleday, 1959).

30. Richmond, *From Nyet to Da,* p. 43.

31. Ibid, p. 40.

Individuals and Groups in Business Cultures

Sheila Graham is a businesswoman from New Zealand whose work in sales requires her to travel. Her company makes quality stainless steel food processing equipment. Today her marketing effort has brought her to Warsaw, Poland. She is meeting at 1:30 P.M. with Jan Zamoyski, vice president of a firm with whom she has been corresponding about the possible purchase of several mixers. Sheila wants to make the most of her visit, which is expensive for her company, and so she has learned what she can about the market in Poland for food processing equipment and even something about the financial picture and how international transactions are usually carried out. She doesn't know much about Jan Zamoyski except that he is in his 50s, at least 15 years older than she is, and speaks English.

So she is a little unsure how to take his behavior when she introduces herself to him—he takes her proffered hand and kisses it, instead of shaking it. Is this an attempt at humor? Should she laugh or take this seriously? Then he compliments her on her appearance. This is unexpected too; after all, she only arrived early that morning and knows she could look better. She doesn't want to be perceived as unprofessional because she is a woman, so Sheila's manner becomes a bit more distant. Both use formal address, last names and not first names, so that makes her feel she has things in control as a professional woman. But again Zamoyski has an odd (comic?) way of asking her if she'd like a coffee: "Would the lady drink a coffee?" (For a sec-

ond, she wonders what lady he means, and then realizes he is addressing her.)

After a little conversation about her flight and the weather, Jan Zamoyski begins to tell her about Warsaw, and to make references to various historical events that are obviously vivid to him. Sheila wants to talk about their business together, but isn't sure how to introduce it into this conversation. He seems to want her to respond with emotion to his rather emotional statements about Poland's history and heroes. She doesn't know anything about Polish heroes, apart from knowing a cardinal became Pope John Paul, and since she isn't Roman Catholic she doesn't feel comfortable entering into a discussion about him. So instead she replies that the language is very unusual to her ears. He promptly asks her to repeat a series of sounds she knows she cannot imitate ("W Szczebrzeszynie chrzaszcz brzmi w trzcinie"), and tells her being able to say that was once a test of true Polish identity.[1] Again, she can't decide if this is a joke or if it is completely serious and some kind of test of her.

Zamoyski next produces a small gift for her, and Sheila experiences new doubts. Should she have prepared a gift too? Should she accept this gift, not knowing exactly what it means? She doesn't want to be rude, but on the other hand she doesn't want to look like she can easily be bribed, either. She takes the small object but does not unwrap it. Now she decides to try to introduce the subject of the purchase and sale of equipment. "I have brought a

101

breakdown of our offer for you to look at," she says, taking papers out of her briefcase.

But Jan Zamoyski's response is to talk instead about the lunch he proposes they now enjoy. Sheila ate before she came to the meeting, assuming lunch would already have been eaten by 1:30 P.M. She puts her papers back in her case. He escorts her to a new dining room in the company's grounds, where he introduces her to six other people, and they sit down to an enormous meal. Sheila protests that she can't eat, but her host keeps offering her food. Her host also offers her vodka, along with a toast to the relationship they are starting. Sheila doesn't like straight vodka, but sips a little of the cold alcoholic beverage from her glass to be polite while the others all down their glasses in one gulp. The glasses are immediately refilled. She picks at the abundant food and tries to ask questions of appropriate persons at the table to facilitate the sale of her company's equipment. She doesn't have much time in Warsaw and needs to make the most of this contact opportunity.

Sheila finally manages to give specific details about the sale to the young man on her left. He listens attentively. The meal finally ends and Zamoyski has another engagement, so she goes back to her hotel. When she phones Jan Zamoyski next day, she learns he cannot meet with her, and that he regrets that the sale will have to be postponed indefinitely. She knows the price and quality of her company's products are good; she knows the Polish company is looking to buy. She anxiously wonders if she did something wrong.

In Chapter 3 we considered question categories of Thinking and Knowing, Doing and Achieving, and Our Place in the Universe. Now we turn to consider how people view themselves, and how their cultural priorities affect the way they interact for business purposes.

CATEGORY 4: THE SELF

In the United States, Great Britain, and Canada, with dominant cultures that are lower-context than higher-context, the individual self is the starting point (or perhaps the final arbiter) for nearly all career and professional decisions that determine working life. To identify a category for inquiry as "The Self" shows the low-context cultural bias of the authors, no doubt. In high-context cultures, group membership is the starting point for decisions.

Culture shapes the idea of self. In high-context cultures, individuals think of the self primarily as an element in a network with others. In low-context cultures, individuals think of self as a single unit of society. To be too aware of what others think—in other words, to be interdependent—is to be weak and lacking in assertiveness. In high-context cultures, to be independent is to be selfish and lacking in social skills.

In cultures that value **independence,** the idea of self includes making decisions for one's own life, taking care of one's self and not relying on others, and taking responsibility for one's own actions. "I can do it myself" is a statement from a self that values independence. In cultures that value **interdependence,** the self consults with others before making decisions; one relies on others for one's sense of well-being; and one takes responsibility for meeting the needs of the group before satisfying one's own needs. "I will do it for all of you" is a statement from an interdependent self.

Culture also shapes the way the self communicates. The person who has an independent self in mind uses communication to present the self and to further the self's goals. The person who has an interdependent self in mind uses communication to further the harmony of the group and the relationships among its members.

The following cultural priorities explore the way the idea of self affects business interactions.

The Basic Unit of Society: The Individual or the Collective?

When businesses in the United States first began exploring the reasons for Japanese success and ways to market products in Japan, they found surprisingly different attitudes in Japanese organizations. In Japan an individual is a fraction of a unit; the group is the fundamental unit. An often-quoted proverb in Japan is "the nail that sticks up will be pounded down." Any assertion of **individualism**—valuing the individual over the group—is regarded as a negative threat to the group and will result in punishment by the group.

Individualism in Japan is tantamount to selfishness. It is the opposite of self-denial for the good of the group, which is highly valued in Japan. That means Japanese managers are closely knit to the departments they manage, which are also highly cooperative and closely knit. Organizations can count on the loyalty and wholehearted commitment of their employees. Organizations have their own songs, their own uniforms, their own retreats for building loyalty and groupness.

Individuals in Western cultures (Canadian, Dutch, French, English, German, to name a few) make career choices on the basis of personal needs and goals. If a job offers insufficient advancement, for example, or a personality conflict arises with a superior, or the tasks become boring, an ambitious individual likely moves to another job. If lifestyle changes—for instance if a child's schooling or care for an elderly relative becomes a priority—an individual may very well change employers. When the employer wants more overtime from an employee but the employee prefers a job that does not require overtime, the employee may change employers.

In Japan, however, none of these situations is reason for a move. Changing employers is an admission of failure and brings loss of face both to the one who could not cooperate in harmony with the organization and to the organization for spawning such an antisocial misfit. In Japan, if personal goals are not met by work, the employee is persuaded to change or defer the goals. When lifestyle changes create new needs, the superior expects to be told and to share the concerns. Child care is typically the responsibility of a wife who stays at home and health insurance is available from all employers, yet employees discuss changes in their personal lives with their superiors. It is not because they may link these changes to a need for more income or housing; it is because the boss is owed the information and is expected to take an interest in the family life of the employee. When the organization demands overtime, employees eagerly respond. In many organizations in Japan, employees come in for overtime work even when they have little actual work to do, just to show their solidarity with other members of their corporate group.[2]

In cultures where the individual is a unit of society, a single person can earn credit or blame for the outcome of an organizational project. In cultures where the collective is important, credit or blame goes to a group. **Collectivism** values the group above the individual, and individuals have a responsibility to the group that supercedes individual needs or rights. The United States and Japan are among the least similar cultures in the individualism–collectivism cultural dimension that attempt to do business together. The United States has individual heroes (in the tradition of Gary Cooper's character in the movie *High Noon,* "a man's gotta do what a man's gotta do") in organizational cultures as well as in U.S. general culture. Japan has samurai-like group heroes: men who act together out of unswerving loyalty to a master but who may not be known by personal name. But between these two is a wide range of other heroes of other cultures.

Throughout Asia, in varying degrees, collectivism is celebrated. This is not surprising considering the high value given to relationships in these cultures. What matters is the close-knit interlocked human network. Individual recognition is less important, particularly if it means a penalty or some kind of ostracization. Harmony among the interdependent group members is the key, and it takes priority above nearly all other values. In collectivist cultures where interdependence is valued, individuals do not seek recognition and are uncomfortable if it is given. The reluctance to be singled out, even for praise, can present obstacles to a manager who is trained to motivate subordinates by offering personal rewards. A study of joint ventures in Shanghai in 1997 revealed that Chinese are motivated by a sense of belonging. This is especially motivating when combined with prospects of long-term employment. "Relationships facilitate results" is the way one interviewee put it.[3] One way a sense of commitment to long-term relationships is cultivated in one Japanese–Chinese joint venture is through company functions such as family picnics where everybody is included. Employees feel they are valuable to the company when they and their families are invited to socialize together.

In the United States, where individualism is valued, competitiveness is encouraged as a means for determining the best competitor. (The implication is that the best competitor is also the best, period.) When individuals compete against one another, inevitably there are many more losers than winners, but the competitiveness principle asserts that as long as you can enter into competition again and again, you too may one day win. In other words, consolation for losing lies in having a chance to compete. The United States has passed legislation for equal opportunity that is probably based in part on the value of having a chance to compete.

Individualistic cultures in general tend to include everyone rather than single out winners. When teams are exclusive, they still come together at a larger group level. At Sony, for example, departments form teams whose members are in a closely bonded relationship that excludes members of other Sony departments unless the concerns are divisional or organizationwide.[4] Foreign managers of branch operations need to look at motivation issues carefully in terms of whether individualism or collectivism is more important in an organization's host culture. Managers of multicultural workforces also need to consider what motivates employees of different cultural backgrounds.

Obligation and Indebtedness: Burdens or Benefits?

The individualist–collectivist priorities mean cultures interpret what obligation means differently. Everyone has had an experience in which someone came to the rescue and offered help just when it was needed. Maybe it was a stranger who offered that last coin you were short for the bus fare. Maybe it was a friend who agreed to drive you to an important event when your own arrangements for transportation failed. Maybe it was a colleague who agreed to represent you at a meeting so you could attend another important function. In the United States, a slang expression sums up the feeling that accompanies gratitude: "I really owe you one." It means one feels indebted to the favor-grantor. But obligation has rules, determined by different cultural priorities, and that can cause problems in intercultural encounters.

To consider the issue of indebtedness, we'll turn to a situation that generates obligation. Person A must meet a visitor at the airport, but finds the means of transportation relied upon to get to the airport is not available. So Person A asks Person B to provide transportation to the airport. In India, friendship means entering into a willingness to be indebted. In fact, in some languages in India, no word exists for "thanks"; if one is in a relationship, one incurs indebtedness and one is expected to repay the debt owed. No words are necessary. Nor does one hesitate to request a favor of a friend; that's what friendship means.

Compare this with obligation in the United States where someone might preface a request with, "I really hate to ask you, but . . . " or "I wouldn't dream of asking you, only. . . " This opening is usually followed by a detailed explanation of why the asker has no alternative but to become indebted. The request finishes with elaborate thanks: "Thanks a million; I'm so grateful." In a culture that values individual achievement, independence, and control over events by personal action, a request that puts someone in another's debt is almost an admission of failure. Sheila Graham, in the Warsaw sales situation, regarded accepting a gift as acknowledging indebtedness, which made her uncomfortable. She wanted the sale to go through on an impersonal business basis, not because of a sense of obligation she personally felt. The Poles, on the other hand, want to build relationship before entering into a business agreement.

People in cultures like Sheila's are not happy about being indebted, and often try to repay and thus erase the debt as quickly as possible. Perhaps too many obligations make people feel that their personal freedom is threatened and that they have lost some control over choices they could have made. Some independent individuals may go to lengths to avoid putting themselves in someone else's debt and to avoid making others indebted to them. For example, Person A who wants to go to the airport but doesn't have transportation might hire a taxi rather than ask someone to make a special trip. Similarly, rarely are gifts given for no apparent reason; on occasions when they are given for no specific reason, they are made to seem unimportant by a casual giving style. The reason: the giver does not want to make the receiver feel too heavily obligated.

Scholars observe that these characteristics are true of the dominant culture in the United States. They observe that African-Americans differ, however; this group is much more likely to enter into relationships of obligation (by someone or to someone).[5] Latino-Americans also are more comfortable with reciprocal obligation; two neighboring households may share a garbage-collection contract, for example, by pooling their garbage and each household paying every second month instead of every month. Their view is that non-Hispanic neighbors wouldn't like sharing the cost because they would be too concerned about who created more garbage and therefore should pay more.

The dominant culture in the United States, with its value of individual responsibility, invented the pot-luck dinner (everyone brings a dish and thus nobody is host and nobody is indebted), and "going dutch" (people who go to a restaurant together or attend other entertainment and pay their own bill). Asians, Europeans and Middle-Easterners are appalled; their values of hospitality and of indebtedness as the mark of a relationship are offended. This view is also discussed in depth in Chapter 7.

In fact, in most cultures of the world significant relationships are those that involve webs of obligation. Relationships of two or more individuals—or groups—can last for decades and even generations. In China, Japan, and other Asian countries, a first act that places someone's family under an obligation leads to a reciprocal act and so on throughout years, and the obligation responsibilities are passed down to succeeding generations. The obligations are the responsibility of everyone in the group, not only the individual who first became indebted. To terminate the indebtedness once and for all, to clear and erase the debt, is to end the relationship. This is serious. In fact, ending a relationship is an event of such magnitude that usually every measure will be taken to avoid it. The webs that bind a group together as well as the whole network of connections between groups are threatened when one connection is severed.

In modern Japan a wedding invitation may be greeted with horror and dismay, because it means the guest family must present the bride's family with a very large gift. The choice is either to give a large sum of money or to lose a close relationship. Indeed, some Japanese deliberately cool relationships with families that have daughters of marriageable age. Once they are safely married, relationships are resumed.

In Filipino culture, indebtedness because someone has done you a favor is *utang no loob*. This generally refers to indebtedness outside the family. The repayment may be in a different form from the favor received and may be spread out over several occasions, according to the wishes of the original grantor of the favor.[6] The obligation is shared by the whole group.

Japanese culture distinguishes between two kinds of indebtedness: *giri* and *on*. An example of *on* is the indebtedness a new employee incurs. He spends the rest of his life working to repay the debt he owes for being hired, through looking after new employees.[7] *On* is the obligation a child owes to its parents for the nurturing they give throughout the years the child is growing up. Because of this obligation, the child will take care of the parents when they are old, to repay the debt. Or again, in an organization a senior looks after a junior, which means the junior incurs *on*. But the junior shows loyalty to the senior, which repays the *on* or reverses the debt. *Giri* is also obligation. It implies self-discipline is necessary to overcome personal feelings and fulfill the debt owed to others. For example, *giri* requires an employee to agree with a superior, not argue.

Obligation and indebtedness are taken for granted as part of business relationships, too, in most of the world's cultures. This means that a business organization may incur indebtedness by asking a favor—say, extended terms of payment. In return, that business will continue to buy from the organization to which it owes a debt of a favor. Similarly, individuals in business organizations often ask special favors of individuals in cooperating business organizations, based on the ongoing relationship between the two larger entities.

Obligation can involve issues of ethics when cultures disagree about how far obligation can go. A foreign company offered an information systems manager in a firm in the United States a regular monthly payment into a bank account in a third country in return for informing the foreign company whenever his firm had a contract to fill. The foreign company then knew to submit a bid. The information systems manager didn't have to lobby for the foreign company, only give them the information that his firm was in the market for products or services. It was up to the foreign company to compete successfully. Of course, the manager's firm didn't know he was taking money from the foreign company. The foreign company earned over $12 million simply because they knew about the potential for selling to the manager's firm. The manager did well too; he had enough extra money to send his children to expensive universities.

Where does one's obligation lie? Would the obligations of the manager have been different if the information-seeking company were not from a different country? What if the information-seeking company were owned by a relative of the manager? Perhaps being paid (obligated) to supply information seems acceptable; after all, the information systems manager did not try to influence the purchase decision. But then why didn't he want his employer to know he was taking money from the foreign firm? In fact, the employee subsequently found he couldn't carry on with divided loyalties; his obligation to his employer won and he ended his deal with the foreign firm.

Age: Is Seniority Valued or Discounted?

In cultures that value age, the older a businessperson is the more credibility he or she has. Seniority in an organization is directly linked to seniority in years. Organizations send senior members to negotiate with other senior members when business transactions are held. Elders are treated respectfully, which means that nobody disagrees openly with what a senior person says. Meetings are never occasions where the younger members challenge positions or opinions of senior members, and the result is a harmonious unit.

When a senior person seems to be in error, quiet behind-the-scenes discussions take place in which the senior is shown alternative ways the position can be carried out, or is given several possibilities both positive and negative, in order to allow a reinterpretation of the position. Never is anything done or said that could cause loss of face to a senior person. On the contrary, extraordinary measures sometimes are taken to ensure face is saved and even gained.

This is true in Asia where older members of organizations enjoy great freedom and power. They can make choices for themselves and others in a way not open to younger people. Since others must listen to them and be directed by them, they have a degree of freedom from the need to conform that only comes with age. They have the most impressive job titles and often the most responsible jobs.

When U.S. organizations send executives to Asia, they often risk not being taken seriously unless their representatives look appropriately senior. In a delegation to a Vietnamese trading corporation, for example, the oldest-looking person will usually be assumed by the Vietnamese to be the leader of the group. In cultures that equate youthfulness with vigor, some people change white hair to more youthful colors; in Asia white hair earns respect. In a delegation of three people, one of whom has white hair, that one will be first to be seated, first to be greeted, first through doors, and so forth. Young executives puzzle Asian hosts, since in Asia one only becomes high ranking with age.

By contrast, in youth-oriented cultures being young seems to mean having more choices, more power, more energy, and more freedom than being old. Advertisements for consumer products in the West—cars, liquor, clothing, watches, fitness equipment—

appeal to the desire to be vigorous, healthy, and powerful, and these are related to looking young. Young corporate heroes are profiled in weekend newspaper supplements
because they are young. Middle-aged people even appear at times to take lessons from
their children on how to dress, what activities to pursue, how to wear their hair, and what
slang to use, in an attitude of respect for youth that baffles members of seniority-oriented
cultures. The word *old* has bad connotations: it means loss of power—physical, mental,
political, sexual—and with it, loss of respect, loss of capability, loss of status, loss
of position. Old employees are "kicked upstairs," "put out to pasture," "waiting for
retirement."

The great differences in how age is valued are important for businesspeople to understand. If your employees include a number of Asians, you may not be prepared for their
dismay when older workers are laid off. On the other hand, Asian managers who retain
older workers out of respect for their age, when younger workers are more productive and
more adaptable, risk the scorn of employees from youth-oriented cultures.

Manufacturers, distributors, and retail sellers of products designed to help mature adults
look younger may not have the market they assume in age-respecting cultures.

Gender: Are Women Equals or Subordinates?

In most cultures of the world, women do not achieve key business positions. The priorities
of cultures where women do not earn executive titles cannot simply be dismissed, however; members of those cultures do not all regard women as lesser beings, unworthy of
power.

In the United States, where equal opportunity is an official policy and where women can
perform in every area of employment, the view is that women and men are equally capable of achieving organizational goals. Women and men are equally intelligent, equally
competent, equally worthy of recognition for jobs well done. The fact that women do not
enjoy equal status or equal pay with men is often deplored, although tolerated. A majority
of single and married women work outside the home, and most two-parent households rely
on two incomes for meeting basic costs of housing, food, utilities, transportation, and personal needs.

Nevertheless, much is written about the differences between genders, and there is evidence that men and women select priorities differently from the general culture. For example, women are reported to be more consultative in their management style and less directive than men. They are said to have more interest in the emotional well-being of
subordinates and co-workers than men, to listen better and cultivate personal relationships
with co-workers more than men. Men who also exhibit these behaviors are said to have
"feminine" characteristics, while women who lack them are called "masculine"; their
behavior is sometimes explained as being more masculine because they have had to learn
to compete in a men's world. Managers—male or female—who have so-called feminine
qualities (cooperativeness, intuitiveness) are looked upon more favorably by so-called
"feminine" cultures, while managers who are "masculine"—again, male or female—and
who have "masculine" characteristics (assertiveness, decisiveness, competitiveness, and
aggressiveness) are valued primarily in masculine cultures.[8]

Cultural attitudes toward women vary, but the status of women in a society is not always
linked to their roles in the same way from culture to culture. Nurturing children is virtually

always the women's role. In some cultures this carries with it very high status, for instance in Muslim cultures. There the home is a sanctuary from the rough and dirty world outside, where women can live in security and peace with their children.

Men have the responsibility of protecting their women from outside dangers, of providing for them and giving them children. Women enjoy a high status within Muslim culture as childbearers and family nurturers. In some countries, unmarried Muslim women may work outside their father's home until they have a home of their own. Nevertheless, as Islam dictates, devout women will only appear in public in modest dress, which means some sort of veil in many Islamic countries. A Muslim businessman who arrives for a meeting with a co-worker in a veil will not usually introduce her, and she will not speak or shake hands with others. In part, this is because she deserves protection by her co-worker and the respect that comes from practicing Islam as shown by social distance on the part of men who are outside the family. It also represents a cultural priority that assigns decision-making roles outside the home to men.

In presently and formerly communist countries, women enjoy much more equal status with men. Chairman Mao's famous statement, "Women hold up half the sky," is often quoted as evidence that women in China are not excluded from any professional achievement. As a matter of record, however, women rarely rise to the top ranks of the party or of government. Nevertheless, they can have considerable professional status. Women are all expected to be employed outside the home. They are also expected by most families to do most of the domestic work, in spite of working full time. (Similarly, in modern Russia a familiar image in fiction is an overworked mother who has to be committed to a sanatorium. Luxury means staying at home with the children and not having to go out to work.) The extended family pattern in many cultures in which grandparents live with or near their children and grandchildren means child care for working women is usually built in. Women must retire from government jobs in China at the age of 55; men retire at 60.

In Japan, women often work in business organizations but in low status jobs; as OLs (office ladies) they perform clerical and even hostess duties. Many choose to work so they can find husbands, and large organizations encourage marriage between employees since wives will then understand their husbands' loyalty to the company. Employees are acceptable wives (having already been screened for employment) and should get along with the wives of other employees—an important consideration since the couple's socializing will be almost exclusively with other employee-and-wife couples. Young married women may continue to work until the arrival of their first child, but then will not usually remain employed.

As mothers, Japanese women enjoy high status in society; the bond between mother and child, called *amae,* is regarded as the most important in life. Japanese sociologists describe it as a basic dependence upon uncritical acceptance, such as mothers give children, which in turn fosters a desire for the security of acceptance. They attribute the Japanese drive toward conformism to *amae.* The desire for acceptance and the dependence upon others to provide acceptance is apparent in the polite Japanese greeting at a first meeting. It translates, "Please take care of me." But in general women have lower status in Japanese society than men. An indicator of this is that women in Japan use a different vocabulary from men in referring to self and others. Women bow lower than men to show their status is not as high (although their relative power may be greater).

Yet women typically hold the purse strings of Japanese homes, which gives them some power. In fact, women often enjoy economic power that is greater than male family members' power in a number of cultures, ranging from West Africa, to Ethiopia, to Thailand and the Philippines. With economic power comes other forms of power; women may not fill the high-profile positions but women may be the determiners of key decisions.

In cultures where women do not have status or power and rarely figure in management levels of business organizations, people from gender-equity cultures may have a tendency to view inequity of women as morally wrong. In these cases it is important to recognize that "wrong" is a culturally based attitude. Certainly professional women in the United States and Europe find inequity on the basis of gender unacceptable. But other cultures view women differently and not necessarily as of diminished worth.

CATEGORY 5: SOCIAL ORGANIZATION

The way society is organized has great impact on how members of that society interact and how they treat outsiders to their culture. Members of multicultural workforces, managers in foreign subsidiaries staffed by native employees—and conversely, employees with managers from foreign cultures—and workers in global organizations who deal with people around the world all carry with them expectations about business behavior based on the social organization they learned in their native society. Like attitudes toward gender, age, and relationships, these notions about how people ought to interact are learned young and are thought of as normal.

Group Membership: Temporary or Permanent?

Individuals in the United States are members of many groups simultaneously. Work associates generally are not all social friends. Friendships develop from a variety of contacts: school, neighborhood, place of worship, clubs, and community service organizations.

Furthermore, group membership is impermanent. If you lose interest in an activity, you drop out of the club and may lose contact with the friends with whom you shared that activity. If you move to another neighborhood, change religious affiliation, or get a new job, your friendships can wane. If your personal goals are no longer being met by a group, you move on and probably look to new associates for the benefits you used to receive from the former group.

In fact, even membership in families is subject to personal choice. Spouses often choose not to remain married, children occasionally decide not to continue in relationships with siblings or even parents, and even parents occasionally determine not to relate to offspring. The breakdown of family groups is regularly deplored in the United States, but nevertheless it is tolerated. A majority of members in the dominant culture of the United States agree the individual's needs come first. When one's own needs are met to an acceptable degree, then one can fulfill responsibilities to others.

In other cultures, where group membership may not be subject to choice, the responsibilities of membership come before the rights of individuals to expect their needs be met. For example, the notion of choosing to loosen family ties simply never occurs to members of collectivist cultures. In cultures where group membership is permanent, belonging starts with the family.

Social organization in Chinese culture has been described by a famous Chinese sociologist, Fei Xiaotong, who studied the culture of the Midwestern United States in the 1930s for his fieldwork.[9] He characterizes Chinese culture as a series of concentric circles with the family at the center along with *I,* the ego. (In Western countries, the innermost circle would probably be *I* alone.) The individual's parents, grandparents, spouse, siblings, and offspring are all in the center of the pattern. The next circle may include spouses of siblings, aunts and uncles, cousins, children's in-laws. The next circle is for one's dearest friends, perhaps from earliest school days; subsequent circles include work colleagues (who are also usually neighbors in China today) who are especially trusted. Then come those who are familiar but not so close, and so on until everyone has been placed in a circle—everyone, that is, to whom one might possibly be under obligation because of a relationship. Everyone else in the geographical area or nation or world is on the outside of the concentric circles: One has no obligation to respond to their needs. While the circle inside which someone is located may change, with a person becoming nearer to or farther from the center, the circles themselves do not.

Social organization in China is relatively stable because everyone understands the pattern of concentric circles and knows the key: If you want to enter into a relationship with someone and therefore be able to incur reciprocal obligation (which is the essence of a relationship), you must locate yourself somewhere inside a circle. You need to present yourself as the friend of a friend of a relative, or the classmate of a former colleague, or at the very least a co-worker of someone who was in a relationship with a co-worker of the other person. Once you can identify yourself as having some place in the social structure of another person's circles, that person has a responsibility to enter into a relationship with you. The Chinese word for relationship, *guanxi,* also means *connection.* The way business gets done in China is through connections.

In contrast, Fei described American culture as *contractual.* Instead of a network of responsibilities ranging from most to least important, he said people in the United States regard all relationships as contracts. They can be broken whenever one party chooses. Even close friendships and family relationships can be severed when they threaten the individual's personal goals. Work relationships, club memberships, ties with schools and former classmates tend to wither if an individual moves away. Americans do move away a lot; it is rare nowadays for an individual to live a whole life in one place. This makes social organization loose and impermanent. You can get lost in the United States. You can even move to a new location and change your identity.

Part of the stability of communist China's social structure comes from the fact that people begin working in a work unit, a *dan wei,* at the beginning of their career and do not change employers unless the employer arranges a change. This employer-for-life pattern is starting to break down as free enterprise grows. Some Chinese deliberately choose to sever connections by buying out their commitment to the *dan wei* in order to start an independent business.

The *dan wei* is not only the employer; it also provides housing, schooling for the worker's child, day care if needed, and allowances for personal needs (hair cuts, books and magazines, transportation). The *dan wei* also takes care of holiday destinations and times (which vary depending on rank), in some cases provides buses for employees' commute to work, and pays pensions upon retirement. Finally, the *dan wei* is where workers obtain certain commodities, and formerly obtained the ration tickets once a month that were necessary to buy staples such as flour, rice, oil, and meat. As more and more private organizations flourish, these functions of the *dan wei* are losing the critical importance they once had. But the entire country was organized in this system as recently as the late 1980s. It may be that new, private organizations will have to appeal to employees by operating in this paternalistic pattern.

Chinese who have had experience in study or work in the United States report astonishment when they once again revisit the United States and find their former colleagues have moved to a new job in a new city, and nobody in the former workplace knows their new address. For them, the obligations of relationship mean not only a lifelong commitment, but one that may well last to succeeding generations. The children of people with close *guanxi* are expected to sustain the same reciprocal obligation pattern, and their children as well.

Communication, especially within permanent groups, has specific functions. We'll now consider three functions of communication.

COMMUNICATING TO NURTURE GROUP RELATIONSHIPS   The permanent nature of relationships affects communication in collectivist cultures. Members of groups do not seek to speak up, to set the record straight, or even to express a contradictory point of view; instead, social harmony is a hidden goal of every communication.

This is very different from the tendency in individualist cultures to verbalize—that is, to put things in words whether written or oral. Westerners may seek to express a different point of view to be recognized or to triumph in presenting a point of view that carries the majority with it. In collectivist cultures, being right isn't as important as being in concord with the group.

In cultures throughout Asia as well as Africa, *losing face* is a terrible thing to suffer. Besides expressing agreement, various other ways of communicating diminish potential loss of face also, such as laughing to discount the significance of some word or act and therefore discount its ability to cause loss of face. Simply choosing not to hear is another ploy.

The profound desire not to be the cause of someone's losing face results in many cultures in a great reluctance to say no or bear bad news. Where the unspoken objective of every transaction is to create and nurture harmony so the relationship can thrive, bad news is a serious threat to that objective. Or to be precise, the *communication* of bad news is a serious threat. The news itself may or may not turn out to have disastrous consequences; maybe the context can be changed and the party need never know the actual bad news. But uttering bad news has to be, well, bad news. Delivering criticism to someone who might lose face by it becomes tricky. Indirectness is the usual policy when one must point out weaknesses or make criticisms of another, in order to *save face.*

Face is collective, not only individual. Children are taught not to lose the family's face. If an employee makes an error that causes the company problems, the company loses face. Often the blame for an error is diffused so no one individual is responsible, but the group loses face.

Similarly, the importance of *giving face* in collectivist cultures is often overlooked by members of individualist cultures. Giving face means making someone look good in front of others of the same collective, particularly (but not exclusively) superiors. Using titles, recognizing special achievement or expertise, praising a job well done, acknowledging an obligation—these are all ways of giving face. Not disagreeing publicly with superiors is a way to give face.

Face can also be borrowed. That is, when someone is at risk of losing face, that person can claim a connection with someone who has face, thereby "borrowing" face. A young person in an unfamiliar business situation who mentions an older, experienced, and known businessman is borrowing his face. A company that is initiating a business association with a foreign company may borrow face from another company with a long history of relationship with the foreign firm.

Some of these communication differences emerged in a cross-cultural training program delivered by Canadians for Chinese participants. When the trainees' lateness inconvenienced guest speakers, the trainers became angry and scolded the trainees. The trainees' response was bewilderment and—as emerged after some delicate questioning—shame for the trainers who let themselves behave so emotionally! So the trainers asked how the Chinese would themselves behave if, say, a friend repeatedly arrived late for a movie date, so late that it wasn't possible to see the film. The appropriate way to deal with such a person, the trainees agreed, would be to go see films with someone else and to become cooler and more distant from the person who behaved so irresponsibly. They said they would feel angry but it was not appropriate to show anger. The other person would certainly lose face if anger were directed toward him or her, and the angry person would look foolish and childish, and therefore would also lose face. Social harmony would be disrupted twice. (The trainers apologized the next day for their angry words.)

DISPLAYING EMOTION Showing emotion in nonverbal and verbal communication varies in degree along the lines of high-context and low-context cultures. In China, Japan, Korea, Thailand, Vietnam, and other collectivist cultures, culture socializes people from an early age not to show emotion publicly. No doubt this is because a display of emotion could have potential consequences of disrupting the harmony that is so important to collectivist cultures.

Obviously this attitude toward emotions can have consequences in work environments where an emotion-expressive culture is in contact with an emotion-repressive culture. When someone from an emotion-expressive culture—say Polish—carries on a communication transaction about a perceived wrong with someone from an emotion-repressive culture—say Japanese—each can be sending messages the other has trouble decoding correctly because of the communication style. The Pole may be perceived to be immature, out of control, and egocentric. The Japanese may be perceived to be cold, unsympathetic, and uptight. These perceptions then form the context for the worded message, which is subject to distortion and misinterpretation, or in other words, faulty decoding.

Egyptians display only emotion that is socially acceptable. The emotion of anger is not socially acceptable. But not to show emotion, for example in the face of another's grief, or jubilation, or disappointment, is self-centered and egoistic. That is, to be impassive is to deny group membership.

SHAMING OR CAUSING GUILT Some who study cultures divide them into those that cause shame in order to make people behave according to cultural rules, and those that cause guilt. Both these emotions can be powerful elements in cross-cultural business interactions. Shame is an emotion of embarrassment experienced by a group, or a member on behalf of the group, when the honor of the group is called into doubt. It is in public view, the result of (alleged) misconduct. Guilt is an emotion of self-reproach experienced internally and privately at the recognition of misconduct. (This is not the same meaning of guilt as responsible for wrongdoing, the opposite of innocent.) Some cultures use the painful emotion of guilt to punish members. The guilt-ridden suffer in private until their guilt is admitted in public and then the behavior about which they feel guilt is forgiven or punished or dealt with in some way. The guilt may or may not go away as a result of getting its cause out in the open. Where individual responsibility, results, and privacy are valued, guilt is a potent way for a culture to enforce rules of behavior.

Where group membership, relationships, and public knowledge of one's life are important—in other words, in collectivist cultures—shame enforces the rules of conduct. These rules may have origins in Confucianism in Asian cultures. In shame cultures, group members suffer the disgrace of belonging to a dishonored group. Shame is not the same thing as *face,* which involves status. A group may be shamed but still not lose face. For instance, if the oldest son of a family incurs a debt and creditors are known to be pursuing him, the family is publicly shamed. But if the debt is paid, there is no loss of face.

Members of shame cultures may not be able to give answers to questions from foreigners without losing the collective's face—questions about their business organization's technological capability, expertise, manufacturing experience, ecological progress, or human rights achievements. Persistent questioning can cause shame if it implies wrongdoing. Similarly, any public comment—even in a joke—that refers to a person's, company's, or nation's failings causes shame for the group (family, employer, country).

It is quite possible for people who are not members of a shame culture to cause shame without realizing it. Dr. Wong, one of a group from China working temporarily in an Australian hospital, reported to a Malaysian surgeon. The surgeon's secretary was Australian. The surgeon and doctor happened to meet and pause for a brief conversation at the secretary's desk. The secretary interrupted, saying, "Dr. Wong, where were you yesterday? I looked all over the hospital for you!" The doctor had been in a lab elsewhere in the hospital—a perfectly reasonable place to be—but hadn't informed the secretary. He felt shamed, on behalf of all the visiting Chinese medical staff in the hospital, by the secretary's question in that situation. He thought she was trying to make him look bad in the eyes of the surgeon. He felt accused of misconduct that reflected on the Chinese group as a whole. But the secretary had no intention to cause him shame. She was simply saying what occurred to her when she saw him and remembered she hadn't been able to reach him the previous day.

Form: Important or Untrustworthy?

Form means protocol, the rules of etiquette and manners for doing something. It is related to communication issues for permanent versus temporary group membership: Form is usually more important in cultures where preservation of harmony in permanent groups is critical. Behaving with form means behaving *correctly.* Cultures that make form important ensure that everyone can operate by the same knowable rules, which reduces the risk of losing face through some unintentional mistake. Everyone is more comfortable because the rules are well established and comprehensive. Trustworthy people follow form. In some cultures, doing it by the book is an essential mark of maturity, adulthood, responsibility.

Form is the reason why Thais do not show anger in public words or actions. Form is what requires Indians to greet one another with *namaste,* which is a gesture that accompanies the greeting, putting the palms of the hands together with fingers pointing towards the chin, and slightly bowing the head. In Thailand the same gesture is called the *wai.* Form requires you to offer your right cheek for a token kiss to every social or business contact you meet in Argentina. Form is why Jan Zamoyski kissed Sheila Graham's hand in greeting and used formal language to offer her coffee in the situation that opened this chapter. The deliberate setting aside of form—which could be called a form in itself—accounts for the Israelis' using first names right away. Form is what dictates that overcoats must be checked at the door in Russia.[10] Form may even determine when it is acceptable to talk business (at dinner? on a train ride? at meetings only?). Some cultures seem to follow form when the substance itself is not significant—this is form for the sake of form.

For example, Japanese businesspeople bow to one another each time they meet, and the depth of the bow registers to a precise degree the relative status of each person. Business apparel is uniform—often literally "one form" of dress. Certain companies provide a company jacket for employees, who change from street clothes upon arrival at work. Delegations of Japanese businessmen abroad are also virtually identical in dress: dark suits, white shirts, about one inch of cuff showing, sober ties (no bow ties). Gifts are elaborately wrapped, even ones that may be of low monetary value, following expected form.

In negotiations, correct form dictates that only designated speakers speak; others are silent unless invited specifically to participate. One correct form for saying "no"—which Japanese employ reluctantly—is to draw in the breath through the teeth with a hiss, and then expel it, "Sahh!" while looking sadly at the table. The proper form for addressing someone is by title (Vice President, Engineer, Teacher) and family name. Given names are only used in intimate relationships, never by business associates.

This is in addition to the speech registers used in the Japanese language, which has six different vocabulary patterns to say *Good morning* depending upon who is speaking and to whom: superior to subordinate, elder to younger, male to female, or vice-versa. Japanese has 14 synonyms for *you,* to allow proper attention to degree of form.

Form also means that family names only are used. Given names are only used by intimates, not work colleagues. One Japanese business researcher commented about the odd use of given names when the Prime Minister of Japan, Yasuhiro Nakasone, met with President Ronald Reagan:

> It made an interesting news item in Japan when then Prime Minister Nakasone reportedly mentioned that he dealt with President Reagan on a first-name basis and termed the two men's relationship as the "Ron-Yaso Relationship." . . . The fact remains, however, that no one, including his cabinet ministers, ever called him by his first name in Japan.[11]

In European cultures, which are generally diverse but share alike a respect for form, business contacts almost never address one another by their given names, even when they work together for long periods and see one another regularly. In written messages, correct form means required use of certain phrases and formulae. French business letters invariably include subjunctive verbs, to show politeness, and close with an expression of warm wishes to the reader that British and American correspondents find florid. In Mexico, business letters not only use elaborate language, they also tend to be extremely courteous.

On the other hand, some cultures mistrust form. *Standing on ceremony* is perceived as giving oneself airs and substituting etiquette for sincerity. To the recently invented culture of the United States, emphasis on form looks mannered. It is dangerous sophistry, even deceit. Businesspeople from the United States are known around the world for their preference for addressing business colleagues by given names rather than family names. An attempt at genuineness, at leaving behind stuffiness and formality, can come across as presumptuous intimacy. The goodwill gesture of putting an arm across another's shoulders can translate as boorish bonhomie. To the venerable cultures of Asia and Europe, lack of form looks unmannerly. It is dangerous naivete, even ignorance. By the same token, members of other cultures may find the behavior of U.S. businesspeople to be a "form" of informality with rules about informality that have to be learned in much the same way as rules of formal protocol have to be learned.

To communicate effectively, businesspeople need to be aware of the different attitudes toward form and to adjust their reactions to other cultures' communication messages.

Personal Matters: Private or Public?

The degree to which possessions, programs, and organizations are private or public varies with culture and can affect how business is carried out. This is a cultural priority, not a description of how companies are structured; we aren't talking about privately held shares versus stock traded on an open market. We are discussing the degree to which people believe work and private life are separate.

Personal privacy is another of the priorities that people the world over take for granted, assuming their view is universal until they are confronted with another view. In Europe as in Anglo cultures—Canada, the United States, Australia, and New Zealand—a person's work life is kept fairly separate from private life. Workers are not expected to bring private concerns with them to work; employees do not bring children to the office to play at their feet while they work; personal phone calls and visitors are not appropriate. Hours that the organization pays for belong to the organization and its concerns.

On the other hand, lunch breaks and even coffee breaks are not paid time in many jobs, and therefore are the employee's personal time. This is when an employee receives and makes personal phone calls, keeps personal appointments and so forth. In some offices, considerable effort is expended to keep employees from discussing personal issues as they work. Organizational policy usually implies, if not directs, that workers should not even be *thinking* about personal issues on company time if such thoughts may adversely affect work.

Not surprisingly, cultures that emphasize relationships, view group membership as long term, and value harmony have a blurred distinction between what is private and what is public (or at least what is "group"). As illustrated by the Japanese worker with the hangover in Chapter 1, in Japan superiors are expected to be paternalistic counselors in matters to do with private lives of employees. The same is true in China, where an employee would appear secretive and deliberately destructive of group harmony for failing to share the particulars of personal problems—serious ones that might interfere with work—with a superior. (Nothing is actually secret and the superior would find out from someone else anyway, in that collectivist culture.) In China where the work unit provides so many of the commodities of personal life, the line is even more blurred. In Argentina, which is strongly influenced by European values, employees are expected to put work priorities first, but family and private concerns are treated with a somewhat flexible attitude.

An expatriate working in China recalled sitting in a medical clinic in a particular *dan wei* when a doctor rushed into the large consulting room. In great agitation he went from doctor to doctor asking each one something in hurried tones. Several of the doctors nodded; others shook their heads. The visitor asked later what the commotion was about. Was it some medical emergency? No; it seems a truck with jars of preserved plums was at the west gate, and anyone who wanted some had to speak up right away. The doctors had been placing their orders. (In the same organization, the woman who ran the photocopy room also took orders for cotton-filled quilts for members of that organization.)

In much of China the summer weather is very hot and humid; typically workers have a long break in the middle of the day during which many go home and sleep. The hot and humid nights mean workers don't get enough sleep between dark and dawn. Workers who live too far away to go home frequently have their siesta at their desk or work station. The organization understands; after all, it provides housing (with or without roofs for sleeping) and perhaps even fans, and knows that employees need sleep.

In Great Britain, by contrast, an employee who comes back to work from lunch and sprawls over the desk for a nap will be under fire from the employer. The employee is expected to sleep in private, on personal time. And even if it is the employee's time, sleeping at work looks bad for the organization in a culture that values achievement and activity.

Finally, differences about public and private touch the question of ownership of intellectual property. In a socialist country, ideas and intellectual products belong to the people, like everything else. Individuals may be recognized for their books or inventions or other creative acts, but their products belong to the people. The creators ought not to seek to get rich at the expense of the people from whom they themselves have come. This is a problem for exporting countries, where intellectual products are commodities just like manufactured goods. Creativity is valued, and creativity deserves recompense.

This can be a critical difference when a company's proprietary information is concerned. Some organizations have experienced problems with trainees and even employees from China and from formerly communist Eastern Europe sharing technological information such as patented processes with colleagues back home. Since costs for research are theoretically shared by everyone in socialist states, the results of research, it can be argued, belong to everyone. In Western countries where research costs are borne by a specific organization in order to compete, there is a need to protect that investment. Each viewpoint is understandable within its own context, but it's important to recognize the cultural variations in the line between private and public.

Social Organizational Patterns: Horizontal or Hierarchical?

Social organization in cultures tends toward one of two extremes: At one, there are rigid vertical levels in society and movement between them is very limited; at the other extreme, society is horizontal and operates pretty much with one social level. In modern history, hierarchical social organization is associated with monarchies, and horizontal organization with democracies. Of course, most cultures are somewhere between the extremes.

As we saw in Chapter 3, India has a system of vertical steps called *castes.* In most business encounters between Indians and non-Indians, however, *castes* play a small role. That is partly because foreign businesspeople have limited contact with them in the course of doing business. It is also because the *caste* system has been officially ended by law, and so it is not easily visible to a non-Indian. The stratification of society by castes still exists, however, and is of sufficient concern that non-Indians should be careful how they ask questions about it.

Monarchies today vary in mobility between levels of society. In Holland and Denmark, for example, the distance between monarch and subjects seems small. Queen Beatrice of Holland frequently stops her car and gets out to shop at town stores, in the midst of her subjects who have great affection for her. In Thailand, however, the royal family is regarded with deep awe and reverence; the lives of all of the king's family members are recorded and followed by subjects who think of them not as familiar but as vastly superior, almost divine. In Japan the Emperor was, until 1945, viewed as divine by his subjects. When Emperor Hirohito broadcast his announcement of surrender to the allied forces, most of his subjects had never heard his voice. (Since the imperial court used classical Japanese, not the common language, most of the country didn't understand his broadcast.) At his funeral in 1991 many mourners confessed that his renunciation of divine status had not persuaded them; they still believed he was the direct descendent of Japan's divine female founder.

Japan is conscious of hierarchy in all things. This is fitting for a country that has had only one dynasty in its entire history. As mentioned earlier, Japanese contains different words to say the same thing, depending upon one's status compared with that of the person to whom one is speaking. Similarly, there are degrees of depth of bow, degrees of elegance in dress, degrees of restaurants, degrees of gifts, degrees of social occasions, degrees of status of universities, and degrees of manufacturers, banks, and other businesses.

Japan also derives some of its levels of hierarchy from Confucian ideas imported from China. Other Confucian cultures—Korea, Vietnam, Taiwan, Hong Kong, and Singapore—also preserve the orientation toward hierarchical organization. In Confucian teaching, man is superior to woman, who owes obedience to the man. Parents are superior to children who owe parents respect, obedience, and reverence—the famous "filial piety." An employer is superior to the employee, and so forth. These attitudes can still be seen in Confucian cultures, 2,500 years after that teacher lived.

The highest status in the traditional Confucian society belonged to the scholar. Only scholars were trusted with the task of administrating the country and carrying out the emperor's justice. Next highest were the farmers whose labor provided sustenance for everyone. After farmers came soldiers and artisans, and at the bottom of the ladder were those engaged in commerce. Strange as it may seem in view of the rapid economic growth and dynamic businesses in formerly traditional Confucian cultures, Confucian teachings held businesspeople in contempt. They were parasites who would seek financial gain from merely brokering commodity exchanges, being merchants and traders, creating nothing by their labor. Even today in villages of western China and Tibet, merchants do not sell to their own family members. If the entire village is related in some way, nobody lives by commerce.

In Russia, even after the dissolution of the Soviet Union and the control of the communist party, commerce is a kind of exploitation. One of the authors was told in Russia that retailers who buy goods from the state, produced by Russian labor, and sell them at a profit, are engaging in "speculation," not business.

The difference between horizontal cultures and hierarchical cultures lies in what birth means. If you are born into a level of society that you cannot leave no matter what your education or income, you are a member of a hierarchical society. If you are able to rise to a higher level (or fall to a lower level) of society than you were born to, with more status, more power, or more wealth, based on merit rather than social origin, you are a member of a more horizontal society.

People of the United States value social mobility because historically most immigrants to the United States were escaping a more rigid system that worked to their disadvantage. The United States proudly calls itself "the land of opportunity" and its people tell stories about individuals of humble birth who began with nothing and became known and powerful and rich. The Horatio Alger stories—Alger wrote in the early 1900s for a young male audience about boys who worked hard and single-handedly changed their level in society—became widely accepted as a true type for citizens of the United States.

Generations in the United States were raised on the twin ideas that everyone ought to be able to rise in society through hard work and achievement, and that rising to the top is unquestionably desirable. For them, hierarchical social organization common to other cultures has been baffling. Why would anyone embrace a system that keeps you in one level all your life? (However, as young people face the prospect of not rising, and even of not attaining the level of their parents, the permanence of class membership has an appeal that may have been previously unrecognized.)

Both Australia and New Zealand have proudly let it be known that they have had prime ministers whose education ended with high school but who have nevertheless risen to the highest level of political achievement. Australia and New Zealand have flexible, horizontal societies where birth does not determine what level an individual may attain in the society. This attitude toward mobility is very different from Great Britain, from which a majority of the populations of both Australia and New Zealand trace their roots.

In England in the 1940s, for example, servicemen from the United States had a hard time grasping the fact that the English had ideas about who could eat appropriately at what restaurants or vacation in what hotels, according to membership in a class. The attitude held by the majority in England has been that everyone has a place or station in society and that is where one is most comfortable. To try to rise above one's station is to ask for discomfort or even pain. To lower oneself is equally wrong and brings about disastrous consequences.

Material wealth is not the critical factor in class membership. Having a big house, an expensive car, and a holiday villa is not as important as having the right family tree. Education is usually linked to class membership since children from different classes go to identifiably different schools, but educational level is only a slight factor in class membership. A member of the working class with a doctorate is always aware of membership by birthright in the working class. Former Prime Minister John Major is an example of someone who rose to the top from a working-class background. He was never allowed to forget it. An upper-class member who has only a high school education also carries that upper-class membership throughout life regardless of low academic achievement.

A stock figure in comic British literature is the titled ignoramus who has been to a good school, yet bumbles around trying to do the simplest tasks in high places. This figure is usually accompanied by a lower-class person who is cleverer, and either outwits the other or gets the other out of trouble. The stories by P. G. Wodehouse about Bertie Wooster and his servant Jeeves are from this literature. Set in the 1920s, they were dramatized for television by the BBC in the 1990s. In general, membership in the upper class entitles one to positions of responsibility in influential organizations. Membership in the lower class in general entitles one to relative freedom from responsibility for decision making outside of one's own family. The majority of people in hierarchical societies don't seek a change in status out of their birth level. They are comfortable knowing what the levels are and where they fit. In Central America, for instance, millions of people of humble birth seek not to move to another level of society but rather to carry out their lives taking responsibility for the things within their scope. Business organizations in hierarchical societies reflect the same hierarchical structure. People have no desire to lose the security of knowing who is where, in relation to everyone else. They do not wish to exchange that security for a wide-open, unstructured system where everyone is on an equal footing. In Indonesia, business-people were alarmed by the familiarity with which an Australian joint-venture representative treated them, asking them to call him by his given name, for example. Where was his sense of self-respect? Didn't he have a high regard for his subordinates? If he did, surely he wouldn't insult them by treating inferiors the same way as he treated their betters. An intention to appear friendly and egalitarian on the part of an Australian can come across as foolish and dangerous to his subordinates.

Approach to Authority: Direct or Mediated?

Authority means different things in different cultures.

A Pakistani-based Canadian manager was approached during office hours by a cousin of one of his employees, complaining that a neighbor had cheated him over a land deal. By virtue of his status as a manager he was expected to fill a vital function of social leadership, which was not restricted to the company.[12]

The relative importance of hierarchy and the priority assigned to form both relate to another factor. How does one approach an authority figure in a culture? Is it by simply and directly appealing to that person? Or is access appropriately through mediators and representatives and lobbyists?

In many cultures the approach to authority is indirect. Only certain avenues lead to the seat of power; only approved escorts can take you to their leader. In Latin American cultures, a mediator is typically the way to reach authority. Often this is also one's patron. The patron–client relationship is a reciprocal one in which the patron looks after the interests of the client and helps to smooth difficulties and further the client's career. The client is loyal to the patron and supports the patron without swerving; the client helps build up the patron's power base through this loyalty. The patron–client relationship functions when the authority to be approached is high above, in a hierarchical structure.

This relationship also was typical of business organizations in precommunist China, where the senior would *ti ba* (pull up) his junior person, through mediation on his behalf (it was always men) and through creating opportunities for the junior. In return, the junior gave the senior man absolute loyalty and assiduous work. In the patron–client relationship, the client moves upward with the patron's promotions. The patron–client relationship is one of expert and protege, master and disciple, but it exists within the larger context of a hierarchy at the top of which is the great power.

Another common hierarchical pattern requires an individual to approach authority only through the established channel of superior to SUPERIOR to **SUPERIOR.** There is no formal patron–client relationship, and usually the hierarchy operates by status and job title as much as by inherent individual status. The position—the rung on the ladder—is more significant than the individual who holds the position. This is particularly true in organizations and cultures where there is job mobility. In a German organization, for example, the manager of a department may move to a different department or a higher position or a new employer. A subordinate nevertheless will go first to the manager, whoever that is, who will then go to a superior, and so forth. In Mexican organizations, the manager is owed respect because it has taken some effort (good performance) to reach the position of manager, or it is a result of birth, or both. The power distance between manager and workers is large, so the manager is somewhat remote from workers. Often intermediaries open doors so the worker can approach the manager, or intermediaries may carry the message for the worker.

In hierarchical cultures where the approach to authority is by mediators, low-level employees rarely have any communication with high-level employees. Communication tends to be mostly downward, occasionally lateral. Messages are often directive, or a combination of directive and informative. Sending a message from the many at the bottom upward to one of the few at the top is difficult because there are many restrictions and inhibitions to unsolicited upward messages. When messages from below are solicited, there are constraints upon the content: Those at the top do not favorably receive messages that are contrary to what they want to hear.

In the United States, in which horizontalism has priority, approach to authority is direct. An individual who wants to get a message to the boss simply walks into his or her office and speaks to him or her face to face. Or rather, people in the United States have a fondness for this image of easy access by anyone; in fact, in large organizations hierarchy can be rigid and access to authority restricted. (In the late 1980s a movie maker documented his unsuccessful efforts to gain access to the president of General Motors in *Roger and Me*.) Small organizations lend themselves more easily to lateral power and communication structures. Nevertheless, the ideal continues to thrive, even in the White House, where in the 1990s President Clinton repeatedly encouraged ordinary people to speak to him and encouraged them to believe their messages were heard.

Presidents aside, people in the United States tend to operate on assumptions about equality that do not always hold in other cultures. For example, a consulting engineer from the United States on a hydroelectric dam joint-venture project in Brazil may assume equality with a Brazilian who is also a consulting engineer, and may further assume direct access to that person. But in fact, the Brazilian may think that the correct channel for official communication is from the consulting engineer to a superior—say the project manager—and then to the highest-level person from the United States partner of the joint-venture, who communicates with the highest-level Brazilian who will communicate down to a Brazilian project manager who will communicate to a Brazilian engineer. This tooth-pattern communication often seems ridiculous, time-consuming, and inefficient to U.S. businesspeople. But then they are not as concerned with hierarchy and status; they place a high cultural priority on direct access to authority.

CONCLUSION

This chapter and the one preceding it have given 24 questions to pose of cultures in order to gain an understanding of business priorities. Whether you know a lot or nothing about a culture, you can use these categories in order to discover the why: why they act that way or think that way or have that belief.

These categories of questions can help you come to terms with aspects of an unfamiliar culture in a way that will enable you to make good guesses about how people will behave in situations you have not foreseen. No list of do's and don'ts can do that for you. The five categories give you a framework for finding out in an ongoing process what things matter in business transactions and relationships with another culture.

Some dimensions cluster together, as we have pointed out; for example, cultures that prefer individual achievement and activity also often tend toward a direct approach to authority, a view that humans are at the center of events, a view that change is positive, and finally, that planning instead of luck determines success.

Cultures that are collectivist have long-lasting group memberships, tend to prefer form, are hierarchical, use mediated access to authority, tend to be less averse to uncertainty, may wish to keep things the way they are and avoid change, and often bend the rules to accommodate relationship needs.

To repeat what we said at the beginning of Chapter 3, learning about a culture is an ongoing experience. You may never feel you know a culture completely. In fact, after reading this chapter you may feel you have learned things about your own culture you didn't recognize before. However, the more cultures you understand, even with a little insight, the more you'll know your own. And now you have a five-pronged tool for learning about any culture.

SUMMARY

Chapter 4 first discussed the category of Self questions.

- *Is the basic unit of society the individual or the collective?* This is perhaps the most researched dimension of culture.
- *Is obligation a burden or a benefit?* Collectivist cultures tend to see it as a benefit to nurturing relationships.

- *Is age valued or is youth valued?* In hierarchical cultures, often age places people at the top of the ladder.
- *Are genders equal or unequal?* The answer to this question may involve finding out how roles and status are attributed to women; Islamic cultures discourage participation in business by women but nevertheless accord women high status as mothers.

This chapter then looked at the category of Social Organization.

- *Is group membership temporary or permanent?* An insight into this cultural dimension comes from attitudes toward family membership.
- *Is form important or distrusted?* Form, or protocol, tends to be highly valued in cultures that are hierarchical, where face can be lost by not conforming to etiquette, where harmony in the group is important, and where relationships matter. It is distrusted in cultures that associate emphasis on etiquette with phoniness and superficiality, and often where individual results matter.
- *Are personal activities private or public?* Employees in some cultures assume personal circumstances should be shared with everyone. These tend to be relationship-oriented collectivist cultures. In individualist cultures, an employee may wish to keep some personal facts private and not even tell the boss.
- *Is social organization horizontal or hierarchical?* The general pattern in society will also be reflected in companies. Where hierarchy characterizes the national or social culture, companies also will have a clearly defined corporate ladder. The levels are generally agreed upon by members of the collective. In horizontal cultures, people can move from their birth level up (or down) as their individual achievements warrant. Mobility depends on the accomplishments of individuals, although their families may partake of the new status.
- *Is approach to authority direct or mediated?* This is related to how hierarchical an organization is and how much weight an individual has. In collectivist and hierarchical cultures, business organizations tend to be hierarchical and authorities are remote, making one or more intermediaries necessary. In individualistic and horizontal cultures, organizations tend to be more horizontal with authorities more directly accessible.

You can ask these questions of a culture, assign the culture a place along the continuum represented by the question, and see how a culture's profile takes shape. Once you have plotted a culture somewhere on the dimension between the basic unit as self or as collective, for example, you can slide the marker of the culture one way or another based on new information you receive. Your placement of a culture along a dimension can shift with your growing knowledge.

NOTES

1. Yale Richmond, *From Da to Yes: Understanding the East Europeans,* (Yarmouth, ME: Intercultural Press, 1995), pp. 51–62.
2. Gary Katzenstein, *Funny Business: An Outsider's Year in Japan,* (New York: Prentice-Hall, 1989), pp. 74–75.
3. Linda Beamer, "Bridging Cultural Barriers," *China Business Review* 5–6 (1998), pp. 54–58.

4.   Katzenstein, *Funny Business.*

5.   Edward C. Stewart and Milton J. Bennett, *American Cultural Patterns: A Cross-Cultural Perspective,* rev. ed., (Yarmouth, ME: Intercultural Press, 1991), p. 96.

6.   Larry A. Samovar and Richard E. Porter, *Communication between Cultures,* (Belmont, CA: Wadsworth, 1991), p. 131.

7.   Dolores Cathcart and Robert Cathcart, "Japanese Social Experience and Concept of Groups," in *Intercultural Communication: A Reader,* 4th ed. Larry A. Samovar and Richard E. Porter, eds. (Belmont, CA: Wadsworth, 1985), p. 193.

8.   Geert Hofstede, *Cultures and Organizations: Software of the Mind,* (Berkshire, UK: McGraw-Hill, 1991), p. 94.

9.   Fei Xiaotong, *Shi Hui Diao Cha Zi Bai [Statement About Social Investigation]* unpublished trans. by David Tsow (Shanghai: Zhi Shi Chuban Shi, 1985), Chapter 4.

10. Yale Richmond, From *Nyet to Da: Understanding the Russians,* (Yarmouth, ME: Intercultural Press, 1992) p. 120.

11. Hiroki Kato, "From FOBs to SOBs: Japanese Vary Too," *Newsaction* (Northwestern University, IL) 36 (1988), p. 30.

12. Richard Mead, *Cross-Cultural Managment Communication,* (New York: John Wiley & Sons, 1990), p. 73.

Organizing Messages to other Cultures

When American Express writes to potential customers for its credit card in the United States, the letter begins with mention of milestones on the road to individual success. Results-oriented cultures value measurements of success like the carved stones on English highways that told travelers how far they were from London, the presumed goal of every journey. American Express tells letter readers that only those who have already achieved a certain "measure of financial success" merit their credit card, along with the benefits American Express offers. One of the benefits it offers, to those who have already proven by their results that they merit it, is no set spending limit. Another benefit is the ease of application: Just complete the short form and sign. People who are busy obtaining results want simple steps to getting the credit card. The letter uses a symbol, a centurion, that is recognized as a logo of American Express. His helmeted profile signals responsibility, fearlessness, and strength.

When American Express writes to potential customers in Mexico, however, the emphasis is on membership in the society of cardholders. Not everyone can appreciate its true worth, the letter says. Members are only those who can—and by implication the receiver of the letter is one of that select group. "Now you, like [equal to] those" can count on the incomparable services and benefits of the card. The reader is invited to take a few minutes to look at how the credit card can help in various

situations. The letter urges the reader to "ask anyone" about the wide acceptance of this card in fine establishments. The message is that anyone in the know recognizes the membership that this credit card confers. The letter goes on to say "you have seen" that cardholders don't need to worry at the moment of paying, when taking family or friends out, because there is no credit limit. (While it is true that many people in the United States "max out" their credit cards, embarrassment from not being able to pick up the tab for a family dinner is perhaps a less compelling selling point than in Mexican culture where the embarrassment is probably more acute. Television ads in the United States do make this point, however.) "Surely anyone knows . . . " that the medical and legal assistance you can obtain when traveling is worthwhile, says the letter. With a few phrases the letter sketches a host of knowing people who form an in-group of cardholders. A nonverbal symbol, the image of the card itself—badge of membership—appears but no rugged, individualistic centurion. The appeal is to Mexican collectivism.

Furthermore, although both are direct mail sales letters, the U.S. letter underlines specific phrases for emphasis to make the main points stand out. The Mexican letter is gracious in tone and has no underlined points or bullets to grab the reader's attention. Instead it guides the reader through various scenarios in which she or he will benefit from being a cardholder.[1]

This chapter examines the way culture impacts business correspondence and other documents. After a review of the communication process, the chapter looks at how communication is organized for routine, persuasive, unwelcome, and problem-solving messages. It then considers the force and role of words in various cultures, the channels of business messages, and finally cultural factors in writing style.

REVIEW OF THE COMMUNICATION MODEL

How does communication take place between organizations? We can discuss organizational communication with the same terminology and the same model we use for communication between individuals. As with communication between individuals from different cultures, when organizations from different cultures communicate, the potential for failed communication is multiplied.

The Tricky Issue of Meaning

Communication is usually modeled as a process. That is, although the model itself is a static, two-dimensional diagram on the page, in fact it represents constant movement. The basis for most communication models is that an **Idea** travels from **Sender** through **Channel** to **Receiver.** To these four basic components are added (a) the notions of *encoding and decoding* the idea into a message, in verbal and nonverbal vocabularies, (b) the idea of *noise* as interference with the transmission, and (c) *feedback* from the receiver to the sender. The process of communication thus has come to be thought of as circular and simultaneous.

Exhibit 5–1 shows the receiver as the sender, too. The process operates in double circles, each starting and returning to each communicator. Both parties are at once the sender and receiver. Both sender and receiver develop the meaning of the message, through the worldview each has. The worldview, of course, includes schemata of other cultures. Schemata are discussed in Chapter 1.

A few sentences ago, you read that an idea travels from sender to receiver. This isn't really the best way to think of communication, however. In fact,

> The idea itself does not really travel, only the code; the words, the patterns of sound or print. The meaning that a person attaches to the words received will come from his own mind. His interpretation is determined by his own frame of reference, his ideas, interests, past experiences, etc.— just as the meaning of the original message is fundamentally determined by the sender's mind, his frame of reference.[2]

The words on the page or the sounds as they travel in waves through air are what actually move. The meanings do not. They remain in the data bank, the worldview, of the sender and of the receiver. This describes communication between individuals, and the same holds for organizations. When the organization that receives a message has a similar frame of reference as the organization sending it, then they are both likely to assign similar meanings to the message. The more different the stored experiences, categories, attitudes, values, beliefs, and behaviors—and the more different the operating environment of

EXHIBIT 5–1 Process Model of Communication

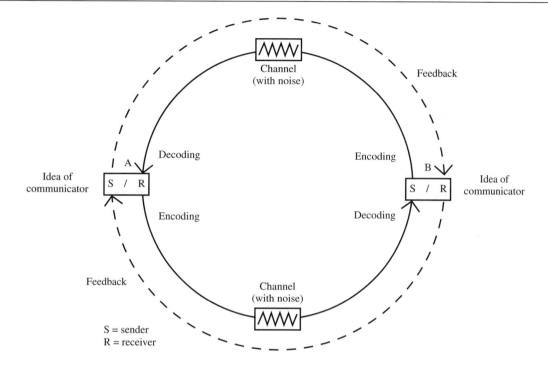

the minds—then the more likely it is the members of the organizations will assign differ-ent meanings. The message will not be understood. This is what happened to the company that sent a message in English that they would like an order filled "right away"; their Korean receiver anxiously responded, saying they would be happy to fill the order, but asking what *was* the "right way"?

The fact is, organizations and the people who issue messages on their behalf operate from a set of cultural priorities and meanings that cannot be assumed to exist in the receiv-ing organization. But at the same time, we *have* to assume some similarity in meanings or else we can't begin to do business. So, simply put, the intercultural business communica-tor has to be able to get the assumptions right, or as nearly right as possible. One way to improve your chances of understanding the meanings of the other organization is to use a matrix of intercultural dimensions.[3] That is what we have just seen in the five categories of questions to pose of cultures outlined in Chapters 3 and 4. When you understand where a culture's priorities lie along the dimensions of value, you can begin to make informed guesses about what messages mean.

This chapter looks at how intention and consciousness affect the way organizations structure and encode-decode messages, both as senders and receivers. It is a chapter about process, more than meaning. In other words, it considers the who, why, how, when, and where of intercultural business communication.

The Purpose and Factors of Communication

This book comes out of the premise that business functions require communication. That means business communicators send messages because they want to perform certain functions for the organization. A basic fact about business communication is that it has a purpose related to the organization's goals; it is *purposeful.* Senders of business messages have the following purposes:

- Instructing.
- Directing.
- Informing.
- Reporting.
- Eliciting information, opinions, authorization.
- Generating enthusiasm.
- Resolving conflicts.
- Analyzing situations and problems.
- Motivating.
- Negotiating.
- Selling.
- Reprimanding.
- Refusing.
- Evaluating.
- Persuading.
- Agreeing.
- Granting requests.
- Proposing.
- Transmitting other messages (documents).

These are largely task-oriented purposes. Purposes that contribute specifically to nurturing relationships are also important. They include

- Praising.
- Expressing concern or sympathy.
- Encouraging.
- Coaching and mentoring.
- Thanking.
- Rejoicing with the receiver.
- Warning about possible problems.
- Guiding around pitfalls.
- Apologizing.
- Expressing acceptance of apology.
- Reconciling.
- Expressing hope.
- Congratulating.

All business functions require communication. That's why organizations value communication skills highly. For example, in goals-oriented cultures, the function of planning and the function of implementing strategies for achieving goals are both important to organizations. People who do these jobs have to communicate about them, and they are valued when their communications are successful. Measuring progress toward goals is also important to these organizations. People who can communicate their cost estimating, monitoring, and justifying are valued. Those who communicate their identification of obstacles to the organization's goals and speedy methods for removing obstacles are valued. Finding ways to motivate workers to want to achieve the goals is important and managers who can motivate are valued. Timing of steps is important and of course money to pay for them is important; employees who communicate about scheduling and financing are valued. Selling the product or service to the largest or best market is important. Therefore, people who can promote and sell are valued by the organization. Since the organization needs to know when goals have been reached, people who can quantify terms (dollars earned, market share in percent, numbers of clients) are valued. Others who can evaluate employees' performances are valued.

Organizations value employees' knowledge and try to capture that knowledge for the benefit of others who serve the organization. The methods employees use for communicating what they have learned vary, but the goal is to have effective communication in place so what employees know about working in a specific position is not lost when they move from that position.

*Purposes are the **why** of business communication.* They exist in all business cultures, although goals vary. Agreement across cultures about **how** the purposes are accomplished is rare, however. ***How** involves the way messages are organized and encoded,* and that will be our subject for the rest of this chapter. But before we turn to it, we'll look briefly at the other process aspects of communication.

When organizations agree about the purpose(s) of a message, they are likely to assign similar meanings to it. When they agree about **who** is involved, they also lower the risk of an unintentional message—say, about status—interfering with the meaning. They can agree whether communication is one-way, as from a superior to a subordinate organization (perhaps a head office to a subsidiary in another country) or two-way, as between subsidiaries of similar status. This is related to the notion of access: If one organization makes its access open, so several levels can communicate with the other organization, then the other organization can agree to be open. Closed access means the messages have to go through one person or one job function.

***Who** within an organization is the appropriate person to receive or send a message?* Questions of status are tricky. In organizations that value hierarchy, the status of the communicator is important. But in organizations that are horizontal, the role (the job function) of a person may be more important than status (the job title).

As we saw in Chapter 4, definitions of **who** may come down to family relationships. You may be the son of the company CEO, and therefore able to speak for her, which will make your message different from someone who is a junior employee and not a family member. Similarly, you may want to know that the receiver of your message is the son of the CEO.

Organizations can also agree on the *channel of communication, or **where** it will take place.* Channel involves the issue of what should be put in writing, and what should be communicated orally. Will messages be communicated by fax? Telephone? E-mail? Face-to-face exchange? When communicators agree about the channel, they can avoid misunderstandings on that score. Such misunderstandings may seem trivial, but they can be significant. A more detailed discussion of channel appears at the end of this chapter.

Organizations are always running up against problems that could have been avoided had the channel been agreed upon. Americans are contract-makers, and usually don't think any agreement exists unless a contract has been written and signed. But in other parts of the world an oral statement is as good as a contract, if it is within the context of a relationship. A member of a United States organization can innocently say, "Oh, I'd really be interested in that new product," meaning (conditional tense) at some future time it sounds worth looking into more closely. But a member of an Asian culture, where relationships make contracts possible, may understand such a comment as, "I *will* be looking forward eagerly to receiving that product." If an oral channel, like the telephone, is used for making agreements by one communicator, and a written channel, like a contract, is used by the other, misunderstanding can result. Agreeing on the appropriate channel can save companies trouble.

When *to communicate* is more complex than simply keeping time zones in mind, although that can be complex enough in a worldwide organization. It also means choosing the right moment for a particular message. Can you raise a business issue during lunch? When riding in a host's car? During a casual moment? Or only in a formal environment? Often this is related to the question, "**Who** is communicating?" You may choose a formal moment to discuss sales figures with the executive vice president, but an informal moment with the manager of accounting.

The question of who goes first in negotiation is in part a **when** question. North Americans often assume that everybody wants to go first and get their position out on the table because frequently they do. Teams in Japan or China usually want to be last so they can hold back their own position until they've heard the other side.

When communication takes place involves the issues of time that we looked at in Chapter 3, such as being on time. And it involves the issue of a simultaneous versus sequential approach to tasks. If you are expecting exclusive attention from someone whose typical method of operating is to carry on several communication tasks at the same time, you may be disappointed. Someone who expects you to be carrying on simultaneous tasks may be uncomfortable with exclusive attention.

ORGANIZING ROUTINE MESSAGES

Direct Plan

Business communication books come mainly from Western cultures, particularly the United States. Accordingly, the authors tend to emphasize the things that are important to business communication in the United States.

For example, they urge writers to avoid ambiguity and get the message across clearly. *Clarity* and *conciseness*—choosing words with care for exact and precise meanings, and eliminating unnecessary words and phrases—are keys to successful business writing style in the United States. Clear and concise sentences are short and use a subject–verb–object pattern in preference to complex structures. Active-voice verbs signify doing and achieving; passive voice verbs are passive, so a culture that values doing and achieving prefers active voice. Concrete nouns have shape, weight, and mass. What's more, you can experience them, if only in imagination, with your senses. Abstract nouns are shapeless, weightless, and amorphous. You can't see or smell or touch them. They are very hard to measure. Achieving, goal-oriented, can-do cultures prefer concrete nouns. Such cultures often express abstract ideas in metaphors that are more concrete, such as the sports metaphors discussed in Chapter 2. "Success" is a less compelling term to results-oriented cultures than "hitting a homerun" or "scoring a goal."

Business communication books also often urge directness in delivering the message. Cultural priorities in the United States include sincerity and openness; going straight to the point displays both. Beating around the bush, on the other hand, suggests you have something to hide, in the dominant culture of the United States. This can be useful, when indeed the point of the message is one you'd rather conceal. But when the message involves a straightforward request or good news or information the receiver has been waiting for, indirectness seems unnecessarily complicated, even devious. Directness also shows consideration for the receiver of the message, since he or she is also busy doing and achieving, no doubt, and probably values time too much to waste it on unnecessary paragraphs or speech.

Business communication texts instruct writers to put the main message in the opening paragraph of correspondence, unless there is a particular reason not to do so. If you put the main message at the end of the document, the busy reader may never get to it. He or she may well have stopped reading by then. Direct-plan reports, written and oral, relay the conclusion and recommendations *first,* before the slower information about why the report is being made and what it covers.

After the main message comes the explanation. In correspondence, this may be one or more paragraphs. In reports and proposals, it includes several sections: purpose, scope, and methodology including persons, facts, analyses, and interpretation. The tendency among low-context cultures is to explain in a linear, often chronological, sequence. Background information can help make the main message clearer, but the direct plan stipulates that background information come *after* the main message (see Exhibit 5–2).

David Victor, in his book *International Business Communication,* calls the direct-plan approach "an example of culture-bound business communication."[4] That isn't to say it is useless; on the contrary, it is the very best way to organize routine business messages for most American, Canadian, Australian, British, and New Zealand readers. It is also probably the best organization for Northern European readers.

But it isn't necessarily the best way for members of other cultures, or the plan they would follow. To high-context culture communicators, a direct-plan message may seem rude and abrupt. The writer may be perceived as unfriendly or unwilling to be in a relationship with the reader, "just wanting to do business, not to get to know us."

Indirect Plan

The indirect plan does not put the main message in the first sentence. It has other priorities than the quick delivery of ideas, such as nurturing a relationship or developing some other context for the message. Japanese business messages often begin with a reference to the season: "Now it is autumn and the red leaves are covering the ground with color." In Muslim countries, the opening paragraph of business letters frequently invokes Allah's

---

EXHIBIT 5–2   Sample Letter #1

Here is a direct-plan letter from Taiwan, translated from Chinese.

Dear Members, and Dear Members' Wives,

The Social Service Committee and the Mountain-Climbing Committee decided on the 82nd year, 4th month and 25th day (Sunday) to organize the Social Service and Mountain-Climbing Activities.

(We) would like to announce the following:
1. Meeting time, 4th month 25th (Sunday) morning, 9 A.M. sharp.

2. Meeting place, the Inner Lake of the Big Lake Garden, the arch bridge.

(We) respectfully invite all members to bring their spouses to *join us actively to celebrate* [this phrase is in Classical Chinese] the event.

Secretary _____

82nd year of China Republic
4th month
1st day

The main message is given before the specific detail. Note the dating system which is specific to Taiwan.

blessing on the reader and the reader's family members—particularly when the business is family operated.

Indirectness is often accompanied by deliberate *ambiguity.* This can diffuse responsibility. Even in routine situations, such as a request for information, indirectness saves face in case the request is denied or ignored. Indirectness signals the writer's intention to take care over things, including care not to make the reader lose face. Ambiguity means that words are chosen for their ability to mean more than one thing, and patterns of words can have more than one interpretation. This has another function: It reveals the subtlety and sophistication of the writer. What is not said may be as important as, or more important than, what is said. Indirectness and ambiguity mean a writing style that favors circumlocution rather than straightforwardness. Sentences may seem to ramble because ideas are developed in relation to each other. Metaphors are preferred because they infer a context of concepts and principles. They suggest unfolding possibilities.

Indirectness may also mean *digression,* or what may be termed side-conversations and ramblings by results-oriented cultures. These added bits of circumstance and situational description help develop a context for business communication for members of relationship-oriented cultures. Edward C. Stewart writes,

> Particularly in some African communication styles, excursions into related subjects are normative, and listeners are expected to embellish the theme rather than to prod for the main point or the problem. In the words of one African student, "I know I have been understood when the other person makes statements that express the same idea as mine."[5]

Specific wording showing consideration for the reader often appears in indirect-plan letters. Expressions of courtesy can become quite elaborate. Even the standard French complimentary close, for example, for someone who is not a close associate contains far more elaborate courtesy than English letters:

> Veuillez agreer, Monsieur, l'expression de mes sentiments devouee [Would you please accept, Sir, the expression of my devoted feelings][6]

Developing a context for communicating information is very important to members of Asian cultures. This is based on the conviction that context is what gives meaning to information, and without the context, the information cannot be properly understood. In a study of Chinese-authored letters in the 19th century written to the Jardine-Matheson Company, a British-owned trading company in South China, indirectness correlates with the writer's desire to establish a context.[7] For instance, one writer named Kean Wo Cheong, inquiring about the status of a shipment of silk in 1874, begins: "It is now about six months, no information has been given us, for that two cases of Silk which was sent to Europe for sale through your Company on our behalf." Only after establishing this context in this sentence does the writer continue with his main message: "We beg that we may be informed the amount realized from the sale of the silk . . ." Establishing the context is perceived to be a way of ensuring the main message is not ambiguous, mysterious, and misunderstood. By contrast, a direct-plan request would simply begin, "Please inform us of the price obtained in the sale of our silk." It would then go on to give the details: the consignment made six months ago, the lack of information to date, and so forth. What remains unsaid in the indirectly organized message is the writer's concern that the ship carrying the silk has encountered some mishap and the silk has been lost at sea or been pirated away. Direct-plan users often are low-context communicators who may put such worries into words.

To communicators who are members of low-context cultures, indirect-plan conversation can seem tedious, slow, and unfocused. Indirect-plan business correspondence (see Exhibit 5–3) can suggest to a low-context reader that the writer is not able to come to terms with the communication task. The reader may question the writer's thinking ability as well as writing ability.

ORGANIZING PERSUASIVE MESSAGES AND ARGUMENTATION

Persuasion is accomplished through an indirect approach in low-context cultures, as can be seen in U.S. business communication textbooks. This is when beating around the bush is preferable to directness. You give the explanation first, and then work your way to the main message. The rationale for using this organization is that a reader will be persuaded by *reasons*. If you marshal your reasons together in a logical sequence and support them

---

EXHIBIT 5–3   Sample Letter #2

This is an example of an indirect plan. The letter is a request for information, with many of the characteristics of indirectness such as elaborate courtesy and detail. The writer has taken great care to follow communication principles important in his or her culture. The capitalization and punctuation are deliberate.

DATE: JANUARY 10, 1994

TO
OFFICE OF ADMISSION
CALIFORNIA STATE UNIVERSITY
5151 STATE UNIVERSITY DRIVE
LOS ANGELES
CALIFORNIA 90032
U.S.A.

SUBJECT: *APPLICATION FOR ADMISSION IN M.B.A.*

SIR,

WITH DUE RESPECT AND HUMBLE SUBMISSION, I WOULD LIKE TO INFORM THAT I'M A STUDENT OF DEPARTMENT OF MANAGEMENT IN DHAKA UNIVERSITY AND HAVE COMPLETED THE GRADUATION SUCCESSFULLY, AND NOW I'M STUDYING MASTERS OF COMMERCE (M.COM.) IN MANAGEMENT, THE MASTERS FINAL EXAMINATION WILL BE HELD THE LAST WEEK OF FEBRUARY, WITH GREAT ANTICIPATION, I WOULD LIKE TO GET ADMISSION IN YOUR FAMOUS AND WELL REPUTED INSTITUTION IN THE COURSE OF M.B.A. (MASTER OF BUSINESS ADMINISTRATION) FROM NEXT AVAILABLE SESSION, I ALSO INTEND TO INFORM YOU THAT I HAVEN'T TAKEN TOEFL AND GMAT YET. I HOPE TO APPEAR FOR TOEFL ON 14TH MAY '94 AND FOR GMAT ON 18TH JUNE '94 WITHOUT HAVING THE TOEFL AND GMAT SCORE, WILL YOU ISSUE THE I-20?

IN THIS REPECT, I HOPE YOU WILL EXTEND YOUR KIND CO-OPERATION AND FURNISH ME DETAILS AND MAKE ME EVER GRATEFUL TO YOU.

THANKING YOU.

YOURS FAITHFULLY,

_____

OF
DHAKA – 1100, BANGLADESH

with facts, you can persuade. This works in a culture where persuasive arguments are based on objective facts. But not all cultures give facts high priority, and persuasion may depend upon who the persuader is, rather than the reasons.

Argumentation and Logic

In low-context cultures, objective facts reside outside the communicator or the organization. They have an independent existence. Facts often can be quantified and measured. (Chapter 8 develops this notion in relation to the collection of information, its reliability, and its validity in different cultures.) Since emotion is slightly suspect, you are better off basing your argument on facts. After all, you can go to court—an ultimate kind of persuasion—based on facts. You can count on them.

Exhibit 5–4 is an example of a persuasive letter that argues by marshaling facts. The writer is unwilling to pay a parking fine incurred for not filling in the car registration form completely for a parking lot. The reader is an ombudsman (*Skasbeh*); her job is to hear complaints and attempt to give individuals with relatively little power some assistance in dealing with the organization.

The writer of this letter appears to present information objectively. He uses a numbered list and takes an objective position about the "facts": his car is new, it was raining, he followed the receptionist's instructions, and therefore he cannot be held responsible for the error and the fine. His argument is constructed like a syllogism: The facts lead to a conclusion that the writer puts in boldface type for emphasis.

This letter also uses sarcasm, something that may not always achieve the writer's objective and persuade the reader, even in a low-context culture. The writer says he cannot be held responsible for the *fact* that parking staff do not understand the question-mark symbol. Nor can he take blame because the parking staff fails to wonder why the word *number* is underlined on the form while at the same time the make of the car is entered on the form—showing he knows the make but not the number. This kind of sarcasm is very common in Norwegian communication and is a customary way for someone to proceed in a complaint. Another sarcastic dig comes from the use of the informal "you" singular pronoun rather than the formal "you" in point number 4.

In high-context cultures, facts are not so objective or impersonal. Words and arguments are not separate from the writer or speaker who expresses them. Facts come with a person wrapped around them. If you argue against those facts, you are arguing against the person who uttered them. In cultures that do not put a high priority on litigation, you can't count on facts to help you achieve your goals in court; you have to count on people. Relationships are how things get done.

Since status is usually important in high-context cultures, the person is always a key factor in how a message is understood. Words cannot be distinguished from their source, and influential people can influence and persuade by virtue of their status. Furthermore, in high-context cultures the web or context of relationships and obligations is ever present. A tug on one side of the web sends vibrations throughout the web. How can a receiver refuse to be persuaded, when the entire network—other people—know about the attempt at persuasion?

EXHIBIT 5–4   Sample Letter #3

This letter argues by carefully organizing facts into logical sequence. The writer dates the letter by putting the day first, then the month, then the year (March 7, 1997). The writer puts key items in boldface type: the addressee (inside address) and the "therefore" conclusion of his argument at the end of the letter.

7.3.1997

Saksbeh. Mona glosli
AutoPark A.S.
Postboks 30 Stovner
0913 Oslo

Vedr.:   Klage på kontrollavgift 0011031

Deres ref: 0011031

Jeg takker for brev datert 6.mars 1997, og ønsker å opplyse om følgende:

1. Jeg har en nesten ny bil og husket derfor ikke skilt nummeret.
2. Det regnet ganske kraftig og det var defor ikke spesielt hyggelig å løpe ut for å sjekke om nummeret på bilen var riktig.
3. Resepsjonsdamene sa at det ikke var nødvendig å skrive hele bil nummer ned, hvis jeg skrev hvilken biltype jeg hadde. De sa videre at jeg bare kunne understreke numrene og sette enn "?" tegn ved siden av. Jeg fulgte deres råd og gjorde som jeg ble bedt om.
4. At dine parkeringsfolk ikke forstår at ett "?" tegn betyr at vedkommende ikke var sikker på nummeret, kan ikke jeg belastes for. Heller ikke at dine parkeringsfolk ikke skjønner hvorfor en understreker nummerene samtidig som en skriver ned hvilken bilmerke det er, kan jeg heller ikke belastes for.
5. **Jeg kan ikke akseptere at jeg skal betale for denne boten etter at jeg fikk godkjennesle i resepsjonen for hva jeg gjorde. Denne må være en sak mellom dere og resepsjonen I Nixdorf.**

Med vennlig hilsen,

B. A. Smith
Church Road 100
361 Oslo

(continued)

Persuasion Tactics

People and organizations in relationships play certain roles. For example, business organizations in India may play the *role of the Morally Superior* in negotiations with the United States and Japan.[8] They are an old and venerable culture, with well-established regulations for

7.3.1997

Saksbeh. Mona glosli
AutoPark A.S.
Postboks 30 Stovner
0913 Oslo

Re: Complaint on Registration Fee 0011031

Your reference: 0011031

I thank you for the letter dated March 6, 1997 and wish to inform you of the following:
1. I have an almost new car, and therefore do not remember the license plate number.
2. It rained quite heavily and it was therefore not particularly comfortable to run out to check whether the number was correct.
3. The receptionist said that it was not necessary to write down the whole vehicle number, if I wrote which type of car I had. She further said that I could just underline and put a question mark "?" sign on the page.
   I followed her advice and did what I was asked.
4. [The fact] that your [informal pronoun] parking staff does not understand that the question-mark sign means that the individual was not sure about the number, cannot be blamed on me. Furthermore, the fact that the parking staff does not wonder why one underlines "number" while simultaneously writing down the make of car, I cannot be held responsible for.
5. **I cannot accept that I should be required to pay this fine after I got approval in the reception area for what I did. This must be a matter between you and the reception function.**

With friendly regards, [formal closing]

B. A. Smith
Church Road 100
361 Oslo

social behavior and deep-rooted expectations for business behavior. They have not been responsible for atrocities or immoral behavior, in their own view. They cast both the United States and Japan in the role of Morally Inferior. This means they persuade with great moral authority, not on the basis of facts but on the basis of what is morally right. This gives them higher status than their Japanese or U.S. counterparts, and status has priority in India. In 1984 a pesticide manufacturing company in the city of Bhopal, India, experienced a disastrous leak of toxic gas. Thousands died and thousands more suffered terrible injuries. The episode was viewed as morally wrong by the Indians who felt the company had failed to behave responsibly. The company was a joint venture, 50.9 percent owned by Union Carbide, a U.S. chemical company, and 49.1 percent owned by Indian investors and the government. Some Indians called for the extradition of the American president of Union Carbide at the time. The morally outraged victims who survived continue to charge the company with not releasing information about the gas and about possible treatment. (You can read the arguments by Indians at *<http://www.ucaqld.com.au/community/bhopal>*.)

The United States, which assigns a high priority to equality, may not be persuaded by India's moral posture. Union Carbide, in the case mentioned above, awarded $470 million dollars in settlement, although it claimed (1) no Americans were present in India at the plant when the disaster occurred, (2) the plant was Indian built and operated, and (3) an investigation showed the reason for the gas leakage: deliberate sabotage by a disgruntled Indian employee. According to the facts collected by Union Carbide, it was not at fault. Americans also value sincerity and right behavior, and likely resent being cast in the role of morally wrong. Resentment makes it hard to be persuaded.

Japan, like India, values status. Moral high ground is not what the Japanese express with status, however; the Japanese go for protocol and etiquette as a result of status. They are deeply angered at being labeled "sinner," a charge that has been made in view of some World War II atrocities committed by the Japanese, for instance. They are not persuaded by this tactic.

Another tactic for persuasion may come from organizations in cultures that feel they have been *the wronged party in international relations.* They may also adopt a dependent posture with a country like the United States and the corporations that represent American values. Mexican organizations, for example, may suggest they are owed favorable treatment—and make persuasive requests based upon this notion—because the United States organization is bigger, has more capital, or is gaining a great concession with access to Mexican markets. (They are likely to reject any notion of inequality, however.)

Persuasion also comes from emotions, which are not separable from people either. Facts alone seem cold and impersonal, and therefore unpersuasive, to people from cultures that value emotional involvement. So the very characteristic that is suspect in low-context cultures, emotion, is what moves the receiver in other cultures. Leaving out the emotion will have the opposite effect to what is intended. One emotion that can motivate in Asian cultures is pity. A Japanese tactic is to describe the persuader's pain and misfortune. For instance, a small supplier may run into problems with delivery schedules and wish to persuade the customer to accept delayed delivery. The argument may run: "We are so small a company, we have little power to force our agents to deliver promptly. Please consider how small we are." The company being persuaded is supposed to respond with pity. In a U.S. context, such persuasion tactics may seem pathetic.

Persuasion is important because, in a sense, ***every communication task a manager performs involves persuasion***. Even when the manager communicates information, the purpose is usually partly persuasion: "giving away purposeless information is a symptom of irrational behavior."[9] You could argue that even small talk has a persuasive undercurrent: Trust me, I'm on your side, be my supporter. Making an oral presentation also has a persuasive element: "Believe me to be a credible speaker, take seriously my message, trust me." Persuasion in intercultural business negotiation is discussed in Chapter 9.

Persuasion begins with establishing the credibility of the party doing the persuading. As we have seen, this can be accomplished in different ways: using facts, taking the moral high road, needing special consideration. The next step is for the party doing the persuading to *establish common ground,* so the party being persuaded feels there is something to be gained for them also. Successful business persuasion usually involves *the revelation of some benefit for the party being persuaded.* How much the benefit is valued is, of course, dependent on the culture. Subsequently, *the persuading side must make its case* and engage the appropriate emotions of the other side.

ORGANIZING UNWELCOME MESSAGES

Communicating about Problems

When visiting management professor Ron Kelly, from St. Lawrence College, experienced conflict with his Chinese hosts in Sichuan about the number of courses they wanted him to teach, or number of students per class, he would arrange to meet with them. He would begin with expressions of gratitude for their assistance in making his experience of teaching in China so rich. He would praise their work, their students, and their institute. He would mention the comfortable accommodations and good food and the excellent sights within an easy bicycle ride of the institute. Near the end of their meeting he would mention "just one little thing" that was a cloud on his horizon, and he would express confidence they would be able to help him sort it out, for the sake of the good relationship they all enjoyed. Rather than press for immediate action, Ron would indicate he'd ask again in a few days. He would usually "forget" a package of cigarettes, or leave behind a bottle of spirits, and depart with warm smiles all around. He had few lasting difficulties in China.

Talking about what's wrong is not easy for people in any culture, but people in high-context cultures like China put high priority on keeping harmony, preventing anyone from losing face, and nurturing the relationship. That is why letters and meetings often include references to past solidarity. Historical references to episodes between organizations and nations may be frequent.

In low-context cultures where information typically is encoded in explicit wording, the tendency is just to "spit it out," get it into words and worry about the result later. Senders of unwelcome messages use objective facts, assuming, as with persuasion, that facts are neutral, instrumental, and impersonal. You can say "the order arrived with 30 percent of the contents damaged" and not point fingers of blame, in low-context cultures. Business communication textbooks suggest a direct plan for talking about a problem that is the other party's responsibility: "Your overdue balance is still outstanding."

Ron Kelly had to learn a different organization of the message when he was in China. At home in Canada he would have been polite, professional, and have gone directly to the point. But in China, as in other high-context cultures, going directly to the problem carries a piggy-back message that is even stronger: You have failed to live up to your responsibility; the honor of your organization is in question; the very relationship between us is in doubt. In high-context cultures, such a message is serious and damaging. Occasions do arise when the direct message is appropriate in high-context cultures, but they are not always the situations a member of a low-context culture would identify for directness. For example, a manager might issue a command to a subordinate with a directness that could seem harsh: "Fill the following orders and ship them before noon."

Indirectness is the way members of high-context cultures communicate about a problem (also see Chapter 8). Stewart reports that according to Japanese informers, a husband would suspect his wife was upset if "a flower was askew in the entryway arrangement, but he would be sure of it if his teacup were only partially filled with lukewarm tea."[10] The Japanese Stewart consulted said they would take special pains to be attentive in such circumstances, but would avoid bringing up actual incidents. Asking, "What's wrong?" would cause unnecessary disruption of harmony and potentially loss of face. In Holland, a husband might suspect his wife was upset if she clattered the knives and forks unnecessarily loudly when setting the table, or banged down the plates with more force than necessary. Signals vary and so does the response to them.

Two Swedish delegates to an organization in China had an experience in which the bad news simply was never communicated at all. The bad news was that the boiler for the residence they lived in would be out of service for at least two weeks. That meant no hot water and no heat, during November when the weather is cold. They only found out the bad news indirectly, from someone unconnected to the Outside Affairs office that was designated to communicate with them. Once they heard about the boiler, they went to see a person from the Outside Affairs offices and began a conversation about an invitation they had received to go to another organization for a visit of about two weeks. The visit was discussed, and dates were proposed for the visit (which not surprisingly happened to coincide with the dates of the boiler repair). The host officer agreed; the Swedes agreed; everyone was happy. Nobody ever mentioned the boiler until after the visit had taken place. By then the delegates were back and the hot water was on.

Although the bad news in this situation was not communicated at all, not even at the end of a message, it was communicated *about* indirectly in the discussion of the visit to the other organization for the very two weeks their boiler would not be operating. The boiler was an unspoken item; the context for that item was the conversation about the visit elsewhere.

When an unwelcome message has to be delivered in a high-context culture, and context alone cannot deliver it, the message will probably be indirectly organized in circumlocutory words. Where someone from a low-context culture would probably begin correspondence about an order that arrived too late to be used with a request for a refund, someone from a high-context culture might give an entire history of the business dealings between the organizations and of the order in question before asking for a refund.

Saying No

Saying no is also done with delay and indirectness in low-context cultures, and the U.S. business communication textbooks agree. They advise writers to "say no slowly." The rationale is to explain *why* first, and since facts persuade readers, by the time the reader gets to the no, he or she is persuaded to accept it. Not all businesses in the United States have caught on to this practice, however, which argues that it isn't a priority everywhere in the culture.

Asian cultures are renowned for saying yes. In fact, in Japan, Westerners have heard yes and gone home happily when the Japanese knew they really meant no. It is much easier for Japanese and other high-context cultures to say yes. Cohen calls it the "social affirmative."[11] It is "yes, I'm listening," or "yes, you have a good point," or "yes, I see (but don't agree)." Often it has the function of the American "uh-huh" to encourage someone to keep talking (this unworded communication refers to the meaningless sounds that indicate social involvement with the speaker's act of speaking, like "mm-hmm"). Sometimes, of course, "yes" means "I agree; I will carry out your request." The problem for low-context communicators is they can't always tell which meaning is meant. When people from a high-context culture receive a yes response, they often seek to verify it, so they can tell which meaning to give it. A Korean manager in a U.S. firm was given the opportunity for a new and more prestigious job. He responded, "I will be willing to do it, if nobody else will." He was saying, "Yes! I accept!"

Saying no is more difficult for high-context cultures. As when they communicate about problems, they would rather not actually have to put a refusal into words. In Chinese, a no may reside in the words: "That may be difficult." The Japanese equivalent to that would be a drawn-out hissing breath, and drawn out words: "Sssaaaah...muzukashii naaaaaaa." (Also see Chapter 4.)

In cultures that put a high priority on face, a refusal is a potential loss of face for both the refusal-makers and those being refused. The refusal-makers lose face because they have failed to perform according to the expectations of the party they have a relationship with—a web of obligations and favors. They are shamed. The refused lose face because they have been turned down by the very party with whom they have a relationship, and they go away empty-handed. They are shamed. The balance of obligations is askew. The relationship itself is momentarily at stake.

No in high-context cultures is frequently couched in an expression that turns the situation around. For example, a person who has to refuse an invitation to dine out with a business associate may say, by way of refusal, "You must be very tired and want to have a quiet evening." This way the refused person does not lose face, although the refusal is clearly understood in a high-context culture.

ORGANIZING PROBLEM-SOLVING MESSAGES

Storytelling

One way to communicate about a solution to a problem is through narrative. An ethnographic study in the 1980s involved the problem-solving communication of photocopy machine repairmen in the United States.[12] The repairmen would be sent out on jobs, where customers would greet them with relief and high expectations. They would start to take the machines apart and try to identify the problems. If the problems persisted, they often would attract other men who would stand around and offer suggestions. Then, according to the study, if the problems still were not solved, the men would start telling Vietnam War stories. Many repairmen had been mechanics in the army, and they had had experiences trying to fix equipment with little more than their ingenuity. Pretty soon, after a number of stories, the solution would be found and the equipment would be fixed. The stories offered guidelines when there wasn't enough data in the manuals. Stories are a way for results-oriented cultures that like to rely on facts to discuss situations in which facts are available only from anecdote and personal experience.

Stories also reinforce common values, so they can be used to talk about solutions to management problems as well. When management wants to introduce change, for example, a story can help employees understand and accept the change. A Ford Motor Company senior executive told a story to 300 managers in Detroit about Willie B, a silverback gorilla, who after 27 years in a small bunker was moved to a new, spacious habitat designed specifically for him. Even though the change was a positive one for Willie B., he spent the first few days taking cautious little steps to get to know his new home. A photograph that hangs on the wall of the executive's office shows Willie B. testing the grass with his toe. The executive's point to the managers was: Remember that change takes time and courage, even when it is for the better.[13]

A general manager at the U.S. department store chain Nordstrom's uses this story: Every morning when the gazelle wakes up in the African plain, she starts running, because she knows if she doesn't outrun the fastest lion she won't see another day. Every morning the lion wakes up and starts running, because she knows if she doesn't run faster than the slowest gazelle she won't eat. So whether you are a gazelle or a lion, you had better start the day running. The story is useful in communicating to staff the importance of staying on their toes, and the manager uses it to address the problem of complacency.[14]

Problems exist in the town of Guryev, on the Ural River in Kazakhstan. This town is perhaps the world's best source of caviar from the beluga sturgeon. In 1991 Kazakhstan achieved independent status as a state, with a government in the capital of Alma Ata instead of Moscow, and the right to sell openly to the West. But unfortunately, the sturgeon are in dwindling supply. A major reason is that they are being appropriated by the officials in the new government—who were the communist party officials in the old government—before they can reach the factories. In autumn there is a "mad beluga season" when the black market does a roaring business. Communication about the problem in this high-context culture is diffused through narrative. Kazakhis do not point fingers at specifically named people. Instead, they tell humorous stories and use proverbs—methods of indirectness typical of high-context cultures—to illustrate the "crazy history" of caviar in Guryev. Here is one example.

The ghosts of Stalin, Khrushchev, and Brezhnev pay a visit to Yeltsin, who naturally has to offer his guests some food and drink. He pours out four glasses of vodka, and then hands round a meager plate of caviar sandwiches.

Brezhnev says . . . "Mr. Yeltsin, When I was in charge, I would put a whole kilo of caviar on the table." Krushchev says . . . "When I was in charge, I gave my friends caviar by the ton."

Finally, Stalin says . . . "When I was in power I had so much caviar that my people went abroad and force-fed foreigners with it."[15]

Russians have a proverb: "Don't count your caviar until you've caught your sturgeon."

Analogy is another way of talking about solutions to problems. Sometimes the analogy is in a narrative, but not necessarily. Military language offers rich material for analogies in corporate problem solving in the United States: operation, briefing, debriefing, offensive, attack, troops, maneuver, ammunition. This language also reflects the action orientation of the business culture in the United States.

Syllogistic and Inductive Reasoning

Narrative and analogy are examples of nonsyllogistic reasoning. But for low-context cultures, reasoning means deductive syllogisms and inductive logic. Induction works from examples to a generalization. Syllogistic thinking is deductive, moving from a generalization to a specific instance. Inductive logic

> reflects Western intellectual traditions of precise, scientific detachment, and appeals to an abstract sense of reason existing outside the relationship between speaker and hearer. Thus it has the effect of establishing the distance between them.[16]

The problem and the reasoning both exist apart from the speaker and hearer, which creates a sense of objectivity about the problem-solving discourse. Individuals' feelings appear not to be involved. In low-context cultures, problem-solving finds expression most often in *reasons why,* leading to *therefore.*

Deductive reasoning is used by French, Spanish, and Italian communicators who prefer to argue from abstract concepts and principles. They tend to dislike an approach like that taken in the United States, finding it too pragmatic and too quick to rush to application before the theoretical framework is in place.

High-context cultures do not see reasons as outside and apart from the relationship between communicating parties. Any problem-solving discourse has to take the relationship into consideration. If a solution ignores or jeopardizes the relationship, it cannot be a good solution. Reasons by themselves are not persuasive; it is the context of the relationship that gives significance to reasons. So, for example, inductive organization may be used in talking about a problem out of deference to the relationship, because it moves from specifics to a generalization. That may be less likely to cause loss of face or wound someone, whereas an accusation could do both.

Bargaining Discourse

Problem-solving discourse in an Arabic-speaking culture may follow the model of the Arab *suq* or market. This discourse is a kind of bargaining that begins with an opening bid from each side, which is far beyond what each expects to settle for. After haggling the two sides finally arrive at a point of convergence in their bids. Although it resembles negotiating a compromise, this bargaining discourse is not confined to purchase situations; the marketplace is an analogy. Problem solving can occur when each side presents a position, then bargains to modify it in response to the other side's position, until a solution to the problem is reached. This is communication exchange that involves two or more parties. It cannot be carried out by only one party, unlike narrative or analogy or syllogistic reasoning, which can be from one to one or from one to many. But bargaining takes at least two. It is a problem-solving approach favored by collectivist cultures, where the process of reaching a solution is a collective one, rather than a task for one individual.

THE ROLE AND FORCE OF WORDS

The Relative Importance of Encoding Messages in Words

Words are inventive tools for communication and the enjoyment of using this toolbox of symbols varies from culture to culture. In low-context cultures, the role of words is informational; in these cultures, "Subtlety and allusiveness in speech, if grasped at all, serve little purpose."[17]

Meaning is encoded explicitly in low-context cultures. The purpose of most communication is to transmit meaning using words. Communication can also be achieved without words, of course, but actions *instead of* words are employed fairly frequently in high-context cultures.

In a training session to orient mainland Chinese to North American work practices, one of the authors delivered a half-day session about "putting messages into words." The theme was that in North American business environments, if you have a problem, you should articulate it to someone rather than struggle along trying to cope in silence.

At mid-day the trainer and trainees sat together around their conference table to eat lunches they had brought. The room had a kettle along with a box of Chinese tea so the trainees could enjoy a cup of tea with their lunch and throughout the day. The trainees were not accustomed to having trainers eat lunch with them, but nevertheless they graciously asked her if she would like some tea. She said yes, thank you very much, she would like tea.

A few minutes later, she was politely presented with a cup of boiled water. Where was the tea? she asked. All gone, she was told. When? A few days ago. Why, she asked, didn't anyone say anything sooner?

After some exploratory discussion, several reasons emerged. One trainee volunteered that they weren't sure the trainer, a teacher who automatically had high status in their eyes, was the right person to ask about something like tea. They didn't want to insult her. Another trainee said they didn't want to mention the exhausted tea supply to the trainer in case that made her feel obliged to buy tea, paying out of her own pocket. They weren't certain the program had funds for additional tea for her to be reimbursed if she did buy them tea. They also felt perhaps they should have replaced the tea themselves, but hadn't worked out an equitable mechanism yet for doing so. In any case that meant the risk of an expenditure that might turn out to be unnecessary.

No doubt the unannounced presence of a trainer at their lunch table raised another uneasy question in their minds: Were they supposed to have reserved some tea in case a trainer decided to have some? Finally, a young man daringly offered the opinion that in China the person who identified a problem was then identified *with* the problem and in his words, "became the problem." It was better not to draw attention to a problem, he said, and the others agreed that this could be true.

This episode says a number of things about expectations by the trainer and different expectations by the trainees about communication. The Chinese were conscious of the social impact of their words, and therefore chose to communicate in actions rather than risk a consequence that was difficult for them to calculate accurately. The act of offering a cup of boiled water in a context where tea was expected was as eloquent as any specifically worded message.

In the Chinese trainees' tea episode the communication had at least three levels: the deliberate act (serving boiled water) that followed the invitation to drink tea, the worded messages that contained consideration for the teacher's situation, and the unworded message about unclear understanding of possible obligation on the trainees' part. Multilevel communication is characteristic of Chinese and other Asian cultures, among many, as was discussed in Chapter 1. It is another result of the importance of harmonious relationships among group members, and the desire not to have any one member feel put down or ostracized or shamed.

Not to encode messages explicitly is to risk being misunderstood in North America. The self-deprecation that is appropriate in Chinese culture, where boasting or putting oneself forward disturbs social harmony, is inappropriate in the United States or Canada where people are often taken at their word about their worth—say, in a job interview. From early childhood, quickness in verbalizing perceptions about the world is rewarded in the culture of the United States.

In high-context cultures the purpose of communication is often socially lubricative. That is, communication between organizations and their representatives first has a role in sustaining relationships, and second only within the context of a relationship of transmitting information.

In general, people from Latin cultures enjoy talk as one of the great pleasures of life. Mexicans love to spend time talking with friends. Italians claim talk with friends is a sign of a good life. Not all that is verbalized is taken literally, but enjoyment comes from the act of verbal—and nonverbal—connection with others. Lots of noise characterizes conversation, and often two or more people will talk at one time. Mediterranean and Hispanic cultures are relatively high-context, and that means relationships and connections between people are important.

The Role of Words in Arabic Cultures

Arabic-speaking cultures also enjoy verbalization. Arabic is an old and venerable language. As the language of the Koran, it has the status of the divine. Muslims believe it is precise and unchanging in meaning, and that a critical response to the language is inappropriate. "The reader is not trained to interact with the text as in [English-speaking] cultures, mentally editing and disputing points. He or she does not easily distinguish more or less significant points."[18] The structure of Arabic lends itself to combinations of ideas, strung together. In English this would be something like compound phrases joined by *and*. This can make Arabic writing or speech seem unfocused when translated into a language that encodes separate ideas efficiently. Arabic is superb for elaborations, however, and Arabic speakers value the ability to embellish utterances.

There is wide latitude to express a love of hyperbole and exaggeration in Arabic. For example, Iraq's leader Saddam Hussein in 1989 called for "the Mother of all battles." and promised the desert would run red with blood. Exaggeration, figures of speech, and repetition are some of the ways Arabic lends itself to the exuberant use of words. Arabic-speaking cultures generally exult in the artistry of accomplished writers and speakers. In fact, the language itself has a power over listeners or readers; the words can have more impact and more reality than what they describe. So words can be used for their own sake, not for the meaning they convey.

It isn't surprising that self-congratulation and self-praise are part of the exaggeration of Arabic speakers. Describing one's own accomplishments, the high status of one's friends, or the superiority of one's abilities in exaggerated terms is usual. It shows one's place in the hierarchy through one's connections. All this inflation of language means that Arabic statements may run to a hundred words when English would use 10.[19] Arabic cultures are relatively high-context cultures; members share experiences and memories of famous users of language. When speakers are communicating informally, one may speak before another has finished, and it isn't unusual for speakers to interrupt and overlap each other's speech.

Writers of business documents use many of the flourishes and embellishments of speech. Letters are frequently framed with invocations of Allah's blessings upon the reader and the reader's family.

The Role of Words in Japanese Culture

Perhaps at the other end of the spectrum is Japanese culture. In Japan, words are not trusted. Many Japanese proverbs emphasize this point:

- Those who know do not speak; those who speak do not know.
- To say nothing is a flower.
- With your mouth you can build Osaka castle.
- Sounds like paradise; looks like hell.[20]

Putting thoughts into words has a low value in Japan, where harmony and contemplation are highly valued and members of the culture learn "to hear one and understand ten," as they listen to what has not been said. There seems little need for speaking, and when someone does speak the preference is for understatement. To boast about one's own powers or achievements is very bad taste. It is putting oneself above others, which is shameful in Japanese culture. This use of language is very different from Arabic-speakers' use of language, even though Japanese culture is very high-context.

The Japanese also value indirect expression. Bluntness is regarded as unsophisticated or even rude. To challenge directly what someone has said is also extremely rude. Since people are not separable from their words, an attack on what someone has said is an attack on the person.

Listeners wait until a speaker is finished before speaking themselves. A moment of silence after someone speaks is respectful; it suggests thoughtful contemplation of what has been said. Conversely, interrupting someone is rude. Japanese listeners pay as much attention to what is *not* said as to what is said. They are "listening" to the unspoken context of the worded message.

The Japanese way of encoding messages sparely but understanding messages on many levels is *enryo-sasshi* communication. Messages are sent through a small exit (*enryo*) and received through a wide entrance (*sasshi*). To accomplish this, Japanese communicators use a number of speech patterns such as hesitancy, unfinished sentences, and incomplete expressions of thought.[21]

Japanese thought patterns are clusters or webs; language patterns also move from one idea or cluster to another and another, but the idea clusters may not have an obvious relationship. They are related more by association than by cause and effect, like stepping-stones that lead to a destination but are spaced out from each other and not in a straight line.[22]

The Role of Words in English-Speaking Cultures

English speakers, in contrast, tend to use language in a bridge pattern, which goes more or less in a straight line from the first idea to the next and so on to the conclusion. Unlike Japanese culture, the United States values verbalization highly and seems to have a great need for using language. Above all, using the *right* word, the *best* word to communicate meaning is especially admired. Consider these English proverbs:

- A word fitly spoken is like apples of gold in pictures of silver.
- There is as much difference between the right word and the nearly right word as there is between lightning and a lightning bug.
- A man is as good as his word.

The general preference in the United States is for exaggeration and overstatement, although not to the degree of Arabic-speaking cultures. In the United States it shows confidence in one's own powers, a can-do mentality. Words like *terrific, great, catastrophe,* and *tragedy* occur in ordinary speech and refer to things that are not so tremendous after all. British speakers of English use extreme language far less often, although recently the adjective *brilliant* has come into wide use to mean "very good." British speakers of English find speakers in the United States tend to overstatement.

In English-speaking cultures generally, something exists when it is put into words; if it is not spoken or written, it isn't possible to *listen* to it, the way Japanese communicators do. Words are taken literally, at their face value, in most situations. Bluntness is admired in many situations; showing your best side in a job interview, for example, means saying what your accomplishments and abilities are. In meetings, being able to express your opinion clearly and perhaps persuasively when others disagree often results in praise or reward. Speakers often interrupt each other, especially in informal situations, or begin speaking before another person has completely finished, in a rush to get the thoughts into words and thus into the attention of the others.

The Effect of Language's Structure

In the 1950s, scholars began to explore the relationship between language structure and thinking. Benjamin Whorf wrote:

> We dissect nature along lines laid down by our native languages. The categories and types that we isolate from the world of phenomena we do not find there because they stare every observer in the face; on the contrary, the world is presented in a kaleidoscopic flux of impressions which has to be organized by our minds—and this means largely by the linguistic systems in our minds.[23]

Now 50 years later, Whorf's hypothesis that language organizes reality is largely discredited. Perception is viewed as a habit that can be learned and changed, not something programmed. Perception constructs reality, but the extent to which language limits perception is not clear. We understand our world by categorizing it, and the categories are influenced by our language.

We can see differences in thinking, in a simplified illustration, by comparing an English and a Chinese sentence. In English: "The interpreter, who arrived yesterday, has already visited the factory." The subject is "interpreter," and the verb is "has visited" in this simple sentence. The nonrestrictive clause "who arrived yesterday" merely tells something specific about the "interpreter." We could leave it out and the sentence would still communicate correctly and meaningfully. The destination is in the last words, "the factory." The adverb "already" places the visit in time. The entire sentence moves in linear sequence from subject through the action of the verb to the object. It unravels syntactically the same way it happens in time: First the interpreter arrives, then he visits—the factory. As he himself moves in time, so does the sentence reveal its meaning. The structure of English cause-and-effect sentences is sequential and linear.[24]

The same sentence in Chinese would be structured differently, as a series of frames or levels. It begins with the word and concept that establish the largest possible context in this sentence: "yesterday." This frames the sentence. The next largest context identifies the interpreter as an *arriving* interpreter, as compared with any other kind of interpreter. The next more-specific frame identifies the interpreter, as opposed to anybody else who arrived yesterday. Next, the event is placed in a time-frame by the word "already," which signals a completed action. The next frame is the specific place where the action occurred, "to the factory." Finally, the most specific information of all is reached: The main message, as in English, is the activity that occurred, "visited." A literal translation of the sentence would be, "Yesterday-arriving('s) interpreter already to the factory visit (completed)." (*Zuotian daozherde fanyiyuan yijing dao gongchan jangwen quguole.*) The organization of this sentence is not based on a sequential relationship, but on the spatial relationship of syntactic items to each other. The sentence is a sequence of ever-more-specific levels, like concentric circles, until the heart is reached. Exhibit 5–5 illustrates the concentric circles.

The result of this cultural preference for different ways of structuring thinking is that when Chinese speakers approach communication tasks that require more than routine attention, they tend to follow a general-to-specific sequence. The indirectness typical of Chinese discourse is understandable and even predictable in view of the logic of the sentence structure.

Similarly, English-speaking cultures' preference for linear directness and logic that reveals cause-and-effect relationships (usually inductive, arguing from reasons to *therefore,* conclusions) can be predicted from the way language is structured. Communication itself is often perceived as a stream or continuous flow of coded elements. "Bits" and "bites" of information are sent "like so many billiard balls—from a sender to a receiver."[25]

Here's another example of how language patterns affect business communication. In a culture that has a rich oral tradition, but not a long history of writing business documents, the written discourse will have characteristics of oral communication. Repetition, rhyme, alliteration, imagery, and hyperbole are important in oral communication to help the listener remember. Chronological sequence is easier to remember than another sequence; chronological sequence is what storytellers use.

These preferences and others not discussed here are deeply rooted in the mind and have a strong relationship with cognition—thinking, knowing, understanding. When we are confronted with new experiences and new languages, we tend to structure them according to our perceptions and previous experiences. When you communicate with someone from another culture, you experience these differences. You may feel you understand the words

EXHIBIT 5-5   Spatial Relationship of Syntactical Elements

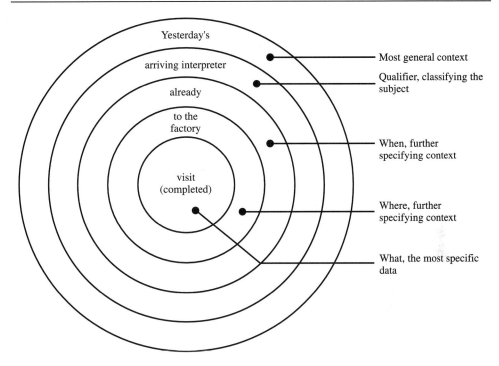

and the message, but you may also feel some uncertainty about the communication because it is organized in an unfamiliar way.

CHANNELS OF BUSINESS MESSAGES

Choosing the right channel and the appropriate form for business messages is a communication skill. When the communication is between cultures as well as organizations, the skill is even more important. In the United States, according to business communication guides, efficiency, clarity, conciseness, accuracy, and accountability are the keys to making the choice. A telephone call may be the fastest way to get clarification. But you may need something in writing before you can act.

Other considerations to keep in mind, when communicating with a high-context culture, are harmony, face-giving and face-saving, status, and ambiguity to allow flexibility. We've seen that these factors affect how messages are encoded. They also affect the choice of channel or medium through which to send the message.

This section considers channels of written internal communication, as from a subsidiary to a head office (memos, E-mail, faxes), written external communication that goes outside the organization (faxes, E-mail, letters, press releases, and customer communication), and oral communication (telephone, voice messages, teleconferences, and meetings).

Internal Channels for Written Messages

Memos, E-mail, networked intranet bulletin boards, printed reports, and other written documents are channels of written communication within companies.

Memos have different roles in different cultures and organizations. In a North American business, memos are the standard channel of communication from superiors to subordinates, subordinates to superiors, and employees of the same level. (Memos can also be written to file or as reminders to oneself.) They can be formal or informal in tone. When informal, a memo is a convenient way of communicating information in writing—so there is a record of it—without the weight of a formal document. Increasingly memos are sent by E-mail.

A New Zealand consultant, Judith, thought memos would provide an accurate record of information without too much formality. So she wrote memos to her client, the owner of a family business in Taiwan. She put her comments in writing in order to reduce misunderstanding. But the owner never acknowledged the memos. So she wrote more. Still no mention of them. Finally she asked Taiwanese friends what this meant. She learned that her status with the owner meant she could have face-to-face discussions with him. Memos are impersonal, and he thought she didn't want to have to get to know him. That made him reluctant to trust her.[26] She was responsibly using an effective communication channel, as far as her own culture was concerned. But it was counterproductive in Taiwan.

As a means for feedback from employees to management, memos (especially E-mail) excel—at least, in cultures where managers expect feedback. Feedback is not easy for managers to gather if subordinates are not used to giving it. Managers who don't solicit feedback will not receive as much as those who do. Memos may not be the best channel in these situations. Face-to-face exchanges, where a wide range of nonverbal signals can be sent along with the worded message, may be a better choice.

E-mail and hard-copy memos are also, perhaps primarily, channels for managerial communication downward. What they signify varies within different cultures. In explicit, low-context, contract cultures a memo may have the force of a written agreement. It can be counteracted with another memo, but once it goes out it is official.

A Thai civil servant was told of an interoffice memo announcing his posting to a regional office. He had not been consulted, had not seen the memo, and had strong personal reasons for not making the move. He tracked the progress of the memo to its final recipient, the director general of his department. He explained his objections and was given permission to destroy the memo and thus cancel the posting.[27]

Apart from the priorities in the Thai culture that allow an employee to be transferred without being consulted, and the authority of the superior to unmake the decision, a third point can be made. The memo lacked the legal force that the same memo would have had in a low-context culture, for example. Its contents could simply be reversed by crumpling up and throwing away the memo itself. All those who had already read it would presumably simply erase it from their minds.

Electronic mail (E-mail) has made an impact on interoffice communication, in format, tone, and content. It can be printed out, thereby providing a hard copy for records. E-mail is less formal a channel than hard-copy memos and letters, without established rules for format, and the tone tends to be informal as well. The content is often less well organized because writers are more spontaneous in creating messages. Sending them involves merely the click of a mouse and rarely includes proofreading. As a result, follow-up messages are often necessary to cover information that was left out of the original message. Study needs to be done on the effect of E-mail on organization patterns: Does the ease of message creation lead to more direct organization? Anecdotal evidence suggests not; writers who wish to open a message by paying attention to relationship building do so with E-mail messages just as they do in hard-copy messages. The culture affects the way technology is used, just as the technology itself impacts the channel. E-mail is not private; managers can read messages presumed confidential by their senders. Employees have been embarrassed by seeing their supposedly private gossip about co-workers reproduced on company letterhead.

Networked bulletin boards allow employees to communicate by an expanded informal grapevine. Fax—facsimile transmission of a document electronically—is also used widely within organizations, especially when people need to see original documents. However, both fax and telephone voice messages can now be delivered to a receiver's E-mail address, and it is no longer necessary to use a computer to receive E-mail.

External Channels for Written Messages

These channels communicate outside the organization. External channels include all of the internal channels discussed above as well as Internet web pages, public announcements in press releases, news stories, contracts, marketing promotions, and user manuals.

E-mail networks enable businesses and private individuals to hook up to the Internet through service providers. Databases such as Lexis/Nexis and ABI/Inform (Proquest) are among hundreds that allow access to thousands of publications, making it possible to retrieve information without leaving one's desk. Web pages give companies a public face unlike any they have had before. The company story is available to anybody who logs on to the corporate website. Customers are able to ask questions about products and services over the Web in a new, direct way that is reminiscent of the old-fashioned local store. Companies are able to track individual customers through electronic databases in a way that gives customers a feeling they are individually recognized by the company. New meanings attach to "relationship marketing" and "customer service." New companies continue to pop onto the screen and new technology is enabling entrepreneurs to move in new directions.

Structured Behavioral Channels

You've already read two examples of deliberately structured behavior to communicate, particularly in Asia: the Japanese husband whose wife communicated annoyance through a flower arrangement; the Chinese trainees who served boiled water to announce the fact the tea was all gone. Here is a third example.

An American lawyer working in a Japanese steel company was part of a group who welcomed a visiting American delegation. But he found himself shut out from the company group deliberations that he had been a part of before the visitors arrived. He had lived in Japan long enough to feel this exclusion deeply.

After the Americans went home, however, senior members of his company invited him to Tokyo for a lavish dinner—the cost for eight people was over $5,000. Although the company behavior toward him during the Americans' visit was never mentioned, he understood the lavish entertainment was the company's way of apologizing and reassuring him that they still valued him.

These acts of communication are carefully planned, with a beginning and an end, as an alternative to written or oral channels. This behavior occurs frequently in cultures in which to discuss the situation would cause potential loss of face. But behavioral communication exists in all cultures and can be eloquent in getting a message across. A subordinate may signal unhappiness about an assignment in the way he or she dresses for work or participates in the social life of the office. A manager may signal pleasure with an employee by an invitation to lunch or gift for the employee's workplace.

This structured activity is a communication channel that replaces worded messages. Thus it is different from nonverbal codes in communication, such as facial expression, tone of voice, gesture, and physical distance. They are discussed in Chapter 6.

Oral Channels

When do you prefer oral channels in your job? When do you phone, drop into someone's office, catch someone at the elevator or in the parking lot in order to communicate a message? Chances are it's when you put a higher priority on keeping things running smoothly than on the information itself. In low- and high-context cultures, oral communication has a more lubricative function, oiling relationships, than written messages. In cultures in which relationships are more important than results, word-of-mouth and face-to-face channels are more frequently used. You may choose business partners because of oral recommendations; you may come to a decision after talking it over with others; you may deliver unwelcome messages orally so you can establish a personal tone at the same time. As we saw earlier in the discussion on memos, written messages can seem impersonal and unfriendly to some recipients.

Low-context culture managers need to keep in mind that employees from cultures with strong oral traditions will probably prefer oral channels to putting things in writing. Their priority for having things in writing so they can be acted upon in good faith may be set aside, legitimately. Members of oral cultures place high priority on their word, and will follow through no less willingly than if it were in writing.

On the other hand, in some cultures some kinds of oral communication presume too much familiarity for some situations. A follow-up telephone call from a Western salesperson in Tokyo who sends a mailing to prospective buyers will seem too aggressive. The proper contact is through a go-between or reference who makes an appointment and is present at the face-to-face meeting. That is an appropriate oral channel.

Voice mail is another oral channel, although the line between voice mail and written messages is blurring with new technology that translates voice mail onto a computer screen. Voice mail allows the caller to leave his or her voice in the receiver's electronic mailbox. Unlike a message noted down by a third party (or no message at all), voice mail transmits some of the nonverbal characteristics of the message directly from the speaker. The listener hears it later in time but complete, with the nonverbal qualities such as pitch and volume, pronunciation, pace, and pauses intact.

Teleconferencing transmits many nonverbal communication cues that E-mail, fax, electronic bulletin boards, or even telephones cut out. When it is too costly for a company to send people thousands of miles to meet face to face, teleconferencing can be a good alternative. However, certain restrictions exist: It is not always possible to see the nonverbal behavior clearly; of course both locations must have the appropriate equipment; time differences can mean one party is up in the middle of the night; and only one person can speak at a time. This may mean having to learn a new set of rules for turn taking in oral communication for some participants.

This leads to our final consideration, the formality or informality of communication style.

COMMUNICATION STYLE

Formal or Informal: Hierarchical or Horizontal

In some cultures, a manager has reached that position through hard work and the status is important. So managers employ a formal writing style that emphasizes power distance and authority. Formality stresses the hierarchy of the organization and the manager's superior status in that hierarchy. Paradoxically, the very hierarchy reinforces social harmony by reducing uncertainty about status. Subordinates expect managers to use a formal style; not to do so is to risk losing the respect of the lower ranks. They want to be confident their manager is indeed firmly fixed above them, being accountable on their behalf and looking out for their best interests. This style lends itself to quick decisions, since subordinates are not likely to question them.

Memos written from managers in these hierarchical cultures—Arab, African, Asian—sound authoritarian to members of horizontal cultures that emphasize equality. Horizontal cultures—English-speaking cultures, cultures from Northern Europe—give more priority to the equal status of employees. Their style is inclusive and they play down the power distance between manager and subordinate. Indeed, the power distance may be slight and the manager's authority may rest on the will of the subordinates to acknowledge it. This style tends to be less efficient than the authoritative style. If everyone has a valid voice and can contribute feedback in two-way communication, issues can take a long time to discuss.

Business communication textbooks from the United States instruct memo writers to adopt a friendly tone and an informal style in order to get the most cooperation from readers. When an issue is serious, formality indicates a writer's commitment to the issue rather than to friendly relations.

Subordinates in North American organizations try to develop sensitive antennae about style of communication with superiors. Generally, they equate formality with distance and

informality with greater friendliness. But formal or informal, employees in these organizations welcome the opportunity to express their views and make their wishes known. A
common complaint from employees is that management doesn't listen to or care about
their concerns; the assumption is that management should care.

Managers who want feedback from subordinates may find difficulties, however, when
subordinates are accustomed to treating managers as authorities who do not make decisions based on subordinates' wishes. The notion of two-way communication may be unfamiliar and uncomfortable. Employees may wonder why managers ask them for information; they may suspect managers have hidden purposes for it.

Where communication is structured with little flexibility for feedback or other response
or for other channels of communication, in other directions, a grapevine communication
system develops. In contrast to the official, formal system, the grapevine is informal. The
more rigid the structured system, the more the informal system flourishes. Studies indicate
that the grapevine has more credibility than the official communication network and is
often more accurate. (See also Chapter 8.)

You can see a flourishing informal network in organizations that have a hierarchical culture; the informal system usually involves someone in the office of the most powerful person, and also involves people who have access to more than one department or location in
the organization. The same is true in a general culture, where the system is naturally more
complex. Chapter 8 deals with the nature of information in detail, but here it is appropriate to point out that the informal information network may be the one you need to pay
attention to in an unfamiliar culture.

Framed Messages

"Framing" is explaining the context of the message before delivering it. It lets the receiver
know how to interpret the message. Is it a serious criticism? Is it a joke? The frame—like
a picture frame—can be nonverbal, but here we'll consider verbal frames. The opening of
a letter that transmits a proposal, for example, "Here is the proposal as you requested . . ."
is a frame for what follows. Frames are widely used in English-speaking cultures in oral
communication: "I hate to bother you, but the courier will be here in five minutes. Could
you please . . . ?" They pay attention to the status of the other party and to the grooming
of the relationship. "The temperature seems to have gone down and I didn't bring a jacket;
would you please close the window?" Frames are particularly useful with requests, to
soften the authoritative tone. Even the context (frame) must be verbalized in low-context
cultures so nothing is left ambiguous or open to misinterpretation.

Because frames attend to the relationship, they seem appropriate for high-context
receivers. But be careful. They can make the sender—if a superior—sound too anxious,
and can make the power distance between superior and subordinate seem too small. A
high-context receiver may prefer the ring of authority in the request: "Have the report on
my desk by 5 P.M. today." Authority is a piggyback message on the worded message; it
says, "I make this request because I am your superior and since you are my subordinate
your role is to fulfill this request." A frame that suggests the roles of superior and subordinate are fluid may make a high-context receiver uncomfortable: "I have a meeting at 8:30
tomorrow morning when I'll be presenting our ideas on the information you have been
gathering, so could you please share your findings with me later this afternoon?"

Framing adds explanatory detail to a message. Detail is an aspect of style, and the question of how much detail to use has its answer in the culture of the receiver. Detail, the volume of information, in a request suggests equal status between sender and receiver and common goals. On the other hand, detail in response to a request shows concern for cooperating, building trust, and entering into a relationship.

SUMMARY

Chapter 5 has looked at the way culture affects how messages are organized.

- The model shows that communication, interpersonal or interorganizational, is a *simultaneously reciprocal process.* Senders of messages are at the same time receivers of messages. However, the meaning of the message depends on culture and context. Organizations from different cultures experience greater potential for miscommunication.
- *Business communication is purposeful.* All business functions require communication.
- *Why, how, who, when, and where* are critical factors in understanding communication differences in organizations. When these factors can be agreed upon, miscommunication is minimized.

Chapter 5 then discusses ways messages are organized:

- *Direct plan is favored largely by results-oriented cultures* such as the United States.
- *Indirect plan is favored by relationship-oriented cultures* such as Asia, Latin America, Africa, and the Middle East.
- Persuasive arguments are based on different approaches in different cultures; logical arguments persuade some, while adopting the moral high ground or taking a dependent posture or making emotional appeals persuades others.
- Unwelcome news is generally presented indirectly; no may not be said at all in cultures where harmony and saving face are important.
- Problem-solving messages may be organized in stories (narrative), in syllogistic or inductive reasoning, or in bargaining discourse.

Cultures vary in the role they assign to words, as well as in the impact words have.

- *Low-context cultures encode meaning in words, while high-context cultures rely more on nonverbal communication.*
- Arabic-speaking cultures enjoy the use of words in elaborations, exaggerations, self-congratulations, and other creative patterns.
- Japanese speakers place little confidence in words and rely more on implied meanings.
- English speakers in Britain use less exaggeration than speakers in the United States, but nevertheless both tend to encode meaning explicitly in words; something has reality when it is worded.
- *Language structure is related to the way meaning is structured and understood.*

The organization of business messages also is connected to the channels those messages take.

- *Internal channels* (within an organization) of written communication include E-mail, networked bulletin boards, memos, voice mail, printed reports and other written documents, and fax.

- *External channels* of written communication include all of the above as well as Internet web pages, public announcements in press releases, news stories, marketing promotions, and manuals.
- *Structured behavior* refers to carefully planned nonverbal communication acts that have a beginning, middle, and end and are used instead of worded messages.
- *Oral channels* include face-to-face encounters, telephone, and teleconference exchanges.

Finally this chapter looks at the formality of messages and the framing of messages.

- Formality emphasizes status; informality emphasizes equality. In hierarchical cultures, formality prevails. In horizontal cultures, the messages managers write do not call attention to their status.
- Framing is explaining the context of the message before delivering it, so the receiver knows how to interpret it. "I really hate to impose, but . . . " is a frame that suggests an awareness of the obligation the request-maker is about to incur.

NOTES

1. Linda Beamer, "The Cultural Basis of Persuasion: Case Studies of Mexican and U.S. Correspondence for Sales," *International Business Practices: Contemporary Readings.* The Proceedings of the 1995 International Meeting of the Academy of Business Administration, pp. 126–133.
2. Lorand B. Szalay, "Intercultural Communication—A Process Model," *International Journal for Intercultural Research* 5 No. 2 (1981) p. 135.
3. Raymond Cohen, *Negotiating across Cultures* (Washington, DC: United States Institute of Peace, 1991) p. 22.
4. David A. Victor, *International Business Communication,* (New York: HarperCollins, 1992), p. 2.
5. Edward C. Stewart and Milton J. Bennett, *American Cultural Patterns: A Cross-Cultural Perspective,* (Yarmouth, ME: Intercultural Press, 1991), p. 156.
6. Based on Iris I. Varner, "A Comparison of American and French Business Correspondence," *Journal of Business Communication* 25 no. 4 (1988), p. 59.
7. Linda Beamer, "Directness, Context and Facework in Chinese Business Communication," *Journal of Business and Technical Communication. In press.* By permission of Matheson & Co. Ltd.
8. This discussion is developed from Cohen, *Negotiating across Cultures,* pp. 73–74.
9. Richard Mead, *Cross-Cultural Management Communication,* (New York: John Wiley & Sons, 1990), p. 62.
10. Stewart & Bennett, *American Cultural Patterns,* p. 153.
11. Cohen, *Negotiating across Cultures,* p. 114.
12. Marietta Baba, "Decoding Native Paradigms: An Anthropological Approach to Intercultural Communication in Industry." Presented at the ABC Midwest-Canada Regional Conference, luncheon program, April 27, 1990.
13. Nancy K. Austin, "Story Time," *Incentive,* December 1995, p. 2.
14. Ibid., p. 1.
15. Aurea Carpenter, "What Comes First," *London Times,* Features Section, 22 February 1992.
16. Mead, *Cross-Cultural Management Communication,* p. 115.
17. Cohen, *Negotiating across Cultures,* p. 27.
18. Mead, *Cross-Cultural Management Communication,* p. 87.

19. Larry A. Samovar and Richard E. Porter, *Communication between Cultures,* (Belmont, CA: Wadsworth, 1991), p. 157.

20. Sheila Ramsey, "To Hear One and Understand Ten" in *Intercultural Communication: A Reader,* 4th ed. Larry A. Samovar and Richard E Porter, eds. (Belmont, CA: Wadsworth, 1985), p. 312.

21. Satoshi Ishii, "Enryo-Sasshi Communication: A Key to Understanding Japanese Interpersonal Relations," *Cross Currents* 11 (1984), pp. 49–58.

22. Satoshi Ishii, "Thought Patterns as Modes of Rhetoric: The United States and Japan," in *Intercultural Communication: A Reader,* p. 100.

23. Benjamin L. Whorf, *Language, Thought and Reality: Selected Writings of B.L. Whorf,* J. B. Carroll, ed. (New York: John Wiley & Sons, 1956), p. 213.

24. Linda Beamer, "Teaching English Business Writing to Chinese-Speaking Business Students," *Bulletin* LVII, no. 1(1994).

25. Cohen, *Negotiating across Cultures,* p. 20.

26. Mead, *Cross-Cultural Management Communication,* pp. 89–90.

27. Ibid., p. 181.

CHAPTER SIX

The Nonverbal Language in Intercultural Communication

Rana Zarvi from Lebanon has been working for a Swedish firm for several months. When she arrived in January, she did not think she would last very long; the short days and the cold winter made her wonder how anyone could live in such an environment. But now summer has arrived, and she is getting used to her surroundings. She likes her work, and her colleagues are friendly, but she has no real feel for them. What do they think? How do they live? In her previous job in Beirut, for example, she would socialize with her co-workers after hours. She knew about their families, and in the office there was an easy-going camaraderie. In Stockholm, her co-workers are friendly but more distant. Rana is used to speaking with her whole body, using her arms to emphasize her points, and showing her emotions through her facial expressions.

Increasingly she is wondering how she is doing. Her boss, Arne Gustafson, seems to appreciate her work, but sometimes she has doubts. In their last meeting, he went over the agenda of an upcoming negotiation session with managers from Malaysia. She knows that the firm faces tough competition and a joint venture with the Malaysian firm would help open the Asian market. Arne discussed the negotiation strategy and gave her several assignments for the negotiation. He was all business, correct but without emotion. Rana is wondering: Is he confident? Does he have any doubts? What does he think is going to happen? Is she doing her part? His words sound confident, but during her time in Sweden she has found that she has not been very successful at reading the thoughts and emotions of her co-workers.

How often have we listened to someone speak and wondered what the speaker really was saying. We may agree intuitively with the words, but in the back of our minds we feel that there is more to the message than the words. We may even come to the conclusion that the speaker means the opposite of what she says. We may base our judgment on an evaluation of tone, intonation, emphasis, facial expressions, gestures and hand movements, distance, and eye contact—in short, nonverbal signals or the silent language.[1]

Although nonverbal signals tend to enhance and support language, they can minimize or even contradict the verbal message. For example, the phrase, "I would love to meet with you and discuss this issue in more detail," can take on different meanings depending on the nonverbal signals accompanying the words.

1. A smile while pulling out a calendar will support the words.
2. Going on without pausing to the next topic after the statement may very well indicate that the speaker is not serious and not interested in meeting, at least not now.

3. A frown and a search for something on the desk while uttering the words may contradict the message altogether.

Some researchers maintain that in face-to-face communication up to 93 percent of an oral message is communicated nonverbally and that the nonverbal elements are a much better indicator of the true meaning than the actual words.

Yet, the true meaning and the interpretation will depend on a variety of factors. As we will see in this chapter, people from different cultures attach different meanings to nonverbal signals. As one example: In Western cultures eye contact can signify honesty, whereas in Asian cultures it may indicate rudeness.

The interpretation of nonverbal signals is further complicated by the fact that within a culture not all people use the same signals. Men and women often use different nonverbal language. Men in Western cultures tend to be more outspoken than women; however, with women asserting their rights more, women's communication is changing. People from different social classes within one culture also may use nonverbal signals differently. People from the upper classes or people in leading positions may be more assertive and outspoken in many cultures when communicating with people from lower classes and lower positions.

Nonverbal communication is influenced by a number of factors, including

- Cultural background.
- Socioeconomic background.
- Education.
- Gender.
- Age.
- Personal preference and idiosyncrasies.

All these factors complicate the interpretation of the nonverbal aspects of communication.

Needless to say, valid generalizations are difficult and always must be reevaluated and seen in the context of the situation. For example, in a Western cultural setting, crossing one's arms may be interpreted as being defensive, rejecting the other person, or being closed-minded. However, it is also possible that the nonverbal signal simply means that the speaker is cold. The isolated symbol may not carry any deeper meaning.

Other nonverbal symbols are interesting but not that important. For example, when Europeans use their fingers counting to five, they start with the thumb and go in sequence of the fingers to the little finger. Americans, on the other hand, start with the index finger, go on to the little finger, and count the thumb last.[2] While this difference is interesting, it does not influence the meaning of what is being said.

You may wonder why we are concerned at all with nonverbal communication if the interpretation is so difficult. The point is that nonverbal communication, because it varies so much and because it carries so much of the meaning, needs our close attention so that we can decode and get our message across more effectively. While we examine nonverbal language of several cultures in this chapter, keep in mind that these are generalizations, and while the descriptions are true generally for a culture, there are many variations within a culture. As you learn more about a culture and as you meet more people from a culture, you may adapt and adjust your interpretation of the nonverbal language signals.

What exactly is nonverbal language? Researchers, while agreeing that nonverbal communication refers to nonworded language, use a variety of definitions that can be divided into two major categories:

1. Nonverbal or nonworded communication includes *all* communication beyond the spoken or written word. It includes aspects such as the language of friendship and material possessions and the nonverbal aspects of written communication, such as weight and color of paper, format, typeface, and binding.
2. Nonverbal communication only includes nonverbal language using the body, including paralanguage.

In this chapter, we will specifically examine

- Paralanguage:
    Vocal qualifiers.
    Vocalization.
- Nonverbal conventions in face-to-face communication:
    Eye contact.
    Facial expressions and gestures.
    Timing in spoken exchange.
    Touching.
    Language of space.
    Appearance.
    Silence.

PARALANGUAGE

Paralanguage lies between verbal and nonverbal communication. It involves sounds but not words. Researchers divide paralanguage into three categories: voice quality, vocal qualifiers, and vocalization.[3] Voice quality seems to be more an individual than a cultural characteristic. We will examine vocal qualifiers and vocalization.

Vocal Qualifiers

The term *vocal qualifiers* refers to volume, pitch, and overall intonation or "melody" of the spoken word. For example, does the speaker raise or lower his voice at the end of a sentence? Does the speaker vary the speed of what she says, or does she speak evenly? Does the speaker vary the volume between loud and soft; in other words, does he speak softly or does he shout? Vocal qualifiers differ from culture to culture. For example, a non-Japanese person listening to a Japanese man can get the impression that the Japanese speaker "spits" words out in clusters. The cluster comes very fast followed by a slight pause before the next cluster emerges. Japanese women, on the other hand, may seem to speak more evenly.

In English as spoken in the United States, a speaker raises the pitch at the end of a question, signifying a nonverbal question mark. If the rise in pitch is accompanied by a pause, the listener interprets this to mean that the speaker is waiting for an answer. On the other hand, if the speaker asks a question without the pitch going up, he may not expect or want an answer. The speaker may be asking a rhetorical question and then be ready to make the next point. A speaker who has finished expressing an idea typically lowers her pitch signifying she is done. Someone else can speak now.

Ending sentences with a high pitch in American English may indicate self-doubt and uncertainty. In French, on the other hand, sentences tend to end on a higher pitch than in either German or English. The French speaker may be very certain of what she is saying, yet a listener from a U.S. or German cultural background may have a different impression.

Vocalization

All cultures use nonword noises such as "aham," "um," "er," sucking in one's breath, or clicking one's tongue. These noises may be used as connectors between ideas; they may also be used to indicate that someone is ready to say something or that more time is needed to think things over. Generally speaking, the interpretation of these noises does not present a major hurdle in intercultural communication. The frequency of their use, however, varies from culture to culture.[4]

Related to the nonword vocalizers are fillers. For example, in English "okay" and "you know" are often used as fillers. The words have a meaning, but the speaker who uses them does not attach the specific meaning to them. The words simply build a bridge to what the speaker says next. The use of *hai* (literally translated *yes*) in Japanese serves the same function. Most Japanese use *hai* as filler without particular meaning. It serves as a lubricant for the flow of the speech. In intercultural communication people must be aware of appropriate frequency and meaning of fillers.

NONVERBAL BUSINESS CONVENTIONS IN FACE-TO-FACE ENCOUNTERS

Nonverbal messages can be broken down into subcategories. While this makes the discussion easier, we must be careful not to assume that speakers use nonverbal signals in isolation. In most cases, speakers use many different signals at the same time. We may move our hands, nod with our head, smile, and keep close eye contact, all at the same time. The nonverbal messages that give listeners the most trouble are those that accompany words. It's the tone of voice, the look on someone's face, or the lack of eye contact that makes you wonder if you understood. As we discuss the nonverbal conventions in face-to-face encounters, we will start with those nonverbal signals that most closely accompany the verbal message and go to those that are not connected with words, such as the use of space, appearance, and silence.

To some extent we are able to manipulate the signals consciously—we may smile because that is expected of us although we may not feel like smiling. In many cases, however, we send nonverbal signals without being aware of doing so. Those signals, the experts agree, are a reflection of our true feelings and reactions. One of the goals in intercultural communication is to interpret *all* nonverbal signals.

Eye Contact

In most cultures superiors are freer to look at subordinates than the other way around. Traditionally, men can look more at women than women at men. In the United States, for example, "ogling," looking at the other sex, may be interpreted as a form of sexual harassment and even have legal consequences. Eye contact, as a result, is becoming complicated within that culture. European women sometimes comment that men from the United States are cold and don't know how to flirt, the innocent game of looking and establishing eye contact. At the same time, women from the United States who visit southern European countries are often uncomfortable when men look at them, which they interpret as offensive staring.

Rules governing eye contact are different in different cultures, and the difference can make people feel uncomfortable without being aware of why they are uncomfortable. In the United States it is customary to look at the speaker's mouth when listening but make intermittent eye contact with the eyes of a listener when speaking. In China, it is the opposite: A speaker rivets the listener with sustained, unbroken eye contact, but a listener does not make eye contact or look at the speaker's face consistently

Since several cultures consider the eye to be "the window of the soul," eye contact or lack thereof is interpreted to have special meaning. In these cultures eye contact is related to honesty. In other cultures eye contact is seen as an invasion of privacy.

EYE CONTACT AS A SIGN OF HONESTY "He couldn't even look me in the eye" is a common phrase that in Western cultures indicates the speaker had something to hide. In North American and northern European cultures, eye contact shows openness, trustworthiness, and integrity. One doesn't have anything to hide. If a woman from the United States looks directly at someone, she allows that person to see her eyes and decide whether she is trustworthy. Someone who does not make eye contact is considered shifty and makes the listener suspicious. People from all cultures carry their cultural attitudes towards eye contact with them, and like most nonverbal behavior aspects, eye contact does not easily travel across cultural boundaries.

Arab cultures, even more than Western cultures, use very intense eye contact and concentrate on the eye movement to be able to read real intentions. The feeling is that the eye does not lie. To see the eye more clearly, Arabs will move closer and that makes non-Arabs feel uncomfortable. A person from Japan, for example would feel uncomfortable both with the intense eye contact and with the close physical proximity. The Japanese person will feel even more uncomfortable if the Arab, in addition to making close eye contact and standing very close to the listener, also touches the listener. In this case the Arabs send three very strong nonverbal signals, all of which run counter to what is acceptable nonverbal behavior in Japan.

In many cases the Arab speaker may want to disclose his innermost feelings, yet given the culture, he cannot refuse eye contact. Therefore, he may look for other means to protect his feelings and intentions. Some people say that Palestinian leader Yasser Arafat, for example, always used to wear sunglasses so that the people he was talking to could not follow the movement of his eyes. They argued that the sunglasses were an attempt to hide true intentions and motives.

EYE CONTACT AS SIGN OF INVASION OF PRIVACY   To look someone in the eye in Japan is invading someone's space. It is rude. When samurai held power, a strict code of behavior was enforced regarding who could look at whom and for how long one could look, and one violated those codes at one's own peril. This has carried over into modern society. The Japanese may sit close together in an office, but they seldom look each other in the eye.

The Japanese feel uncomfortable with direct eye contact, and they want to avoid it. In addition, not looking someone in the eye preserves that person's private space or bubble. In a crowded country the preservation of privacy by any means is considered important. When greeting someone, one bows and looks past the other person. The degree of American eye contact would be considered staring and rude. Even on the crowded subways and trains, nobody makes eye contact. People look past each other.

Facial Expressions

Words are often accompanied by distinct facial expressions. In many cultures, when people are surprised, they may open their eyes wide and open their mouths. When they like something, their eyes may beam, and they may smile. When they are angry, they may frown and narrow their eyes. While many facial expressions carry similar meanings in a variety of cultures, the frequency and intensity of their use may vary. Latin and Arab cultures use more intense facial expressions, whereas East Asian cultures use more subdued facial expressions.

SMILING   People in all cultures smile at times; however, the meaning of a smile may vary. Depending on the culture, it can indicate joy and amusement, but it can also indicate embarrassment.

In an attempt to appear open and friendly, people in the United States smile a lot. Everyone smiles at everyone. To other cultures, the American smile often appears insincere and frozen. Why, for example, should a waitress smile? Restaurants in the United States go to great lengths in training to ensure that all employees practice the appropriate smile. Americans are surprised and puzzled that the rest of the world does not seem to share the American emphasis on the smile. McDonald's, for example, had a hard time teaching waitresses in Moscow the importance of the smile and the proper type of smile.

In Japan people don't smile the way people from the United States do. One does not freely show feelings and force one's emotions on anybody else. Men don't smile in public, and women are not supposed to show their teeth when they smile. To guarantee that the teeth are hidden, Japanese women tend to put a hand in front of their mouths when laughing. The women who greet customers in banks and stores with a deep bow do not really smile by U.S. standards. They look pleasant, but they don't really smile at the customer the way an American would.

Germans smile, but not nearly as much as people in the United States. They will say bluntly, "Life is severe and there is very little to smile about." Germans are much more reserved but for different reasons from those of the Japanese. The Japanese don't want to intrude; the Germans recognize that the world is not necessarily a pleasant place. Life is doing one's duty, and duty does not lend itself to smiling.

Koreans consider it inappropriate for adults to smile in public. Smiling at strangers is something the mentally retarded do or children do before they are properly trained. In addition, for Koreans, as for many other cultures in East Asia, the smile often is not an expression of pleasure but of embarrassment. When a person from the United States or Europe might blush with embarrassment or become defensive, an Asian might smile. To avoid serious misunderstandings, people who engage in intercultural communication should be able to interpret a smile appropriately.

Related to the smile is the laugh. Americans can have a very deep-felt belly laugh that comes from the deepest emotions. In Arabic and Latin cultures the laugh is often accompanied by expressive gestures, such as arm waving and touching. The Japanese seldom laugh that way except among intimates. A laugh is not necessarily an expression of joy and happiness. Like the smile, the laugh often is an expression of being uncomfortable, nervous, and embarrassed.

SHOWING ANGER   The expression of anger also varies from culture to culture both in terms of intensity and type of expression. In addition, cultural values dictate who can show anger. Older people, men, and people in authority may show anger more readily than younger people, women, and subordinates. The boss may get angry at the subordinate, whereas the subordinate is well advised not to react in kind. The result is that the interpretation and the display of anger are influenced by culture.

One of the milder forms of showing anger in Western cultures, for example, is frowning. Depending on the context, frowning can indicate anger, doubt, questioning of authority, suspicion, or disagreement. In cultures where the open expression of one's feeling is not appreciated, frowning may be much more subdued. The Japanese, for example, avert their gaze so as to hide anger; to show anger openly even through frowning is considered inappropriate in business contexts.

Another way of showing anger is shouting and gesturing. Germans, Canadians, Arabs, and Latins often raise their voices when angry. The Japanese seldom raise their voices when angry. Instead, they may show anger by sucking in their breath rather than letting it out with a scream. When Germans are angry, their faces may get red; they may shout; but typically they are still fairly correct in how they address the opponent. Many would still call the opponent "Sie" (the formal address for you) even if they throw all sorts of epithets at him.

Some cultures use intense and expressive gesturing to show anger. People from the Middle East accompany their verbal tirades with big gestures. The whole body is involved in showing anger and outrage as if to illustrate that the entire person is affected. Showing anger means not just a battle of words but also a battle of one's entire existence.

Research in Korean companies has revealed the surprising fact that Korean managers often show anger toward subordinates not only with verbal criticism but also with nonverbal acts of violence—even to throwing coffee on a subordinate or causing physical injury![5] This is surprising behavior because it is so different from what is known of Asian attention to face and harmony.

Asian cultures tend to restrict the range of facial expressions by Western standards. As a result, anger is not openly expressed in work environments in many Asian cultures. People from Asian cultures are able to read the message of the subdued nonverbal facial communication of anger, but people from Western cultures tend to have a hard time deciphering the code. Compared to Japanese culture, facial expressions in Arabic cultures, on the other hand, tend to overstate feelings, such as anger. From the facial expression, an outsider may find it hard to determine how angry a person from the Middle East really is. The point is that people from the same culture have no problems reading the message. The problem comes when people cross cultural boundaries and enter a different system of communicating through facial expressions and gestures.

Gestures

HEAD MOVEMENTS   In most cultures nodding one's head is seen as agreeing and shaking one's head is seen as rejecting, although Bulgarians do the opposite—they shake their heads when agreeing. In southern India, moving one's head from side to side is not a negation. So even in this one area where most cultures agree there is some disagreement.

A speaker may nod her head to affirm what she is saying and emphasize the verbal message. The listener may nod to signal understanding and approval. Nodding can be a signal that the listener understands and that the speaker can continue with the discussion.

A lowered head in Western culture can signify defeat or uncertainty. In Asian cultures lowering one's head may mean accepting one's place in the hierarchy. In contrast, tilting the head upward in Western cultures is interpreted as being arrogant, as illustrated in the expression, "His nose was in the air."

ARM MOVEMENTS   Arm movements take up space and thereby enlarge the size of the speaker. A speaker who uses big arm movements can intimidate the listener and appear more powerful. In most cultures men tend to use larger gestures than women.

When a businessman from the United States wants to emphasize a point in a discussion, he may pound his fist on the table and underline his statements with staccato-like drumming on the table. Businesswomen in the United States in the same situation use far fewer arm and hand movements. However, compared to Japanese women, American woman use very expressive arm movements.

Japanese men use far fewer arm movements than both men and women from the United States. Personal space in Japan is limited, and big arm movements could easily invade someone's private space. In addition, big gestures draw attention to the speaker and single him out from the group, thereby threatening the harmony of the group. Someone from a more openly expressive culture may interpret the subdued arm and body movements of a Japanese person as submissive or timid. A non-Japanese negotiator may even think that the Japanese businessperson is not interested and does not care about the discussion. Yet, by Japanese standards, this person may be quite expressive. People who are used to expressive gestures often have difficulties recognizing and interpreting subdued gestures. They may be so busy talking with their arms that they don't hear the body language of the other person. The person from the subdued culture, on the other hand, may be overwhelmed by the gestures that he too has difficulties understanding. The gestures seem to scream at him.

Arab men use their arms even more than men from the United States do. Gestures and waving of the arms accompany almost every spoken word and seem to embrace a wide space. Arm movements can signal happiness but also anger (see the discussion under

Anger in this chapter). In the process of waving his arms, the Arab may touch the listener occasionally. For Arabs words themselves do not seem to be sufficient to express thoughts—the nonverbal signals do not just accompany the spoken word; they are an integral part of the verbal message.

One of the authors videotaped students making oral presentations in English and in their native languages to see if the nonverbal codes differed in the same speaker. These presentations seemed to indicate that nonverbal codes learned with a specific language did not transfer to another language. For example, an Iranian student, when speaking Farsi, put his hands behind his back in a gesture of respect, straightened his back, and spoke with his chin up making eye contact only with the professor, the authority figure. When that same student gave his presentation in English, he looked like an ordinary American student, one hand in his pocket, occasionally shifting his weight from one foot to the other, and keeping eye contact with everyone in the room.

It would be interesting to see to what extent the change in body movements was a conscious effort to fit into American culture and to what extent it was a subconscious connection of English with a certain set of nonverbal signals.

POSTURE   The way we sit, stand, and walk sends a nonverbal message. In Western culture to stand tall conveys confidence. The confident person stands erect with shoulders back and head up. The posture signals, "I am not afraid of anything." Appropriate posture is related to a person's status in society. For example, the manager may stand erect when talking to subordinates, but the subordinates may drop their shoulders when talking to the manager. In traditional societies the person lower in the hierarchy may be expected to prostrate himself in front of the tribal chief or village elder to show respect. While this form of showing respect and submission is not practiced in intercultural business communication, the international manager does need to know what posture is acceptable in a given culture.

While in most business situations people sit on chairs, in many Arab cultures men conduct business while sitting on the floor. In traditional Japanese businesses people may also sit on the floor. The Japanese style of sitting with legs tucked under can be very taxing for outsiders who are not used to this posture.

In many cultures women of middle and upper class backgrounds are supposed to sit with their legs and ankles together and arms close to their bodies. Women are to be modest and take up little space. When women sit in an easy chair, they seem to "borrow" the space; men, on the other hand, seem to "own" the space. In Western cultures this has changed to quite an extent over the last two decades, and young women often sit as relaxed as men. When Western women do business in more traditional societies, such as Japan or India, they need to adapt the way they sit and stand so as not to give offense.

The way we use our bodies when communicating indicates how we perceive our power, authority, and position in relation to the person we are communicating with. If the other person comes from the same culture, she can read the signals fairly accurately. If the other person is from another culture, she may have difficulties. She may interpret the lack of body language as rejection or the expressive body language as threatening when the speaker was simply using his or her own cultural style.

Timing in Spoken Exchanges

A conversation is verbal exchange between people. While the words are obviously important, the timing of the exchange also carries a significant nonverbal message. To examine the timing of nonverbal communication, we must answer several questions:

1. Who initiates the communication?
2. What are patterns of frequency of exchange?
3. What is acceptable behavior for interrupting the speaker?
4. What are the patterns for terminating the exchange?

In their own culture, people know what the typical patterns for verbal interaction are. For the outsider the timing issue becomes more complex because it is closely related to issues of gender, status, and hierarchy. In many cultures men initiate verbal exchange more frequently than women; older people are more likely to start the exchange than younger people, and people with authority are more likely to initiate communication than subordinates, and this behavior is carried into the office.

Questions 2 and 3 are connected. Whoever interrupts also controls the exchange. Again, in most cultures patterns are similar, but Japan is an exception—interrupting others there is not acceptable. In cultures where interrupting the speaker is acceptable, businessmen tend to interrupt businesswomen more often than the other way around. Older people interrupt younger people more often, and people in power positions will interrupt subordinates. While anyone can end the communication, frequently men, older people, and people in positions of authority are the ones who control the termination.

The roles that gender, age, and authority play in timing communication in all cultures might suggest that culture-based differences in timing are small, yet the differences are significant. For example, even though research has shown that in the United States men tend to dominate the timing of communication,[6] American women are much more assertive and outspoken in business and in public than Saudi or Japanese women.

The following examples illustrate the timing behavior in three different environments:

- An environment that emphasizes equality.
- An environment that emphasizes seniority and hierarchy.
- An environment that emphasizes the role of men.

These areas overlap; Japan, for example, values seniority, but life is also dominated by men. In Saudi Arabia, women are almost banished from public life, but seniority plays a role in the lives of both men and women.

EMPHASIS ON HORIZONTAL RELATIONSHIPS   For most people in the United States, a discussion is a give-and-take procedure where people take turns speaking. The speaker gives clues when he expects the other side to come in, when to wait, when to be silent. The listener also sends signals when he wants to get in. These signals are internalized, and most people don't think much about them unless the reality clashes with their expectations. One of the signals an American may use to indicate readiness for a reply may be lowering the voice, pausing at the end of a phrase or sentence, gesturing for a response, or looking expectantly at the other person.

Women and young people in the United States have become more assertive and outspoken over the past few years and increasingly influence and even control the timing of communication. Many companies proclaim open door policies and strive to empower employees in an effort to tap the creativity of their workers. They encourage subordinates to initiate communication with supervisors and to express their ideas more openly. As a result, employees have gained some control over the timing of both verbal and nonverbal communication.

EMPHASIS ON SENIORITY AND HIERARCHY   The timing in a Japanese conversation is dominated by the person with seniority, who also typically is higher in the hierarchy. The younger person will wait to be addressed and avoid eye contact while being addressed and while speaking. For a non-Japanese person the timing of a Japanese interchange is difficult to follow because much of the conversation is nonverbal and the nonverbal signals are difficult to decipher for outsiders. The timing signals are more subtle than in the United States. The verbal duel, common in Western culture, is frowned upon.

EMPHASIS ON THE ROLE OF MEN   In contrast to Japan, Arabic cultures are more verbally oriented. People enjoy the lively exchange of ideas. At first glance, one may get the impression that everyone can interrupt everyone and jump into the conversation. Yet, older men clearly dominate the exchange and timing. While many people, including younger ones, may speak, a few older men control the process. Women in many Arab countries do not speak in public, and in business settings women are seldom participants. The timing of communication is typically controlled by men. Women appear more reactive than proactive participants.

Touching

In many international business settings, the handshake has become an accepted touch between businesspeople when they first meet, replacing or complementing traditional greeting rituals. But the type of handshake varies widely (see Exhibit 6–1). The Germans and Americans prefer a firm handshake, which is seen as a symbol of strength and character. The French generally have a much softer handshake. They may feel uncomfortable with the grip of a German, and the German may wonder about the limp handshake of the French. Middle Easterners may put the free hand on the forearm of the person with whom they are shaking hands. As a result, the distance to the other person diminishes. The Japanese, used to bowing, may shake hands with foreign business partners but keep their arm firmly extended to keep a greater distance. In addition, they may slightly bow and thereby combine the Japanese and Western greeting ritual. German men traditionally would also bow when shaking someone's hand. The German bow, however, differs significantly from the Japanese bow.

The handshake with the bow illustrates that greeting rituals in many cases combine different types of nonverbal communication. As mentioned above, the German and Japanese bow differ (see Exhibit 6–2). The Japanese bow from the hip with a straight back. Men keep their arms at the side with the hands extended at the side of the upper legs. Japanese

---

EXHIBIT 6–1 The Handshake

Country or Region	*Type of Handshake*
United States	Firm handshake
France	Soft handshake
Germany	Firm handshake, for men, traditionally accompanied by a slight bow
Japan	Handshake with arm firmly extended, accompanied by bow
Middle East	Handshake and free hand placed on forearm of other person

---

women put their hands on the front of the thighs when bowing. During the bowing the neck remains straight. In German bowing, on the other hand, the hips remain straight; the bow comes out of a lowering of the head. The German bow is called a *Diener.* This means it is a bow to and recognition of authority. The word *Diener* means servant, so with the bow the German says "at your service." Older Germans may still do a *Diener,* but most people today just give a slight nod of the head. The bow does not fit with notions of democracy and equality. Former Chancellor Helmut Kohl was criticized by a number of people and magazines because he did a *Diener* when greeting former President Bush. The gesture was seen by many Germans as unacceptably servile.

In Argentina, when women meet work associates or friends they stretch forward so their right cheek is touching the other person's right cheek, and perhaps kiss the air below the other person's right ear. Women do this when meeting men or women; men only do this

---

EXHIBIT 6–2 Greetings

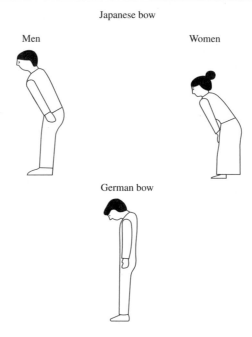

Japanese bow

Men

Women

German bow

when meeting women. Not to perform this greeting ritual is to appear cold, unfriendly, and even angry. In Lebanon, typically men will kiss the right cheek, the left cheek, and perhaps the right cheek again of other men. In Estonia, however, cheek kissing is not approved. Estonians expect a firm handshake upon meeting, and again when taking leave of someone.

The German culture uses the handshake more frequently than almost any other culture. In fact, this form of touch is the acceptable and expected form of touch in virtually every situation, whether meeting a stranger or greeting one's family. Not following the custom is viewed negatively.

Ulrike Schumacher, a German student, worked as an *au pair* girl with an English family for a summer. She had had a very good experience and had improved her English tremendously. The host family had welcomed her and had been rather generous. In many ways she was part of the family. However, she thought it strange that throughout her entire stay she never once shook hands with the family, neither at the beginning nor the end of her stay. She became accustomed to the lack of touch though and did not think much about it; she adapted. When she returned to Germany her family gathered, eager to hear about her experiences. As Ulrike entered the living room where everyone was congregated, she said, *"Guten Abend, schön wieder daheim zu sein"* (Good evening, nice to be back home again) and nodded to the group. Afterwards her parents criticized Ulrike for being distant and uppity in not going around the room and shaking everyone's hand.

In Germany, shaking hands is an accepted and expected greeting ritual; however, Germans seldom embrace. Hugging, even among family members, is rarer than in France or Latin cultures. The handshake establishes touch, but at arm's length, whereas an embrace is just too much invasion of the personal bubble.

The Maori of New Zealand, on the other hand, expect touching as part of the greeting ritual. Maori businesspeople may feel left out of business meetings if the traditional greeting, the *hongi* or pressing of noses, and the *karanga* or formal cry of welcome, are not performed. They serve a similar function to the handshaking in German society, setting everyone at ease. It would be unthinkable for a Maori function not to begin with both *hongi* and *karanga,* however many non-Maori are present.

People from low-context cultures tend to feel crowded by people from high-context cultures, and the people from high-context cultures feel left out and rejected by people from low-context cultures. People come with certain expectations that frame their behavior, and when those expectations are not met, they feel confused, resentful, or left out. All people from all cultures bring their unique cultural baggage with them. However, as people learn more about another culture, they adjust their expectations. They become more sophisticated and adjust their behavior according to the context and their degree of awareness of this context.

A Bolivian and a Dutchman who meet for the first time to do business will both be dissatisfied unless they understand each other's touching behavior. The Bolivian comes from a culture that is close, where people touch each other frequently while speaking. He will approach his Dutch counterpart with this background and act accordingly. The Dutchman, on the other hand, comes from a much more reserved culture. People are more distant and cold. He too will bring this background to the meeting and act accordingly. If they want to work together, they need to come to terms with these differences.

How do we know what the "right" distance is and what acceptable touch is? As in childhood, we learn by observation in individual situations. Books can help, but lists of do's and don'ts, while providing some initial guidelines, do not give the underlying reasons for individual differences, variations, and changes.

Touching behavior can and does change as people adapt to new cultural environments. Sometimes they very consciously decide to change to fit in. When Vittorio Sanchez goes to Chicago on business, he refrains from touching the businessmen he meets because he knows that businesspeople in the United States touch each other less frequently than Latins do. In other cases the adaptation occurs more at the intuitive level where people are not necessarily consciously aware of changes in their touching behavior. Urs Luder, a businessman from Switzerland, has noticed that his past few visits to Abu Dhabi were much more pleasant. He is not as tense and nervous as before, and the atmosphere is more relaxed. His hosts seem more pleasant. What Urs may not be aware of is that his nonverbal behavior has changed. He does not avoid being touched by people he talks to, and he himself approaches people more openly and feels comfortable putting his hand on someone's arm.

If we understand that touching is natural to some cultures, we will be less offended if someone touches us. By the same token, if the other person knows that we need our space, he will allow us more room and breathing space.

Above all, we need to keep things in perspective and not get offended each time we deal with someone who has a different relationship to space. Men in Africa hold hands with other men walking down the street. Men in the Middle East kiss the cheeks of other men in greeting. Russian men embrace in a bear hug. Doing business with people from other cultures may mean setting aside ideas about touching learned in one's own culture. During a television interview, the late Egyptian President, Anwar Sadat, in the excitement of the discussion, slapped former British Prime Minister Margaret Thatcher's knee. Most of us think of Mrs. Thatcher as properly British and fairly distant, but she was not offended. She correctly interpreted the gesture as acceptable in the Egyptian culture.

The Language of Space

The language of space is powerful. How close can we get to people; how distant should we be? Most of us never think about space; we intuitively know what the right distance is. Our use of space in communication is an excellent illustration that culture is learned and not inborn. Though our parents may have given us some verbal instruction on space, we have learned most of our behavior by observation. We simply do what is "right."

Arabs learn the same way, and so do Japanese, Mexicans, Russians, and members of all other cultures. The problem is that the acceptable use of space varies widely among cultures. What feels right for us may be totally offensive to someone else. Space in many ways becomes an extension of us, and we feel uncomfortable with people who play by different rules.

PRIVATE SPACE   Our private space is sacred, and we feel violated if someone invades that personal bubble. In the United States that bubble is about the length of an arm and we talk about arms-length relationships, meaning that we keep someone at a distance and don't allow them into our personal sphere. That bubble is a little bit smaller in France but larger in the Netherlands and Germany. It is even larger in Japan but much smaller in Latin countries and the Middle East (see Exhibit 6–3). The size of the private space is also influenced by social status, gender, age, and level of authority, further complicating the interpretation of space in communication.

Our attitude toward space reflects our attitude toward privacy. If we understand how people arrange their personal space at home, we will gain insight in how they communicate through space at work.

Northern Europeans cherish their privacy and arrange their dwellings accordingly. Property boundaries are carefully marked, and everyone ensures that they are not violated. Fences and hedges separate gardens. Traditionally, a German house had a fence around the front yard with a gate that was closed and in many cases locked. Over the past years, the front gate was increasingly left open, and today it frequently has been removed altogether. As more and more Germans acquired automobiles, dealing with the gate became inconvenient.

When Mr. Schubert came home from work, he would have to get out of the car, unlock the gate and open it, unlock the garage door and open it, get back into the car and drive the car into the garage. Then he would have to lock both the garage door and the front gate. This process became just too inconvenient; hence, the changing custom.

In Germany, elaborate laws detail rules on the use of the garden. Fences must be on the property line, and their height is regulated. In a country that is crowded and where sun is

EXHIBIT 6–3   Personal Space in Several Cultures

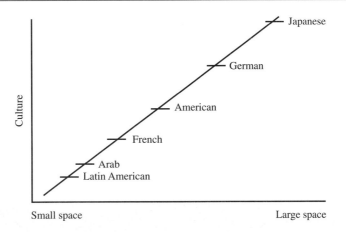

cherished, the fence must be low enough so as not to hinder the growth of vegetables in the neighbor's garden. Trees must be planted at a prescribed distance from the lot line so they don't shade the neighbor's property. Germans send a strong signal that they don't want anyone to invade their space. If necessary, legal regulations will enforce the cultural predisposition towards privacy.

In the German house itself, the emphasis on privacy also becomes obvious. For example, all rooms have doors with locks, and the doors are closed and often locked. It would be inconsiderate to enter someone's room without first knocking on the door and waiting for the invitation to come in. In the common areas, one may enter without knocking, but the doors are still closed. As more and more houses have central heat, the doors to the common living area tend to remain open, but bedroom and bathroom doors are always closed.

In contrast to Germany, houses in the United States may have fences or hedges surrounding the backyard, but the front yards are wide open and inviting. Doors tend to be open, an open invitation to come in. If someone wants to be alone, then the door may be closed.

In Japan, privacy is defined altogether differently from the United States and Germany. Japan is a crowded country, and space is costly; therefore, houses and apartments are smaller. Walls and doors are thin, traditionally made of wood and parchment paper. Sound carries easily. Yet, within this crowdedness, the Japanese are able to create their private sphere. The private bubble and the personal space are more a creation of the mind than an actual existence. Americans connect privacy with physical space, whereas the Japanese connect privacy with mental space.

Middle Eastern and Latin cultures also reflect their attitudes towards privacy and personal space in the way they arrange their houses. A house in the Middle East traditionally has few or no windows to the street; all windows open into an inner courtyard. The family is protected from the outside world by walling itself off in a realm of privacy. Within the house, however, personal space for the individual is often limited; family togetherness is emphasized. To remove oneself physically and insist on one's own space is not acceptable and is not easily tolerated. Individuals are first and foremost part of a family, and the living arrangement emphasizes that concept. Within the family space, men's and women's areas are also separated in Islamic homes. In many ways men and women dwell in the same compound, but they live separate lives in separate quarters.

OFFICE SPACE   Our attitudes towards private space are also carried over into our attitudes towards office space. Generally, cultures that value a big personal space value large and private offices. In cultures where personal distance is smaller, the size of the office is not as crucial. Japan does not quite fit into this pattern. The Japanese prefer a larger interpersonal distance, yet they tend seldom to have private offices. We must keep in mind, however, that the Japanese, as mentioned earlier, do not so much emphasize actual physical distance to attain privacy but rather mental distance. In addition, the emphasis on the group orientation in Japan carries more weight than any privacy consideration. The whole issue of office space in the case of Japan is influenced by other cultural values and considerations. The following examples illustrate that the arrangement of office space is a reflection of underlying cultural values.

In the United States the size of the office and its location are indicative of the business-person's success, importance, power, and status within the hierarchy. In a country where many offices do not have windows, windows become a status symbol. Top managers have their offices on top floors with plenty of windows. In a Midwestern university, for example, offices are assigned by seniority, and a goal of every professor is to ultimately have one of the rare outside offices with a window.

In addition to office size and location, furnishings also signify level of importance. A Midwestern insurance firm in the United States has three grades of wastebaskets. The kind of desk, desk lamp, art work, and plants employees can have in their work spaces is dictated by status and level of importance.

The French are horrified when they look at typical American offices with their artificial light. Both in France and Germany, every employee is entitled to a workplace with natural light. They are puzzled how human beings can work and concentrate in offices without natural light. Schools in Germany, by law, must have windows large enough that the square footage of the windows equals at least two-thirds of the square footage of the room. American schools without windows look like prisons to Europeans.

Office size and furnishings are also important in Europe. A manager who has a private office with a *Vorzimmer* (outer office) and a secretary is important, and everyone knows it. Similar to private houses, German office doors are closed. It would be unthinkable to just barge into an office without first knocking at the doors, both the boss's and the secretary's, and waiting for "*Herein*" (come in). An office is a private workplace that one does not enter uninvited.

French offices tend to reflect the cultural value of centralization. Just as France is centralized with every major road converging onto Paris, offices are spatially organized around the manager who is at the center. The manager is the controller and observer of everything going on in the office. Currently, most companies are headquartered in Paris. The top managers control all activities at headquarters, and headquarters in Paris controls all company activities across France. Most French people agree that anyone who wants to get ahead in this environment must move to Paris. Ambitious people are petrified at the idea of being "banished" to the provinces. The centralized office arrangement reflects historical developments and realities of France.

Office space in the Middle East and in Latin America can be quite different. Big multinationals in the Middle East and high technology oil firms have a more Western approach to office space, but the attitude in smaller and mid-sized Arab firms is quite different.

The Arab office is a meeting place. A businessperson thinks nothing of having several different persons in the office at the same time and doing business with them simultaneously. Westerners, who might be offended by the informality and lack of privacy and total attention may have a hard time coping, but the Arab businessman sees nothing wrong with the arrangement.

Two German women living with an Iraqi family for a summer had to see a doctor; one had an ear infection the other suffered from laryngitis. The family contacted a specialist, and the son of the host family accompanied the two women to interpret. The doctor had a long line of patients waiting outside the office, all of whom had applied for work at the Baghdad airport and needed vision and hearing examinations. The Germans and their friend were whisked past the line of people and taken directly into the office. The doctor, who had studied in Europe, was delighted to see them and interrupted the examination of a patient to serve tea to the new arrivals. He invited them to sit down and then finished the examination of the man. Next he examined the German women and gave them each a shot of penicillin. He asked them to stay longer and visit with him. During that time he continued his examination of the other patients, and nobody seemed offended (also see Chapter 3 on simultaneous performance of tasks).

This scene is unthinkable in North America or Europe. It is important to keep in mind that the patients were there for a routine check of vision and hearing and that they did not have to undress or discuss personal matters, but even so, a Western patient would expect total attention from the doctor and resent other people sitting in the examination room. Yet this is acceptable behavior in the Middle East and also in China.

Offices in the Middle East tend to be crowded. Importance is not necessarily reflected in the size and location of the office, and the typical American status perks may be meaningless. That does not mean, however, that there are no symbols to indicate the level of importance. Since in many ways status is conveyed by the importance and number of connections one has, a manager who has many visitors and many phone calls during your visit may show his importance that way.

Fred Brunell, a French manager, is visiting Ayub Rabah in his office in Amman, Jordan. They intend to discuss possible joint venture opportunities. They are still in the beginning stages and are trying to get to know each other and determine relative status, position, and power to negotiate. While Fred Brunell sits in the office, Ayub Rabah receives several phone calls, one from a friend in the government office for foreign investments to arrange an evening together, another from an old school friend who is a banker. The banker is discussing some financial arrangement. The phone conversations are personal and illustrate that Ayub Rabah is well connected and has clout. Fred Brunell is impressed by the prospect of working with someone who can get things moving. In a culture where connections are important, Ayub Rabah has shown that he is somebody. He has sent important signals to Fred Brunell, but it is up to Fred to interpret these signals in the context of doing business in Jordan.

Japanese offices also reflect cultural values. In Japan, the individual is expected to fit into the group and respect group goals and group norms. Harmony is an overriding principle. As a result, private offices in Japan are rare and reserved for upper managers, and even then, depending on the firm, managers may sit or work in the same area with their employees. A typical office arrangement puts file cabinets along the outside walls of the office. The employees sit in groups at large tables in the center of the room (see Exhibit 6–4). In many cases, these are regular tables rather than desks with drawers, and everything is out in the open. The employees are facing each other with the leader of the group seated at the head of the table. Unless the nature of the business requires a phone, individual employees typically do not have a phone at their work station.

EXHIBIT 6–4 Japanese Office Layout

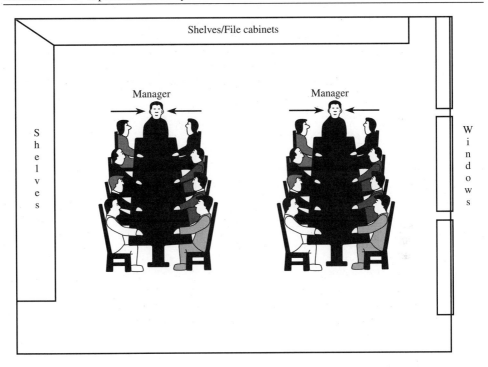

The Japanese believe this arrangement emphasizes the importance of the group and the need to work together. When an employee needs to discuss something with a co-worker from the same table or from another table in the room, they go to one of the tables near the file cabinets so as not to disturb the rest of the group.

From the Western viewpoint, with its emphasis on individuality and privacy, this arrangement seems oppressive. With everyone watching, one can't even use the phone without the rest of the group listening. And, of course, private phone conversations, such as calling the children when they get home from school or making social arrangements with friends, are out of the question. Many Westerners would resent this arrangement, seeing it as a lack of trust (also see Chapter 3).

Another typical arrangement of the Japanese office is to have everyone sit at individual tables or desks facing in the same direction. Sometimes the manager sits in the front of the room facing the employees, but in many cases the manager sits in the back, behind the employees (see Exhibit 6–5). Again, businesspeople from the United States or Canada would be uncomfortable with this arrangement and would feel as though someone were looking over their shoulder the whole time they were working. Japanese, who are accustomed to the group watching and to being expected to follow norms, have far fewer problems with this arrangement. At work, the employee is first and foremost a member of the team rather than an individual with individual rights to privacy and territory.

EXHIBIT 6–5   Japanese Office Layout

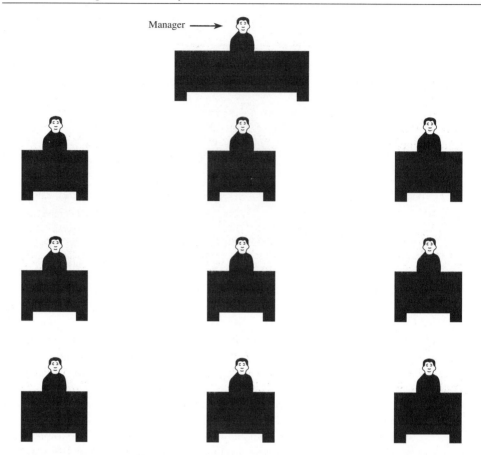

Manager ⟶

If the Japanese manager has a private office, it often has windows to the large common work area, where the manager can look out at the employees but the employees can also look into the manager's office.

The Japanese office layout sends a strong symbolic message: "We are in this together." The welfare of the whole is more important than the concerns of individuals. While behind the scenes there may be quite a bit of maneuvering for individual recognition, on the surface harmony rules and everyone works for the common good.

As a result, the furnishings in Japanese offices are not as important as in U.S. offices. Even in big companies, the office decor usually looks rather modest by Western standards. Businesspeople from the United States, used to more lavish furnishings, may misinterpret the signals and question the importance or profitability of the Japanese business they are dealing with.

PUBLIC SPACE   The way people arrange and use public spaces also reflects cultural attitudes towards space and privacy. Businesspeople from the United States going to Japan or China often comment how crowded the cities are and that there just is not enough breathing space. That may be true by U.S. standards, but the Japanese and Chinese may interpret the conditions differently. Two people from different cultures may look at the same space, yet they may come to different conclusions as the following example illustrates.

Aki Hayashi, a Japanese visiting professor at a university in Illinois, was going to a convention in New Orleans. His American colleagues were all flying, but he was going to take the train. He wanted to see something of the country. Brian Ober, one of his American friends, warned him that the train would be very crowded and that he would not like it at all. Mr. Ober was very surprised when Professor Hayashi told him that his compartment on the train had been very nice and so spacious.

Numerous articles have illustrated the prime example of crowdedness in Japan: rush hour on the subway in Tokyo. They usually show a picture of a person whose job it is to push people into the train so that the doors can close. (This phenomenon has been greatly exaggerated in the American press, however. In 1989 only two stations in all of Tokyo had pushers, and only during rush hours.) When looking at these pictures one wonders how the throngs of people fit with the cultural emphasis on personal distance and private space. How do the Japanese cope with that? Many Japanese do not like the crowded conditions, and increasingly people are moving from Tokyo back to their hometowns to have more space.

Most Japanese have found a way of coping with the overcrowded public space of the subway system. In this environment, filled with people pushing and shoving one another, the Japanese riders each become an island. Each is alone as long as he does not acknowledge any of the other people; the others do not really exist in his space. As pointed out earlier, space becomes a psychological phenomenon. The Chinese deal with the crowded public space in similar fashion.

People from the United States carry their idea of individuality over into public spaces. They consider it their right to walk and play on the grass in the park. After all, it is their park; their taxes paid for it. Government buildings in the United States are open to the public. Anyone can go into the Capitol in Washington or the various state capitols. In no other country is the residence of the president open to the public. Scloss Bellevue, # 10 Downing Street, and the Elysee Palace are all closed to the public. In the United States, right to access is considered important. In contrast, ordinary citizens are not allowed entry into the new Shanghai City Hall. It is where the mayor and vice mayors, as well as all the key officials for the city, work. Ordinary people have no business there, and are turned away by security officers.

The Germans organize their public spaces like their private lives. *Alles muß seine Ordnung haben* (everything must have its order). Order is an overriding concern, and detailed provisions are made to guarantee that order. Germans tend not to have problems with this control because they grew up with an emphasis on order. As a result, parks tend to be clean and neat; the grass is not trampled down. This order is achieved through the use of numerous signs; *Betreten des Rasens verboten* (It is forbidden to step on the grass) is typical and strictly enforced. For most Germans there is nothing wrong with the content or the tone of the rules, most of which are issued as clear orders in a negative tone. The emphasis is on clarity rather than friendliness. However, during the last decade the universal acceptance of the tight regulation of public spaces began breaking down. This change in behavior indicates that the nonverbal language of space can change over time. The study of nonverbal communication must, therefore, be an ongoing activity.

Germans tend to be very aggressive in crowds. The British queue (line up) at the bus, in stores, and at theaters. Theater-goers in London, for example, follow strict unwritten rules on queuing to get tickets; it is expected that everyone follow the unwritten honor system. Germans, in contrast, form throngs and push and shove without any order at all, and they are surprised at the voluntary order of the British. One evening during rush hour, two friends, a German and an Englishman, wanted to take the *Tube*, subway, in London. As they approached the station, they encountered a long line of people waiting to buy tickets. As the Englishman turned towards the end of the line, the German said, "Waiting in line is going to take forever; let's just get to the front." The Englishman was horrified and explained that such a move was absolutely unthinkable and could not be done. The German, in turn, was amazed at how fast the orderly line moved; waiting in line did not take so long after all.

In public spaces Germans also emphasize their rights. Individuals are expected to protect and insist on their rights. Children must be prepared for a rough and cruel world; therefore, they must practice insisting on their rights from an early age.

A German woman who had lived in the United States for many years was visiting her hometown and took her two young children to a *Schulfest*, a school carnival. When her children wanted to ride the merry-go-round, they waited on the side until the merry-go-round came to a stop. Even though they had been in front of the other children, they were swept aside and did not get on. The same scene repeated itself several times. German parents were saving places for other children or they pushed their own children on. Finally, the visitor used her elbows too and got her children on the ride.

In the United States this whole scenario would have been entirely different. First of all, all children would have waited in an orderly line. Everyone would have taken one turn and would have been expected to get off after one ride. If the child wanted another ride, he would have had to go to the end of the line again. Everyone would have understood that the procedure had to be fair to everyone and not be based on bullying.

As conditions in big cities become more crowded, traditional etiquette and rules of acceptable verbal and nonverbal communication behavior may face major challenges. The pushing and shoving on Japanese subways, as pointed out earlier, does not fit the traditional value of personal distance and harmony.

Japan is not the only country that must deal with a breakdown of traditional behaviors. In Mexico City, for example, the subways are overcrowded with commuters on weekdays during rush hour, and with families on weekends. Traditionally, unrelated Mexican men and women do not mix in public. Particularly, unmarried women are protected by their families to preserve their virtue. In this traditional environment, men are seen as protectors of women, and women are expected to behave modestly and shy away from public places. In modern Mexico, many women, young and old, married and single, have jobs. They must get to and from work on their own without any chaperon or male protector. In the past, young women moving about on their own were suspected of dishonorable behavior. Men knew that such women did not require the same courteous treatment as their own sisters. Today the lines are blurred, and many men do not know how to behave. In this case, the changing social environment has had a profound influence on nonverbal communication. During rush hour many female riders were being molested by men in overcrowded subway cars. The solution came by separating women and men on the subway during rush hour. Now men are not allowed into cars reserved for women, and women who go into the men's cars do so at their own risk. The crowded conditions encouraged nonverbal behavior that was not acceptable under normal circumstances. As the environment of a culture changes, society must reevaluate its standards of nonverbal communication and develop safeguards to protect the standards.

Behavior in public spaces is carried over into offices and business practices. One cannot separate general cultural behavior from business behavior. The two go together. How we approach people and how we deal with space and issues of privacy have deep cultural roots. We may not agree with or like what others do. That is not the issue; the point is that we must understand what the others are doing and why they are doing it.

Appearance

The way we dress also communicates. Dressing according to custom and expectations shows respect for form and establishes a foundation for future dealings. Subtle aspects of dress can let people know where one is from.

Two professors from the United States were sitting in the office for foreign trade in former East Germany waiting for an appointment. A businessman entered and sat down, obviously also waiting for an appointment. Without having spoken to the newcomer or without having heard him speak, the two professors looked at each other and agreed, another American. How did they know? The button-down collar, the style of the suit and the wingtip shoes were clear signals. They were right; he was American.

When examining appearance in intercultural communication, one must ask a number of questions, such as

- What is appropriate business dress for men and women in a given culture?
- What is the difference in attire when doing business in one's own culture and doing business with another culture?
- What degree of importance is attached to one's attire?
- What are the penalties for inappropriate attire?

In some ways, business dress for men is universal around the globe, yet there are differences. The suit, the dress shirt, the tie are generally acceptable. But the styles may vary widely. Europeans tend to wear suits that are more tailored and youthful than businessmen in the United States do. The severe business suit, sometimes described as the IBM-look, is disappearing in Europe. The Japanese, on the other hand, remain conservative. They tend to wear either grey or dark blue suits with white shirts. Arabs may wear Western suits, but when doing business in Arab countries they usually wear traditional dress, the white flowing robe and the headdress. In Southeast Asia, the European business suit, with its origin in cool and cloudy England, is giving way to a new uniform, slacks and a short-sleeved shirt worn outside the pants with collar and attached belt. However, when a businessman from this part of the world travels to the United States or Japan for business, he will wear a conservative business suit.

For women dress is more complicated. Businesswomen from the United States tend to wear suits. Even though the suits have softer lines and are less masculine and dresses have become more acceptable, business dress for American women in managerial positions is still more severe than in Western Europe.

A German student, after finishing her MBA in the United States and looking for a job in her native Germany, discovered very quickly that her American business suit was totally inappropriate for interviews. It was too severe and too conservative. No young businesswomen was wearing that kind of suit. A short skirt with a stylish blouse was the norm.

French female students going back to France from the United States make the same comment. They too find that French businesswomen dress more femininely than their American counterparts. These returning students feel uncomfortable in the typical American business dress; however, they also point out that while women in French or German business tend to be dressed more fashionably, very few are in managerial positions. That, of course, is another question, a matter of tactics perhaps. If women want to succeed in business, they have to dress and look the part.

In Japan, women often work as Office Ladies serving tea and greeting customers. They do not have to worry about what to wear; the company provides them with a uniform, usually a conservative suit with a blouse, white gloves, and a hat (also see Chapter 1).

In most cultures, dress also identifies a person as belonging to a specific group and having a certain status. Dress can offend, but it can also protect. With the growing assaults on foreigners in Germany, the Japanese issued a dress code for after-business hours for all Japanese employees in Germany. Immediately, all Japanese had to wear dark conservative suits with white shirt, tie, and dress shoes at *all* times to establish them as businesspeople and distinguish them from other Asians who might be in the country illegally and involved in illegal dealings. The business dress, it was assumed, would identify and therefore protect the person as merely doing business in Germany rather than wanting to immigrate illegally.

With the growing emphasis on comfort and leisure time activities, attitudes towards appearance and dress are changing in many cultures. In many cases, young people around the globe have more in common with young people from other cultures than with the older generation of their own culture when it comes to dress. Jeans, tennis shoes, and sweatshirts are invading the former place of formal business attire.

A few years ago, Germans were very conservative in their dress, both in business and in their private lives. It was expected that one dressed up for the office and on Sundays. Every German man from age 14 on owned a black suit to be worn for weddings, funerals, and other important occasions. During final examinations in the Gymnasium (high school) and in the university, both men and women were expected to wear black suits to acknowledge the importance of the occasion. Much of that has changed today. The young people are very informal, and many go to interviews in jeans and tennis shoes. Even doctors applying for positions in hospitals show up in faded jeans for their interviews. While older Germans may bemoan the casual dress as a sign of lack of respect and the general decline and downfall of behavioral norms, young people are enjoying the more relaxed attire.

If a person from a more casual culture with emphasis on comfort does business with someone older from a conservative and formal culture, dress can become a serious issue.

A group of professors from the United States attending a four-week seminar in Taipei were moaning about the heat and the lack of air conditioning. The seminar leader, a Chinese woman professor, at first did not say anything; she simply assumed that everyone agreed on what appropriate dress was for the seminar lectures and company visits. When some of the professors, however, started showing up in shorts and T-shirts, she asked them to dress up, meaning suit, shirt, and tie. The Americans immediately tried to negotiate down the expected level of formality. As a Chinese woman she felt very uncomfortable telling the mostly male group what to do, but finally she had to be direct. The group was to visit Chiang Kai-shek's tomb, and there was no compromise. She ordered suit, dress shirt, and tie, and the Americans finally gave in.

Silence

Many people connect communicating with doing something—verbally, nonverbally, or both. Communication means action, such as encoding a message, decoding the message, sending a message, sending feedback. At first glance, silence does not indicate action, yet communication through silence plays an important role in all cultures. The importance of silence as a communication tool and the interpretation of silence vary from culture to culture, but all cultures use silence at times to get a point across.

The differences in the use of silence can be best examined by looking at high- and low-context cultures.

SILENCE IN LOW-CONTEXT CULTURES   In low-context cultures where ideas are explicitly encoded into words, silence is often interpreted as the absence of communication. It is *down time*. Silence means the act of actively worded communication has stopped.

Yet even in low-context cultures silence is not necessarily without meaning. When someone is silent after being asked a question, the silence is an answer. The English phrase, "The silence was deafening," describes this interpretation. When someone falls silent in conversation, another person may well ask, "What's wrong?" The silence does communicate a message. It may indicate that the receiver of the message did not hear the message, is angry at the message, needs time to think, or is embarrassed. Usually, low-context cultures view silence as communication gone wrong. To them it indicates a rupture has occurred in the communication process.

Phrases such as *Reden ist Silber, schweigen ist Gold* (speaking is silver; being silent is gold) seem to contradict the view of silence as being negative; however, when given a choice, people in low-context cultures tend to choose speaking over being silent. Silence is ambiguous; it must be interpreted, and the interpretation of silence is more difficult than the interpretation of words. Silence does not fit with the low-context culture emphasis on precision and clarity.

For this reason, people in low-context cultures generally are uncomfortable with silence. They often feel responsible for starting a conversation or keeping it going, even with strangers. Passengers on a train that makes an unscheduled stop in the countryside, for example, may start a conversation because they feel uncomfortable just sitting there.

SILENCE IN HIGH-CONTEXT CULTURES   High-context cultures have a different attitude towards the use of silence. Perhaps the most obvious example is Japan, although other Asian countries share the Japanese attitude about silence. The Japanese believe that silence is preferable to conversation. It is through silence that one can discover the truth inside oneself. Contemplation and meditation take place in silence. Buddha taught that words make truth untrue, and there is a view in Japanese society that words contaminate understanding. Reading another person's inner core, a kind of communication without words, can only take place in silence. Speech distracts from true understanding. This attitude towards the use of silence can become a serious stumbling block in the progress of negotiations between businesspeople from Japan and the United States. Most of the discussion in Japanese negotiations is in groups, and much is said through silence, facial expressions, and body gestures among the Japanese team.

Silence to the Japanese is not empty. While Westerners typically view silence as gaps in conversation, the Japanese believe silence is part of conversation. In a crowded country, silence evokes space; a person can be in his or her own realm through silence, even though surrounded by others. Japanese speakers are comfortable with silence in communication and do not hurry to fill it up with speech.

SUMMARY

This chapter has examined the major aspects of nonverbal signals in intercultural communication. Much of what people say in all cultures they say without words or in addition to words. In many cases the nonverbal symbols support the spoken word, but they can also contradict what is being said.

Paralanguage lies between verbal and nonverbal communication. This chapter has looked at

- *Vocal qualifiers.* The term refers to volume, pitch, and intonation. Different cultures use different vocal qualifiers.
- *Nonverbal business conventions* in face-to-face encounters.
    - Eye contact. Conventions relating to eye contact are related to position in the hierarchy. Eye contact has implications for perceptions of honesty and importance of privacy.
    - Facial expressions. Facial expressions have different meaning in different cultures. The smile can express friendliness or embarrassment. A frown can be an indication of anger or doubt.
    - Gestures. Head movements, arm movements, and posture communicate a message to the other side.

- Timing in spoken exchanges. Our timing behavior reflects the importance of equality, hierarchy, and gender relationships.
  - Touching. Cultures have different conventions for touching in social and business situations. Touching is typically related to status, gender, and seniority.
- *The language of space.* We communicate through our use of private, office, and public space.
- *Appearance.* Dress sends signals relating to respect.
- *Silence.* High-context and low-context cultures differ in their interpretation of silence. In low-context cultures silence is frequently seen as absence of communication, whereas in high-context cultures, silence is an important communication channel.

The interpretation of the nonverbal language is complicated by the fact that different groups within a culture often use different nonverbal signals. To be successful in interpreting the nonverbal language of a culture, you need to go beyond memorizing do's and don'ts of touching, using space, making eye contact, and using facial expressions and gestures. To be successful in reading the nonverbal symbols, you must understand the cultural values that give rise to a specific nonverbal language.

NOTES

1. Edward T. Hall, "The Silent Language in Overseas Business," *Harvard Business Review* 38, no. 3, (1960), pp. 87–95.
2. David Victor, *International Business Communication,* (New York: HarperCollins, 1992).
3. Ibid.
4. Ibid.
5. In-ah Ha, unpublished paper presented at the IAIR inaugural conference, Kent State University, April 1999
6. D. Tanner, *You Just Don't Understand,* (New York: Ballantine Books, 1992).

CHAPTER SEVEN

Variable Rules of Engagement

The U.S. company Homecrafts was in the process of buying the Swiss firm Alpine Treasures. The talks had been going on for some time. David Goldstein, negotiating for Homecrafts, was getting rather frustrated. Several months ago it had looked as if the deal could be signed within days, but then things just slowed down. David had invested a lot of time and effort and would like to close the transaction.

When they first met, Alpine Treasure's owner Louis Semar seemed surprised that someone as young as David would be in charge of negotiating a transaction of such magnitude. Mr. Semar was used to working with people about his age who had proven themselves for a number of years. How could a young person have the experience? David, on the other hand, thought that Louis was a bit stuffy and old-fashioned. The use of last names and the formality of the interaction made him feel uneasy. But in spite of the differences, they informally agreed to conclude the deal. David E-mailed headquarters to announce that the deal would go through shortly. He was excited and figured that the conclusion of this purchase would be a step towards his next promotion.

When they met to work out details, David assumed they knew each other well enough to do away with the last names. But when he opened the discussion with, "Well, Louis what do you think?" he could not understand why Mr. Semar addressed him as Mr. Goldstein. What was his problem? David simply could not understand why Mr. Semar was so distant. He had invited Mr. Semar to eat

with him on numerous occasions and he had inquired about his family and hobbies, but Mr. Semar remained distant. He answered all the questions politely but never gave more personal information than necessary. David considered himself a friendly guy who took pride in his ability to make people feel at ease, but in this case, nothing seemed to work.

At the same time, Mr. Semar got rather frustrated with this pushy American kid. Why was he always inquiring into his private life? And the young man kept up the pressure to sell, to convince him that he should take the money and retire. David Goldstein was young enough to be his son, and here he acted as if he was a close friend. It seemed that David had no personal commitments to anything but his job and money. Mr. Semar could not bear to think that his life's work would come down to a cold business transaction.

After another round of discussions, when David thought surely things would work out, Louis Semar withdrew even more. He had built this company. The offer was good financially; he stood to make a lot of money. But that was only part of it. His heart was in that firm, and to sell out, and to Americans at that, just did not seem to be right. In addition, he was disturbed by talk of reorganization and changes in employment practices. The firm employed about 100 people, most from the little town where the company was located. He knew these people; he had gone to school with them. He relied on them, and they trusted him. What would happen once the Americans took over? David could not understand these concerns. Mr. Semar would be very well off; he could retire in comfort and do whatever he wanted to do. In his opinion this indecision on Mr. Semar's part was simply ridiculous. After all, this was a business, not a family affair. And from a business viewpoint this was the right thing to do.

David was willing to offer more money. In his opinion the Swiss firm would be a great addition to Homecrafts. He decided to approach Mr. Semar one more time and put on some pressure to settle the purchase. He carefully laid out his approach; he prepared charts detailing the financial benefits. He pulled all the arguments together showing why this was an excellent business deal that would benefit both sides.

Mr. Semar listened politely. He did not disagree with anything David said, but he asked for some more time to consider. Several weeks went by, and David did not hear from Louis again. As he began to realize that Louis Semar would never sell, he started to think what he might have done differently to make it easier for the Swiss owner to sell his stake in the company.

In previous chapters we have examined how various cultures communicate verbally and nonverbally and how they organize their messages. In this chapter we will examine how people establish relationships. As the opening scenario to this chapter illustrates, people from different cultures have different ideas on what is important and who is important. They have different ideas on who has authority to make decisions. As a result, the rules of establishing relationships and working together differ as well.

RESPECT FOR AUTHORITY AND THE STRUCTURING OF MESSAGES

Different cultures use different symbols to show respect towards authority. As pointed out before, those signs are neither correct nor incorrect; they are different. They are learned, and they may change over time.

Signals of Respect

The nonverbal signals for respect can be obvious or more subtle. For example, as discussed earlier, consider the Japanese bow. The depth of the bow clearly indicates who ranks higher. The subordinate must bow lower, and if the wrong person bows lower, then the ritual will be repeated until everything is right. It can be an amusing scene with both sides continuing to bow when one party is a Westerner who does not understand the rules of the game.

In some cultures, people of lower status kneel in front of superiors and authority figures or even prostrate themselves in front of rulers. People from the United States with their notions of equality may have trouble with those types of rituals. A man from the United States who worked in the Peace Corps in Nigeria married a Nigerian woman. As part of the ritual in seeking to marry the woman, he was expected to prostrate himself in front of the woman's grandfather who was the village chief. Although those traditional signs of respect for authority may have vanished in cities and urban centers, it helps to be aware of expected behaviors towards authority both in social and business relationships.

If a person expects certain signs of respect, he or she may be upset if those expectations are not met. At best the situation may be awkward; at worst it may lead to tensions or even open hostilities. The following examples involving Queen Elizabeth of Great Britain did not result in an international crisis, but they do illustrate the point.

When Queen Elizabeth II visited the United States, people who were to meet her were given detailed and careful instructions on how to behave on the occasion. Protocol prescribes how to address royalty and how to walk and talk in the presence of royalty. This carefully choreographed ritual was rudely shattered when a woman in Washington, D.C., pushed protocol aside and hugged the Queen. The Queen was gracious, but it was an obvious breach of etiquette that only "barbarian" foreigners would commit. The American woman was not disrespectful, but clearly her way of showing respect and welcome was different from the ancient tradition of keeping physical distance from superiors.

When Queen Elizabeth visited Sydney, Australia, in 1991 as the honored guest for the country's 150th anniversary celebration, the Prime Minister, Paul Keating, put his arm around her when ushering her into a room. The gesture was seen around the world on television. Mr. Keating had previously publicly stated that he believed Australia should be a republic and no longer accept the queen as Head of State. Throughout Britain, Australia, and New Zealand the gesture was discussed widely in the context of Keating's viewpoints. The British tabloids saw it as unforgivable rudeness, but many Australians saw it as the behavior of a strong, independent leader. The controversy continued long after the event.

In both examples, the people who "violated" the expected ritual of showing respect came from egalitarian societies that believe in individual achievement rather than the inherited power of a monarchy, and both, in their way, expressed that they considered themselves equal as human beings.

In another example, Suzuki of Japan and General Motors built a joint venture plant in Ontario, Canada, to manufacture a car called Cami. During the construction of Japanese-style apartments for some Japanese engineers, the Japanese project manager went to the surrounding farms to apologize in advance for any inconvenience the neighbors might experience from the construction noise and heavy equipment. He knocked at the door of a farmhouse across the road, carrying a large box, beautifully wrapped, that contained a cake. He introduced himself with a bow and explained to the farmer's wife what his visit was about. Then he presented the package. This was all perfectly within his cultural tradition. The farmer's wife was Hungarian. She responded from *her* cultural tradition—she threw her arms around the surprised Japanese man and hugged him.

Positions of Authority

In all cultures certain positions and professions enjoy a high level of authority. In many societies medical doctors carry prestige because they can help the sick. In some cultures poets and scholars demand respect. In Asian societies teachers carry authority. They are considered wise, and their teachings are not questioned. A Korean student would not think of questioning his professor. The professor is older and more experienced and, therefore, must know. These attitudes are also true for China, Japan, and most of Southeast Asia. Teachers are persons who command respect as illustrated in the following example.

A professor from the United States had attended a four-week seminar on Chinese business culture in Taiwan. At the airport, things got hectic, and she was worried about missing her plane. The line for the security check was long and moved very slowly. On her jacket she carried the Chinese badge identifying her as a professor and member of a special group. When she asked whether the x-rays were safe for film in her carry-on luggage and voiced concern over missing her plane, the official looked at her, saw the badge, and passed the entire carry-on luggage around the checking system. He said to her as she passed, "Good-bye, Teacher." She did not receive such treatment upon arrival in San Francisco!

When doing business with people from other cultures you need to find out what kinds of people and what professions are accorded special respect. Their views may carry more weight, and their opinions may be asked before decisions are made. A senior manager in Japan, for example, is not just considered a manager by the new recruit. The new recruit will also look up to the senior manager as his *sensei* (teacher).

In many cultures authority figures are not to be interrupted when speaking, and their opinions carry a lot of weight. The conditioning starts very early. Businesspeople must be aware of the implications of this cultural value on business decision. A Thai job applicant who seems quiet is not necessarily wrong for the job. He may simply reflect his culture's acceptable behavior towards someone who is in charge. To ask many questions or speak a lot during an interview might be interpreted as arrogance and egotism and disqualify the candidate with a Thai firm in Thailand. An interviewer from the United States, on the other hand, may interpret the behavior as lack of drive and ambition. Unless the job applicant is familiar with employment communication in the United States, he is at a disadvantage. At the same time, unless the interviewer is familiar with the behavioral patterns of the applicant's cultural background, the interviewer may miss a good employee.

In contrast to Asians, businesspeople in the United States are expected to be assertive. While authority figures in the United States carry more clout and typically set the tone and speed of interchange, employees can interrupt and give their own opinions and comments. Children are raised to be assertive and to discuss options freely. Likewise employees are encouraged to speak their mind. In the interview process for a job in the United States, for example, individuals are aware of their accomplishments and will emphasize their possible contributions to the firm. Job applicants are expected to present themselves to the potential employer and highlight their potential contributions to the success of the firm.

A business professor from New Zealand commented that American business communication texts on the job search are not usable in New Zealand. The letters come across as too assertive and egotistic. New Zealanders, as well as Canadians, prefer a less pushy approach. A job applicant states his or her accomplishments and skills and lets them speak for themselves. "To sell yourself" is traditionally inappropriate in these cultures. In the future it will be interesting to see how the growing globalization of business will affect the traditional cultural communication patterns. For example, business students from Indonesia point out that they tend to use an American approach when they apply for jobs with an American multinational and a more traditional Indonesian approach when applying for a job with an Indonesian firm. This development also illustrates that international businesspeople need to distinguish traditional cultural behavior from "international" business behavior, which is influenced by traditional culture but also by international business culture.

Dress as Symbol of Authority

As we have said elsewhere, the standard business dress around the globe is the suit, shirt, and tie for men and some sort of suit or dress for women. That sounds easy enough; yet there are enough variations indicating authority that businesspeople must be aware of local customs and traditions.

Tom Sides is flying to Tokyo for a business meeting. He will meet a potential joint venture partner for the first time. The flight from Chicago is about 13 hours, long and exhausting. Tom has packed several suits, shirts, and ties in his luggage. But for the long flight he wants to be comfortable, so he wears jeans and a sweatshirt and tennis shoes. He knows that someone from the Japanese firm will meet him at Narita airport, but surely that person will understand the need to relax on a long flight. Kyuofumi Katsuki, who meets him, does not comment on Tom's dress, but Tom is beginning to wonder whether he did the right thing when he sees Mr. Katsuki's formal business attire even though it is the weekend. Tom is getting a sense that his casual dress may have eroded his authority and credibility as a business partner.

When traveling, businesspeople from the United States tend to emphasize comfort and practical clothes. The Japanese partners may, however, wonder how to read someone who is so set on personal comfort that business etiquette is put second. The formality of dress is also crucial in Taiwan. Not to dress appropriately, which is to say conservatively, is easily interpreted as lack of interest and disrespect for the *person with whom you are meeting* and one's own authority (also see Chapter 4 on business form).

You show respect and sincerity by the way you dress and by respecting certain rules of appearance of the host culture. That does not mean you have to adopt the local dress, but it does mean you should adapt your clothes to the customs of the host culture. This can present a particular issue for women in positions of authority because rules for appropriate dress for women can vary widely across cultures. In Arab countries, even in the less fundamentalist ones, women are expected to dress modestly. Mini-skirts, sleeveless blouses, sleeveless dresses, tight skirts, and tight dresses would not be considered appropriate. A woman who wants to do business in the Middle East must be aware of the basic rules and make sure that she does not undermine her credibility and authority, not to mention insult her business partner. Offensive dress can easily lead to embarrassment and loss of status.

A university official in Malaysia invited a visiting professor from Sweden and her teenage daughter to a formal lunch. The arrangement was for the daughter to meet the host, the host's wife, and her mother at the restaurant. The daughter arrived wearing a modest but sleeveless dress. The host was extremely gracious, ushered his guests to seats, sat with the group until everyone had ordered, arranged for the payment, and then departed and sat elsewhere for lunch. Even though his wife was there, he could not eat lunch in the company of an undressed woman. Eating with the guests under these circumstances would have not only embarrassed him but would also undermine his professional standing and authority.

In a sense it is easier for women to choose appropriate dress in Afghanistan than in more liberal Islamic countries because the dress rules in Afghanistan are spelled out very clearly. Arms, legs, and hair *must* be covered in public. There is no room for variations. The rules in other countries may be much more vague and less official. In Taiwan, for example, women may wear slacks, but they should stay away from sleeveless blouses. There is no law, but it is simply not done by people in positions of authority. Two women professors from the United States who attended a seminar felt very uncomfortable wearing their sundresses and decided on their own that this was not appropriate attire for sight-seeing and definitely unacceptable for visiting businesses and government offices.

Businesspeople must be particularly sensitive to dress in other cultures because of the often negative image that tourists have created. For example, Westerners often assume that their leisure dress is appropriate everywhere. Many come in shorts to visit churches and museums. Hordes of tourists flock to the beaches of Greece, Sri Lanka, or Morocco and promptly go topless or entirely nude. After all, the tourists have the money, which they suppose gives them a right to do whatever they want to do including disregarding local customs and norms of behavior. At best that kind of behavior shows insensitivity, and at worst cultural imperialism. In no case does it foster mutual respect and understanding. In fact, it may undermine the credibility of a businessperson even if that particular person is sensitive to cultural attitudes towards dress. As a result, businesspeople, in addition to doing the business at hand, may also have to overcome negative cultural images created by mass tourism.

POWER DISTANCE AND SYMBOLS OF POWER AND AUTHORITY

According to the work of the Dutch researcher Hofstede, power distance in the United States is comparatively small. That means that, true to a democratic society, Americans are less tolerant of inequalities in power than people from cultures with high power distance. Cultures with a smaller power distance are more horizontal, less hierarchical, and less authoritarian than cultures with high power distance. Understanding where a culture ranks on the power distance scale can be helpful when dealing with a businessperson from another culture. The differences in power are expressed in many different ways, some obvious and some more hidden.

Tone and Behavior of Power and Authority

In spite of all claims to democracy and equality, symbols of power are everywhere in U.S. businesses. The size and location of the office and the type of furniture indicate power. An employee entering the office of a powerful manager will read the nonverbal signals and act accordingly. Plants, real wood furniture, and original art work all spell out a higher position in the U.S. context.

While the person in power in many ways controls the interaction, the position of power also brings with it an obligation to be gracious. In many cultures, the subordinate is expected to remain standing when entering the office of a superior as sign of respect; the gracious host is expected to offer a seat. Letting the subordinate stand during the discussion while the superior is seated indicates that he is busy and would not like to be disturbed, or that he might not consider the matter or the person important enough to engage in a discussion. Any particular meaning will depend on the context. If a boss whom you have known for many years does not invite you to sit as you enter, you know how to read the signal. The unfamiliar is more difficult to read, specifically if you deal with someone from a different culture.

At the end of a meeting in the United States, the superior will send the message that the discussion is over by standing up. The subordinate will get up and leave after the appropriate leave-taking ritual. In cultures where hospitality is important, it may be impolite for the host to send signals that a get-together is over. In that case it may be the guest's duty to announce his or her leaving. The host then will press him to stay, but the guest who knows what is expected will politely decline. This is a typical ritual in Arab countries. The difficulty for a foreigner is to know what the right time is and how to read the invitation to stay a little longer.

Businesspeople in the United States, used to a more egalitarian society, prefer a collegial to an authoritarian tone in business dealings. This is made easier by the fact that modern English, in contrast to many other languages, does not distinguish between a familiar form and formal form of address and that most people after a short time call each other by first name.

A friendly and considerate tone is important in business communication in the United States, but clarity is the overriding goal. If there is any concern that a pleasant tone might cloud the meaning, U.S. businesspeople opt for clarity. The major goal is to get the meaning across. The purpose of Western communication is the transfer of meaning and the establishment of rational and logical relationships between ideas. To assure that the message is clear, businesspeople from the United States may use many words and lots of examples, typical characteristics of a low-context culture. Ideas are encoded explicitly.

Germans have a tendency to establish their authority by giving very clear, precise, and often blunt directions. Germans tend to spell everything out; nothing is left to chance, and the language is very precise and definitive.

A gymnastics school in the south of Germany ran summer programs for teachers from other European countries. Most of the participants came from England, and all participants stayed in the residence hall. In the opening session the director of the school welcomed everyone and then proceeded to announce the rules that everyone would be expected to follow. She asserted her authority by the tone and words she used. She gave strict guidelines on expected behavior in the residence hall, which kinds of linens were acceptable, when to use the showers, what to wear for the gymnastics sessions, and so on. Her comments were packed with *verboten, nicht erlaubt, Sie müssen* (forbidden, not allowed, you must). The leader of the English group had to translate the comments for the English participants. It was remarkable to see what she did. In her translation all the words such as *must, don't,* and *forbidden* became *it would be nice if, you might want to, please consider,* and the like. She never once commented on the tone, but she certainly changed the tone of the message for her audience. The regulations were made palatable to people who were not used to being ordered around by an authority.

In German business, managers have a remarkable authority. They are in charge of their departments, and interference from outsiders is not common and not easily accepted. Employees generally accept the authority of managers and don't argue. As long as the law is followed, Germans are often very willing to do as told.

Titles are important in Germany, and they are used. The distinction between *du* (you) and *sie* (you), the familiar and formal address, and the use of last names further position people much more clearly in the hierarchy than in the United States. People know their place, and they want to find out what someone else's place is in business and in society at large. Companies, for example, regularly ask on employment applications about the profession and place of employment of the applicant's parents and siblings. While accomplishments are important, family status and connections also demand respect.

The Japanese like to point out that theirs is a society without class distinctions; however they also emphasize that ranks and levels of society are very important. The individual is clearly subordinated to the common goals of the group. Indeed, Japanese use the word *harmony* whenever possible when describing their relationships. Clarity, so important to Westerners, is not the overriding issue. If clarity might cause loss of face or weaken harmony, harmony is considered more important. A superior will not openly criticize a subordinate, he will not emphasize his superior status, and he will not issue directives with *must, will,* or *shall.* The subordinate is supposed to understand the situation and accept his or her place in the hierarchy. This, of course, requires tuning into the fine points of cultural discourse and a sensitive reading of nonverbal messages. The power distance is definitely present, but it is seldom verbalized. As is typical for high-context cultures, Japanese businesses assume that people know their place and will act accordingly, but the reality may be somewhat more complicated.

First of all, there is a tremendous difference between smaller and larger firms. Small, family-owned firms can be very authoritarian. There is no question in anyone's mind who is in charge. The owner tends to make decisions and expects that they are carried out. The system of consensus, typically known as *the* Japanese decision-making model, is practiced more in larger firms. But even in the large firms someone is indeed in charge, the hierarchy is enforced, and the final decision is often the boss's. It is the discussion process leading up to the announced decision that gives the impression of equal participation. Everyone gets an equal chance to express his opinion, but the discussion is often aimed at bringing everyone around to the boss's opinion in the end. Additionally, the process is influenced by the history of the firm. If the firm is bureaucratic and run by managers, the power of groups is larger. In a firm such as Sony, which has a distinct individual founder, the imprint of the founder is stronger. While groups are important and while harmony is important, the original founder has a much more active role and more say in all company decisions. People at all levels listen to what Mr. Sony has to say.

In typical Japanese fashion, power and respect are a part of *amae* and reciprocity. Managers and employees know that they depend on each other, and they are willing to accept the dependency. The relationship is very similar to a parent-child relationship. The child needs the parent, but at the same time the parent needs the child to fulfill the role of parent. The relationship is a complex web of obligations that is central to Japanese interpersonal relations, including business relationships. The firm guarantees a job and decent wages; the employee promises top performance. Each knows that the other has a certain amount of power, but as long as both sides subscribe to the same set of values, they will get along. If that common bond begins to break, the situation changes. If employees no longer commit themselves to the firm and keep their eyes open for better opportunities, the companies will decrease their commitment also and move away from lifetime employment.

In reality the touted lifetime employment system has never covered more than 30 percent of Japanese employees. It is only practiced by large firms and only applies to men. Women are not part of the system, and neither men nor women in small businesses are guaranteed lifetime employment. Furthermore, even in large firms, lifetime employment is only for regular employees, not for part-timers and temporaries, who are an ever-growing part of the workforce. During the last few years the lifetime employment system has come under additional attack. A number of Japanese firms have concluded that, in order to be competitive in the global market, they need to focus on performance and merit rather than mere longevity with the firm. The changing employment patterns will bring with them a new power structure and relationship between employees and employers.

While people in a firm know very well who has power, the issue is not openly discussed. To people on the outside, the facade of harmony must be maintained at all costs, and saving face becomes an overriding issue. Companies go to great lengths to present an image of harmony.

Kazuo Ota, an employee in a Japanese subsidiary of a U.S. firm, gave notice that he wanted to leave the company. This seemingly simple act started a flurry of activities. Mr. Ota's boss, Masataka Abe, refused to accept the resignation because Mr. Ota did not have "valid" reasons for leaving. As it turned out, Mr. Abe was glad to get rid of Mr. Ota, but as he explained, this was Japan, and appearances were important. He said that he would talk to Mr. Ota in a few days, and they then would agree that they would part with mutual respect and satisfaction. This way nobody was to blame; there would be no fault on any one side. To Mr. Abe this saving of the reputation was extremely important.

An American working for a Japanese firm in Chicago ran into a similar problem.

Brent Weber, a recent graduate with a degree in international business, was excited about his job offer from a Japanese firm in Chicago. He had heard about the excellent training Japanese companies provide for their employees, and he was looking forward to a promising future with the firm.

After some time with the firm, however, Brent became disillusioned. He felt he just did not get the training to move ahead, and he started looking for another job.

Somehow his Japanese manager found out; he called Brent in and made it clear to him that he was expected to leave. Before Brent left the firm, however, the Japanese manager met with him once more. He went to great pains to point out that, even though Brent's actions had been disloyal to the firm, they were parting on good terms, that Brent was not fired but that they had come to mutual understanding that parting was best for both sides. The appearance of harmony and agreement were important.

Japanese firms have a tremendous power over suppliers. The big firms buy exclusively from the supplier, and the suppliers depend on the firms for their business and economic well-being. The suppliers are the ones that are expected to absorb excess workers in hard times; they are the ones that must absorb fluctuations in business. In return, they know that they have a customer for their goods, and they know that they will receive help with development costs and technical changes. As a result, however, they are totally dependent on one manufacturer. Traditionally, in Japan the buyer has been in a considerably more powerful position than the seller, and the seller tends to accept the power position of the buyer, as the following example illustrates.

Two Norwegian businessmen were visiting a kimono wholesaler in Nagoya. On the day of their visit several suppliers were in the offices of the wholesaler who was in the market for luxurious and very expensive kimonos. The layout of the offices and the atmosphere were very traditional; all floors were covered with tatami mats, and everyone had taken off their shoes at the entrance of the building. People were sitting on the floor in traditional style.

The Norwegians discussed several aspects of the business with the wholesaler. While they were talking, a newcomer approached, but the owner of the business barely acknowledged him. After a deep bow, the "intruder" stayed at a respectable distance. When the Norwegians asked a question about the production of kimono belts, the owner waved to the person and asked him to come closer. It turned out the "intruder" was a kimono belt manufacturer who exclusively manufactured for this particular wholesaler. The supplier bowed several times and answered the questions asked of him. When the discussion went on to other areas, he was waved away and quietly withdrew. To someone watching the scene, the more powerful partner was easily identifiable.

The buyer is sometimes compared to the father who has authority over the supplier, the son. The father has the authority, but because he loves his son, he will not harm him. That means the buyer has the power, but he will see to it that the supplier is treated fairly. Nevertheless, they are not equal in stature and status, and both sides are keenly aware of their respective levels of authority and power.

Language as Symbol of Power and Authority

In addition to tone and behavior, language itself is an indicator of authority in most cultures. Japan is a good example of how language is used to establish authority.

In Japan, power becomes obvious through such nonverbal symbols as bowing, as pointed out earlier, but vocabulary is also an indicator of power. The Japanese society is a hierarchical society. The language that subordinates use differs from the language that superiors use. The vocabulary can be quite different, and everyone is aware of what the connotations of words are. For example, when a manager addresses subordinate men, he will add the suffix *kun* to the name rather than the respectful *san* (the equivalent to Mr.). The subordinate will address the superior with the last name and title or title and *san*. For example, the boss will call the employee *Nakasone-kun,* but Mr. Nakasone will call the boss *Abe-kacho* (*Abe* being the name of the boss and *kacho* meaning section chief).

Address reflects one's standing in the group. This is even more emphasized by using a person's title or position plus *san* rather than the name plus the title. In this situation the boss is not *Abe-kacho* but *kacho-san,* not *Tanaka-bucho* (department head) but *bucho-san.* This practice is even carried over into family relationships. A boy will call his older brother *ani-san* (older brother) rather than Wako, his older sister *oni-san* rather than Noriko. In a way the person loses his or her individual identity and takes on the identity in relation to his or her position in the group.

Lately, several Japanese companies have started to move against the extreme status consciousness in addressing people. They are promoting the use of the suffix *san* for everyone regardless of position. Nakasone-kun would become Nakasone-san; Abe-kacho would become Abe-san. It is interesting to note that the Japanese, who have emphasized their group membership by pointing out that everyone from president to storeroom clerk wears the same uniform, are now talking about the need to equalize the language. The United States is cited as a positive example in this effort.

The hierarchical thinking of Japanese society also is apparent verbally in the way people refer to themselves. In Western cultures people refer to themselves as *I*. This identity stays with them and does not change. It does not matter whether a man talks to his parents, spouse, friends, co-workers, or boss. When he refers to himself, he uses the pronoun *I*. That is different from Japanese culture. First of all, it is considered egotistic and impolite to refer to oneself because that draws too much attention to oneself. If at all possible, one should avoid any reference to *I*. The subject *I* will become clear in the context. If the speaker does use the personal pronoun, the pronoun changes depending on the people he or she is addressing. The Japanese have many words for saying *I*. Each depends on the relationship of the speaker to the listener, and each indicates the hierarchy of the group. The particular word that is used depends on status, gender, age, and familiarity. Boys, for example, will use *boku* for *I* when talking to each other. A man will use *temae* for *I* when talking to his boss. Young men talking to each other will refer to themselves as *ore*.

A discussion of groups in Japan must take into account that group membership is permanent (see Chapter 4). Groups are important because they help define one's identity and role and establish authority relationships that last one's lifetime. This helps explain the importance of university clubs. All Japanese universities have a variety of student clubs, from soccer to martial arts, fencing, rock climbing, theater, and politics. The Japanese take these clubs very seriously. Joining is not casual or temporary but for a lifetime. When graduates go their separate way after graduation, they do stay in touch. They belonged to the same club; they had the same experiences. If one works for MITI and the other for Mitsubishi, they know they can count on each other.

Westerners often complain about the close ties between Japanese business and industry. What they may not understand is that this is not necessarily an official tie but an unofficial tie based on group identity and personal relationships that have grown over many years (also see Chapter 4). And these relationships are often the basis for power in Japan.

What appears harmonious on the surface, however, is not necessarily harmonious underneath the surface. Japanese business involves an amazing shuffling for power and position, but all behind a facade of harmony. Employees know very well where they stand and what their chances of success are in a firm. While the older generation still emphasizes seniority and promotion based on seniority, younger people are increasingly disillusioned with this approach. Japanese who have studied abroad or worked abroad are rebelling against the seniority system. They want more power based on knowledge and experience rather than number of years with the firm. With the growing global competition, the Japanese elite is beginning to review the issues of merit and group harmony. Any changes will have far-reaching consequences in traditional business culture and behavioral norms.

Family and Societal Structures as Indicators of Power

So far we have discussed the tone and language of power, but in most cultures, power is also conveyed by social groupings and structures of groups, as the Japanese example just discussed indicates (see also Chapter 4).

While Islam stresses the equality of all believers, the Islamic social structure emphasizes hierarchy and authority. The symbol for the underlying power structure is the extended family or clan, which is tightly ruled by the senior male member. For younger people who may have studied abroad and who have gotten used to questioning authority, the return home can be a tremendous culture shock. No matter how much they know, they will be expected to bow to seniority. The head of the group officially has the say.

Most Arabs are used to this structure and accept the authority of a person as long as it is clear that this person is officially in charge. However, Arabs have a hard time dealing with people when there is no clear indication of who the leaders are. Free-flowing discussion in the Western sense is difficult in Arab culture. In the severity of the desert environment only the strong survive, and therefore one has to constantly protect one's position. In this context, give and take are seen as a sign of weakness. As a result, Arabs stick to small talk when lines of authority are not clear so as to avoid confrontations and arguments.[1] Group decision making using the Japanese approach would probably not work because the Japanese approach does not have an obvious leader who is in charge.

Western businesspeople doing business in the Middle East will be much more successful if lines of authority, power, and responsibilities are clearly spelled out. They can also help discussions along if the Arab businessperson realizes that the Westerners have the full support and confidence of their companies back home. Arabs will respect clearly identified authority, but any sign of insecurity will be interpreted as weakness and ineffectiveness and will be relentlessly attacked.

Similar to the Arab tradition, the Latin tradition is male oriented and based on a strong, authoritarian leader. The tradition evolved out of the strict hierarchical organization of the Catholic church and the system of large haciendas.[2] Traditionally, the hacienda is run by a patron, a father figure who takes care of the people living on the hacienda. It is a very paternalistic model, based on reciprocity and loyalty. The employees owe duty and obligation. Their loyalty is a personal loyalty to the owner rather than to a group as in Japan. Loyalty is not abstract but real and shows up in the carrying out of orders. In this system both sides accept their place: the owner–manager who makes the decisions and the subordinate who carries them out. The patron clearly is the authority figure, and he also is expected to take care of the employees; however, the employees have some power also, even though it is more indirect. They control important information that they will pass on only in return for certain favors.

Because the patron as the authority figure is supposed to know what to do, he cannot ask for information in the Latin cultural tradition. Asking would be interpreted as weakness. As a result of the traditional communication pattern, communication in Latin organizations even today is not very effective. People try to protect their reputations and positions; people do not freely work together to achieve common goals.

Decision making by consensus or setting common goals in a group is difficult in Latin cultures because managerial practices do not take the cultural realities and constraints into account.[3] Many a North American management consultant has failed in Latin America when preaching the advantages of an open communication system where the boss asks for input from the employees and employees freely share their opinions. Communication patterns are culturally conditioned. The one higher in the hierarchy takes care of the lower one who, in turn, owes obedience and carries out orders. The lower one does not interrupt and ask questions. That is not his place. If the superior asks for input, the subordinate may legitimately question the ability of the superior to run the firm.

ASSERTIVENESS VERSUS PEACEKEEPING

Standing up for One's Rights

U.S. businesspeople believe in assertiveness training. Assertiveness is seen as a positive value, and the emphasis on assertiveness highlights individual rights over obligations to groups and society. If in doubt, Americans often push for truth rather than peace and harmony. They believe it is better to know the truth. "The truth will set you free" symbolizes the faith in asserting what is true and right.

Germans, even more than people in the United States, emphasize the importance of standing up for their rights, of consciously asserting their rights. In many cases, outsiders can see those characteristics much more clearly than insiders.

An Iranian doctor who had lived in Germany for many years commented on the German need to assert oneself. From childhood on, she noted, German children are taught to defend their rights as people and their right to property. *Was recht ist muß recht bleiben* (right must remain right) indicates this attitude. One should never give up one's right or give in. The Iranian formed the opinion that in Germany, giving in stamps the person as weak and incompetent. As a result, life is regulated and rules govern the most minute details of life. The Germans may have their possessions, but in the process of gaining and keeping them, according to the Iranian doctor, they miss out on the interpersonal warmth that comes with sharing.

The example illustrates that people approach other cultures with their own set of values and priorities. The Iranian doctor evaluated the German culture based on her own background, which firmly places the individual into a hierarchical group that emphasizes interdependence.

Germans tend to see life as tough and not always fair; therefore, children must learn to fight early (also see Chapter 6). A German mother once said that it was important that children learned to cheat on tests because life is hard and often cruel. Everyone cheats; therefore, it is important to learn how to do it too for self-protection. While not all Germans may agree with the attitude of the mother, it nevertheless illustrates the point.

This need for assertiveness can be humorous but it can also be more severe. In the extreme it leads to individuals who believe they are the expert on everything. Germans find it difficult to say they don't know or to admit that they were wrong. When a person in the United States might say, "I'm sorry, I guess I was wrong," the German would be quiet or explain why he was right. Insecurity frequently leads to an exaggerated assertiveness.

A group of German and U.S. students discussed construction of houses in both Germany and the United States. The Germans were horrified by how thin the walls of American houses are. Given the temperature extremes of the Midwest continental climate, they thought that the walls should be thicker to conserve energy. The U.S. students pointed out that the thickness of the walls did not automatically mean better insulation. They explained the significance of the R-value and how thick a stone wall would have to be to reach the equivalent insulating value of a six-inch fiberglass pad. The Germans listened until the Americans had finished, and then one of them simply said: "This is wrong. Thicker walls are better." He probably knew nothing about R-values and insulation values, but he "knew," and he asserted his knowledge.

This behavior can also be observed in business. The German subsidiary of a U.S. pharmaceutical company regularly sent reports and requests for additional funds to headquarters. The manager at headquarters in Chicago repeatedly told them that they needed to justify their requests, that to say they needed the funds for effectiveness and competitiveness was not enough. The Germans continued to send requests without the justifications. If they said they needed the funds, they needed the funds. They were right. The U.S. manager in exasperation suggested some training in American-style business report writing. The Germans were furious; how dare he suggest they needed to change!

In another case, the German manager of a German subsidiary of a U.S. firm refused to go to European regional meetings. He knew his job; why should he waste his time to go to France or Great Britain? If they needed help, they could come to him. In contrast to Americans, the Germans tend to be more production oriented; public relations is often a distant last concern. German advertisements typically assert product superiority in a technical sense. Companies, like individuals, seem to say, "We know we are right, so why bother about appearing nice."

For example, a German manufacturer of high-quality steel products was unsuccessful at selling its products in Shanghai. The firm could not even sell its products through a joint-venture company. On sales calls, the Germans would simply state the superiority of their products and give the price. The Chinese, on the other hand, were looking for an advantage, a special favor, a sign of some consideration due to them because they were entering into a buyer–seller relationship. The Germans reputedly stated, "You can't have a Mercedes at a Volkswagen price," packed up their brochures and specifications, and walked out. The Chinese had thought they were negotiating, and had only just begun the process. The Germans had no time to waste: they knew their product was of high quality, they said so, and they named the price. Nothing further remained to be said, as far as they were concerned.

Preserving Harmony

In contrast to Western assertiveness stands the concept of peace and harmony in Asian cultures. The Japanese proverb, "The pheasant would have lived but for its cry," is symbolic of that concept. One is quiet and fits in. To tout one's rights or superiority is not acceptable. The emphasis is on duty, obligation, and loyalty rather than on rights. Both Confucionism and Buddhism have emphasized duty over rights. The verbal assertiveness of Western cultures is alien to Eastern cultures.

Assertiveness only makes sense if there are absolute rights and wrongs. Assertiveness implies that I assert my rights because I am right; therefore, I must maintain and defend my rights. In cultures that believe that circumstances define what is right and wrong, the insistence on absolutes becomes hollow and makes no sense. Businesspeople from Eastern cultures may consider the Western emphasis on absolute principles as unrealistic and pushy, and the Western businesspeople may view the Eastern emphasis on circumstances as an attempt to avoid commitment.

Different cultural backgrounds influence how both sides approach each other and present their ideas. The businessperson from Western cultures is likely to assertively and openly push for acceptance of a proposal. East Asian businesspeople fight for their proposals also, but typically the fight is more subtle, more quietly persuasive than openly assertive. Unless both sides understand the reasons for their behavior, they may not be able to communicate effectively and they may miss business opportunities.

RECOGNITION OF PERFORMANCE

Recognition of performance can be divided into two major groups, monetary and nonmonetary rewards.

Monetary Recognition

Cultures that emphasize relationships over individual achievement and material possessions tend to play down the role of money in recognizing performance. Cultures that admire individual performance tend to connect salaries with recognition. In the United States, for example, recognition of achievement is reflected in one's salary. Surveys over the past few years have shown that American executives are the highest paid in the world, not just in terms of absolute dollars of compensation but also in terms of what other people in business make even though surveys show that interesting work rather than salary is their prime motivator.[4] The differentials between pay for manufacturing employees and CEOs is highest in the United States and lowest in Japan and Germany. However, the gap between U.S. chief executives and their foreign counterparts is closing fast as foreign firms have started to add stock options to executive pay. Today executives of multinational firms in many countries, among them Argentina, Germany, and Japan, have included stock options in the pay package. This development is another example of the impact of globalization. In an era when business seeks talent globally, compensation packages have to be competitive at a global level.

As European firms are hit by "merger-mania," more and more executives are receiving golden parachutes. German, French, and British CEOs have made international headlines when their severance agreements were disclosed. Traditionally these CEOs might have received a cash payment for the loss of compensation in a takeover and a nice pension, but the multimillion-dollar parachutes were virtually unknown. This is definitely changing.[5]

The big pay differences between lower-level employees and executives have become an issue in several countries. In the United States, for example, employees and stockholders are more and more disillusioned and complain about managers taking rewards but avoiding punishment. Managers are accused of giving themselves huge salaries, bonuses, and stock options regardless of performance. Even the Securities and Exchange Commission (SEC) has entered the discussion. Increasingly, American critics argue that the system needs to be more participative and consensus oriented.

In many developing countries, pay differentials between managers and lower-level employees are tremendous and are an expression of the traditional hierarchical class structures. Since class membership is often attained by birth rather than individual accomplishments, the salary structures reinforce the existing system.

Nonmonetary Rewards

Appropriate recognition must be based on cultural motivators and culturally acceptable norms. In a culture that considers individuality as positive, singling individuals out for praise is positive. U.S. firms, for example, may recognize the salesperson of the month or the employee of the month. Singling out an individual both praises the individual and provides incentive for the others to do well so that they too may be recognized. The successful saleswoman at Mary Kay Cosmetics gets to drive a pink Cadillac. The whole world can see that she is a top performer. Local newspapers regularly run columns on who has been promoted in the community. A brief description and a recent picture duly recognize the individual achievement. Americans want others to see what they have done. In contrast, at Beijing Jeep, some workers actually turned down a pay increase because the apprehension they felt about the resentment of less-productive workers outweighed the benefit of more money.

Some U.S. companies offer other types of nonmonetary incentives as well, such as organizing special trips and retreats for successful employees. Company-paid trips to Hawaii or Florida, particularly in January if the firm is located in the northern parts of the United States, indicate appreciation and success.

In cultures that do not put a high value on individuality, the open recognition of individual achievement may not be desirable. To single out one salesperson as the top performer in a Japanese firm would be embarrassing for the employee and would not endear him to the other employees. What he achieved was a result of group interaction and cooperation. Nobody can reach the top alone. As a result, companies tend to reward everyone. Everyone gets a bonus; everyone gets to go on a trip. A small subsidiary of a U.S. firm in Tokyo, for example, sent all 54 employees for three days to Hong Kong. They went in two groups so that the business could remain open, but everyone down to the lowest clerical employee went. Any other arrangement would have been unthinkable. Similarly, in 1998 a software company in California, owned by several Taiwanese, made headlines when it awarded a Christmas bonus of nearly $60,000 to each employee! This is a monetary reward, but also a collective one.

In a Japanese firm one of the women was asked whether she was willing to accept a position as manager in training. She would have been the first and only woman in that position in the firm. Most businesswomen in the United States would have jumped at the opportunity. She declined, saying that she did not think it appropriate to be singled out from among all the other women. For the sake of harmony and for the sake of not being the object of criticism by others, she felt it was more important to remain a member of the group of women. The Japanese emphasis on fitting in does not mean that there are no personal ambitions and maneuvering for positions. The difficulty for Westerners is that the surface seems to be so harmonious and smooth that it is difficult to recognize and interpret any undercurrents. They are there, however. A Japanese businessman described the Japanese approach thus: "Like a duck—serene above and paddling like hell below."

Pay differentials in former communist countries were small; however, much of the compensation in those societies came in privileges rather than salaries. A Russian manager might not make much more money than a first-line supervisor, but the manager might have access to special stores, vacation spots, inexpensive and heavily subsidized theater tickets, and travel within the communist block countries. In this kind of environment, salaries alone do not give a clear picture of actual power and authority.

In developing countries, recognition may come in the form of products that are difficult to get. For example, an employee may be much happier with a VCR, cell phone, or a television set than the equivalency in the local currency if these products are not readily available. Having them may indicate prestige and connections. Sometimes better apartments, houses, vacations, and automobiles may be coveted possessions, and employees may go to great lengths to get them.

Any firm employing people from diverse cultural backgrounds needs to be aware that people from different backgrounds look at rewards differently. What may be a dream come true for one person may be disappointing to the next. Some companies have tried to avoid problems abroad by implementing the same policy for recognition worldwide, only to find out that this does not work. Just as with the other aspects of communication, the reward process must be adapted to the cultural norms of the people one is dealing with. Any policy must be soundly based on a study of what is culturally appropriate and acceptable. In addition, the firm must be fair to all subsidiaries. If individual recognition is not appropriate, a more group-oriented approach may solve the problem. However, it would not be appropriate to give no recognition at all.

Increasing globalization has made recognition of performance more complex. Small and medium-sized firms may continue to follow traditional patterns for recognizing performance, but many large multinational firms may need to combine approaches from several cultures. If an Australian firm practices polycentric staffing and employs Australians at headquarters in Brisbane and Japanese people in its subsidiary in Osaka, Japan, the firm can design a reward structure that fits the Australian culture at headquarters and the Japanese culture at the subsidiary. If, on the other hand, the Australian firm uses a staffing pattern where Japanese and Australian employees work both at headquarters and the subsidiary, both locations must take both cultures into account. Developing an award structure that corresponds to cultural priorities requires sensitivity and careful study of the culture.

HOSPITALITY

Hospitality plays an important role in establishing business relationships. Much intercultural business communication takes place through social gatherings and gift-giving. Appropriate behavior in the social setting is crucial in order to be successful.

CONVENTIONS FOR EXTENDING INVITATIONS

Business relationships, especially in international dealings, often involve entertaining businesspeople from other cultures. Whom does one invite, when does one invite people, how well does one have to know people to invite them?—these can be complicated points in business relationships across cultures. In the United States, people are fairly open and invite people easily into their homes. Even if they have not known the other person very long, many extend an invitation.

This openness is not universal. At an elementary school picnic in the United States two American parents met the parents of a Japanese student. The Japanese father was a visiting professor at the local university. They were new in town and didn't know anyone. The Americans, to make them feel welcome, invited them for Sunday afternoon. The couple came with their son, and the afternoon was very pleasant. In the course of the conversation the Japanese expressed their surprise at having been invited after just having met the host. In Japan that would not happen they pointed out. Indeed it is much more difficult to receive an invitation into a Japanese home. Typically, if the Japanese have been to the United States, they will open their houses more readily. However, it is not uncommon that Japanese employees who have worked together for years have never been in each other's houses. Any socializing takes place outside the private home either in a public place or at the place of work.

The Japanese are expected to fit in the group, to share, and not to insist on private space, but families are kept very separate from work life. The work team may be a second family for the employee, but the private family and the company family in many cases do not mix. Part of the separation may be a result of crowded living conditions. With small apartments it is difficult to entertain at home, but the reasons for the separation of work and family seem to go deeper.

It is a nightmare for the Japanese if a foreign businessman announces that his wife will accompany him on the next trip. The Japanese do not know how to deal with this situation because wives are not typically included in business functions. To ask a Japanese wife to take care of the visitor's wife also poses problems. The foreign woman may feel uncomfortable, and the Japanese woman may resent having to be involved in her husband's business affairs, not to mention having to overcome language problems.

Guests in Japanese homes must follow certain customs. At the entrance one takes off one's shoes. Perhaps this goes back to the time when the entire floor was covered with tatami mats. These mats are delicate and difficult to clean; therefore, to prolong their lives, people would take off their shoes when entering the house. Even though today most people in Japan have carpeting or wooden floors and usually just one tatami room, the custom has survived. All guests are expected to take off their shoes.

Many families provide slippers for guests. For this purpose, most houses have a set of shelves at the entrance filled with a number of pairs of slippers. Men find out very fast that the best shoes to wear are slip-on loafers rather than shoes with laces. A separate pair of slippers is provided for use of the toilet—the slippers that are worn in the rest of the house must never be worn in the bathroom. Exchange students typically infuriate their hosts before they catch on and change slippers intuitively.

The ritual of taking off one's shoes and putting on slippers provided by the host is perfectly natural to the Japanese. The host shows hospitality by providing slippers; the guest shows respect by taking off the shoes. People from other cultures, on the other hand, may view the ritual somewhat differently especially if they want to present a certain image.

A group of businesspeople from the United States was invited for a Fourth of July party by Mitsubishi in Nagoya. At the entrance everyone took off his or her shoes and put on the provided slippers, olive green. In the eyes of the Americans, the slippers merely looked odd with the business suits the men were wearing, but they ruined any ensemble and color coordination the women were trying to achieve. The businesspeople from the United States felt as if they lost all their dignity when putting on the slippers. The Japanese, on the other hand, did not even seem to notice. To them it was quite natural—what else would one do?

Arabs may invite outsiders into their homes more easily than the Japanese, but the outsider will only see the official or public places of the house. Women typically will not be present and will not appear while the outsider is in the house. The Arab may entertain at home but still separates the public and private aspects of his life.

Mixing Social Engagements and Business

Typically the host sets the agenda and guides the visitor through the course of engagement. The host determines whether to meet for dinner, at a bar, at a night club, or in his or her home. The host also invites the appropriate persons. These arrangements may be fairly easy. More complicated is the question on how fast to proceed to business. Businesspeople from cultures that consider time a perishable commodity want to move fast—after all time is money. They may invite the potential partner into their house for dinner but then proceed to talk business most of the evening.

In cultures where business is based on trust, the personal relationship must be established before any business discussions can begin. Businesspeople from these cultures will use the social gathering as a way to get to know the other person and will avoid business discussions during that time.

No one culture is right or wrong; cultures are different and approach business differently. They develop different norms and expectations. Businesspeople should learn how the other side approaches business and what the principles of hospitality are. Then they can make the necessary adjustments or openly talk about the differences and come to a mutual understanding. Generally, however, the rules of the host culture carry more weight. If you are doing business in another culture, you may have to be the one who makes most of the adjustments.

Appropriate Behavior for Hosts and Guests

A typical U.S. symbol of hospitality is the cocktail party. A manager may invite employees, clients, and customers so that they can get to know one another. The goal at a cocktail party is to meet as many people as possible. Nobody expects to get into deep discussions. In fact, it would be rude to monopolize any one person. One makes small talk and "works the room," exchanging business cards and phone numbers so one can get into contact later and establish future business relationships.

To Europeans the cocktail party is a curious phenomenon. In Germany, for example, one invites only as many people as one has chairs for. To invite crowds and expect them to stand would not be hospitable and thus not acceptable. The art of small talk is not a forte of most Europeans either. They tend to view the U.S. style of entertaining as superficial and lacking sincerity.

A U.S. firm that hosts a cocktail party in Japan creates all sort of problems because the cocktail party is based on the premise that one can walk up to anyone in the room and introduce oneself. In Japan, with its hierarchy and protocol for how to address others, it is almost impossible to introduce oneself without knowing the age and status of the other person. What was intended as a friendly gesture by the manager from the United States may cause discomfort and embarrassment for the Japanese guests.

In cultures where the development of personal relationships is important in doing business, the offering and acceptance of an invitation imply that both host and guest exclusively devote themselves to that particular engagement. In cultures that look at entertaining simply as a prelude to business, the implication may be quite different. For example, invitations in the United States may announce: "Cocktail party 5–7:00 P.M." Unthinkable in cultures where hospitality is supposed to be unlimited! To invite someone for a set time period is rude. Americans, on the other hand, find this arrangement very considerate and efficient. The guests know that they don't have to reserve the entire evening for the event; they can make other plans for the rest of the evening.

A couple of German businesspeople who were visiting the United States were troubled after their second day. They finally approached their American friends and asked for help. They had been to a party arranged by their U.S. client the night before. Somehow, they felt they did something wrong. They also felt that they should have left earlier than they did but they did not know what was appropriate length of stay. In the discussion it came out that in Germany guests show appreciation by staying until the end. Since the guests from the United States dropped in and left, not all the guests were there at any one time, and the Germans just did not know what to do and how to get away. They did not know what the expected social behavior was in this setting.

In their own cultures people know when to arrive for business meetings and business-related social functions. In the United States, one is expected not to be too punctual for cocktail parties, and one can leave after a short stay. For a dinner party, on the other hand, one is supposed to be on time and stay for the evening. In cultures that don't live as much by the clock the invitation for seven o'clock does not mean one must be there at seven o'clock. In fact, nobody in Spain or India would expect the guests to come at seven. An hour later or even two is common, and nobody thinks anything of it. Dinner typically is served late in the evening. A hostess from the United States or northern Europe would be very upset by this same behavior and vow never to invite those people again. After all, if the invitation is for seven, then dinner will probably be served at 7:30 or eight at the latest. The evening is much more programmed, and the hostess does everything to make things "run smoothly." Her reputation as a hostess depends on the smooth functioning of the event.

In the United States guests may linger after the dinner, whereas in Japan and China the host and the guests will get up shortly after the meal is over and say their good-byes. The ending to social functions in Japan and China strikes Europeans and Americans as abrupt. They often feel the evening has barely started and wonder what to do with the rest.

As with most other aspects of intercultural communication, one needs to be aware of the customs in the other culture. An Australian who is insulted for not being invited to a Japanese partner's house even though he was in the Australian's is petty. The businessperson from New York who insists on inviting a client from Saudi Arabia, a culture that keeps business and families separate, to his home may not foster his business interests. In Brazil it is normal for a person to give a little party with drinks and hors d'hoevres for his friends from the workplace before leaving on vacation, usually on Friday evening. Not to do so is unthinkable. So the issue of *when* to invite is also a cultural minefield. In many cases you can overcome problems by saying something like, "In my culture it is the custom," or "it is appropriate," or similar phrases. Similarly it is acceptable to ask what is appropriate behavior for a visitor. Most people will praise you for your sensitivity and the goal not to offend, and they will be much more forgiving of mistakes if they know that you want to do what is right.

Gift Giving

Many companies have specific rules on gift giving in a business context. They may have items on hand that managers can use for gifts; calendars, pens, clocks, and golf balls are popular items. When giving business gifts, businesspeople from the United States also must be aware of legal restrictions based on the Foreign Corrupt Practices Act, which outlaws bribery and strictly limits the value of gifts one can give and accept. The official company rules on gift giving may not answer what to do if the employee is invited to attend a social event such as a dinner party.

In many cultures it is appropriate to take small gifts when one is invited to enjoy hospitality. In northern Europe a fitting gift is flowers or chocolates for the hostess. A bottle of wine, especially in France, could, however, be viewed by the host as the insult that he does not serve good wine. In Germany roses and chrysanthemums are not considered appropriate. Roses are for lovers, and chrysanthemums are for funerals. Flowers also must be in uneven numbers in Germany, and they must be taken out of the paper before being presented, unlike the custom in Britain.

In Japan gifts are important. Twice a year, at New Year's and in July, people present gifts to work associates, friends, and family members. These two times coincide with the payment of the twice-annual bonus. An unwritten protocol dictates what is appropriate on these gift-giving occasions. Levels of hierarchy are closely observed. People know what to give to a subordinate or to a boss. Importance is attached not only to what one gives, but also to where the present was bought. A present from a prestigious and expensive department store counts for a lot more than the very same present bought at a small neighborhood store. However, the Japanese are beginning to change their behavior somewhat—they are becoming more price conscious and increasingly even buy gifts at discount stores. But a gift bought at Mitsukoshi in the Ginza, for example, still carries a certain prestige with it. A Japanese business professor presented a visiting professor from the United States with several gifts—books, tea cups, and a fan—all nicely wrapped. As he gave the presents, he pointed out that the presents came from the best department store in town.

The problem for the outsider is to determine what is appropriate gift giving. If one is not familiar with the ritual, one is at a loss as to what to select. Japanese businessmen appreciate gifts of whiskey. Given prices of whiskey in Japan, however, a foreign visitor may want to buy the gift outside Japan. Nicely packaged food items, such as fruit and meat, are also welcome gifts. Personal items are taboo; gifts should be neutral.

Packaging is another issue. Elaborate wrapping is considered very important in Japan, less so in the United States and Canada and even less in Great Britain. With packaging laws in Germany, for example, wrappings may completely disappear. The law requires stores to take back any packaging that is considered superfluous. Under this provision, a store has to keep the toothpaste carton and cartons for six-packs of soft drinks and beer. Germany, which already restricts the amount of household garbage, is contemplating charging garbage collection fees by the pound of garbage. Given the situation, a host might not appreciate elaborate wrapping of presents.

In the United States the recipient of a gift is expected to open a gift immediately upon receipt. Doing otherwise would show a lack of interest and appreciation; it would be rude. Children are taught early on to open gifts and acknowledge the gift with elaborate praise. "How wonderful; just what I always wanted!" Germans open presents also, but they are more reserved in their comments. The Japanese and Chinese, on the other hand, never open presents while the giver is around. This would be very rude because of the potential loss of face for the giver and even receiver. Parents take great care to emphasize the appropriate behavior with their children. One Chinese mother explained that it was hard at times to ensure that her daughter would not jump to open the present. It was difficult, but for obvious reasons it was necessary. Chinese or Japanese who are familiar with the custom in the United States may go ahead and open presents from foreigners. If you are not certain, your best approach is to explain the custom of your culture and ask if it is acceptable to open the present. Most people understand that customs are different in different countries. They may find it strange, but they will appreciate that the foreigner asks.

In the United States it is typical to ask whether one can bring anything when being invited. The hostess will say no unless she knows the guest very well. It all follows a ritual where the actors know their roles. The institution of potluck dinners where everyone brings a dish is unheard of in Europe. If one invites, the assumption is that one can prepare the food and generally handle the work associated with entertaining. In China it is unthinkable to bring something for dinner. The host is gaining face from offering hospitality to guests and is storing obligation debts to his credit.

The way people from different cultures express appreciation for hospitality varies. In the United States, a businessperson who is invited for dinner to the private home of a business contact is expected to write a thank-you note shortly after the event. The Japanese tend to not write thank-you notes. Giving and showing hospitality are part of reciprocity. It is an ongoing process that never ends. To thank someone with a thank-you note could be interpreted as a signal that the writer wants to settle the "debt" and close the relationship. Germans hardly ever write thank-you notes. They say "thank you" at the end of a visit. They are sincere in their appreciation, but they don't send notes.

Dealing with Controversy in Social Settings

In other parts of the book we have discussed how people from different cultures deal with controversy in business settings. In social settings behavior is very much influenced by attitudes towards hospitality. In Arab countries, hospitality is a sacred duty. One must be polite and considerate to visitors. Open disagreement is not acceptable. That does not mean that Arabs cannot loudly argue and disagree among themselves, but with a guest in the house, the rules are different. Both sides should avoid controversial subjects.

The French, on the other hand, love to introduce controversial topics and are eager to make their points clear and to disagree with each other. Open disagreement is a sign of a successful evening, and everyone enjoys the verbal game. The Japanese are much more careful and disagreements are avoided. One does not argue at social functions, and as host it would be impolite to disagree with the guests; therefore, controversial topics are taboo.

Businesspeople in the United States, who often pride themselves in being outspoken, avoid controversial topics at social functions. The other side, they feel, is entitled to its opinion, but increasingly, businesspeople also worry about being accused of insensitivity to people who hold different views. It is therefore considered best to stay away from discussing certain topics.

Hospitality in the United States is important and shows openness and friendliness, but it does not have the same far-reaching obligations it may have in other cultures. Opening one's house does not mean unlimited hospitality. Americans look at hospitality more pragmatically. It facilitates social intercourse and establishes pleasant relationships, which make it easier to conduct business. Americans generally are more concerned about creating a pleasant atmosphere even if only for a specifically prescribed time and for a specific purpose.

Holiday Greetings

Many firms in Western countries send Christmas cards or season's greetings to their suppliers, customers, business associates, and government contacts. The Japanese send New Year's cards; the Taiwanese send Lunar New Year's cards. When a firm starts doing business in a different culture, it must ask when and if it is appropriate to send greetings and who should receive a card.

You may wonder whether it is appropriate to send cards that celebrate a holiday in your culture to business associates in cultures that do not celebrate that same holiday. This becomes a particular issue if the holiday has religious significance and if the other culture does not practice your religion. The answer will depend on how well you know the country and the individual. In most cultures it would be appropriate to send best wishes for the New Year or season's greetings for the holidays. Japanese firms often send their best wishes for the New Year to their Japanese business partners, but many also send Christmas cards to their Western business associates and friends. The mainland Chinese, most of whom are non-Christian, also send Christmas cards. Even Chinese organizations send them—although for most, Christmas has no spiritual significance. Sending the greeting and best wishes is seen as respect for the other person's traditions and cultures. Therefore, Chinese and Japanese want to honor their foreign business partners by acknowledging their special holidays.

If you add your foreign partners to the list for your own culture's holidays, they may feel honored that you include them, but they may also be offended. You need to find out what is acceptable. For example, Saudi Arabia does not allow any Christian symbols, such as the cross or the Bible, into the country. Even secular symbols of Christmas, such as Christmas trees, Christmas cards, and Santa Claus are banned. An American businessman reported that the rubber Santa Claus he had taken to Saudi Arabia for his son was confiscated at the airport. Iran, on the other hand, appears less strict these days. The popular assumption is that Iran is the most fundamentalist Islamic society, but a Western woman doing business in Iran explained recently that there was a Christmas market in Teheran and that one could buy Christmas trees in the streets. People were also free to gather for worship regularly, although for practical reasons they did so on Fridays rather than Sundays.

The timing of greetings is important also. Holiday greetings in most countries are expected to arrive on time, preferably before the holiday. In France, however, season's greetings can be sent until the end of January.

ETHICAL CONSIDERATIONS IN INTERCULTURAL ENGAGEMENTS

As we have discussed the various ways people from different cultures establish business relationships, you may have started to wonder what the right or ethical foundations of these relationships might be. What do businesspeople from around the globe consider ethical behavior? What is considered ethical depends on the cultural background of the partners involved.

For some this may be difficult to accept. After all, many of us assume that ethical standards are universal. We may define ethical behavior as being honest, being fair, telling the truth, and being considerate and caring, and we may think that these values are culture-neutral. Yet, as we have seen throughout this book, none of these terms exist in a vacuum; they are influenced and shaped by the cultural priorities of the people who use them.

The philosophical foundations of ethics in various cultures help to illustrate this point. For example, Aristotle, a Greek philosopher, argues that a person can find the "good." In fact, the virtuous person will see it as his or her highest goal or *summum bonum* to find and do what is good or virtuous. Furthermore, Aristotle maintains that people can be taught to do what is good and that they will gain happiness from doing the virtuous or the ethical.

Kant, a German philosopher, holds that a person is not only capable of knowing the good or the right, but also has an obligation to do what is right. This is known as the categorical imperative. Like Aristotle, Kant sees the good and the bad, the ethical and unethical, as opposites.

Much of Western thought has been shaped by the conviction that knowledge to do the good will lead to the good and that there is a rational way of getting there. Therefore, people from these cultures will have strong opinions on what is right and wrong. As a result, they have a tendency to look at ethics as an either-or concept. They know that there is a gray area, but generally ethical standards are seen as absolute and objective. This view holds that ethics can be legislated, as the United States has done with the Foreign Corrupt Practices Act. If there is a universal ethical standard, a universal set of right and wrong, then it should be possible to clarify the standards through rules and laws and thus ensure that everyone understands and accepts the standards. The Aristotelian human relations (HR) manager would recognize that there is a "good" that is knowable. At the same time the manager also tries to ensure that employees act according to company rules and guidelines. The HR manager will attempt to inculcate good or virtuous habits in the employees to carry the company to the good.

Philosophers in East Asia have taken a different view. Daoism, for example, sees reality not as an either-or proposition but rather as a holistic unity that encompasses all aspects of reality. In Daoism, as in Western philosophy, people have an obligation to do the virtuous; however, the virtuous is not an absolute. It is impossible to have the absolute good or the right because reality consists of both opposites. Daoists, therefore, are concerned about an appropriate balance in the universe, and the appropriate balance always depends on specific circumstances that require a careful weighing of options. Westerners, not understanding this background, frequently refer to this view of ethics as situational ethics or opportunism. The argument is that if the circumstances dictate what is ethical, there are no standards for ethical behavior. People from East Asia, on the other hand, view Westerners as narrow-minded and unrealistic. In this system the HR manager will weigh what the best or virtuous practices are under the given circumstances.

Islamic culture draws on yet another source for determining what is ethical and unethical, right or wrong: religion. Islamic ethics is ultimately based on revealed truth. Allah provides appropriate guidance for all actions. The virtuous HR manager acts based on religious principles. In the increasingly secular Western world this is easily interpreted as old-fashioned and fundamentalist. However, in order to understand Islamic views on ethics, it is necessary to recognize the role of religion in shaping ethical thought. The philosophy of ethical behavior is also influenced by other cultural variables, such as group orientation or individualism.

Businesspeople from relationship-oriented cultures may have a very different view of what is ethical than people from results-oriented cultures. They may use the same terms but assign radically different meanings to those terms. Honesty may not be an absolute term but rather may be seen in the context of the group a businessperson is coming from. For example, fairness does not signify some abstract ideal; instead fairness means that one is willing to fulfill one's obligations to one's group or family. Thus, in a results-oriented society fairness might dictate that a manager hires the person with the best credentials for the job, an almost clinical decision that is separate from the person. In a high-context society, on the other hand, fairness would dictate that a manager hire a family member, the child of a friend, or someone who has special connections. Likewise, honesty is dependent on the context as well. Honesty may be what it takes to establish the relationship to do business together.

One of the challenges of international business is that all businesspeople from all cultures judge ethical behavior by their own self-reference criteria. It is tempting to apply one's own definition of ethics to what the partner from another culture does and conclude that the partner is unethical based on these standards. Not understanding the ethical framework of the people you are dealing with can lead to misunderstandings and frustrations.

For example, firms from the United States frequently try to avoid nepotism, the hiring of relatives of employees, because this is seen as providing an unfair advantage, which is bad. These views are related to the value the United States places on social equality. To hire someone based on his or her family relationship to an employee seems to be unequal treatment, favoring those people who have employed relatives and disfavoring those who do not. Managers are afraid that the relatives might stick together and that the resulting cliquishness might hurt morale of the work unit.

When a U.S. company went into Mexico, the managers took their standard against nepotism with them and made it a point not to hire relatives; it seemed to be the ethical decision. However, the firm found out that the Mexican view of nepotism was very different. Employees had an ethical obligation to help relatives obtain a well-paying job in the U.S. firm. Everyone accepted that obligation. In fact, it would have been unethical not to try to help one's family. In return, family members understood and accepted the obligation that they had to work hard not to bring shame to the family member who helped them get the job. What had originally been seen as an ethical dilemma, giving an unfair advantage by hiring relatives, turned out to be a motivator to do good work. The company changed its standards and accepted a practice that made sense in that environment.

Businesspeople from results-oriented backgrounds typically separate the business deal from the relationship with the other side. The goal is the business connection, the contract, the sale. The relationship is superficial, just enough to do business. It is a connection with a very specialized purpose. They may very consciously avoid any personal connections so as not to muddy the waters. This strikes people from high-context cultures as odd. Each side may attach the label *unethical* to the behavior of the other side and strain the relationship even further.

While Americans groan about high taxes, most accept that it would be unethical not to pay the taxes owed. After all, taxes are needed to run the government and to carry out programs that will help society as a whole. Chinese have a somewhat different opinion about those kinds of societal obligations, and many feel that they can do more good by helping their families directly rather than paying taxes whose workings they cannot observe directly.

How people from different cultures handle obligations also sheds light on attitudes towards ethics. Where the building of relationships is crucial to doing business, obligations are typically seen as ongoing. By not repaying a debt immediately the partner signifies that he is interested in a continuation of the relationship. In Japan, for example, the willingness to accept an obligation is a positive sign. In fact, the concept of *amae* refers to both the willingness to take care of someone and the willingness to be dependent on someone. In this view the individual is clearly tied into a relationship. Repaying the debt would end the relationship because it would signal that the person no longer is willing to accept the obligation. This attitude is in great contrast to the American ideal of self-reliance. Here the goal is not to be a burden on anyone. It is expected that one repays one's debts promptly (also see Chapter 4).

As we will discuss in greater detail in Chapter 10, human resource issues, including rules on hiring, promotion, and safety, are tied to specific laws, but there is also an ethical element involved. Most industrialized countries have outlawed child labor, and condoning any type of child labor would be seen as a violation of ethical norms. Not all cultures share this viewpoint. In industrialized countries childhood has been expanded into an age group that a century ago would have been considered young adults. In developing countries, children grow up faster and are considered adults at an earlier age, frequently around age 14; therefore, it is acceptable and expected that they contribute to the family income. (We are not talking about young children working in sweatshops many hours every day.) The idea that young adults should be allowed to play when they could contribute to the well-being of the family would be considered irresponsible.

In group-oriented societies, seniority plays a major role in establishing ranking and order. It gives belonging and clarifies one's status in the group. With industrialization merit and individualism tend to gain in importance. As a result, the basis for promotions may change from seniority to merit, and with it what is considered ethical may change as well.

As businesspeople engage in relationships with partners from other cultures, they need to be aware of the cultural foundation of what is considered ethical behavior. One of the most crucial steps is to examine why a culture has certain ethical standards and what they mean in that particular context. As the following story illustrates, different views of what is ethical can lead to problems for everyone involved.

David was conducting a seminar in Los Angeles for a delegation of mid-level civil servants from China. The seminar on trade was scheduled for two weeks, and as time went on, fewer and fewer Chinese showed up for the sessions.

One evening, David's associate received a phone call from an office of the state Department of Motor Vehicles. They had one of the delegates, a woman, in their office. They wanted to go home and did not know what to do. She spoke no English but became very distraught. Here is what she told them after they had found an interpreter.

She had read an ad in a Los Angeles Chinese-language newspaper by an organization that promised it was able to get people documentation papers to enable them to stay in the United States. She phoned the number and was told someone would come to the hotel and meet her. She waited and in about one hour two men came. They asked her to bring all her documentation papers—her Chinese passport and her visas, both the Chinese exit visa and the U.S. entry visa for a visitor—and they took her by car to an impressive office. It was a DMV office, but apparently they told her that it was their organization. She could not read English. They sat her in the outer office and took all her papers saying they needed to

make copies and would be right back. Apparently they left the building through a back door. She sat for hours waiting. Finally she called the hotel, and the hotel informed the delegation organizer.

She was the victim of Chinese scam artists, but she also was trying to circumvent the U.S. Immigration system by using unofficial channels. This willingness to circumvent, to do things by making your own arrangements, is typically Chinese, and typically leads to trouble. A lawyer who was called in assured her that she would not have any problems leaving the United States without a passport. However, in China, the passport is the property of the work unit rather than the individual. She would have to account for the loss to her superiors. She would certainly report the loss as theft, but she was also trying to do something unethical and illegal in the United States. By doing what she considered to be in her best interest, she did not consider the ramifications. Defections from official delegations can get seminar organizers into big trouble with the Immigration and Naturalization Service in the United States. In addition, her defection would make it more difficult for other Chinese to get permission to attend seminars in the United States.

The above example does show legal standards that were not observed by the woman and ethical standards that were not observed by the fly-by-night operators who took advantage of her and crossed the legal line when they stole her passport. Similarly, Chinese companies negotiating joint ventures with U.S. firms often expect the U.S. company can use its "influence" to enable the joint venture to circumvent U.S. import–export law. They believe influence exists when in U.S. law it does not.

We all behave according to our own code until we bump up against somebody else's code. At that point, we need some way to reconcile differences and point to a common code we can use. Businesspeople have to make decisions regarding ethics all the time.

Richard Mead suggests there are two approaches to ethical issues across cultures:[6]

- *Ethical universalism*—a single ethical code everybody should follow. Hofstede connects this to individualism. The United States seems to be the key proponent of this view, since U.S. culture is a legalistic, individualistic culture that thinks one system can operate everywhere (universalistic). The Foreign Corrupt Practices Act is one example of this view. The problem is that this approach fails to consider that other cultures may have different definitions of ethical behavior in business.
- *Ethical empiricism*—behavior is related to the group and your responsibilities to it; so you maintain a higher standard of ethical behavior with in-group members. You have different standards for the different groups you interact with. This extends to different cultures also. This view easily comes across as patronizing, unprincipled, and ethically suspect.

Mead also suggests some practical ways an international manager can identify ethical norms in another culture, such as

- Comparative analysis of ethical norms.
- Reference to institutional norms, such as a national legal system, religious leaders' teachings, professional associations, family.
- Informal behavior guides, such as "face" in Asian cultures.
- So-called tests (the "secrecy" test—if your partner insists the deal be kept secret it may not be ethical; the TV test—would you want your deal on TV?; the test of asking how people you admire would view it, and so on). These tests aren't very useful, however, because they do not come to terms with underlying ethical issues and definitions of ethical behavior.

SUMMARY

This chapter has illustrated that appropriate social and business behavior is dependent on cultural orientation.

- *Respect for authority and structuring of messages.* Businesspeople will be well served to understand the symbols of authority and power. Nonverbal behavior, position, and appearance signal level of authority and power.
- *Power distance and symbols of power and authority.* Understanding where a culture ranks on the power distance scale can be helpful when working with a businessperson from another culture. The use of language is an indicator of authority in most cultures.

- *Assertiveness versus peace keeping.* Businesspeople from assertive cultures may lose out on contracts and alienate partners who come from cultures that emphasize harmony. At the same time, businesspeople from cultures that value harmony and peace may come across as weak and indecisive to people from assertive backgrounds.
- *Recognition of performance.* Rewards for performance are based on cultural priorities. In some cultures the major sign of success is the monetary reward, such as salary. In other cultures, the nonmonetary rewards, such as recognition by powerful people, may be the more significant recognition of performance.
- *Hospitality.* Businesspeople meet in both work and social settings. Each culture has its own unique rules and customs as to what is acceptable social behavior. For example, is it acceptable to mix social life and business life? What gifts are appropriate and when?
- *Ethical considerations.* Different cultures have different views of what is ethical. What is considered ethical behavior depends at least to some extent on cultural priorities and philosophical viewpoints.

NOTES

1. C. Pezeshkpur, "Challenges to Management in the Arab World," *Business Horizons* 21 (1978), pp. 47–55.
2. W. Woodworth and R. Nelson, "Information in Latin American Organizations: Some Cautions," *Management International Review,* Winter 1980, pp. 6–69.
3. Ibid.
4. K.A. Kovach. "What Motivates Employees: Workers and Supervisors Give Different Answers," *Business Horizons* (September–October, 1986), pp. 58–65.
5. Ragharen, A. and G. T. Sims, "Golden Parachutes Emerge in European Deals," *The Wall Street Journal* (February 14, 2000), pp. A17, 18.
6. Richard Mead, *International Management,* 2nd ed. (Malden, MA: Blackwell's, 1998), p. 196.

CHAPTER EIGHT

Information, Decisions, and Solutions

1

In 1768, three Scottish printers cooperated to produce a compendium of knowledge that would bring into one set of books all the basic information on all the topics they could possibly think of. The result of this massive undertaking was *Encyclopaedia Britannica.* In the subsequent 200 years, all over the English-speaking world the *Encyclopaedia Britannica* became the most trusted source of information for schools and libraries. After being revised 14 times, it is still considered the most comprehensive of all its imitators worldwide. In 1990 global sales were U.S. $650 million. Since then, however, sales have collapsed by over 80 percent.

Why? Information is no less valuable today—in fact, in the Information Age, we consult sources of information even more avidly. The answer, of course, is information technology. The CD-ROM appeared in the early 1990s, and in five years it dealt the venerable global hard-copy brand a crippling blow. In early 2000, the company announced it would no longer publish its multivolume set.

Britannica's most recent edition sold for between U.S. $ 1,500 and U.S. $2,200 per set. In contrast, CD-ROM encyclopedias such as the Microsoft-licensed Encarta usually are free with the purchase of a personal computer. People—usually parents—who bought an encyclopedia set in past generations were primarily doing something to help their children excel in their homework assignments. The encyclopedia gave readers a single-source access to high-quality information. Today, parents buy their children a computer for the same reason. (Computers, which usually include an encyclopedia CD-ROM, now cost less than a set of the Encyclopaedia Britannica.)

The Britannica story shows how evolving knowledge, changing technology, and innovation turned the print-encyclopedia world upside down. It is a story about how a company that sold knowledge was itself slow to learn from its own store of expertise and knowledge about the encyclopedia market. The World Wide Web opened up at about the same time Britannica began losing sales. What began as a communications experiment by a bunch of geeks in four universities back in the 1960s became the Internet of the early 21st century, and the force behind the New Economy.

Britannica is not dead yet, though. Under new ownership and management, it has produced a fairly successful CD-ROM that also has Internet connectivity. Once again *Encyclopaedia Britannica* is setting standards for quality knowledge content. Britannica may become a leader in the new market of readily accessible information. It is not just knowledge any more that is important, but the access to knowledge that gives power. Furthermore, the management of knowledge is crucial. Britannica did not manage the knowledge it had.

Information is important to business because it is used to attain business objectives. In the past decade information technology—IT, or infotech—has been the powerhouse behind the information revolution. Globally, information access through technological advances has transformed the way people work, as well as the way they interact and recreate. But it is a mistake to assume that because technology can be transplanted using the same hardware and the same software, the value of "information" is the same worldwide. As we have seen in previous chapters, businesses have different priorities because of the cultures in which they operate. That means they place different priorities on information and on processes like making decisions. Even the need for a decision is not perceived the same way.

Information is useful for solving problems, and in turn problem-solving skills are related to decision making. Problems that involve people and their relationships to power, resources, and decision making are called "conflict" in Western culture. Needless to say, not all cultures define problems the same way, nor do they perceive conflict the same way. Similarly, business information is not the same in all cultures. And yet when people do business in a new environment, they rely on the kind of information they are used to in their own culture. If that kind of information is not available or is not as accurate as information they are used to, businesspeople can't make decisions that work. It isn't surprising that problems arise.

This chapter examines the nature of business information and differences in how information is gathered, assessed, and valued by managers and their organizations. Next, since information is used for making decisions, various decision-making processes will be discussed. Then the chapter looks at problem solving and resolving conflicts across cultures.

BUSINESS INFORMATION GATHERING

Business information is goal oriented. Businesses gather information for business purposes, and not simply for the sake of general education or collecting statistics. They want the information in order to do something that is more effective because of the information. But as we'll see, different cultures look for different kinds of information for different reasons to reach different goals.

The Nature of Business Information

What constitutes information? It differs along the continuum between high-context and low-context cultures. High-context cultures value relationships, teamwork, and long-term group membership. People in these collectivist environments seek information about groups in order to make business decisions. Of course, they also look at costs, benefits, processes, suppliers, markets, and management structure. But knowing *who* is involved is critical.

Furthermore, high-context cultures rely on subjective information that is internalized; that is, it is information that exists within human hearts and minds. It is made up of opinions, attitudes, deductions, and insights based on personal experience. Most importantly, information in high-context cultures is always viewed with reference to the context: the relationships of the group, the history of group, the long-range goals for the group, and so forth.

In Japan, a businessman might introduce the art of calligraphy as a topic of conversation over a meal with a counterpart from the United States. The American may think such a topic indicates a lack of seriousness about doing business. But the Japanese businessman may be looking for qualities in a business partner such as a level of refinement, taste, and sensitivity to the parallels that can be drawn between art and business. He may believe he can discern these qualities in another person by listening to that person's conversation on the topic of calligraphy. The American may value these qualities no less, but she won't look for them as qualifications of a business partner.

Low-context cultures value independent decisions, activity that achieves goals, and individual accountability. They rely on objective information that is externalized; that is, it consists of data that exists independently of the person who gathers it. It is made up of opinions, attitudes, deductions, and insights based on measurable units. Tests of reliability and validity assess the value of data.

The U.S. business culture is more low-context than high-context, and it probably devotes the most effort of any culture to considering the nature of business information. After all, this is a culture in which members like to define terms and pin down explicitly what they mean. Information in the United States is explicit and quantifiable.

Some business information is specifically sought for communication objectives. That is, it forms the basis of communication acts and products. It may be information for a persuasive proposal or recommendation. It may be information for a justification report, a problem report, a periodic report, or an analytical report. The report or proposal may be written or oral. Information may be gathered for an annual report, a corporate brochure, or advertisements. Managers need information about new trends in order to evaluate information that comes from internal sources about sales, market share, costs, profitablility margins, strategic plans, customer feedback, and moves by the competition.

Information used for specific communication objectives is usually assessed as to its reliability and validity. Both high-context and low-context cultures look for reliability and validity of data, although ways of defining these characteristics may vary.

Reliable generally means that the information is consistent, timely, and stable. The same information could be gathered again at another date from the same people using the same means, provided the factors in the situation are the same. It doesn't depend upon emotions affecting the sources. Reliable sales figures for the month of March are not subject to variation depending upon whether or not the sales manager is angry with the production manager.

Valid means that the information is about what it purports to be about. Information from a parts supplier about availability of a part for an assembly job is valid when it refers to that specific part and not another part. Unless the information is indeed about *what* it claims to be about, it is not valid—even if the measure (say, the quantity of that part manufactured per month) is reliable.

People who make decisions value information. Managers want lots of information, and they want it to be useful in the decision-making process. Managers ask subordinates to supply information so they have the benefit of a wide range of viewpoints. Some managers deliberately develop a communication style that encourages information sharing. Everyone's opinions and ideas are sought. The more breadth of information the better the decision.

Effective managers give their subordinates lots of information when they explain decisions so their subordinates understand the direction of the decision. Then subordinates can act to carry out the decision. When subordinates have information about the larger objectives and goals, they are more likely to feel a commitment to them. Their commitment can be encouraged to grow if they are informed about the background to a decision: the history, the reasons, the long-term objectives. Managers also feed information to subordinates in order to generate feedback of information.

Information can be characterized as *formal* and *informal.*

FORMAL INFORMATION   Formal information comes from four sources:

- Publications and public information.
- Observation.
- Interview and survey.
- Experimentation.

The methods for accessing information from these sources are agreed upon. For example, experiments must follow certain procedures to yield valid results, such as control of variables, selection of subjects, and explicitly identified equipment or situations. Then another researcher could exactly repeat the experiment. Use of published information involves documenting the sources carefully so that another researcher could also consult the same sources. Observation similarly has to be described so another researcher could duplicate the observation and get the same results. Interviews and surveys involve questionnaires that should be designed carefully and pretested before data are gathered. They also should be open to scrutiny by other researchers.

The information yielded by these four methods is thus presumed to be untouched by the researcher's personal and subjective bias. In other words, it is considered objective data. Low-context cultures think that objectivity ensures a greater degree of accuracy.

INFORMAL INFORMATION   Of course, businesspeople also gather informal information that is used for making decisions about doing business. For example, a business wants to know what deal a competitor has made with a domestic company in a target country. Or an organization wants to know who has recently been hired in a key position by a company that buys from it. Organizations want to know who is marketing a new product or repositioning to a new market or using a new advertising agency. Often this information comes from talk with contacts outside the business, but isn't always published information or the result of experiment, survey, or observation. Nevertheless, its value is still based on whether or not it can be verified by another source. It still may be *objective* data.

Informal information that is *subjective* often comes through a "grapevine" or other informal network inside or outside an organization. Subjective data can also be useful because the emotional bias, as well as the data, are information for the gatherer that can affect a decision. If the informal talk about the implementation of a training program carries emotional messages of suspicion and fear, a manager can respond to the emotion and allay fears and suspicions, thereby possibly increasing the likelihood of success of the program.

In high-context, hierarchical cultures, as well as low-context, horizontal cultures, businesses gather this information through informal channels. In fact, this talk-with-contacts information may be more valuable to an organization than the formal information that comes from formal sources: publications, on-line services, observation, experimentation, and survey. One reason is that the information from informal sources is always within a context. The source understands the information within a context and delivers it within a context. The information gatherer receives it and assigns it meaning within a context.

With the Information Revolution, informal information from the Web is easily available to just about anyone with an Internet service provider (ISP). The informal communication channels such as chat rooms and bulletin boards give people who have not been introduced the opportunity to discuss pretty much anything. This is a greatly expanded grapevine that gives access to a breathtakingly broad range of informal information. For example, you can find out what's happening at a company by chatting or exchanging E-mail with an employee there, even if you never learn that person's name. You can learn what people really think about someone they worked for, before your company hires that person. You can find out what people who bought a product really think of it. Chat online involves participants in an immediate, personal dialog carried in an authentic "voice." People communicate in an unmediated and direct on-screen conversation that seems to give more trustworthy information than the official company press release or memo. The popularity of Ananova, the British Press Association's news droid on the Web, suggests that even low-context cultures prefer news from a humanlike source.

Electronically facilitated conversations also go on among employees of companies, often through an intranet or a network that serves specific users. But the unfiltered information also introduces a whole host of new problems. Verification of information may be more difficult.

Companies are noticing the enhanced communication among employees. The Xerox company ran a series of TV ads in the late 1990s that depicted a "conversation" in some idealized classical setting outside of time involving people in togas who observe and comment upon modern-day employees' needs and solutions. The 1950s had gossip at the water cooler; in the 21st century talk is electronic and reaches a far wider potential audience.

The authors of *The Cluetrain Manifesto* predict, "In just a few more years, the current homogenized 'voice' of business—the sound of mission statements and brochures—will seem as contrived and artificial as the language of the 18th century French court."[1] Our current language of business conforms to norms of business discourse that very well may seem dated and quaint in the future. The typical company's voice is authoritarian, aloof, and arrogant, whereas customers and employees alike are engaged in a conversation through informal communication channels like the Web in the "real" voice of everyday people. *The Cluetrain Manifesto* warns companies that once people have become part of that conversation, they won't be willing to be listen to companies speaking in the 20th-century voice. The father-knows-best tone of one slogan in the early 20th century may be the most obvious example: "What is good for General Motors is good for America." People today are not persuaded by that argument.

Possession of Information

Information is a useful resource in competitive situations. The person or group that knows what another does not know has an advantage. Let's say you are one of two candidates for a position and your interview with the hiring team is next week. You'll want to find out everything you can in order to strengthen your candidacy. If you are working within a low-context, results-oriented culture, you'll want to know the job description, the qualifications the team is looking for, and the things they value in an employee at that position. You'll also want to know what strengths and weaknesses your competitor has, if possible. This will give you some power in the interview to respond and perhaps even direct the conversation.

If you are working within a high-context, relationship-oriented culture, you'll also want to empower yourself for the interview, but you may want different kinds of information. You'll want to know who the people are on the hiring team and who will have the greatest say. You'll want to find out what links (connections between people, such as common interests, acquaintances, and experiences) your colleagues have with the hiring team and with the others you'll be working among if hired. You'll also want to know what links your competitor has with the hiring team and the organization. Of course, there are many other factors you'd want information about as well, but in both high- and low-context cultures information is power and gives an advantage—even when the nature of the information varies.

In organizations from high-context cultures where the career path of the individual is closely tied to the team or group of which the individual is a part, information is "owned" by the group. Individuals share information. This is related to the cultural priority discussed in Chapter 4 about what is private versus what is public. In a high-context culture like China, for example, little is *not* shared. Information belongs to the group, not the individual. That way, individuals are linked together into a collective.

In China, one of the authors, a visiting professor, discovered a different attitude toward confidentiality, to her chagrin. She had written a personal assessment of each student at the end of a course. She had given each student a personal copy and given the whole document, labeled "Confidential," to two people only: the chair of the department in which she taught and the president of the university. She was amazed when she saw her confidential evaluations *published* in a universitywide periodical—complete with the "confidential" heading duly translated! As a Westerner, she had not understood the collective ownership of information.

Human resources management implications come out of this different attitude toward information about people. In the United States, people assume that personnel matters are private. Teachers go through elaborate procedures to assure that students do not have access to each other's grades. In business it is the same. Evaluations are confidential. The right to privacy, like many other rights in the United States, comes from an individualistic cultural dimension.

Information is a link that joins people in a collective or group. For example, Thais seeking employment include not only university education on their resumes, but also high school education.[2] That's because they may have gone to a school that a member of the royal family or some other nobility attended. That links the candidate to a high social status and would link future co-workers as well.

From secret handshakes and codes in social organizations to vacation experiences in specific locations to membership on boards or committees, information that is shared by the group, but not by those outside the group, defines membership. In group-oriented cultures, what is known by one member of a group is known by all members of the group. In individualist cultures, what is known by one individual is not automatically the property of the group. One who knows has a power others do not have, and when one chooses to share the information, a link is forged.

In low-context cultures where the career of the individual is to a greater extent the individual's own responsibility, information is owned by the individual and shared judiciously where the individual will benefit. In a low-context culture like Austria, for example, individuals value confidentiality of information and do not share it. If a job candidate has had a link with a prestigious person, the candidate might use that to enhance his or her status, but co-workers would not expect to be included in the linkage or benefit from it.

Ambiguity versus "Hard" Data

Another characteristic of information that varies with cultures involves what is known in English as "soft" and "hard" data. Hard data are often numerical. Of course as you know, statistics can be used to mean anything. Meaning is influenced by assumptions, by statistical tools used, and by personal bias in interpretation. Nevertheless, numbers are valued because they appear to be objective and verifiable. Numbers supposedly could be duplicated by another statistician looking for the same information in the same places. The fact is, however, that any two statistics-gatherers may have different results.

Figures that show quarterly earnings, for example, seem to be incontrovertible. But in fact they may not measure the same things in different organizations. Market share figures can include or exclude factors, and so they can vary from company to company and product to product.

In some cultures, statistics mean very little because other factors that are not quantifiable are the important factors. In Russia, in the 1980s when factories produced according to state-determined quotas and didn't worry about markets, an important statistic was the production quota. Productivity, cost, supply of materials and labor, warehoused unsold inventory, and sales were all of far less importance, and these data were typically not gathered. Today, the important factor may be personal ties—who the factory manager is close to, or on poor terms with. Changes in government policy, rather than anything quantifiable or measurable, may be important factors.

For businesspeople from the United States who attempt to do business in Russia, frustration often develops over the lack of hard data. But people in Russia are inexperienced at gathering hard data other than production figures and at putting this data to work for business objectives. The same is true in some former Soviet block countries without recent histories of market-oriented economies. Vietnam and China, which are still communist countries, for example, are trying to come to terms with information needs for decision making in market-based economies.

In planned economies, certain hard data may not only be hard to come by, but also may not be considered relevant. It isn't just a question of planned or market economies, however; relevance and appropriateness are culturally defined. High-context cultures with market economies may identify "relevant" data differently from low-context Europe or the United States. For example, issues involving family or obligations may count more than hard data. The Korean father who founded a family noodle shop may not be the fastest worker (most productive), but it may be important to him to make noodles, and the loss of face he would suffer if his children were to decide to replace him would make such a decision impossible.

"Soft" data are estimates, nonnumerical projected trends, guesses, and suppositions. Businesspeople in the United States sometimes talk about "flavor" or "feel" when discussing imprecise characteristics of a product or market or partnership. For example, a Middle-Eastern company that wants to import cotton fabric may order more patterns with green because of a guess that consumers will prefer the color green. A Canadian company would prefer to rely on hard research data from market studies, surveys, and focus groups.

Much information is *not* quantifiable, but nevertheless it is important. Employees may report they enjoy working in a particular department within an organization, but they may not be able to answer exactly why they prefer it to another department. Questions that ask for numerical responses (degree of lighting, number of times employee birthdays are celebrated a month, total minutes taken for lunch on average) cannot contain the information or communicate it meaningfully.

Business Information Sources

Who collects information? Where is information available? The issue of availability of information rarely concerns business information-gatherers in Western cultures. The West is overwhelmed with information. Managing the information tidal waves that threaten to drown gatherers is a big job in itself. In fact, an industry exists to offer information about how to manage information. In the West the problem is identifying which sources to spend time on, since there are so many. Rarely is information unavailable (except of course where it is private and confidential).

It is also assumed in the United States that collection of information about people is acceptable in many situations. Europeans have a rather different attitude. For example, the United States keeps detailed cancer statistics concerning follow-ups, effectiveness of treatment, and the like. Patients are not identified by name, but the information is collected and managed. In Germany, no such research bank exists because hospitals are not allowed to collect it. It is considered a violation of privacy. This has ramifications for determining the effectiveness of treatment options.

Public Information Sources

Information is gathered by a wide range of information services and made available in libraries, newspapers, and other publications, nonprint media like radio and television, and online databases like Lexis–Nexis. Information is gathered by private companies who sell it, such as J.D. Power and Associates, which analyzes and compiles market information about automobiles. Information is gathered by independent researchers, often funded by public sources, who make findings public. Journalists gather information for publication. Academics gather information for publication. And information is gathered by governments and published in documents available in libraries.

Not all cultures offer public information. In China, for example, information is gathered by separate government ministries; each has its own publication and makes public only what it chooses. When a Western import–export company wanted figures about the export of leather work gloves in the late 1980s, for example, they had to go to the National Native

Produce and Animal By-Products Import and Export Corporation of the Animal By-Products Branch of the Department of Animal Husbandry and Health within the Ministry of Agriculture. Figures were not available from any centralized government publication or in any newspaper. Information is not released to just anyone who asks. Even determining where to go for information is difficult—information about who has information may be hard to obtain.

In contrast, the Canadian government publishes *Statistics Canada* regularly; monthly figures are available for all export commodities. An individual or organization wanting to know about Canadian exports or imports of leather work gloves can look up monthly figures in any public library. While exporters in Canada complain about the amount of paperwork demanded by the federal government, Canadians value open public access to such information.

Gathering information is taken for granted as a valid business activity in Western cultures. It is necessary and reasonable for businesses to gather and use information. In non-Western cultures, however, and especially in societies with governments or research institutions that look upon their information as exclusively theirs, gathering information can be dangerous. It threatens the sources that control information. Since information is power, holders of information don't like any dissipation of that power. In addition, the act of gathering information can seem threatening to people who have had information about themselves used against them. In different cultures, people who gather information about others and hold it secretly, from Iraqi or Afghan secret police to the powerful military rebels in Sri Lanka and central Africa, generate fear.

Imagine a culture that views change as negative, that values being rather than doing, that considers the group a basic unit of society and individuals as fractions of the whole basic unit, and that looks upon its own cultural priorities as the only ones worth holding. Then imagine someone—probably a foreigner—coming in to ask questions and gather information about behavior, preferences for products, prices paid for goods, and other market data. Such inquiries will almost certainly be treated with suspicion and hostility. The way business information is defined and gathered has to be put in the context of a specific culture.

This imaginary culture, as described in the preceding paragraph, is probably a high-context culture. But high-context cultures are not alone in valuing information as a source of power:

> In all cultures, information creates and reflects power, depending on who has it, how it is used, and to whom it is transmitted or not transmitted. It distinguishes the "ins" from the "outs" and so whether or not you share the secret reflects your social standing. And vice versa, any information restricted to an elite is perceived to be important, perhaps even when it has little instrumental value.[3]

Information is power. Businesspeople speak of the importance of "getting all your ducks in a row"—an image from a fairground shooting gallery—to refer to the need to have all the pieces of information possible and to understand how they fit together before revealing one's intentions to others. That is a way to minimize the risk that a powerful person with more information could come between you and your objective.

A young Thai executive in a finance company came up against a boss who refused to tell her what was involved in his job and refused to train her. After all, status came from what he knew that nobody else did. She reported, he will not tell anybody what he is doing, even me. He is frightened that we are going to take his job. He's old, he has to retire in four years. Everyone respects him because he's old and he's the only one who has the information. He just likes to give orders and nobody can say anything because we don't properly understand. Even [*sic*] he won't help me although our managing director told him to . . . When he goes the company can easily go bankrupt because we don't have his knowledge. So I have to go abroad for training and then come back and train other people.[4]

Information and the Knowledge Economy

In recent years, the availability of information has transformed not only how businesses operate, but the very economic environment in which businesses exist. Computers linked by the Internet to vast databases access information that software easily converts to useful business knowledge. Small businesses can compete with big companies, if they just use some ingenuity and creative ways of serving the customer. Larger brick-and-mortar companies like the U.S. retailer Wal-Mart have reinvented themselves on the Web. Employees have access to more information and as a result express greater satisfaction with their work. Productivity is up and so are profits. In this new economy, knowledge is the major factor in the creation of wealth. Processes and labor, capital and investors will obviously continue to be important, but it is knowledge that is most highly valued in the New Economy.

What is "knowledge" in a company? The example above from Thailand illustrates what this means: the accumulated experience, understanding, contacts, and information that all exist within the minds of employees. Companies are right to view this intangible resource as valuable. For example, an employee who has experienced a posting overseas has gathered considerable knowledge that she can pass on to the person who replaces her.

In order to capture and capitalize on this knowledge, companies must come up with a way to manage it. In many organizations, this is an IT function and knowledge is stored in databases so others can access it.

Here is a story. A village sits at the edge of a river. The people depended on the river for everything: fish for food, water for drinking, and irrigation for farming. One day, 500 kilometers upstream, somebody had the bright idea of building a dam. The villagers knew this was a serious threat. What would happen to the river if the dam was built?

The choices were obvious: Either they adapted to a new way of life by the river or they perished. The villagers who changed moved on to dominate the valley. Those who didn't were swept away.

The New Economy is like the dam. Information today is like the river. If the villagers (or companies) don't change, they will be wiped off the landscape. The pursuit of knowledge is the solution—he who controls knowledge rules the river. The pursuit of education, or, more broadly, human capital, is paramount.

This story is told by futurist Alvin Toffler, who believes knowledge as a critical factor of production will redefine work.[5] Here are 10 ways Toffler says knowledge will continue to change the workplace:

- The definition of work is no longer muscle power but rather mental power.
- Work can happen anywhere and at any time. It no longer occurs only in offices or factories, but in homes, hotels, trains, planes, and taxis.
- Workers, instead of being followers, now are changed to thinking innovators.
- Workers are no longer wage-slaves but instead are becoming entrepreneurs, operating as free agents and selling their labor.
- Workers no longer depend solely on an income from an employer; they earn from multiple streams, such as investment and other incomes on the side.
- The nature of careers also is changing. If in the Old Economy workers stuck to one career, in the New Economy they continually change their jobs and their careers.
- Companies are changing from permanent or fixed, stable entities into changing, nimble organisms, and the continuous change means new relationships every day.
- Products are changing at lightning speed; before one product is finished, change takes place, demanding different sets of skills.
- Markets are being redefined as companies learn to specialize to meet local micromarkets.
- The nature of learning is changing so that "nimble" companies learn, unlearn, and relearn quickly.

The availability of more timely information in recent years has enabled business management to reduce inventory and eliminate unproductive workers that were a security "cushion" but in the end produced nothing of value. The New Economy is the result of the extraordinary surge in technological innovation, particularly for information access, that developed through the latter decades of the last century. According to longtime chairman of the United States Federal Reserve Bank, Alan Greenspan, these developments emphasized the essence of information technology. The result is the expansion of knowledge and the reduction of uncertainty.[6] Because knowledge is essentially irreversible, the recent gains in productivity appear permanent. Expanding E-commerce is expected to accelerate these gains, as companies sell more and more products. Already consumers can buy automobiles, groceries, toothpaste, and wine on the Web, and many businesses rely on the Web to locate suppliers, customers, and partners.

The technology that makes the knowledge economy possible is spreading quickly around the globe, but should still be kept in perspective. In 2000 there were more telephone lines in Manhattan than in all of Africa. The global population is about 6 billion, and half of those people live on less than U.S. $2 per day. Many have never seen a computer, let alone used one.

However, technology is spreading fast. On a visit to India in 2000, President Clinton was amazed to see a computer that a person with basic literacy skills in Hindi and English could operate in a small poor village. A young mother demonstrated that she could access a website from the Indian Health Department for information about what a mother should do in her child's first six months, complete with good graphics. She printed out the information and took it home. In another village, a dairy co-operative was tracking its output by computer and satellite-delivered information. In Hyderabad, India, the chief minister has a goal to have every village and every state service on the Internet by 2002. In Bangladesh the Grameen Bank is launching a project to finance a cell phone in every village. That way poor villagers can be connected to the rest of the world. Internet cafés have sprung up in many underdeveloped countries, challenging ideas about technology in poorer parts of the world.

Recently a World Bank representative went to Ethiopia to determine how the World Bank could assist on the development of E-business. He thought that he was going to deal with people who had no experience or understanding of E-business, and said to a group of local businesspeople, "Does anybody here know what a website is?" Someone raised a hand and said, "I do; I have a website." The World Bank employee asked how he could have a website in Addis Ababa, since there are no connections. The Ethiopian said, "It's very easy. In the United States, cab drivers in Chicago, New York, and Washington are Ethiopian. And what they want to do is to send goats to their families in Ethiopia. So I've opened a website in New York. I go to my cyber-café here every day and I collect the orders from the cab drivers in the United States to send goats to their families in Ethiopia."[7]

Informal Sources

Where information travels freely by open channels, organizations can sift, verify, and select information for business goals. Where information is restricted and access is not open, organizations rely more heavily on informal sources. Where information is withheld from workers and only made available in limited supply, workers rely on the organizational grapevine—the informal network. The grapevine flourishes where formal, official information is limited. The secretary to the president or vice president, the mailroom, a good friend of a relative of the chairperson, a confidant of the director—these are the kinds of sources with greatest credibility in an informal network. Informal Internet sources also have greater credibility when they are known persons or entities.

People from open-information cultures who are used to formal sources that offer reliable and accurate information have tended not to place much value on factual information that comes from informal sources. For example, a German Swiss firm may disregard sources' *opinions* about the prospects of success for a proposal to raise the price of a service in Japan. But informal sources of information may be much better at reading the context than foreigners, and informal information may be more accurate than the official version. Internet sources and informal personal E-mail contacts have made informal information much more important than only a decade ago. In some cultural environments, unofficial spokespersons, unsigned newspaper articles, and references in an organization's internal documents can be reliable sources. They not only provide data but also interpret that data, and interpretation means putting the information in context.

For example, in China in the spring of 1983 foreigners who hoped to do international business there were (indirectly) given to understand their hopes should not be too high. Visitors in the Beijing Hotel noticed that suddenly, overnight, not a single waitress was wearing make-up. When they asked about this change, they were told that the woman who read the nightly news on Beijing television had appeared without make-up the night before. Thus the change in policy toward the West was signaled, although a formal statement of the cooling toward the West didn't come for several months. Businesspeople unaccustomed to reading contextual signs were at a disadvantage; those with context interpreters who were able to decipher the signs had information earlier than their competitors who relied on "hard" facts and published sources.

Criteria for Business Information

A number of criteria exist for assessing business information, whether from the Internet, published sources, informants, or surveys:

- Verifiability.
- Trustworthiness.
- Accuracy.
- Credibility.

We'll consider each of these criteria.

Information-gatherers often wonder whether data **can be verified.** That means confirming the information from another and unrelated source. When Mitsubishi receives information about the success of its North American advertising campaign for the Galant car from its advertising agency, it will ask its sales department for confirmation. When Dow Chemical Company receives information from the construction contractor about the scheduled completion date for a plant in Kuwait, it will ask for information from other divisions with previous experience for confirmation.

Another criterion is **trustworthiness.** This is related to the source of information. If the source has proven correct in the past, then the source is probably trustworthy now. Newspaper articles frequently quote a "reliable source"; the author of the article has had some previous reason to believe the source's information is correct. Sources are trustworthy if they are accountable, that is, if they can be called upon to verify their information. Nationally known publications or news media that are shown to be untrustworthy lose credibility (and therefore market). Trustworthiness also applies to the information itself—the degree to which one can count on or have confidence in it.

Is the information **accurate?** This is a key criterion for the usefulness of information. A businessperson who asks about the market for cellular telephones in Nairobi wants as accurate data as possible. Obviously the answer depends to some extent on the source and the verifiability of the information. In some cultures, accuracy is not verifiable and businesspeople have to make do with the best information they can get. If they wait for what they believe is accurate information, they may never make the decision.

Another criterion is **credibility.** Can the consumer of information have confidence in it? If information seems too good to be true, it probably is. When production turnaround, construction schedules, cost, or potential market figures are much more favorable than you had believed they would be, they probably are not believable and you are right not to believe in them. Information that looks odd may *be* odd.

These four criteria—verifiability, accuracy, trustworthiness, and credibility—have been discussed from the point of view of the authors of this book. That point of view is low-context, with a priority on hard data and information sources that meet the criteria discussed here. But the criteria are culturally defined. They mean different things in different cultures. Information from Malaysia may look odd to a New Zealander for whom it may seem to lack verifiability, accuracy, and a degree to which it may be trusted, but it may be the only information available. The Malay, to whom the context of the information is well understood and implications for its use are obvious, may think the information extremely helpful.

In the absence of shared definitions of the criteria for business information, business decision makers need to be flexible. They need to adopt new definitions about information. For example, they may need to look at the connections (people) of their sources, or the validity of contextual signals like the make-up of the waitresses at the Beijing hotel. *Information, like everything else in business communication, is culturally defined.*

DECISION MAKING

The ways people in different cultures make decisions is an important factor in cross-cultural encounters. The rules governing decision making differ and are culturally based.

Take the decision 12 people serving on a trial jury in the United States have to make, for example. They may have 12 different ways of arriving at a judgment about the defendant. Some may draw up complex charts of pros and cons, "guilty" and "not guilty" indicators. Others might add some kind of weighting factor and add up the numbers. Still others could lock on to a key piece of evidence and take that as the deciding factor. One or two may go by something more intuitive: The defendant reminds them of a boy they knew in elementary school or a girl they dated in high school.

Within a culture people use a variety of decision-making strategies. In dominant-British culture, decisions that are based on hard data are made one way—people often are methodical about choosing a loan plan or a mortgage, for example. But when decisions are based on luck, the same people may abandon all method and logic, as when they choose a horse at the racetrack, for example. Businesspeople in Western cultures who do not rely on luck for most business decisions often turn to apparently random ways of making choices when luck is a factor. In other words, people follow a wide range of decision-making processes. The variations in decision-making practices come from cultural priorities.

Making Decisions Based on Ends

Companies in low-context cultures make decisions by focusing on results, or ends. The Ford Motor Company decides to lay off thousands of workers because that will result in higher end-of-year profits to shareholders and lower losses. Philip Morris decides to lower the price of its cigarettes in order to increase the volume of sales and stop erosion of the market share to generic brands. A restaurant chain decides to open a new restaurant in one town and close a restaurant in another town because the shift in economic level of the population means the market has moved.

The cause-and-effect thinking of low-context cultures means they argue from causes to effects and back. They measure profits or market share or number of clients and look for reasons; then they identify other reasons that they believe will result in better profit figures or market share or number of clients. For instance, people who make staffing decisions with ends in mind often have to lay off employees who cannot contribute to the achievement of the goals and to hire other employees who can. These decision makers are valued.

People in ends-oriented organizations make decisions based on the organization's goals: better profit, better productivity, greater market share, or more customers. Decisions are also driven by *personal* goals. That is to say, even personal decisions are based on an assessment of results. An employee will decide to work here for five years in order to accomplish a specific personal goal, and then he or she will be prepared to move over there with the purpose of accomplishing a different goal. Dan will be supportive of Lynn's new program so that Lynn will recommend Dan for promotion; personal goals always play a part.

Employees at many levels get to make decisions in organizations in ends-oriented cultures like the United States and Canada. True, at the lower levels they may only be small decisions that are easy to make. But the employees can be held accountable for their decisions, and that helps the organization measure and evaluate them—and employee evaluation is another of the organization's goals. As for their own personal goals, the employees get some practice at decision making on behalf of the organization.

From their earliest years, individuals in Canada, for example, learn that making their own decisions is expected of them. Even very young children are often asked to decide which of the 108 flavors of ice cream sold in the local ice cream parlor they want. Teachers in kindergarten let the children decide what size and shape to draw a house and what features to include. A sign of adulthood is when young men and women make their own decisions about what career to pursue, what education to acquire, what mate to settle down with. Adults in North America have freedom to make decisions without reference to elders or youngsters. Indeed, the individual's right to choose, or to decide things about personal issues, is valued highly by Canadians and even more by people in the United States. It's often used as a political slogan that speaks powerfully to members of these cultures.

Making business decisions in English-speaking business cultures usually involves subdividing points and issues and dealing with the subsections in a specific order until everything has been addressed. Clarification of detail is important so the relationship of subsections to the larger issue can be understood. Cause-and-effect relationships are established. "What if?" questions are posed and potential answers are offered.

In Europe (France, Germany, Holland, to name a few countries), organizational decisions are based on results but not so many people in an organization make them. In France as in Germany, a very few at the top of an organizational pyramid make decisions. In Holland, the few may be a slightly wider circle, but lower levels do not participate. This is a meaningful difference from Canada and the United States. One cannot expect someone in a middle-level position in an organization in Europe to influence a decision of any magnitude. Canadian and United States companies often delegate authority to make decisions to their representatives, even midlevel ones.

Another consideration in some European cultures is that the goals or ends the company wants to achieve may not be entirely quantifiable. Members of European cultures have strong memories about their own past histories, and their consciousness of their historical identities often leads to a sense of honor and pride. Organizational goals may include preserving and boosting the honor of a national or regional culture. Businesses in the United States tend not to place a high regard on such elements as pride in past glories when setting goals. This is likely to result in United States–European misunderstanding and miscommunication.

Finally, in low-context cultures that value achieving goals, making decisions can be a goal. There is a tendency to consider a decision as an end in itself. Management practices often involve making decisions as a form of action. A matter has been dealt with when a decision has been made.

Making Decisions Based on Means

In Asia, Africa, southern Europe, and Latin America, decisions often are based on means, not ends. There is considerable variation among these diverse cultures, but they differ from the United States, Canada, Britain, Australia, and New Zealand, and to an extent from the northern European countries, where ends are more important than the means.

Means cultures are people cultures, where relationships matter more than results. Children are not expected to make decisions about their own lives, for example; issues such as what university to attend or what discipline to study are made by the senior family members, not the student, in Japan, Korea, China, Vietnam, and Taiwan. Japanese schoolchildren draw a house with the teacher's hand guiding theirs; the drawing shows what the teacher decides to include.[8]

Where decisions are based on means, trust is a key issue. Hard information, statistics, and measurements are not as important as trusting a relationship.

Juan Carlos Aguilar has decided to use Luis Calderon's firm as supplier for his graphic arts company because he has met Calderon several times in social situations and over a long breakfast last week Calderon assured him of his firm's ability to supply what Aguilar's organization needs. This decision is in spite of the fact that Calderon's firm is known in the industry as having a hard time shipping promptly and shipping correct orders.

Another firm has sent Aguilar a promotional mailing with impressive figures, but Aguilar knows nobody in that firm. The firm also sent a representative but Aguilar wasn't impressed when they met briefly in his office. He will go with someone he feels he can trust personally.

When Juan Carlos Aguilar wants to promote his ability to produce printed materials using a new color process to a government official, he has a third party arrange a lunch with someone close to that official, say a lower-level official. In this case, the third party happens to be the lower official's brother-in-law, whom Aguilar knows. The friend and brother-in-law is a go-between.

He and Juan Carlos and the lower official will meet, have drinks and order a meal, and talk about family and other things. Then Juan Carlos will inquire about the lower official's responsibilities so that Juan Carlos, in response to what the lower official (and the go-between) say, can appear very impressed with the lower official's position, responsibilities, cleverness, and the like. Then he will ask the lower official—who has thus been established as wise and well connected—to recommend some higher-level official Juan Carlos could talk to about his new color process and printing ability.

If possible, Juan Carlos will get a card from the lower official. Then he will approach the person recommended, and use the lower official's name. The higher official will usually be in a position to make decisions or influence them. That person may be impressed that Juan Carlos knows the lower official (Juan Carlos will say, "Oh yes, in fact we had lunch the other day"). Because of the chain of contacts between people from Juan Carlos, through his friend the brother-in-law of the lower official, to the lower official and then to the ultimate target, a decision may be made in Juan Carlos's favor, to use his company's services. Juan Carlos will owe his friend a favor for his work as go-between.

Chains of relationships linking people in networks of favors owed and granted exist in most high-context or means cultures. In Hong Kong, for example, trust is similarly a key issue.

Another key issue is solidarity with the others in one's group. In the early 1980s an internationally renowned steel company in Japan entered into a contract to supply steel to another Asian government when it was not feasible to do so. The company could not meet the deadline at the agreed price. But the honor of the company and the honor of the country were at stake. The company performed the contract to the last letter, but suffered great financial loss doing it. The contract wasn't so important in itself, but not losing face as an organization and as a representative of the Japanese nation was very important. It outweighed the cost in money.

Taking responsibility for decisions is part of what a manager does in Western cultures. A manager's power comes in part from this role, and when decisions have good results the manager wants to take credit for them. But managers in non-Western cultures are the opposite. As Victor writes,

> In Asian cultures the powerful eschew decision making . . . In the West, power is demonstrated by the ability to override the dictates of social pressure. By contrast, in Asia, the social order is seen as designed for those in power, and thus power is enhanced as it adheres *to*—rather than overrides—that social power.[9]

Lucien Pye describes the Chinese system as operating in order to diffuse decisions and ultimately spare the powerful from having to take responsibility for them.[10]

In China, decisions are made with reference to relationships. The process involves gathering opinions and arriving at a consensus among the group, in an informal way. If a group cannot be consulted, historical precedents are. In other words, the group is expanded to include people who made well-known decisions in the past. Mao Zedong, Chairman of the Chinese Communist Party and leader of China until his death in 1976, used historical precedent for some of his decisions, quoting events that had taken place over 2,000 years before. Although he had extraordinary powers as the head of the party that ran the country, he needed to present his decisions as the result of consensus between himself and a group—in this case a group of famous heroes from China's long past. Decisions thus are linked to former decisions, and decision makers join the company of renowned heroes in Chinese history. Relationships are how business gets done. Results-based issues that occupy decision makers in low-context cultures are unimportant compared to fostering and nurturing relationships—especially relationships between greater and smaller political entities.

In Ceqikou, a village outside a suburb of Chongqing, in Sichuan province, a fine, wide highway crosses a creek that swells in rainy season—and comes to an abrupt halt on the other side of the creek bank. Trucks that bring goods to the village have to turn around and be unloaded onto handcarts since the village lanes are narrow and paved with cobblestones and trucks can't use them. The Chinese built the road because someone in Beijing authorized it. But to continue the road into the village would have meant the demolition of the majority of homes along the narrow lanes.

In the West a feasibility study would have been done, and factors such as the width of the lane between village houses would have been calculated into the final decision of whether or not to build the new road. The goal of providing a road would have been weighed against the difficulty and cost of relocating the villagers into new homes. But the decision to build was made in Sichuan on a political basis—to support relationships—and other considerations were not important compared with keeping relations good between the village, the district, the province, and Beijing.

Where relationships are important, the consensus of the group is also important. The Japanese *ringi-seido* method of organizational decision making emphasizes consensus. This method has been misunderstood by some in the West who apparently think that decisions are made by top management only when low-level groups approve or even initiate decisions. In fact, Japanese corporate decisions do not originate in the mailroom.

The *ringi-seido* works like this.[11] A manager introduces an issue for discussion and proposes a decision. He goes to each department that is affected and discusses it with each department manager, and he also goes to his vice president for approval. If someone has a concern about the proposal, he discusses it with the proposer after work in informal and formal meetings. These informal soundings and exchanges are called *nemawashi,* which in Japanese means "root-binding." The word describes how a plant's roots are gently and carefully shaped to produce the desired plant. Just so are the deep concerns and emotions and principles and goals of employees gently handled. Next the proposer has to get agreement from other department managers who will be involved in any way. This also means after-hours discussions: *nemawashi.*

Once the proposer has talked to everybody individually and resolved any concerns anyone has, he presents the proposal (which may be very different from the original) at a meeting of all department managers and produces a form called a *ringi-sho.* After this form has been issued, the proposer presents his proposal at a vice-presidential meeting. Each vice president has been briefed about the issue by his department managers before the meeting. There is no unresolved reservation in anyone's mind by this time. In essence, the decision has been made. The document, the *ringi-sho,* is circulated to the department managers, the vice presidents, and perhaps the president for signatures of approval.

Approval doesn't take long in Japanese companies, once the document for signatures has been circulated. What takes a long time is the *nemawashi* that the proposer undertakes with any manager or vice president who has a problem with the original proposal. But it means everyone from manager up to the president has had a chance to present concerns to the sponsor of the proposal, and the concerns can alter the original proposal. After official authorization seals the proposal, everyone is in agreement about carrying it out. Nobody has reservations or anxieties that have not been discussed and assuaged. Nobody is excluded from the decision making; everybody is a member of the in-group. (Actually, not quite everybody. Lower-level employees, which usually means all women and some young men, do not participate.)

Final authority for decision making in most Japanese organizations rests with one man, the president. But it is unusual for him to authorize a decision without first assuring himself of the agreement of others. Lower-level representatives of an organization do not have the authority to make decisions. When pressed, for instance, in negotiations, they cannot commit their organization.

Other Asian cultures have less formalized ways of obtaining consensus than Japan's *ringi-seido;* nevertheless unanimity is important throughout Asia. Harmony matters more than putting oneself forward or having a more powerful voice in decision making than one's colleagues.

Two points need to be emphasized. First, as you probably have already realized, the values of harmony and consensus occur most in cultures that are hierarchical. This may seem paradoxical; where people have the least chance to change their social status and where those in power take for granted that their position won't change, harmony is the method of operating. But consider this: Consensus doesn't threaten the hierarchical structure. Those in power do not risk losing power and those with little power do not stand to gain power; so both can agree and present a unified face. In Asia, saving and giving face to individual group members and holding up the group's face is more important than any specific outcome or end.

Second, this discussion about decision making broadly contrasts an *Asian* style with a *North American* style, and an *English-speaking* style with a *Hispanic* style. But in reality, all decision-making methods discussed here can be found in all cultures. Every day in some organization in the United States, a lot of informal discussion is taking place at various levels, problems are solved, consensus is reached, and a decision is made before any formal decision is passed in a meeting. Every day in some Chinese organization, a situation is arising that requires an immediate decision, an individual has no opportunity to consult a group, and the decision is made on the basis of what the desired results are. Every day some Canadian, United States, and Australian businesspeople are following Juan Carlos Aguilar's strategy for getting access to a target person by using a friend as a go-between and by getting a business card or permission to use the name of someone who already is known to the target person. And every day in a Latin American organization, someone makes a decision without regard to personal relationships.

Nevertheless, *in general*, decision making does come from the values of a culture. If a culture values results, encourages individual competition among workers, and quantifies and measures goals, then decisions will usually be made on the basis of goals or *ends*. If a culture values relationships, encourages harmony among workers, and emphasizes trust, then decisions will usually be made on the basis of *means*.

PROBLEM SOLVING AND CONFLICT RESOLUTION

When people from different cultures engage in business, they often have different expectations about what to do when problems and conflicts arise. Ways of defining problems, ways of handling them, and goals for resolutions are all likely to vary depending upon cultural priorities. Ways of handling conflict vary also.

Some authors discuss conflict along with negotiation, but we see conflict and negotiation as separate. Negotiation across cultures is a specific communication task, but it doesn't have to be called "conflict." On the other hand, conflict is an inevitable part of doing business. It occurs regularly, and it is unavoidable. It is even more present and unavoidable in business between members of more than one culture. It crops up in day-to-day activities and isn't limited to negotiations. Therefore, conflict communication is discussed here, along with problem solving.

Defining Problems and Dealing with Them

People in different cultures see problems differently and talk about them differently, as we have seen. What constitutes a problem? And whose problem is it, anyway?

In individualist cultures where people are responsible for the consequences of their own individual actions, problem-solving skills are learned at an early age. Western societies praise and reward the person who solves a problem; some valued employees have the title "troubleshooter" and the responsibility of finding solutions to problems. School exercises in Western cultures involve getting students to compete to see who can reach a solution first.

In low-context cultures, problems are objectified and externalized. They lie outside the plan for accomplishing the goal. They are extraneous to the cause-and-effect pattern of Western thinking. English-speakers talk about "bugs" that have to be worked out, or "wrinkles" that need to be ironed away. Problems need solutions, so they can be erased. Individuals who achieve solutions to problems are valued. Individuals take responsibility for solutions as well as blame for failure to solve problems. Individuals who cause problems also are blamed.

But in collectivist cultures, problems are not an individual responsibility. Blame is not attributed to individuals, unless an individual who calls attention to the problem seeks some individual advantage. In the illustration in Chapter 5 about a problem trainees had communicating the fact that their tea supply had run out, a worker from China remarked that the person who identified something as a problem *became* the problem. Blame is usually generalized to the group, however, and the group works together to find a solution. In process-oriented cultures that emphasize the group acting together, that very cooperation itself is worthwhile. Problems are neither externalized nor considered nuisances that interrupt and interfere with the accomplishment of a goal. Rather, they are part of the context and process in which the group operates. Working on the problem is as important as solving it. Quality circles in Japan are an example of this approach. The line between what is *problem* and what is simply the situation is not as clear in collective cultures as in individualistic cultures that make the problem somehow outside the normal situation. So the way a problem is defined is different.

Problems can be things like a devaluation of the Mexican peso that makes it harder for a gallery owner in San Miguel de Allende to buy art from Canadian Inuit sculptors. When the peso goes down, her costs go up since the Canadian dollar is now more expensive to buy with pesos, and Canadian products are also more expensive to buy. Problems can include unusual weather that disrupts the movement of people or goods. Problems are obstacles to business objectives that do not directly result from disagreements between people.

Managing Conflicts

The whole idea of managing conflicts is a low-context notion. We try to define, resolve, and get on with it. In high-context cultures, conflict is part of life.

When problems involve disagreements among people, they are called *conflicts*. Cultural priorities determine how conflict is handled.

In individualist cultures, conflict is accepted as an integral part of life. Borden writes that although the negative results of conflict are widely acknowledged, nevertheless "some feel that a relationship without conflict is no relationship at all."[12] Conflicts are looked upon not only as inevitable, but sometimes as necessary and even healthy. As a way of controlling outcomes of conflict that may be destructive, members of low-context cultures often verbalize their feelings and discuss conflicts. Results cultures value objectifying, depersonalizing, and analyzing issues apart from the people involved. Disagreement makes discussion possible, in these cultures. Israeli culture is an example: In a sense, the entire tradition of the Mishna is ongoing debate or argumentation based on disagreements. The debaters may have the greatest respect for one another and still disagree. In fact, the attitude is that conflict can *only* be resolved when it is brought out into the open and explicitly discussed.

In collectivist cultures, however, conflict may be viewed as one dimension of the ongoing relationships among group members, not something outside the relationships. Conflicts are part of collective life. But conflict that is openly identified threatens the harmony of the group. Indeed, when conflict is out in the open, it is almost always destructive in collectivist cultures. Instead of verbalizing conflict, high-context cultures use actions to compensate, show goodwill, and restore harmony to the group. Apologies are not asked for or given because they are recognition of conflict. A low-context person who insists on "talking it out" with a high-context person may feel resolution is being achieved. But the other person may feel the open admission of conflict is an irreparable rupture in the relationship.

Say, for example, that a manager in the United States turns down two sales proposals, one from an American subordinate and one from a Japanese subordinate.

The North American subordinate will probably enter the conflict situation with heated discussion and issue-oriented arguments. He or she will probably produce facts, figures, and graphs to illustrate his or her case. In contrast, the Japanese subordinate will probably be dumbfounded by the direct, outright rejection and will then proceed to analyze the conflict episode as a personal attack or a sign of mistrust. In fact, he or she will probably resign as soon as possible.[13]

The American subordinate probably believes the root of the conflict was in different goals and objectives. The Japanese subordinate probably believes the conflict was not in the rejection of the proposal but rather in the way it was communicated.

In the United States culture, conflict is generally said to arise from five areas:

- Disagreement over tasks (what).
- Disagreement over processes (how).
- Disagreement over allocation of resources (with what).
- Disagreement over goals (why).
- Disagreement over power (who).

Let's say a product such as a microwave snack food is losing market share. Perhaps it is due in part to a competitor's new product. But it may be due in part to conflicts between people over resources, processes, goals, and power. Production employees may not feel they were consulted when the marketing department decided to launch the new snack, while the marketing employees may feel they are being held back by production staff, who are cautious about letting a product go (disagreement over process). The production manager may feel she should be the one to stand in front of the microphones and announce the new product, not the marketing manager who did not participate in its creation (disagreement about power). Marketing may wish they could move faster, while production may want more time to test the product (disagreement about the resource, time). The aim of the production people is to develop a product that will not be flawed; the aim of the marketing people is to sell the product in as great a quantity as possible (disagreement about goals). This simple illustration shows how conflicts arise when people are doing their jobs, within one cultural environment. When groups from different cultures disagree, the conflict is more complex.

Results cultures like the United States spend conscious time and effort on conflict resolution. Conflict is brought out into the open and is specifically addressed with "conflict communication." The goal of the communication is to resolve the conflict.

Relationship cultures, which prefer to consider problems within the context of group effort, don't have to spend conscious time and effort on conflict resolution—it's part of the culture to deal with it without calling attention to it. The Japanese don't talk about conflict as the result of five areas of disagreement or create narratives about it. They prefer not to mention conflict directly at all. In the lower-context culture of the United States, managing conflict is a "can-do," measurable goal to be achieved. Accordingly, experts offer managers definitions and categories of ways to manage conflict, such as these by K. W. Thomas:

- Competing (insisting your goals rank above those of others).
- Collaborating (showing high concern for others' goals while being assertive about one's own).
- Compromising(settling for less and making others do so too).
- Avoiding (not pursuing your goals or others' openly).
- Accommodating (allowing others' goals to take precedence).[14]

The choice of approach depends on organizational goals, circumstances, priorities, and corporate culture. This list offers a good description of the options open to a manager for conflict resolution between low-context parties that both have high priorities for encoding messages in words and for achieving results.

Competing is openly encouraged in individualist cultures. Salespeople are challenged to outdo each other, for example. The salesperson of the year is singled out for an award in many companies. But collectivist cultures do not encourage open competition. Individual goals are not to be placed above the goals of the group.

Collaboration is also encouraged in many individualist-culture companies. Being able to work with others, being a team player, is important for success in most organizations. Many corporations that use collaboration to resolve conflict urge conflicting sides to establish a common goal and get away from the focus on one's own interest. Thomas's definition of collaboration is very individualist: One continues to keep one's own goals firmly in view while also accommodating others' goals. This is not the same approach used in collectivist organizations; they encourage commitment by teams and groups to common goals. Individual goals are not worthy of the effort that common goals merit. If individual goals conflict with the group's goals, the individual goals fade or are postponed.

Compromising involves giving up something voluntarily. Both or all parties are expected to do so until finally resolution is reached. The implication is that when goals conflict, different sides give up some things while managing to retain other aspects of their goals. So although the conflicting parties all yield something, they also all gain something. Cultural attitudes toward compromise vary, and this will be discussed more fully in Chapter 9. **Bargaining** and negotiating may be necessary to reach this partial-loss/partial-gain position.

When the parties themselves cannot reach agreement, a *third party* may be asked to intervene. When the third party is a go-between, an information conduit, **mediation** takes place. When the third party is asked to make a judgment and impose a solution to the conflict, the process is called **arbitration.** These third-party roles are typical of a culture that places a high priority on explicit encoding of messages, and on achievement of goals as markers of success. In cultures accustomed to authoritarian behavior and hierarchical power structures, the use of a third party may quickly move to the arbitrator. This is the case, for example, in India where conflicting brothers will appeal to the president of a family-owned company for a ruling rather than sit and discuss their conflict on their own or with a go-between. The resolution of the conflict is the goal rather than conflict management.

Avoiding conflict is another way of resolving it. In individualist cultures it is rarely a satisfactory, long-term solution. The parties simply agree to stop disagreeing openly. Perhaps they get tired of conflict. Perhaps the parties feel no meaningful goal can be achieved if they have to give up anything. In collectivist organizations, avoidance of conflict is the most common method of handling it. When disagreements arise, parties hold back from openly pursuing their goals in the face of opposition. They may continue to work toward goals, but they will do nothing openly that might disrupt the harmony of the larger group.

Accommodating the other party's goals and abandoning one's own is not a common process toward resolution of conflict in low-context cultures. In collectivist cultures, however, such a move may be taken more often because it results in an indebtedness. At a later date, the party that gave up its goals can remind the party that was assisted in reaching its goals of the favor. Such a move is not unknown in individualist cultures. But in collectivist cultures, accommodation of the other is a way to build the network of obligation discussed in Chapter 4.

An employee from an individualistic culture and an employee from a collectivistic culture who disagree thus also may find themselves in disagreement over how to handle their conflict. If a collectivistic person's secret and concealed activity is discovered, the individualistic person will make accusations of underhanded and sneaky behavior. If the individualistic person insists on bargaining, mediation, or arbitration, the collectivistic person may feel threatened with a loss of face and may be shamed by the rupture to the outward harmony of their relations.

When a conflict arises between cultures, one collectivist and the other individualist, the collectivistic people tend not to discuss it as a problem, but rather to consider it as one factor in the context of the whole relationship. They balance it with examples of good cooperation, and they minimize the potential damage from conflict by talking around it and dealing with it indirectly. The individualistic people, on the other hand, want to put a name to the conflict and objectify it so some solution can be identified. They verbalize the details of the conflict and believe that by talking it out and having everyone's views in words, it can be understood from all sides, reduced to its constituent parts, and then the parts, one by one, can be talked away. Obviously, these opposing behaviors dealing with conflict can themselves become a source of misunderstanding.

When you encounter some conflict in your dealings with members of another culture, don't assume your method of resolving conflicts will be the one the others automatically use. Think about the other culture's values and priorities and pay close attention to what the other parties to the conflict do. They may be dealing with it in a way you don't recognize. Furthermore, their method may resolve the conflict.

Communicating about Conflicts

Certain communication strategies can enable you to handle conflict: to talk about it or talk around it and to use communication strategies to resolve conflict. But remember that for some cultures, actions are the best communication. There are five recommended strategies:

- Listen sincerely.
- Express agreement where you can.
- Identify common goals.
- Explain your position.
- Identify resolutions that accommodate cultural priorities.

LISTEN SINCERELY   This is an important strategy for conflict communication when only one culture is involved; it is even more important when the conflict is intercultural. We often assume we understand the other's point of view and don't need to listen to its being presented. Assuming you understand someone else's perceptions, reasons, and values on the basis that they are like yours is called **projected cognitive similarity.** Even when you acknowledge another set of perceptions, reasons, and values, you may be assuming you understand them. But this assumption is especially likely to be wrong when you don't have the same priorities as someone from another culture.

Richard Mead, in his book on intercultural communication for managers, offers suggestions for *how* to listen.[15] First, listen with an *attitude of interest* in what the other party is saying. The interest may be apparent, rather than real, but an appearance of interest will encourage the other side to speak about the conflict. This is important, because in many high-context cultures a public acknowledgment of disagreement is not acceptable. If the other party comes from such a culture and you come from a low-context culture, you may have a hard time getting any discussion about the conflict out in the open. An attitude of interest in the other party's concerns can help. On the other hand, if you are one who prefers to deal with the conflict indirectly and your counterpart wants open and frank discussion of the conflict, you still need to listen with interest. Then you can say you appreciate the statement and appear sincere to the other side rather than indifferent, even if you go on to ask for a postponement of the discussion.

Sometimes the opportunity to express a position is all that is necessary for a party to drop a conflicting position. This is true when one grievance in the conflict is a feeling of not being heard. Writing about United States–Russian conflicts, Yale Richmond advises,

Confrontations over differences of views can often be avoided by letting Russians talk themselves out. After they have unburdened themselves and expressed their righteousness and indignation, their opposition may moderate and the differences may turn out to be not as great as originally believed. In fact, after talking themselves out, Russians and Americans may even find that they have a unanimity of views.[16]

Next, *assess the meaning of what you are hearing.* Don't rush to judgment, but pay attention to the unspoken cultural priorities behind the words. Ask questions for clarification, being careful to avoid making the other side feel defensive. The other party may use a communication style that is ambiguous and indirect on purpose, so listen for style as well as content.

Finally, *think before you respond,* which may mean taking time. Results-oriented cultures tend to encourage quick responses for quick resolutions to problems. Get it fixed! Get over it! Move on! These are attitudes that easily find expression in results cultures. Relationship-oriented cultures are the opposite. Taking time allows one to think carefully about all the ramifications of a response upon the lives of the others. There is also the hope that if enough time passes, the conflict will fade and be resolved without intervention.

EXPRESS AGREEMENT WHERE YOU CAN   This advice means letting the other party know you find the other position understandable and legitimate. Note the words in this advice, *where you can.* The agreement should be genuine on your part. Usually people have reasonable concerns, and if you put yourself in the others' position, you can agree with their view of the issues. Your agreement at this stage is with their concerns, but probably not with their solution—otherwise you don't have a conflict. For instance, with a Syrian it may be sufficient to express agreement on items that you can agree upon for the areas of disagreement to recede in importance.

IDENTIFY COMMON GOALS This is the key to an agreement that is usually labeled "win-win" (discussed in more detail in Chapter 9). It is what happens when sides compromise, or reach some agreement through bargaining or mediation, although something also is given up. When both parties can identify common goals, both can work backwards to processes to reach those goals. Terpstra and David describe a family-owned business in India that entered into a joint venture with a firm from the United States. As a result, an organizational specialist from the United States suggested tightening the loose Indian business structure. He drew up an organizational chart that placed a younger brother who had an MBA in a higher position than two older brothers who did not have MBAs. Conflict immediately arose among the brothers, and the two brothers of the older generation became involved. "They both said, 'What is the business good for if it breaks up the family?' "[17] The conflict could only be resolved when the common goal—the family united in an ongoing business—was clear to all parties, Indian and American. If the business itself threatened the family, the business could go.

EXPLAIN YOUR POSITION   This is where you state your concerns. This is not the same thing as persuasion or argumentation. At this stage, you are setting out your position clearly and neutrally. If the conflict has arisen because of a misunderstanding, this is where it will come to light and your conflict can be resolved. Some conflicts do arise from misunderstanding.

For members of low-context cultures, messages are typically encoded explicitly, and delicacy is not as important as accuracy. If you are a low-context culture member communicating about conflict with someone from a high-context culture, explaining your position can be a step that needs special attention. You want to get your position across clearly, but you do not want to risk losing the goodwill of the other party. Where to draw the line is tricky.

If you are a high-context culture member, your efforts at explaining your position may need to focus on explicit and factual presentation. Appeals to the other party's allegiance to the organization may not be helpful.

A manager in a data-processing company was having difficulty dealing with a conflict between a young, ambitious French Canadian male and his co-worker, an older Chinese woman who was on a special visa from China. She had recently become uncooperative and had made it clear to the manager that she would not be willing to travel to the capitol with her co-worker to hold discussions with legislators about a new product. Yet she had worked on the development of the product with great enthusiasm.

When the manager asked her what the problem was, he received no clear explanation. When he asked her co-worker, the young man had no insights to offer. The young French Canadian was clearly annoyed, however, that the Chinese woman was refusing to share her data with him. That meant he couldn't make the presentation to the legislators because she had all the key data on her computer disks.

The manager's repeated questions to her about her "problem" got nowhere. So he changed his approach. He began explaining his concerns, as manager and as spokesperson for the company, about the upcoming meeting with legislators. His explanation about his position was unemotional. In that climate she then felt she could explain her position. She revealed she felt that as an older—and to her mind, more senior—person, she should not be sent to the capitol with a younger employee who would do the presentation of material she had worked hard to develop. That would diminish her status, she felt.

This was obviously a conflict about power, and more specifically about roles. Because the manager explained his position without blame or emotion, the woman was able to respond with an explanation of hers. Once the manager understood her position, he could take steps to resolve the conflict. He announced through a general memo that the woman was the senior consultant on this project and her name would be first on the documents. The young man would do most of the presentation because he was a native English speaker. This satisfied her and allowed the project to continue.

In addition to explaining your position, you also need to make clear what outcome you desire. Making your wishes clear is *not* necessarily the same thing as explicitly stating them, however. As we have seen in Chapter 5, actions can communicate. Behavior can call attention to issues and reveal feelings without explicit encoding in words.

IDENTIFY RESOLUTIONS THAT ACCOMMODATE CULTURAL PRIORITIES
As we have seen, for low-context cultures *resolution* means a termination of the conflict.[18] This may mean that individual goals are met; it may mean organizational goals are met. Another possibility is that the conflict itself ceases without goals being met; parties simply stop being in conflict. Disagreement may exist about the means to reach the end of the conflict, in other words, but the end itself is recognized by all.

In high-context cultures, however, resolution has quite a different meaning, or perhaps it has little meaning. Conflict is simply seen as an ongoing part of the relationship. It may take one form or another, and it may involve certain issues at one point and other issues at another point, but the conflict itself doesn't "end." It simply is not overt and does not disrupt the functioning of the group. This is implied by Pye, for example, in his discussion about the tendency of Chinese negotiators to see any agreement as simply part of a context of ongoing discussion, and not an end.[19] The goal of conflict resolution may be to diffuse the conflict through ambiguity.[20]

SUMMARY

Business information is culturally defined. Information is valued by businesses because it is used to attain business goals.

- *Information is usually valued when it is reliable and valid;* but of course these are also culturally defined terms.
- *Formal information* comes from publications and publicly available sources, observation, surveys and interviews, and experimentation. Results-oriented cultures look upon it as objective and therefore more accurate than informal information.
- *Informal information* comes from the grapevine or online chat rooms and bulletin boards. It always comes with a context and a personal bias.
- Possession of *information means power.* Being "in the know" makes one a member of an in-group, as compared with out-group members who are not in the know.
- Individualist, low-context cultures value "hard" information, often numerical measurements. Such information is not always available in collectivist, high-context cultures.
- *Sources of information are not always public.* In some cultures, gathering information is regarded as inappropriately invasive.
- Information technology has opened access to information tremendously. Knowledge is now considered a company resource and a key factor in the creation of wealth, which has led to a New Economy based on knowledge. Knowledge management is practiced by more and more companies.
- Business information is assessed on the bases of *verifiability, trustworthiness, accuracy,* and *credibility.*

Businesspeople use information for making decisions. Individualist cultures generally make decisions based on ends; collectivist cultures generally make decisions based on means. Conflicts are perceived differently, problems are defined differently, solutions are arrived at differently in different cultures.

- *Cultures define "what is a problem?" differently.*
- *Conflict occurs in one or more of five areas:* tasks, processes, allocation of resources, goals, and power.
- *Five ways to manage conflicts* include competing, collaborating, compromising, avoiding, and accommodating.
- To communicate about conflict, whether with high-context or low-context cultures, the following guidelines may help: listen sincerely, express agreement where you can, identify common goals, explain your position, and identify resolutions that accommodate cultural positions.
- For some high-context cultures, resolution may mean simply diffusing the conflict by nonconflict-oriented communication and absorbing the conflict into the ongoing relationship.

NOTES

1. Rick Levine, Christopher Locke, Doc Searls, and David Weinberger, *The Cluetrain Manifesto: The End of Business as Usual,* (Cambridge, MA: Perseus Books, 2000), p. xiii.
2. Richard Mead, *Cross-Cultural Management Communication,* (New York: John Wiley & Sons, 1990), p. 74.
3. Ibid., pp. 66–67.
4. Ibid., p. 67.
5. Razali Kassim Yang, "Focus Digital Divide: He Who Controls the Knowledge Rules the River, Third Wave Futurist Says at APEC Meeting," *Business Times (Singapore),* April 7, 2000, p. 3.
6. Alan Greenspan in "Transcript of Remarks at Afternoon Session of White House Conference on the New Economy" (1/9), National Desk, *US Newswire,* April 5, 2000. *http://web.lexis-nexis.com/universe,* Retrieved on May 29, 2000. "The new economy, the impact of information technology and the extent to which it has rewritten the rules."
7. James Wolfensohn, "Transcript of Remarks at Afternoon Session of White House Conference on the New Economy" (5/9), National Desk, *US Newswire,* April 5, 2000 (*http://web.lexis-nexis.com/universe*) Retrieved May 29, 2000.
8. "Doing Business With Japan: Part One, Getting Started," videotape, ITRI, 1991.
9. David A. Victor, *International Business Communication,* (New York: HarperCollins, 1992), p. 174.
10. Lucien Pye, *Chinese Commercial Negotiating Style,* (Cambridge, MA: Oelgeschlager, Gunn & Hain, 1982), p. 16.
11. Robert T. Moran, *Getting Your Yen's Worth: How to Negotiate With Japan,* (Houston: Gulf, 1985), p. 15.
12. George A. Borden, *Cultural Orientation: An Approach to Understanding Intercultural Communication,* (Englewood Cliffs, NJ: Prentice-Hall, 1991), p. 111.
13. Stella Ting-Toomey, "Toward a Theory of Conflict and Culture," in *Communication, Culture, and Organizational Processes,* International and Intercultural Communication Annual, vol. IX, William B. Gudykunst, Lea P. Stewart, and Stella Ting-Toomey, eds., (Newbury Park, CA: Sage, 1985), p. 77.
14. Donald P. Cushman and Sarah Sanderson King, "National and Organizational Cultures in Conflict Resolution," in *Communication, Culture, and Organizational Processes,* International and Intercultural Communication Annual Vol. IX, William B. Gudykunst, Lea P. Stewart, and Stella Ting-Toomey, eds. (Newbury Park, CA: Sage, 1985), pp. 117.
15. Mead, *Cross-Cultural Management Communication,* p. 118.
16. Yale Richmond, *From Nyet to Da: Understanding the Russians,* (Yarmouth, ME: Intercultural Press, 1992) p. 130.
17. Vern Terpstra and Kenneth David, *The Cultural Environment of International Business,* 3rd ed. (Cincinnati: South-Western, 1991) pp. 187–8.
18. Lawrence B. Nadler, Marjorie Keeshan Nadler, and Benjamin J. Broome. "Culture and the Management of Conflict Situations," *Communication, Culture, and Organizational Processes,* International and Intercultural Communication Annual, Vol. IX, (Newbury Park, CA: Sage, 1985), p. 95.
19. Pye, *Chinese Commercial Negotiating Style,* p. xi.
20. Ting-Toomey, "Toward a Theory of Conflict and Culture," p. 81.

CHAPTER NINE

Intercultural Negotiation

A Canadian team of two men representing Canwall, a wallpaper printing equipment manufacturer, went to a town north of Shanghai in the province of Jiangsu, China, to negotiate a sale to a new wallpaper production company. Charlie Burton, president of Canwall, traveled with his marketing director, Phil Raines. The company had never before sold its equipment outside Canada, and the two Canadians were delighted with the warm reception they enjoyed in China.

This wasn't the first meeting between the Canadian company and the Chinese wallpaper factory. The manager of the Chinese company, Mr. Li, had been a member of a delegation to Canada. He had met with one of Canwall's senior salespersons and the director of manufacturing. Subsequently a trade representative from Canada had been in China representing Canwall's interests to the Chinese manager. After these meetings and numerous letters and faxes, Canwall's top people were now ready to negotiate the sale.

The day they arrived they were met at the airport in Shanghai by Manager Li himself and transported in a chauffeur-driven car 90 miles to the town. Their accommodation was in a newly built hotel, and while it was not luxurious, it was certainly comfortable. A few hours after their arrival they were treated to a 12-course banquet given by their host, with several high-level municipal officials present. This red-carpet treatment made them feel optimistic about the sale.

The next day they were taken to see the sights nearby: a large, new port for container ships and several factories that indicated the prosperity of the region. They were eager to begin discussing the sale, but after lunch they were given time to rest. In the late afternoon one of the manager's English-speaking employees came by with the news they would be taken to see a local dance company's performance that night.

The third day they finally sat down to meetings. Progress seemed very slow—each side giving generalizations about itself that seemed unrelated to the sale. The Canadians used an interpreter supplied by the Chinese who was eager to please them, so the Canadians felt comfortable with her, but translation slowed down communication. After listening to various apparently unrelated points, the Canadians thought, "So what?"

The Chinese also spent a lot of time talking about the Canadian trade agent who had been in their town earlier. Burton wasn't able to tell them much about that person, since he had never met him personally.

When the Canadians at last were able to make the presentation they had prepared, they were surprised at the number of people who showed up. There were two of them, but there were 10 Chinese facing them across the table. Still, the Chinese frequently nodded and smiled, and said "yes." Burton and Raines had prepared sales data and showed, effectively they thought, that within five years the factory could double its present production. At the end of the day, the jubilant Canadians returned to their hotel rooms confident they had sold the equipment.

The next day they were asked to explain once again things they thought had been covered already to a Chinese team with four new faces in it. They were confused about who their negotiating counterparts really were. Their jubilation began to evaporate. They were asked to explain the technology in minute detail. Neither Burton nor Raines had been involved in the engineering of the high-tech component that was the heart of the equipment. After doing the best they could, they returned to the hotel exhausted.

Their interpreter also seemed to be unfamiliar with technological terms, since she and the interpreter for the factory spent some time discussing them between themselves. Because the Canadian side's interpreter was a woman, the Canadians had to meet with her in the hotel lobby to discuss their plan for the next day. The two tired men would have preferred to sit in their room while they talked with her, rather than in the noisy lobby where they were the object of curiosity, but she requested they remain in a public place because as a woman she could not meet with them in their room.

The next day the Canwell negotiators were asked again about the technological details of the equipment. This time one member of the first-day team pointed out discrepancies between what they had said and what the manufacturing director, an engineer, had told them in Canada. Burton and Raines were chagrined. The Chinese were reproachful about the discrepancies, as if the Canadians had been caught in a shameful act. At lunch the two Canadians quickly faxed Canada for specifications and explanations. The afternoon session was uncomfortable, although everyone was polite. Burton and Raines were a bit unsettled when a middle-aged woman suddenly burst into the negotiating room and whispered in the ear of one of the key Chinese speakers, who immediately got up and left the room. The Canadians expected some explanation for the emergency but none ever came.

The next day, because of the time difference, the Canadians received some of the documentation they needed by fax, and discussions resumed with the same questions being asked yet again. It all went very slowly. The Chinese appreciated the high quality of the Canadian product but worried they wouldn't be able to fix the equipment if it broke down. They suggested—delicately, so as not to imply they *expected* breakdowns—that perhaps the Canadians could give them some help with maintenance training. The Canadians pointed out the expense and difficulty of keeping someone in their city for several weeks or months and expressed confidence that there wouldn't be any problems the manual didn't cover. The Chinese would be able to look after the equipment just fine.

Finally the technical discussions gave way to the issue central to most negotiations in most countries: price. This proved to be the most difficult of all. The Chinese began by asking for a 20 percent price discount. The Canadians thought this was a simply outrageous negotiating ploy; they stuck to their price, which they knew to be fair, and offered a 3 percent discount on the printing cylinders.

Although Burton and Raines had heard that negotiations took time in China, they had thought a week would be ample. Now time was running out and they were due in Beijing in two days. They already had learned that getting plane tickets wasn't easy, so they were anxious to be on the plane as previously arranged. The Canadians began to ask pointed questions about what the Chinese were unhappy with, and where they needed to go over issues again. During the last two sessions, the Canadians tried to get the Chinese to focus on the unresolved points, but the Chinese seemed reluctant to do so.

A number of issues remained unresolved when the farewell banquet was held the following noon. The question of price seemed near solution, but not the method of payment. That was the final, apparently insurmountable, hurdle since the Chinese couldn't guarantee the payment schedule; it seemed tied to deadlines and requirements of the municipal officials. Nevertheless, Manager Li smiled and spoke of mutual cooperation for the future, past Chinese-Canadian relations, and the great amount he and his factory could learn from the Canadians. They signed an expanded version of the letter of intent that had been signed nine months earlier in Canada. The Canadians left with expressions on both sides of willingness to continue to discuss the sale through mail and fax.

The Canadians were stunned to learn two weeks later that the factory had decided to buy from a Japanese equipment manufacturer. They knew their product was good and their price was fair. What had happened to derail their sale?

Negotiating is a special communication task. It occurs when two or more parties have common interests and therefore have a reason to work together, but when they also have interests that conflict, which may prevent them from working together. More specifically, negotiation is the communication that takes place in order to reach agreement about how to handle both common and conflicting interests between two or more parties. Negotiation always has an element of persuasion in it.

Some authorities on negotiation claim cultural differences are merely one of many factors, and may boil down to being "simply differences in style and language."[1] But this view assumes that negotiating skills are value free and are the same around the world, like the rules of chess for opening moves, middle game, and endgame. Not only does this view mistakenly discount the role of culture in framing the priorities of the negotiators, it also overlooks what happens when people of different cultures interact. The interaction produces a communication situation that is the product of both cultures and of the personalities of both teams. Negotiation, like all communication, is dynamic and not static.

One interculturalist has this to say about negotiation:

> In the USA several books have appeared on the art of negotiation; it is a popular theme for training courses. Negotiations have even been simulated in computer programs, which use a mathematical theory of games to calculate the optimal choice in a negotiation situation. These approaches are largely irrelevant.[2]

This critical view comes from the author's observation that the books and mathematical games are based on the assumption that both sides have values of the United States. Another author refers to the "instrumental and manipulative" style of negotiators from the United States.[3] Negotiating "how-to" books abound. But no intercultural negotiator can assume the same values on both sides. All negotiators bring their packages of strategies to the negotiating table, but the strategies are different because their cultures have different priorities. Culture tells them what is important and what they can block out because it doesn't fit their shape of reality; culture enables them to assign meaning to the other side's communication and to guess at the others' motives.[4] So to negotiate effectively, intercultural negotiators not only need special communication skills; they also need to understand their own and the other team's culture. They need to be able to switch from behavior they use when with their own culture to the behavior that will be most appropriate for another culture.

What Really Happened with Canwall in China?

What happened was a combination of cultural factors that worked against the Canadians, some within their control and some outside their control. Here are a few of the reasons for the outcome of this episode.

CHINESE EMPHASIS ON RELATIONSHIPS   First, the Chinese felt they had already formed a relationship with the Canadian firm because they had formed a relationship with the trade representative. But Burton and Raines, who came to negotiate the sale, were new to them and didn't even seem to know the trade agent very well. The trade representative had actually been an agent who represented a number of Canadian light industry manufacturers, and not a Canwall employee. The Chinese also had developed a relationship with a salesperson and the director of manufacturing of Canwall. They were disconcerted by having to develop new relationships from the beginning, all over again. But the Canadians typically used lower-level people for preliminary discussions, where technical details were ironed out, and then sent in their top-level people to sign the contract.

CANADIAN EXPECTATIONS ABOUT TIME AND EFFICIENCY   The two Canadians had expected a much faster pace of negotiating, and had not expected to spend so much time eating, resting, and sightseeing. After all, their product was familiar to the Chinese and it was a good product, fairly priced. They had looked forward to ironing out any wrinkles about payment and schedules and concluding the sale in three or four days. In fact, Charlie Burton had worried they'd have time on their hands after the contract was signed. The Chinese, however, wanted to get to know these two men they hadn't previously met. Also Manager Li had to make sure the communist party secretary of the municipality would support his purchase from overseas; the party secretary and other government party officials had to be kept informed and also had to get to know these new Canwall people.

DIFFERENCES IN NEGOTIATING STYLE   The Chinese began with generalities about their factory and the local government successes. They gave anecdotal information about other experiences with foreigners and about historical connections between China and Canada. This was to create a context for the negotiation at hand, but it seemed inconsequential to Burton and Raines. On the other hand, the Canadian presentation of specific data, moving to generalized projections, seemed rushed and incomplete to the Chinese.

The Chinese spent a long time on the technical specifications of the equipment, partly because they wanted to learn how it was made and partly because they wanted to be sure they were being given accurate information. When Burton fudged a bit on the details (with which he was unfamiliar), the Chinese suspected he may be trying to hoodwink them. It took a lot of time to undo the loss of trust and to verify the true information with the faxed documents.

The Chinese were painfully conscious of being perceived to be lagging behind in the latest technology, and their sense of national honor made them determined to help China "catch up." So partly, too, the Chinese objective was to learn more about the engineering of the equipment so they could eventually copy the process and produce their own, in a process known as reverse-engineering.

Once the negotiations were well underway, the Canadians focused on points of contention that remained unresolved; the Chinese preferred to focus on what had already been agreed. The Canadians found the Chinese slow and unwilling to be specific about the outstanding problems; the Chinese found the Canadians assertive and too absorbed with the negative, the unresolved conflicts.

DIFFERENCES IN RANKING ISSUES TO BE NEGOTIATED   *Price.*   The Chinese were well aware that the Canadians were more advanced in their technology and wealthier in their resources. It made sense to them in the price negotiations, therefore, that the Canadians should be more generous in their terms since they were dealing with a less-developed country. When negotiations between Chinese and foreign companies were a relatively new activity in the early 1980s, often the Chinese asked for enormous price discounts without being aware of the economic factors that determine price in a free economy. Their own prices had been determined by the central government, without concern for the actual cost, which included prices of resources, labor, and finished products. By the late 1980s, the Chinese had learned that asking for price concessions often meant getting them, and the practice continued. By the 1990s, asking for concessions had become standard negotiating procedure. Li's purchase costs were now market driven domestically, not state determined, but Li was still not very experienced at costing out his expenses or profit. He was not able to rely absolutely on the stability of his financing arrangements. So his inflated opening price gave him a comfortable margin.

When the Chinese reminded the Canadians that other manufacturers—notably the Japanese—could undercut the Canadian price, the Canadians responded with some chagrin that their industry was not subsidized by their government in ways the Japanese were. They were touchy about this fact and their bargaining position as a consequence of it, within the global field of competitors.

Payment Schedule.   The issue of the payment schedule was thorny. The Chinese manager was able to buy with hard currency, a development that occurred in early 1993, but he wanted some leeway so he could make the most of his capital. A decade ago he had had to get government approval to purchase equipment with hard currency. Now he enjoyed the choices open to him, but was wary about being taken advantage of.

Attitudes toward the Relationship.   The Chinese also welcomed a chance to make a relationship that they could pursue further when the government gave them more authority to spend foreign currency. For them the relationship was still "on," even if in a dormant period. They were quite well aware of the high quality of the Canadian equipment, but were happy to do business with the lowest-priced supplier of quality equipment. The Canadians, for their part, felt that when they lost the sale, they had lost their chance in China, after spending considerable time and money to chase it. For them, the relationship was terminated.

FACTORS THAT DETERMINED THE DEAL   The week after the Canadians left, a Japanese manufacturer's representative made his third visit to Manager Li's operation. He was authorized to offer a lower price on the equipment than the Canadians; his price on pattern-printing cylinders was higher, however. He also offered to have a company employee stay in the town for four months and train Chinese employees in maintenance of the equipment. The Chinese manager felt this was a better deal, although he also looked forward to future negotiations with the Canadians. The Chinese party secretary, who also had his own personal agenda to consider, sent a report to the provincial government on the manager's decision to buy the Japanese equipment at the lower price. This enhanced his own standing as a shrewd negotiator. He didn't mention the higher price of the pattern cylinders.

Pattern cylinders were the costliest part of the equipment. Since Li wanted his firm to produce more than one pattern, his expense in the end was no lower than it would have been with the Canadian product. (Subsequently Li felt he had not negotiated well with the Japanese because the pattern cylinders had to be replaced more frequently than originally planned).

As for the maintenance issue, the Japanese firm was happy to supply someone to teach the Chinese how to maintain and troubleshoot the equipment. They planned to keep this trainer in China in order to learn about other market possibilities. Of course, the distance from Jiangsu to Japan is about one-fifteenth the distance to the Canwall head office. The Japanese employee could go home frequently, while for a Canadian such travel would be very costly.

How Knowledge of Culture Can Help

This case illustrates a number of negotiation strategy differences and expectations at work. All interactions with other cultures become more likely to succeed when you know something about the other culture's strategy differences and expectations. You can identify these cultural factors when you have posed the questions of Chapters 3 and 4 about an unfamiliar culture; considered the best way to organize and structure the negotiation communication and how best to persuade (Chapter 5); taken into account the nonverbal and behavioral signals involved; and considered the way decisions are made, information is collected, and problems are solved in the other culture. In many ways, the negotiation communication task is a cumulative one.

For instance, the Canadians could have kept in mind that the Chinese value **relationships** as much as results for their own sake. They are disconcerted when people they have entered into relationships with suddenly disappear, like the agent they mistakenly thought was closely tied to Canwall. The Chinese expect to spend **time** developing the links that knit individuals into webs of relationships. Guests will be treated to sightseeing jaunts and special dinners and entertainment, in order to give the Chinese a chance to share some experiences with them and chat informally. They want to cultivate a sense of friendship and with it, **obligation.** Then they will pursue their goals by appealing to the obligation of friendship.

Relationships need a context in which to flourish, so the Chinese spent time giving background information and reminding the Canadians of historical China–Canada ties. Their value of **harmony** in group interactions means they prefer to focus on the things that already have been agreed rather than on conflicts that remain unresolved. They are careful to **avoid displays of anger** or to express criticism that might cause **loss of face** for the other side. On the other hand, they are masterful at using **shame,** which only works when one side can be alleged to be guilty of misconduct that jeopardizes negotiations. Pointing out the inconsistencies in the specifications was a way of causing the Canadians shame and thereby moving the Canadians to a weaker negotiating position. (The Canadians, however, missed this maneuver, so it didn't produce shame or concessions.)

In negotiations, the Chinese often dwell at length on technical details. They want to understand the technology; they also want to be sure they are being told the same thing each time. Since in general Chinese do **not use question-asking as a primary learning**

method the way Westerners do, they often ask questions in order to verify the accuracy of what they have been told, as much as to find out something they have not understood. Asking questions is also a way to get to know someone, to develop an understanding of someone and build a relationship.

The Chinese **perform tasks simultaneously;** someone on their negotiating team may take a telephone call, disappearing and then reappearing without explanation. The Canadians viewed this as a most unusual interruption, probably an emergency of grave importance, but that is because Canadians tend to do tasks sequentially, devoting their entire attention to only one thing at a time.

The Chinese have a **preference for form** in negotiations, or in other words, for following a specific protocol. This usually means the opening discussion will be very formally conducted. The host side will first describe themselves—who they are and what they do—with many statistics. Then they will expect the guests (in this case the Canadians) to do the same. None of this has any real relevance to the issue being negotiated, but this form is important. The preference for form and correct manner—which preserve the harmony mentioned earlier—derives from **Confucianism,** which also is the source for the following values.

The most important person on the negotiating team from the Chinese perspective is the most **senior in age;** this is a key, along with membership in the Chinese communist party, in the **hierarchy** of the Chinese workplace. This will probably be true of their own team, although the key persons may not be much in evidence during the negotiations. It will also be true of the Chinese perception of your negotiating team.

Since **access to authority is mediated** in Chinese culture, the real decision-swaying power may not be identifiable to a foreigner. The municipal party officials, while not determining the purchase of the wallpaper printing equipment, nevertheless were involved because their goodwill could be crucial to Manager Li. The people with the authority to make decisions—the manager, the powerful municipal officials, and the most powerful people in the factory—were no doubt all communist party members. Their network of obligations would also have played a role.

Interdependence characterizes Chinese social organization, and the members of the Chinese team are conscious of representing a larger collective. The employees of the factory, from the manager down, will probably spend their entire working lives in that factory. The county officials may never change jobs either. Their work colleagues are also their neighbors; many are relatives. Even after retirement, employees are still associated with their workplace, which provides housing, access to food and other products, health care, and many other services.

Since the Chinese value relationships and can accept failure of specific undertakings as long as the relationships are intact, they can **tolerate uncertainty** about outcomes. If success doesn't come this time, it may come the next. As long as the relationship has not been ruptured, there is always a chance for future cooperation. The Canadians viewed the loss of the sale as the end of their dealings with this factory.

Awareness of these cultural priorities can help Burton and Raines prepare for their next Chinese sale, and can help you too, regardless of your own culture or the unfamiliar one with which you want to negotiate. Neither side is right or wrong; they are just different. But as sellers in this case, the Canadians probably need to develop more understanding of cultural priorities than the Chinese.

This chapter will now address the factors in any negotiation. They include expectations for outcomes, the makeup of the team, the physical context for negotiation, and communication and style of negotiating. A discussion of the phases of negotiation concludes the chapter.

FACTORS IN NEGOTIATION

The remainder of this chapter looks at negotiating with these aspects in mind:

- Expectations for negotiation outcomes.
- Team members: makeup and motivation.
- Physical factors.
- Communication and negotiating style.

The aim of this discussion is to show how culture affects negotiations. A number of books on *how to* negotiate exist in your own culture. Primarily, since this is a book about communication, we'll concentrate on the fourth item. But we'll examine all four aspects of negotiating, beginning with expectations for what the negotiations will accomplish.

Expectations for Outcomes

DIFFERENT GOALS   Different sides of the negotiating table often seem to be after very different things. This may appear to be the result of shrewd negotiating tactics in which a side doesn't disclose openly what its goals are—and maybe it is. You may decide the other team is craftily hiding what they want behind some other, seemingly unimportant aims. But another reason for their obliqueness may simply be that they want something different from what you think they want. People from different cultures often are looking for different outcomes. As far as is possible, you need to identify ahead of time what the probable goals are for the other side.

For example, in the case of the Chinese-Canadian negotiation, the Chinese had four goals: (1) to buy the best quality they could find at the very best world price, (2) to develop an ongoing relationship with Canwall, and importantly, (3) to learn as much as they could about Canwall's new technology. Had the contract been signed, the Chinese also would have expected (4) exclusive access to the Canadian equipment. The Canadians understood only the first of the Chinese negotiation goals. The second goal may drive the opening encounters with high-context cultures. As Raymond Cohen explains, "For high-context negotiators, then, the initial concern is to exchange the sterility of the business files that are tossed on their desks for a tangible sense of the humanity of the other side."[5]

FAIRNESS AND ADVANTAGE   As the case shows, the Chinese were interested in developing a relationship. Negotiating teams from Korea, Japan, Thailand, and Singapore—as well as teams from African, Latin American, and southern European cultures—usually are too. A relationship, as discussed in Chapter 4, implies to most Asians a willingness to incur indebtedness. This may help explain the tendency among countries on the lower end of the digital revolution in technology, as illustrated in the case example, to believe the wealthier, more advanced side should give proportionately *more* than the less advanced, less wealthy country. The less advanced team will thus be indebted to the other party in the relationship. The payback date, however, may be far into the future since the collectivist view of relationships is they extend for generations. The Philippines and Indonesia are among the countries today that are looking to bridge the digital divide.

North Americans, British, and other Europeans, among other nations, are not usually happy with an agreement that gives one side greater advantage than the other. They are accustomed to thinking of a "fair" settlement as one that even-handedly splits advantage between the two parties. But obviously the 50–50 ideal is not shared among all cultures. As some researchers point out, the use of the English term "fair play" does not seem to be translatable into some other languages; if the *term* does not exist, then it is likely the identical concept does not exist either.[6]

NEGOTIATION OUTCOMES: WINNING, LOSING, AND COMPROMISING (OR STALEMATE)   Competition cultures, especially those that put a strong priority on achievement, doing, and accomplishing goals through planning and taking control, and national or family honor (powerful in Middle Eastern or Korean companies, for example) look upon negotiations as situations to *win*. *Winning* means not having to make concessions beyond the reserve point—the bargaining limit established by a negotiating team before the negotiations begin—in order to gain the team's objectives. Winning can also mean you have achieved an agreement where the other side gives up more than you do.

Compromise is a standard expectation in bargaining and negotiation in many Western countries (see also the discussion on conflict resolution in Chapter 8). The notion of fairness in these cultures means both sides have to give a bit, and the bits are equal. A good end is achieved when the compromises made by each side are about the same size. However, you may need to be careful about using the word *compromise*:

> In some cultures, such as Iran, the term "compromise" has moral connotations and implies a corrupt betrayal of principle. So it has to be kept out of your vocabulary.[7]

Russians do not view compromise as the fair and equitable conceding of position by each side:

> Russians regard compromise as a sign of weakness, a retreat from a correct and morally justified position. Russians, therefore, are great "sitters," prepared to wait out their opposite numbers in the expectation that time and Russian patience will produce more concessions from the impatient Americans.[8]

Win–Lose.   To some negotiators, however, winning means more than getting everything at the terms desired; winning means beating down the other party so they have to go past their reserve point. This may involve price, schedule, marketing terms, or any of a host of issues. Or winning may mean making a small compromise but demanding a large compromise from the other side. In other words, in this outcome winning means the other side also has to *lose*. This is sometimes called *zero-sum* negotiation.

Win–Win.   Cooperation cultures that value relationships as ongoing between organizations and lasting longer than the lifetimes of those at the negotiating table often prefer outcomes that emphasize advantages gained by both sides. In other words, the objectives are win–win or *non-zero-sum*. When both sides win, nobody loses face or is shamed.

The difference between a win–win outcome and compromise lies in the negotiator's focus. If the negotiator primarily thinks of his or her own team's outcome, the attitude will probably be to expect compromise—what we will gain in return for what we will have to give up. The focus is on our loss as well as our gain. If the negotiator looks at *both* his or her own team and the other team, then the attitude will probably be to expect each side to gain. The focus is on mutual gain. One of these three modes is usually what a negotiator expects: compromise, win–lose, or win–win.

Stalemate. However, negotiators sometimes have to accept a stalemate, when no agreement can be reached. Nobody enters into trade negotiations with this goal in mind. It represents a failure of the negotiation. Negotiators usually expect movement toward agreement. Occasionally one side gains everything without giving up anything, and the other side simply agrees. In this case, rather than having a failed negotiation, no negotiation has taken place. This is a simple agreement without conflicting interests. As Moran and Stripp sum up: "Without common interests there is nothing to negotiate for, and without conflict there is nothing to negotiate about."[9]

Finally, fundamental advice about expectations for the outcomes of negotiation comes from the practical guide by Copeland and Griggs: Make sure what you are negotiating is negotiable.[10] It may *not* be negotiable because the party negotiating with you hasn't the power or access to grant what you want, because it doesn't exist, or because what you want simply cannot be bought or obtained.

Members of the Negotiating Team

According to Moran and Stripp, in their book *Dynamics of Successful International Business Negotiations,* negotiators fit one of two basic descriptors: strategic or synergistic. The **strategic negotiator** is out to win and sees the process as something to be won through cleverness, competitiveness, and even deceit. This negotiator is suspicious of, and hostile toward, the other side. The style is confrontational. The **synergistic negotiator** wants to avoid confrontation and is cooperative rather than competitive. This negotiator focuses on common interests, but allows opposing interests to exist even beyond the point at which agreement is possible. The style is trusting and friendly.

MEMBERS WITH HIGH STATUS   Frequently negotiators are chosen because they are high-status members of the organization. Their presence on the team indicates the organization is serious about concluding negotiations successfully. In the case example, the Canwall president—the highest-status person in that company—led the negotiating team to China. Many firms follow the practice of having lower-level negotiators do the groundwork, and then sending in the top-level people to close the deal. Considerable "face" can be gained for the top-level people when a negotiation reaches a successful conclusion, but having the lower-level workers involved is also useful. A manager of a Japanese–Chinese joint venture in Shanghai told one of the authors that the high-level executives and politicians had initiated that joint venture, following the successful outcome of negotiations, with great fanfare. But it was low-level employees who had to make it work. He said their valuable contributions were not solicited during the negotiation process, at a time when potential problems and conflicts could have been addressed, and their pictures were not in the news!

This practice is usually meant to communicate to the other team the importance of the negotiations to the organization. It can get in the way of smooth negotiating, however, unless the high-status persons are also well informed about the history of past meetings between representatives of the two negotiating sides. The top executive must be thoroughly briefed about people, interests, and previous discussions because the other side will expect that he or she has been involved all along. In addition to information, the high-status member needs to have the same communication skills necessary for intercultural interaction that the other team members need. Status isn't enough.

The presence of a high-level person on the team also signals the authority to make a binding agreement. But some companies delegate this authority to other team members when a high-status person is not part of the team. Negotiators from the United States, for example, value efficiency—achieving goals with the least expenditure of time and money—more than status. Consequently, they view as wasteful the practice of sending a team to negotiate that has to keep going back to higher authorities at home for decisions. They want their negotiating team to be able to conclude an agreement on the spot. Koreans, with their Confucian value of respect for seniority, want their older and higher-status authorities to exercise their judgment about agreements. If the senior person is in Korea and the negotiations take place in another country, time has to be allowed for the senior person to be reached and the progress of the talks discussed.

MEMBERS WITH SPECIAL EXPERTISE   Some negotiators become members of a team because of their specialized expertise. For example, a person with technical or technological knowledge may be very important. Or an expert in financing with accurate cost figures may be able to make the difference between success and failure in Kuwait. Someone with marketing expertise in a specialized product or with legal experience in a particular country can make or break negotiations. For example, one person's experience with Japan's import regulations governing agricultural products and health inspections enabled a German company to negotiate an agreement for the sale of sausages to Japan. The expertise may be knowledge of the culture and values of the other side. Richard Welzel, a German–Canadian broker of food processing equipment, was able to negotiate a purchase of secondhand German-made machinery in Bulgaria because he understood the quality of the machinery.

THE TRANSLATOR   One of the most important people on the team is the translator. This role is also discussed in Chapter 2. Many negotiating teams choose not to take their own translator, but rather to depend on the host country to supply a translator. This is usually a mistake. Obviously, a translator's first loyalty is to his or her employer; the Chinese who supplied the translator to the Canadians in the case example could have asked the translator for daily reports on what the Canadians said when they were alone with her. This would give the Chinese a great advantage in the negotiations. Similarly, a Chinese team in another country would be wise to bring its own translator.

Having your own translator means you have an ear to hear what the other team says in side-conversations and comments among themselves. English-speaking teams frequently rely on the widespread use of English around the globe; they assume it is possible to negotiate in English—and cheaper, if they don't have to take a translator with them.

But they miss out. They don't understand what the other team is saying when they converse in their own language. When the English-speaking team has a side-conversation, however, the other team's translator and English-speaking members can understand what is being said.

Another benefit of having your own translator is that he or she can understand the translations by the other side's translator. This means that errors or omissions—which are frequently unintentional—can be corrected immediately. Translation is extremely hard work, and it doesn't stop just because the formal session is over. At social gatherings the translators work just as hard as at the meeting table. It is understandable that a tired translator may misunderstand or mistranslate. A second translator simply offers a check against errors.

Occasionally a member of a negotiating team uses the translator's mistranslation to display knowledge of the language of the other side. This is done at the expense of the translator's face. For example, a vice premier in China, whose English was excellent, corrected his young female translator's use of *could* instead of *should*—among other corrections—to illustrate his excellent command of English to his audience of foreign academics in 1997. Why would he do this? He was receiving the guests on behalf of the Chinese government, and his words were being officially recorded—in Chinese. His translator was a person of very much lower status than the vice premier, so she had much less face to lose. Moreover, she gained collective face from his excellent English. He made the point about his accomplished use of English and guests were duly impressed.

Translation errors are mines waiting to explode around unsuspecting negotiators. Simple mistakes in translation can cause days of delay while the misunderstanding is identified and cleared up. One key to preventing errors is not only to have your own translator, but also to have a translator who is familiar with the vocabulary of the business. Someone with a degree in language studies may have read bookshelves of literature in the other language, but lack technical vocabulary. In fact, the translator needs to have a technical vocabulary in *both* languages.

Another factor in the selection of a translator is *specific* language skills. Many foreign firms negotiating in China take with them a Chinese who lives in the firm's own country and works for the firm. This can be excellent, providing the language spoken by the Chinese employee is the language spoken in the area of China where negotiations will take place. China is a country of many regional dialects. Many foreign firms use the services of trading companies located in Hong Kong, where the language of more than 90 percent of the people is Cantonese. In China the official language is Mandarin. The two spoken languages are mutually unintelligible. A Cantonese translator in Beijing cannot translate spoken Mandarin, and a northern Chinese cannot translate the Cantonese spoken in Hong Kong or Canton province. The Chinese also, like people in many countries of the world, practice regional snobbery about accents. A translator who speaks Mandarin with a strong Cantonese accent will not be as highly regarded in Beijing as a translator who speaks with a north-China accent. (See also Chapter 2.)

China, like India, is a language of multiple dialects. The regional language in the case study example would have been Shanghai dialect, but in addition the factory town has its own dialect. That means even if the Canadians from Canwall had brought their own Mandarin-speaking translator and even if they had found one who also spoke Shanghai dialect, the opposite team could possibly have exchanged comments in their local dialect that the Canadian translator would not have understood. Similarly, in India your translator may not know the regional dialect (there are over 600 of them). This means the microphone for eavesdropping on the other team's side-conversations—your translator—is closed off.

You can make your translator's job easier, as mentioned in Chapter 2, if you speak in very straightforward language. Consider, for example, how you would translate the warning uttered by a spokesperson for a nongovernment international aid organization who said the United States should continue its involvement in rebuilding the social institutions in a country that had been at war, "or else the line will not be drawn in the sand and we'll be back in the soup again."[11]

MAKEUP OF THE OTHER SIDE'S TEAM   Analysis of the other team is very important. With a bit of application of what you have learned about a culture from the questions you have posed, you can see the cultural priorities that generate communication behavior at the negotiating table.

Take a Kuwaiti negotiator for example. Posing the questions from Chapters 3 and 4 results in the following information. Kuwaiti culture encourages competitiveness among organizations. Women are not usually part of negotiating teams. Achieving goals for the sake of the group honor—or often the royal al-Sabah family honor—is very important, although the will of Allah may intervene. Goals may be long term and Kuwaitis are patient. The society is hierarchical, with members of the ruling family in key positions. Access to authority is mediated. Form and protocol are important and negotiations may have a ceremonial aspect. Courtesy and patience are characteristic of Kuwaitis' interaction with others, since acceptance in the group is an important part of their Bedouin heritage. Language may be used flamboyantly and with an eloquence that is valued for its own sake, beyond or beside the meaning of the words. The way Kuwaitis understand and think about issues is to take several levels into account, rather than to move in a mental linear path. The chess-playing characteristic of some negotiations is renowned. Display of emotion is typical.

Once you have gathered responses to the culture questions and have considered the rules of engagement, a picture of the Kuwaiti negotiator emerges. He will be educated and skilled, a member of the ruling family or valued by it, with a strong expectation that negotiation will involve a need for cleverness on his part in order to win. Suspicion and hostility will probably not be evident because he will display Kuwaiti politeness and Bedouin hospitality. His love of verbal play and the importance of emotion in communication may make the Kuwaiti negotiator's wording of messages seem theatrical to a low-context communicator who shuns ambiguity and strives for directness and simplicity. He will probably possess technological expertise and expect to be given accurate and complete information. His religion, Islam, will frame his thinking and communicating acts and he may quote the Koran as a guide for his behavior. He will be patient and will be ready to spend months negotiating. Finally, he will value a personal relationship with the negotiator on the other side of the table.

MEMBERS' DECISION-MAKING AUTHORITY   You will want to consider as far as possible the question of how much authority rests with the negotiating team to conclude an agreement. In hierarchical cultures the ultimate authority may lie with someone who is never present at the negotiating table. Where hierarchy and consensus both characterize a culture, the most influential person may be present at some meetings but may not be introduced in a way to suggest the power that person wields.

In Japanese negotiations, for example, the senior member of the group may not appear at all—or even at any—meetings. He (nearly always it's a man) will receive regular and detailed reports, however, of all that is said during the negotiations and will direct his team members to proceed in a certain way. No agreement will be reached without his approval. Team members will give no hint that an agreement could exist until they have had a chance to discuss with him. If the senior authority is not physically present as a member of the negotiating team, he may be in a hotel room or office nearby. Or he may be in another city or country. In that last case, obviously consultation with him will take more time than if he were present. On the other hand, the team members you are negotiating with may have full power to commit their organization to an agreement.

TEAM MEMBERS' STATUS   Members of the other team, like yours, may be chosen because of their status. In addition to high status within the organization, sometimes being in a special relationship to someone in power is a reason for inclusion on a team. The relatively young and inexperienced nephew of the president, for example, may have a place on a negotiating team mainly because his uncle owns the company. But this may not simply be nepotism. It may make good business sense—perhaps a family member can be trusted best to look after the interests of the family in reaching a certain agreement. If the family rules the country, as in some Middle Eastern nations, then the family interests coincide with national interests, and family members play key roles in foreign negotiations.

We've already seen that family loyalties can motivate negotiators, and so can company loyalties or national loyalties. The desire to win through clever strategies can motivate negotiators. The wish to develop a relationship that will continue, and that will allow for indebtedness and favors, is a motivator. The value of harmony in human interactions and the avoidance of confrontation can motivate negotiators to reach agreement rather than continue to hold discussions.

Physical Context of the Negotiation

Where the negotiation takes place—the physical context for the communication—has an impact on the outcomes. For example, if the negotiation takes place by telephone or fax, the nonverbal messages have a diminished impact compared with face-to-face negotiation. Indeed, most negotiation involves meetings between parties. The host team for the negotiations has an advantage because the environment is in their control. The guest team doesn't have the same degree of control.

SITE AND SPACE   For example, the hosts can determine what city and what building will hold the meetings. If it's the boardroom of the building where the host organization members work, all the resources of that organization are at the disposal of the host team—from photocopiers to telecommunications, and from files to assistants. So the hosts have an advantage of *convenience*. Handheld organizers and cellular telephones are increasing the convenience of access to one's own office, but there are still advantages to being in one's own setting.

Whether the home negotiators work from an open office with a dozen others, in a cramped space at the back of a second-story building, or in a meeting room with stiff-backed chairs lined against the walls, the space will be familiar to them. It will not be familiar to the visitors. The visitors will be getting used to an unexpected environment, which can distract them from their negotiating goals. The visiting team may experience some *culture shock* (see Chapter 1) that will be greater the longer they stay.

SCHEDULE AND AGENDA   Jet lag can make the visiting team unable to perform well on the hosts' schedule. People whose internal clock says it's midnight find it difficult to stay alert even if the clock on the wall says it's 11 in the morning. Russians, for example, have been known to conduct very long sessions when it is uncomfortable for a visiting team suffering from jet lag.

Control of the schedule also often carries over to control of the negotiating agenda. For example, hosts may suggest postponing certain discussions until guests are more rested, with the result that the hosts control the order in which issues are addressed while giving the appearance of concern for the guests' comfort. The order of items discussed on the agenda can have an impact on the outcome. If the two sides agree to one principle or goal, then subsequent points may be presented as simply subsidiary to what has already been agreed. If both sides agree to use a particular supply source for a raw material in a joint-venture manufacturing project, then including a member of the supply organization on the board may seem a logical subsequent decision. But if the issue of membership on the board were addressed *first,* the decision might be different.

The power of the keeper of the agenda is considerable, determining when meetings take place and what amount of time is allotted to discuss which issues. An issue that isn't on the agenda may never be discussed. The visiting team has to be alert to their responsibility of participating in setting the agenda.

USE OF TIME   Use of time is related to the agenda. Russians often use time to their advantage as part of the nonverbal communication in negotiations. For instance they may delay negotiations in order to make the other side anxious. This behavior towards North Americans, for instance, is based on two assumptions: They "regard compromise as both desirable and inevitable, and . . . Americans feel frustration and failure when agreements are not reached promptly."[12]

Negotiators from the United States are well known for their impatience. Timothy Bennett, a United States trade negotiator to Mexico, says his countrymen and women think that some solution is better than no solution, which leads them to compromise more than their Mexican counterparts.[13] Decades of negotiations have taught Japanese that Westerners, and especially delegates from the United States, are not patient. If the Japanese prolong the negotiations sufficiently, the Westerners will probably agree to whatever the Japanese want. In Japan, however, to take time is to show maturity and wisdom. Haste shows poor judgment and lack of genuine commitment. Foreign negotiators in the Middle East often complain that meetings are not arranged. Foreign negotiators in Latin America complain that they have to wait. In Asia, foreign negotiators complain that they do too much sightseeing and not enough negotiating. In the United States, foreign negotiators often feel rushed.

HOST HOSPITALITY

> [In Hungary] we drink *palinka,* a plum or cherry brandy. It's 200 proof. When we start, the Americans are already drunk. The Hungarians aren't. We're seasoned. In Hungary, the Hungarians use this. They try to influence Americans with good drink to sign a favorable contract. It's an instrument to oil the wheels." . . . A foreign man who can't hold his liquor is probably discarded as a potential business associate . . . [It is] reason to break off negotiations.[14]

Most negotiating involves some socializing. It may be a way to initiate the negotiations and establish some advantage for the host. Sometimes when negotiations are stuck, a meal together or evening out can be a good strategy for refocusing the agenda. Often socializing is done at the end, after negotiations are concluded favorably. The Canwall team was treated to a farewell banquet; in China as in other Asian countries such as Korea and Vietnam, the toasts that are made at banquets carry messages about what items are particularly important to those negotiators.[15] In all cultures, socializing provides an opportunity to get to know the other party better and build relationships with them. However, the food, beverages, and beds in which visitors sleep may be unfamiliar. With jet lag and unfamiliar food may come digestive and sleep disorders, and the visiting team may suffer a loss of *physical wellbeing.*

Communication and Style of Negotiating

Negotiation is a special task that uses special verbal and nonverbal communication skills. We look now at the communication between sides and consider the cultural factors that determine how negotiators communicate.

DIFFERENCES IN FOCUS   Focus may be positive or negative; it may be explicit or implicit; it may be general or specific. Cultures that emphasize communication as a tool for articulating specific goals in order to accomplish them tend to look upon negotiations as a series of points to "settle." Their language in negotiations is explicit and zeroes in on what has yet to be agreed. These explicit statements may in fact be questions and emphasize negative points of disagreement, such as, "What do you still not like about this detail of product design?" Americans prefer this direct approach because their aim is to clarify and resolve an issue.

But cultures that use communication to encourage harmony, preserve face, and develop long-term relationships are not comfortable with direct and explicit talk. For instance, in Japan getting straight to some point about which agreement has yet to be reached might result in confrontation and emotions—even anger. Someone might lose face. Japanese, like negotiators from other Asian cultures, prefer to emphasize the positive points of agreement. They begin with general terms and seek agreement from the other side about general goals. Then regardless of the remaining details, the general agreement holds the two sides together in a relationship. They do not ask—and do not enjoy being asked—pointed questions. They want to develop relationships because once a relationship exists each side has an obligation to consider the needs of the other, so the issue resolves itself.

The Chinese strategist and philosopher Sun Tzu (pronounced "swin zuh"), writing in the fifth century B.C., described the inexhaustibility of indirect tactics, as unending as the rivers and as recurring as the seasons.[16] Conflicts can be diffused by indirectness. In more modern times, Henry Kissinger compared Mao Zedong's indirect, "many-layered" conversations to

> courtyards in the Forbidden City, each leading to a deeper recess distinguished from the others only by slight changes in proportion, with ultimate meaning residing in a totality that only long reflection can grasp.[17]

The metaphor of many-layered courtyards is an apt one to describe the way the negotiations proceeded.

An approach that focuses on particulars, especially unresolved ones, is typically Western. Negotiators look at the unsettled issues, and one by one address them. That approach is logical to the Western problem-solving mind. But it isn't shared by all cultures. In Asia, unresolved issues are part of the whole web of the relationship being woven by the negotiation process. A simultaneous, not sequential, approach means the negotiators look at unresolved issues as potentially resolved because of the developing relationship between the two sides.

Businesspeople from Western cultures need to remember that Japanese, Chinese, and most Asians dislike confrontation and will not argue when they feel they are right. Attacks on statements are the same thing as attacks on people making the statements. Japanese and Chinese and other Asians need to remember that businesspeople in Western cultures prefer directness and the airing of different opinions, and to a large degree consider words apart from the people who produce them. When words are attacked, persons are not necessarily also attacked.

HONOR   Group membership, when it is highly valued, can impact negotiations in a number of ways. Negotiators whose allegiance is to a family group, such as the ruling household of some Arab countries, or to a nation, such as Korea, may be motivated to gain the best advantage for the honor of their group. The fact that something bigger than the individual seems to be at stake can make a negotiating team less flexible.

On the other hand, negotiators who are motivated by a desire to uphold their individual reputation and record can also be inflexible about backing down. The key is for you to understand what motivates your counterparts. Then you can accommodate the needs of the other side. If your counterparts are motivated to succeed for the honor of the group, then you need to send messages that show you understand. Your own group membership will be important to emphasize. In either case, words that provoke a defense of honor can be the wrong words to use.

Not backing down is related to a team's decision-making process. If it is a consensus-based process, then the team's position will have been determined by lengthy group discussions before the negotiations take place. This makes the team less able to change their position spontaneously. They have to go back and consult the others in the group before they can agree to changes in their initial position. If individuals have authority to make decisions, the team's position may be flexible and open to change.

FORM   Form is very important in high-context cultures, as we have seen in Chapter 4, and nowhere more so than in negotiation sessions. In Arab cultures, for example, sessions begin with small talk, and communication is indirect. In some situations, negotiators may sit on cushions on carpets, not on furniture. In other situations, the negotiations may take place in a restaurant or club owned by someone other than the negotiators. Visitors should not refuse an offer of hospitality such as a small cup of strong coffee, nor arrange their feet so that the soles point toward anyone. Proper respect is due older members of the Arab team, and that means not using too much familiarity. Visitors should use titles to address people, and they shouldn't ask about female family members. (If you ask how many children a businessman has, he may give you the number of his male children.)

In Russia, negotiators must follow the protocol of correctly using Russians' names. This means using the full name: the given name, the patronymic or father's name, and the family name. Proper respect is shown when all three names are used to refer to someone. This may require a bit of effort on the part of a foreigner who is unfamiliar with the name system. The names change, depending upon whether the person is male or female: Alexei Fyodorovitch Melnikov is the son of Fyodor; his married sister is Irina Fyodorovna Dunayeva. A similar naming system is used by Mexicans and other Latin Americans, to varying degrees (see Chapter 4).

EMOTION   In some high-context cultures, public display of emotion is a sign of immaturity and a potential cause of shame to the group. Japanese negotiators will close their eyes, look down, or rest their head against their hand and shade their eyes in order to conceal an emotion such as anger. Similarly Thais have learned to keep potentially disruptive emotions from showing in their faces. Koreans, Taiwanese, and other Asians along with Japanese and Thais have earned the descriptor *inscrutable* from Westerners because of their learned cultural practice of avoiding a facial display of strong and disruptive emotion. High-context cultures value harmony in human encounters and members avoid sending any nonverbal messages that could destroy harmony. Other high-context cultures, for example in the Middle East, put a high priority on displays of emotion to emphasize the sincerity of the position being put forward.

In low-context cultures, a deliberate concealment of emotion is considered to be insincere. Members of low-context cultures have learned a large vocabulary of facial expression that signals the emotion a speaker feels. When they see none of the expected indicators of emotion on faces of negotiators on the opposite side of the table, they presume it is not present. If this assumption is discovered to be wrong, and the speaker is indeed feeling an emotion such as anger, the member of the low-context culture feels deceived.

SILENCE   Similarly, silence as a nonverbal communication tool can be very effective in negotiations. As discussed in Chapter 6, in low-context cultures where ideas are explicitly encoded into words and unspoken ideas are more difficult to respond to, silence makes low-context negotiators uneasy. Silence often means unhappiness in low-context cultures. Even when no message about unhappiness is intended, silence in low-context cultures indicates a rupture has occurred, a break in the process of communicating. For these reasons, negotiators from low-context cultures generally are uncomfortable with silence. They often feel responsible for starting conversation or keeping it going.

Japanese speakers are comfortable with silence in negotiations and do not hurry to fill it up with speech. After a speaker from one side speaks, Japanese listeners pause in silence to reflect upon what has been said and to consider the speaker's feelings and point of view. This is how Japanese show consideration for others in oral interpersonal communication, as we have seen in Chapter 6. Similarly, to interrupt a negotiator who is speaking is to show disrespect. Because of this protocol and the Japanese value of silence, negotiators with Japanese counterparts must be careful not to speak too hastily or too much.

THE PHASES OF NEGOTIATION

The foregoing aspects of communication style are employed in specific phases of negotiation. Exchanges proceed according to four phases of negotiation in all cultures;[18] the emphasis and time spent on any one phase are what differ:

- Development of a relationship with the other side.
- Information exchange about the topic under negotiation.
- Persuasion.
- Concessions and agreement.

Development of a Relationship

Cultural priorities differ about how much time is spent on each phase of negotiation; for example, Chinese spend much longer on phases one and two, while Canadians want to get to phase three more quickly.

In the first phase, in which the relationship between negotiating teams is being established, trust is the critical factor. In cultures in which relationships have high priority, time may be spent in nonbusiness activities so you can get to know each other. Sightseeing and a welcome banquet are two typical activities in Chinese business interactions with foreigners. In Argentina the visiting team may be treated to an elaborate cocktail party in someone's home or to a barbecue, called a *parrilla,* in a home or restaurant; again at the successful conclusion of negotiations the teams may enjoy a celebratory meal, usually less formal in dress.

One way to establish a relationship is to identify the common goal both sides have in reaching an agreement. Once the desire or need for the other side to come an agreement is on the table—in words—you can both refer openly to the common goal.

In order to develop trust, you need to have openness in your communication and to experience openness from the other side. This usually involves some gentle questioning by each side to see how willing the others are to reveal themselves. Often the answers are already known to the questioners—the probes are designed not for gathering information so much as for testing the openness of the other side. Usually each side displays apparent candor in these exchanges; whether it can be trusted or not is what each side has to determine.

Face is an important consideration in developing a relationship with someone from a high-context culture, especially from Asia:

> Face may be lost as a result of many developments: a premature or overeager overture that is rebuffed by one's opponent; exposure to personal insult, in the form of either a hurtful remark or disregard for one's status; being forced to give up a cherished value or to make a concession that will be viewed by the domestic audience as unnecessary; a snub; failure to achieve predetermined

goals; the revelation of personal inadequacy; damage to a valued relationship. The list is endless, for in the give-and-take of a complicated negotiation on a loaded subject, anything can happen.[19]

Since face can be lost even without the awareness of the other party, negotiators need to take care. Asking questions that seem designed to expose weakness, making comments that assume familiarity, or giving responses with the wrong degree of coolness can all lead to loss of face for the other party and with it, loss of trust.

Information Exchange about the Topic Under Negotiation

Frank disclosure often can work in your favor and generate trust. For example, if the Canwall negotiators had said, "We're very glad to be talking with you about a sale of our product, because we have a long-term interest in business with China," their Chinese counterparts would likely have considered this a frank admission of Canwall's aims. You need to disclose at least some of your positions. You also need to be able to believe what the other side is telling you.

One way to obtain information is to ask questions rather than wait for disclosure. According to Richard Mead,[20] you can ask questions

1. To determine common ground.
2. To clarify information.
3. To call bluffs.
4. To show you are listening.
5. To show your interest.
6. To control the direction of the discussion.
7. To broach potentially controversial issues (rather than by statement).

Items 1, 4, and 5 particularly have to do with developing relationships; item 2 has to do with understanding facts; items 3, 6, and 7 have to do with managing the negotiation process.

Asking questions can be problematic, however. In order not to seem overly aggressive you may need to "frame" your questions. Framing is discussed in Chapter 5. It means putting a frame of explanatory language around a request that does not change the meaning but makes it less aggressive: "I hope you don't mind my asking for your unit price, but our estimates were much higher and our head office will ask why we were so far off." The frame softens what could be a very hard-nosed question: "Where did you get that unit price?"

Another problem with asking "why" questions, if you expect a "cause" answer, is that in some cultures the typical response is not a cause but an explanation of a pattern—of an organizational structure, market consumption, or an economic policy, for instance (see also Chapter 1).

Let's assume you want to negotiate a purchase from a supplier in another culture. You'll need to ask about technical information, price, discounts, quantity, shipping dates, insurance, payment method, shipping method, repeat orders, and quality control. You'll ask questions about all these items, and each is potentially an issue to be negotiated. As you question, you are refining your idea about the importance to the other side of reaching an agreement and what the other side's *best alternative to a negotiated agreement* (BATNA) is. You are discovering what items the other team is willing to yield about, and what items the other team is inflexible about.

Persuasion

This brings us to the third communication phase: persuasion. At this point you have established what you need to focus on in order to reach an agreement. In other words, you have a clear idea where the conflicts lie as well as the concord. Now you will attempt to persuade your counterparts to accept a settlement that ensures you what you need and perhaps more. They will do the same.

The language of persuasion varies among cultures, as is discussed in Chapter 5. You can employ the language strategy of inclusiveness for persuasion. For example, if the individual needs of your counterparts are to appear tough and persistent because those are cultural values that drive individual behavior, you can avoid using language that forces them to back down. Use the inclusive language *together we can . . .* rather than the exclusive language *you'll have to accept . . .* and *we absolutely require . . .* Avoid *I*-centered messages and *must, should, ought* messages. In other words, use *you-viewpoint* and indicate you understand the others' point of view. Encourage your counterparts to focus on what they can gain, not what they may have to give up.

Differences in negotiation tactics between low-context cultures and high-context cultures are shown in Exhibit 9–1. Obviously many of the tactics used by low-context cultures will not work in high-context cultures, and vice versa. For example, as Chapter 5 discusses, many cultures are not persuaded by objective facts. Silence may signal unhappiness to the other side, or may be understood as a comfortable pause during which you ponder and meditate. Some disagreement is inevitable, since that is why you are at a negotiating table, but how it is communicated varies culturally. Threats, personal attacks, insistence, and being emotional are all subject to cultural priorities.

When members of low-context cultures communicate with members of high-context cultures, they need to be especially aware of the cultural context of communication: concerns for harmony, status, and showing respect. When members of high-context cultures communicate with members of low-context cultures, they need to pay special attention to

---

EXHIBIT 9–1   Low-Context and High-Context Negotiation Tactics

Low-Context Negotiation Tactics	*High-Context Negotiation Tactics*
• Supporting argument with factual data.	• Supporting argument with personal connections.
• Offering counterproposals.	• Offering counterproposals.
• Silence.	• Silence.
• Disagreeing.	• Suggesting additional items.
• Threatening the opposing side.	• Referring to precedent.
• Attacking opponents' characters.	• Deferring to superiors.
• Avoiding certain issues.	• Avoiding certain issues.
• Expressing emotion.	• Avoiding conflict.
• Insisting on a final position.	• Remaining open and flexible.
• Making a final offer.	• Revisiting and reopening items previously negotiated.

---

the words and what the words actually say, not what can be implied or inferred in the words.

Arabic-speaking businesspeople need to remember that low-context cultures attach face-value meanings to words, analyze the meanings, and don't usually discount any words as mere rhetoric. Businesspeople from low-context cultures need to remember that Arabic-speaking cultures enjoy the way words themselves—by their dancing, heaped-up phrases, and sheer volume—can affect people, and that literal, face-value meanings may not be intended.

People from cultures who prefer explicit communication that is direct and to the point tend to persuade with facts (see Chapter 5). This is true of businesses in the United States, for example, where arguments that are based on fact have greater credibility than arguments that are based on opinion or inference. Facts are; they do not need to be proven. So strong is the attitude that facts count that a sufficient number of facts often seems to make an argument irrefutable. You know yourself that statistics can make a business decision seem sound. But you also know that statistics can be used to say anything. Of course, people can also be mistaken and get facts wrong.

Some businesspeople prefer arguments based on inference, which is a conclusion based on fact but not proven. Inferences are assumptions. Some believe inferences or presumed implications generated from facts are more powerful than the facts themselves. When a politician suggests that the plan her opponent has to create new jobs will actually threaten the environment, the politician is inferring consequences.

Inferred consequences are the stuff of advertisements. Ads infer that a consumer will benefit in some way by purchasing the advertised goods. For example, drinking a certain beer will connect you to a more glamorous social circle; driving a certain car will put you in the company of professional racing drivers; using a certain credit card will enable you to join in fun international travel. Your response to these appeals is emotional: desire or perhaps disgust (the advertisers hope it's desire).

Asian negotiators often use inference when they refer to history. Asians, Europeans, Latin Americans, Middle Easterners, and Africans tend to take a long view of current activity, placing it in the context of a history reaching far back, but still having a very real meaning for the present. This enables them to take a long view of the future as well. Americans, Canadians, New Zealanders, and Australians—as well as most Argentines—have a short history, and even that seems remote and unconnected to the present. They often could use their historical contacts as a persuasive tool but they overlook it. In the early 1980s Canadian business negotiators were surprised to learn about the high regard in which Canada was held in China thanks to one man, Dr. Norman Bethune, who had been on Mao's long march but was an obscure eccentric in Canadian history. Bethune was politically correct (Mao had made him the subject of one of his essays) and well known in China. Canadian business negotiators soon began finding links between their organizations and Bethune.

Others prefer arguments based on opinion. Opinions cannot be proven true or false. These are usually also emotional. For some, emotion means genuine involvement on the part of the persuader. Without emotion an argument lacks heart and conviction and is simply cold and impersonal.

Obviously when someone who shuns emotion in favor of facts encounters another who prefers emotion and finds facts alone to be unconvincing, the result can be miscommunication that results in a failure to reach an agreement. Some observers have noted this problem in Arab–Israeli negotiations; Arabs prefer argument based on a mixture of opinion and emotion, with some fact and inference; Israelis prefer an argument based on fact and inference with less opinion or emotion.

The sequence in which items are discussed is often a critical communication factor in negotiations. Research has shown that skilled Western negotiators are more flexible in the sequence in which they communicate about factors than average Western negotiators who stick to a planned sequence.[21] The average negotiator treats items independently, while the skilled negotiator is able to link items. This is called "enlarging the pie"; the negotiator adds issues so the pie is larger and therefore everyone can have a larger piece.

Skilled negotiators also make more frequent reference to long-term concerns than average negotiators. The negotiator who appears to be after a short-term, in-and-out business deal is less likely to succeed than the negotiator who makes reference to long-term goals.

Even with the best motives and the most careful preparation, negotiators who ignore the other culture's priorities can put a foot wrong. In 1983 an article in the *Harvard Business Review* outlined what the authors called the "American John Wayne" style of negotiating, which still has relevance today.[22] Here is a summary.

1. **I can go it alone.** Many U.S. executives seem to believe they can handle any negotiation situation by themselves, and they are outnumbered in most negotiation situations.
2. **Just call me John.** Americans value informality and equality in human relationships. They try to make people feel comfortable by playing down class distinctions.
3. **Pardon my French.** Americans aren't very talented at speaking foreign languages.
4. **Check with the home office?** American negotiators get upset when halfway through a negotiation the other side says, "I'll have to check with the home office." The implication is that the decision makers are not present.
5. **Get to the point.** Americans don't like to beat around the bush and want to get to the heart of the matter quickly.
6. **Lay your cards on the table.** Americans expect honest information at the bargaining table.

7. **Don't just sit there; speak up.** Americans don't deal well with silence during negotiations.
8. **Don't take "no" for an answer.** Persistence is highly valued by Americans and is part of the deeply ingrained competitive spirit that manifests itself in every aspect of American life.
9. **One thing at a time.** Americans usually attack a complex negotiation task sequentially; that is, they separate the issues and settle them one at a time.
10. **A deal is a deal.** When Americans make an agreement and give their word, they expect to honor the agreement no matter what the circumstances.
11. **I am what I am.** Few Americans take pride in changing their minds, even in difficult circumstances. Americans also think it is "phony" to act differently in a negotiation with foreigners than they would act at home.

You can venture a guess about how successful these strategies would be in a high-context culture or in a low-context culture. The obvious U.S. cultural values include individual performance, desire to achieve an agreement, preference for informality and for communication in English, emphasis on direct and explicit communication, and an unease with silence.

Concession and Agreement

Finally, the negotiators' communication task turns to concession and agreement. When making a concession, skilled negotiators link that to a counterconcession, using "if" language: "We'll accept your shipment dates if you'll agree to a discount on future orders." Many experienced negotiators warn that you can't come back and ask for a counterconcession after a concession has been granted to the other side and the discussion has moved to another issue. Once you agree without condition or "if," the issue is settled. You attempt to reopen it at risk of losing what agreements—and trust—you have already gained.

Sometimes the final agreement arrives more quickly than you expect. Many Chinese negotiations, for example, consist of probing the other side's position, testing for firmness and the other side's final position. Then suddenly, you may find that the Chinese side offers a final agreement that solves many of the issues raised, without the need to haggle and bargain or persuade. When this is the case, it probably isn't a good idea to offer too many counterproposals or alternatives, because that weakens your position. On the other hand, the Chinese negotiators in this situation should hold back from commitment to unattractive points to see if the other side will offer counterproposals or if they are really firm. Anglo negotiators are known to be under pressure from their own cultural priorities to settle. They want to achieve an agreement; in some cases they seem to feel *any* agreement is better than no agreement. They can be impatient, but they also can be imaginative about solutions.

Some negotiating teams will be able to live with an agreement that at least gives them the *appearance* of having done well. Cohen quotes an Egyptian proverb:

Make your harvest look big lest your enemies rejoice.[23]

The agreement has to *look* good as well as be good.

Some cultures are not interested in settling the negotiations in a way that terminates them. To these context-oriented cultures, the relationship between organizations is what makes negotiations and agreements possible. Each side has an obligation to nurture the relationship and keep it going. Signed agreements don't do that. Japanese negotiators, for example, prefer escape clauses in contracts—when contracts are necessary at all. Western negotiators are dismayed when Japanese or Chinese counterparts begin making changes immediately after contracts are signed. But in Asian cultures, the documents are far less important than keeping the interdependent, interwoven organizations in a good relationship.

Negotiators from the United States, on the other hand, are keen to sign agreements. Contracts are firm and go a long way toward eliminating ambiguities and misunderstandings. They and other low-context negotiators see unwritten and informal agreements as unenforceable. They may allow the other side to conceal something; low-context cultures give openness high priority.

Time magazine, nearly two decades ago, ran this statement: "The successful negotiation between Japanese and Western businessmen usually ends up looking very much like one between two Japanese."[24] It is still true today. Sensitivity to another culture is still advisable in the 21st century. It takes more effort than simply expecting others to learn your own communication style, but it's worth it.

SUMMARY

This chapter has shown how cultural priorities affect specific communication tasks, in this case the task of business negotiations:

- The experience of Canwall in China illustrates cultural priorities and shows an outcome that was not what the Canadians had expected.
- What really happened involved the way *culture affects communication.* Chinese cultural dimensions (from Chapters 3 and 4) include *relationships,* expectations about *time* and efficiency, the way *obligation* is perceived, the value of *harmony,* the method of *learning,* performance of tasks *simultaneously,* preference for protocol and *form, seniority* and *hierarchy, mediated access* to authority, *interdependence,* and *tolerance of uncertainty.*
- *Expectations for outcomes* is one way cultures differ at the negotiating table. Cultures may have

  Different goals.

  Different views of advantage or disadvantage.

  A preference for one of the four outcomes of negotiation: compromise, win–lose, win–win, or stalemate.

- The *makeup of the negotiating teams* may also differ, but teams usually include

  Members with high status.

  Members with special expertise.

  A translator.

- *Physical aspects of the negotiations* can affect the outcomes also:

  Site and space.

  Schedule and agenda.

  Use of time.

  Host hospitality.

- *By far the most important differences are in communication styles:*

  The focus may be on what has already been agreed or on what remains in dispute.

  Some teams negotiate for the honor of their country or firm.

  Some teams prefer the observance of more form and specific protocol than others.

  Some show emotion and even make a deliberate display of emotion, while others show little emotion.

  Some teams use silence, while others are uncomfortable with silence.

- *Negotiation has four phases:*

  Development of a relationship with the other side.

  Exchange of information and positions.

  Persuasion and argumentation.

  Concessions and agreement.

NOTES

1. William Zartman and Maureen Berman, quoted in Raymond Cohen, *Negotiating across Cultures,* (Washington, DC: United States Institute of Peace, 1991) pp. 16 ff.
2. Geert Hofstede, *Cultures and Organizations*, (New York: McGraw-Hill, 1991) p. 225.
3. Cohen, *Negotiating across Cultures,* pp. 31–32.
4. Glen Fisher, *International Negotiation: A Cross-Cultural Perspective,* (Yarmouth, ME: Intercultural Press, 1980).
5. Cohen, *Negotiating across Cultures,* p. 51.
6. Robert T. Moran and William G. Stripp, *Dynamics of Successful International Business Negotiations,* (Houston: Gulf, 1991) p. 84.
7. Richard Mead, *Cross-Cultural Management Communication*, (New York: John Wiley and Sons, 1990), p. 203.
8. Yale Richmond, *From Nyet to Da: Understanding the Russians,* (Yarmouth, ME: Intercultural Press, 1992) p. 141.
9. Moran and Stripp, *Dynamics of Successful International Business Negotiations,* p. 77.
10. Ibid., p. 84.
11. Tom Getman, *McNeil Lehrer Newshour,* June 7, 1993.
12. Moran & Stripp, *Dynamics of Successful International Business Negotiations,* p. 168.
13. Cohen, *Negotiating across Cultures,* p. 89.
14. Diane Zior Wilhelm, "A Cross-Cultural Analysis of Drinking Behavior within the Context of International Business," in *Anthropology in International Business, Studies in Third World Societies,* no. 28. Hendrick Serrie, guest ed. (Williamsburg, VA: College of William and Mary, 1986), p. 77.
15. Linda Beamer, "Toasts: Rhetoric and Ritual in Business Negotiation in Confucian Cultures," *Business Forum* (1994), pp. 22–25.
16. Sun, T (1984). *Art of War* (S. B. Griffith, Trans.). New York: Oxford University Press. (Original work published 256 B.C.)
17. February 21, 1972, *The White House Years*, pp.1061–62; quoted in Cohen, *Negotiating across Cultures,* p. 123.
18. Graham and Herberger, quoted in Mead, in *Cross-Cultural Management Communication,* p. 189.
19. Cohen, *Negotiating across Cultures,* p. 56.
20. Mead, *Cross-Cultural Management Communication,* pp. 196–7.
21. N. Rackham, "The Behavior of Successful Negotiators (Huthwaite Research Group Reports), in *International Negotiations: A Training Program for Corporate Executives and Diplomats.* ed. E. Raider, (Brooklyn, NY: Ellen Raider International, 1976), pp. 196–7.
22. In Philip R. Harris and Robert T. Moran, *Managing Cultural Differences,* 2nd ed. (Houston: Gulf, 1987), p. 59; boldface added.
23. Cohen, *Negotiating across Cultures,* p. 131.
24. Quoted in Robert T. Moran, *Getting Your Yen's Worth: Negotiating With the Japanese,* (Houston: Gulf, 1985), p. 67.

CHAPTER TEN

Legal and Governmental Considerations in Intercultural Business Communication

Asaji Hasoi is the Japanese dealer for PowerBikes, a U.S. motorcycle company. He speaks good English and gets along well with the marketing staff at headquarters in St. Louis. Over the years he has been in St. Louis numerous times for training and product planning sessions. Mr. Hasoi has just received a fax from a new brand manager at headquarters, Patricia Holter. Patricia introduced herself and announced that she would come to visit in a month to meet Mr. Hasoi. Mr. Hasoi is delighted, and as he communicates with Patricia several times during the next month, he is beginning to look forward to meeting her. She seems to understand his concerns and is receptive to his ideas concerning the marketing of PowerBikes in Japan. At the beginning of their visit, they exchange some small gifts and then start discussing the issues at hand. Mr. Hasoi takes Patricia to several stores that sell PowerBikes and introduces her to the store managers. During the last day of Patricia's visit, they wrap up the discussion. Both are pleased with the outcome. At the very end, Mr. Hasoi, as a token of his appreciation and recognition of their successful relationship, presents Patricia with an expensive leather jacket for a motor bike. The jacket is wonderful, and Patricia would love to have it. However, she also knows that under American law and under company rules, she can-

not accept the present. The Foreign Corrupt Practices Act is very clear on this issue. An expensive present like this could be considered a bribe and is, therefore, not acceptable. At the same time Patricia realizes that Mr. Hasoi's intent has nothing to do with bribery. What should she do? She weighs her options and then politely declines the present. Mr. Hasoi seems to take her rejection merely as a first polite refusal which would be appropriate under traditional Japanese custom. Therefore, he once more offers the jacket. Patricia realizes that rejecting the present would be a personal rejection of Mr. Hasoi. She explains the situation, but Mr. Hasoi does not seem to understand her predicament, and he again insists she accept the present as a token of their working relationship. Finally, Patricia takes the jacket.

Legally the situation is clear. The present is in violation of the law. And yet, from a cultural viewpoint Patricia is in a predicament. One could argue that Mr. Hasoi should understand the legal issues involved or at least accept Patricia's explanation. The reality is frequently different, and businesspeople must weigh their actions. In this case one might say that even though the jacket was expensive, the gift is a far cry from a multimillion-dollar bribery. But the law does not distinguish between a gift to build or celebrate a relationship and a bribe.

271

In this chapter we will examine legal implications for intercultural business communication. In the course of doing business, managers must communicate with governmental offices, other businesses, employees, and the public. In an international environment, these managers must not only understand the culture of the people they are doing business with, but also the laws that regulate business in a culture.

COMMUNICATION AND LEGAL MESSAGES

What makes sense and is legal in one country may be illegal in another country. In the United States, it is illegal to discriminate on the basis of race, sex, national origin, and age. Japanese, Latin American, and many European job advertisements, on the other hand, may specify the preferred age and sex of a potential employee. For example, job ads for office staff in Mexico frequently mention that applicants must be *attractive* young females. When establishing corporate policies relating to employment, managers must have an understanding of how the laws of the countries they are working in will influence these policies.

Legal systems come out of cultural values; laws do not develop in isolation: they are culture bound. As a result, laws relating to hiring and firing employees, property, contracts, dispute settlement, and ownership have cultural roots. How these laws are formulated, communicated, and enforced is influenced by the communication patterns and priorities of a culture. At the same time, the legal system also acts as a stimulus for gradually changing cultural values. Managers working and communicating with employees from different cultures and engaging in international business should have at least some understanding of the legal systems of the countries they are dealing with. That does not mean managers must be international lawyers, but it does mean that they need to be familiar with basic legal concepts and must know when to call in the legal experts.

Legal systems are territorial. Laws apply to a particular jurisdiction, and typically lawyers are educated in a particular kind of law. Australian lawyers are educated in Australian law. If they work for an international firm, they bring their background in Australian law. When a dispute comes up with a French firm, they do not automatically know what the French legal situation is. In that case, the Australian firm may hire a French law firm to interpret the French law. The problem is that the French lawyers know French law but not Australian law. To the challenges of intercultural communication are added the challenges of different legal systems.

The French lawyer has no problems discussing aspects of French law with another French lawyer. They speak the same language, share the same cultural background, and have had similar legal training. This scenario changes dramatically if the French lawyer must explain a French legal concept to a business lawyer from Sydney, Australia. The two lawyers speak different languages, come from different cultural backgrounds, and have been educated in two very different legal systems.

To avoid serious misinterpretation and miscommunication, the lawyers may use a type of back translation. Back translation, as discussed in Chapter 2, is frequently used when questionnaires are translated from one language into another to ensure accuracy. Lawyers can use the same techniques. After the French lawyer has explained the French legal situation, the Australian can back translate the explanation to the French to ensure understanding. Rephrasing the same question using different formulations and seeing whether the answers are essentially the same can bring out possible difficulties and misunderstandings.

However, back translation is no guarantee for effective communication. For example, the word *force majeure* is part of the legal language in both France and Australia. Both sides may use it assuming that the other side understands the phrase as intended. To minimize misunderstandings in the communication process, both sides must ask questions and probe for hidden meanings or different meanings.

When René Chrétien from Lyon and William Brandon from Sydney discuss a business contract, they cannot just look at the literal meaning of *force majeure*. They must take into consideration the

- Literal meaning.
- Legal meaning.
- Implications of the legal meaning for fulfilling a contract.
- Implications of the legal meaning for settling any contract disputes.

Probing for intended meaning and verification for clarity and accuracy are typical for low-context cultures. Greg Turner from the United States has no difficulties with insisting on clarity; that's part of his job. His success will be measured in part by how clear the terms of a contract are. Akihito Hosokawa from Japan, on the other hand, comes from a high-context culture where the insistence on clarity and precision can be interpreted as a sign of mistrust. Traditionally, the Japanese person is not so much after precise legal meaning as after building trust and a long-term relationship.

International business is concerned with both international and comparative law. There are two kinds of international law: public international law and private international law. Public international law, sometimes called law of nations, deals with the relationships between countries. It involves treaties, wars, the sea, diplomats, and expropriations. Since those aspects can affect businesses, public international law and how it is communicated and interpreted is important to businesses. Cases in public international law may be taken by a country, not an individual, to the International Court of Justice in Den Haag, Holland. (I have decided to leave Den Haag, rather than The Hague, since students from other countries may not be familiar with the English term for Den Haag.)

A major issue in public international law is the question of enforcing judgments. The International Court of Justice can render a verdict but has no real power to enforce the verdict. Most of the decisions rendered by the International Court of Justice are followed; however, since there is no international sheriff, the enforcement of decisions is always a question. This was clearly illustrated when civilians from the U.S. embassy in Tehran, Iran, were taken hostage by an Iranian group. The International Court of Justice rendered a verdict, in record time, that the taking of hostages was a violation of international law. However, the Court had no power to enforce its decision. The hostage crisis dragged on for many months.

War criminals in the Balkans are tried under public international law. They are charged under crimes against humanity and war crimes. This case is particularly interesting since a number of nations have agreed to this trial. This is not always the case because a person may be considered a terrorist or criminal by one country but a freedom fighter by another country. For example, the case against Osama Bin Laden, accused of masterminding the bombing of two U.S. embassies in Africa, has been brought by the United States. If he were captured, he would most likely be tried by the United States under U.S. law. Theoretically, he could be tried under international law, but this venue might be more difficult if several countries opposed such a trial.

Private international law deals with laws between persons and businesses. It involves the settlement of conflicts and the enforcement of contracts. One of the most important questions in private international law is which court has jurisdiction. For example, in a contract dispute between a Venezuelan firm and a Nigerian firm, one of the questions to be answered is which court will settle the dispute.

Most international business is more concerned with comparative and private international law than public international law. How are contracts handled in various jurisdictions? What are employment laws? What are import–export regulations? The international businessperson will regularly be involved in interpreting the laws and regulations of other countries in the context of doing business. Laws and regulations are specific forms of communication, and international businesspeople are interpreters. Alfredo Luzero, for example, must be able to explain legal concerns of headquarters in Amsterdam to his managers in the subsidiary in Lima. At the same time, he must interpret employment issues and legal concerns of Peru, the host country, to upper management in Amsterdam.

SPECIFIC LEGAL SYSTEMS

While every country has its own laws and legal system, there are three major legal systems:[1]

- Code law.
- Anglo-American common law.
- Islamic law.

With the political and economic changes in Eastern Europe and Russia, a fourth system, socialist law, is losing importance. However, several of these countries are still struggling to put new legal systems in place. As long as remnants of socialist law remain, it is advantageous to have some understanding of socialist law. In Russia, for example, the legal system is currently in flux. Many of the old laws regulating property ownership have been discarded, but new laws, even if they are on the books, are not enforced consistently. The emergence of the Russian Mafia has made the enforcement laws even more complicated. The uncertain legal situation and constantly changing government regulations create an uncertain environment for both domestic and international business.

In many parts of the world the major legal systems are influenced by indigenous systems and tribal laws. New Zealand, for example, pays special respect to Maori laws. Contracts may well be influenced by traditional considerations of a culture. India, for example, has retained common law, but local traditions play a role also. Payment for goods or services does not follow the tightly regulated schedules of U.S. business firms. The law takes into account the personal relationships of the parties involved. Businesses typically do not press for payment within a specific time period. The assumption is that one does business with people one can trust, and therefore it is assumed the clients will pay when they can.

Code Law

Western continental Europe follows code law. Code law comes out of the French legal tradition. The French code law goes back to 1806, when it was written under the direction of the Emperor Napoleon in an attempt to clarify the legal situation. Thus it is also known as the *Code Napoleon.* While the French code law is based on Roman codes, it also incorporates some of the ideals of the French Revolution, such as the right to private property and the freedom to make contracts. French code law is written in clear and concise style; it is meant for the citizen.

The German code law (*Bürgerliche Gesetzbuch, BGB*) was enacted in 1896. It is a highly structured, precise, and detailed system. In both the French and the German systems decisions are made by expert judges who interpret the law. Previous decisions in similar situations have only limited persuasive authority.

Code law is deductive. The student of code law learns to read the law paragraph by paragraph. He or she gets the interpretation of the law from a law professor or judge. Previous cases involving a similar legal issue are not binding and not overly important in the logical thought process.

Anglo–American Common Law

Under Anglo–American common law, decisions are based on precedent in similar cases. Common law grew out of common practices of the courts of the King of England. Today most of England's former colonies, including the United States, have retained common law. Two notable exceptions are Louisiana in the United States and Quebec in Canada. The state of Louisiana and the Province of Quebec have maintained their French heritage and French legal system. Both use code law.

Common law is inductive. The last relevant case becomes the source of law. The terminology can be confusing. For example, the United States, a common law country, has the Uniform Commercial Code (UCC). The UCC was enacted to guarantee uniform enforcement of commercial law across the 50 states. All, except Louisiana, have adopted the UCC. In the first few years after the passing of the UCC, lawyers had a hard time interpreting the UCC because the case law in this area had not been developed yet. And the meaning of the law comes out of cases rather than the wording of the law itself. The case at the end of the chapter is an illustration of the application of common law to a business problem.

Islamic Law

Islamic law is known as *Sharia*. It is based on these sources:

- Koran, the holy book of Islam.
- Sunnah, deeds and sayings of Mohammed.
- Interpretations of Islamic scholars.
- Consensus of the legal community.

In addition, Islamic law has been influenced by indigenous and tribal laws, such as Arab Bedouin law, commercial law from Mecca, agrarian law from Medina, and Jewish law.

In contrast to Western legal systems, Sharia encompasses the totality of religious, political, social, domestic, and private life. Sharia is concerned with ethics and moral issues rather than strict commercial law and regulations. Islamic law has been static for several centuries; no new interpretations have been allowed. As a result, Islamic law has almost no provisions to deal with modern international business practices and transactions such as credits and interest payments. Nevertheless, several Islamic countries, among them Iran, Pakistan, Saudi Arabia, Sudan, and Libya are having Islamic law as the ruling law. Any international manager doing business in an Islamic country needs to be aware of some of the practices of Sharia specifically as they relate to contracts, banking, and agency relationships. These aspects are discussed in greater detail later in this chapter.

Islamic law applies to all Muslims, but it also covers foreigners living in an Islamic country. For example, Saudi women are not allowed to drive. This rule also applies to foreign women. Saudi women are not allowed to travel on their own. Similarly, Western women cannot travel alone in Saudi Arabia. The ban on consumption of alcohol includes everyone, Saudis and expatriates. When Muslims travel abroad, they are not totally bound by Sharia.

The enforcement of Sharia varies from country to country, and businesspeople need to familiarize themselves with the specific rules for each country. Even in the strict countries, however, the enforcement of traditional Islamic law, such as cutting off the right hand for theft, is rare. Yet violating religious law can have severe and unexpected consequences.

Rene Lafontaine, a businessman from Lyon, France, had been appointed manager of a department in a French subsidiary in Riyadh, Saudi Arabia. He supervised several French men and women and about a dozen Saudi men. He had never been to Saudi Arabia before, and after a month in the new job, he decided to host a party after work on company premises. He had arranged for food, soft drinks, and wine. Things went very well, and everyone was having a good time, when all of a sudden the religious police entered the premises and arrested everyone in attendance.

The entire group was taken to jail, where Rene learned that the group was accused of illegal consumption of alcohol and prostitution. He could understand the first part but not the second until he was told that the attendance at the party by unmarried French women was considered a form of prostitution. He managed to call the French embassy in desperation. Surely, the French ambassador could clear up the whole mess and get them out within an hour. He was wrong; it took the ambassador 24 hours to resolve the situation.

DISPUTE SETTLEMENT

Direct Confrontation and Arbitration

When disputes arise over a contract, the question is whose courts will decide the outcome and which law will be applied. The manager needs to consider the area of dispute settlement from the very beginning of the negotiations and make this a part of the negotiation. Each party will probably want the courts of its own country to settle any disputes in the hope that this will be an advantage. In a dispute between a Japanese and a U.S. business, the Americans will want a court in the United States, for example, a court in Texas, to hear the case. The Japanese, on the other hand, will want the Japanese courts to hear the case. However, given the tendency of U.S. courts to award huge settlements up to millions of dollars, it may be advantageous for the American firm to have the case decided in a foreign court. It is helpful if the parties are aware of the past decisions in cases of conflicts. If opposing parties conclude that the courts in their respective countries have been fair in the past, then the nationality of the court may not be crucial.

The two parties may also take into account the nature of the business. If the joint business dealings involve shipping and the law of the sea, it may be advantageous if a British court hears the case. The British have a very well developed law of admiralty and may, therefore, render the fairest and most objective judgment. As a result, a Portuguese and a Thai firm, even though both firms are in countries that have their own established legal systems, may agree on using British admiralty law in disagreements over shipping issues.

Traditionally, high-context cultures place less emphasis on detailing the rules and legal provisions in case of disagreements. They prefer a style that avoids finding out who is to blame and who should be punished (also see Chapter 3 on rule observing versus rule bending.)

Two Japanese firms doing business together will hardly ever resort to the courts to settle disputes; in fact, a firm going to court, even if the law is on its side, may lose face. As we have discussed earlier in this book, the emphasis on communicating in Japan is on creating an atmosphere of harmony. A lawsuit would severely disrupt harmony. The firm that brings the suit may lose as much or even more face than the firm that is being sued.

However, a non-Japanese businessperson should also know that in international contracts the Japanese may insist on as much clarity as the Australians who come from a low-context culture. Firms around the globe may practice one style within their cultural boundaries and another one outside their national boundaries.

In countries where suing is not a culturally acceptable means for settling disputes, mediation and arbitration play important roles. Even firms in low-context cultures are beginning to turn to mediation and arbitration in an attempt to cut legal costs and avoid disrupting business transactions. Arbitration is generally quicker and more neutral than a lawsuit. Under arbitration both sides agree on certain rules of arbitration before a dispute ever occurs. They also agree to abide by the decision of the arbitrator. The win–lose approach of lawsuits is replaced with a communication style that seeks to overcome disagreements and reestablish common goals.

When negotiating contracts and trying to set up new business ventures in a country, a manager must examine the overall business climate and the government regulations of business. For example, does the government create a positive atmosphere for doing business? Is the government fair, and does it treat locals and foreigners the same way? Or does the government protect local interest each time a dispute arises?

Communication with Agents

International firms frequently hire agents to represent their interests abroad and sell their products. Depending on the cultural environment of the agent, the relationship between the agent and the foreign firm may go beyond a strict business relationship that can be severed at will. In cultures where business relationships are based on personal relationships and trust, firing an agent can cause loss of face for the agent. The agency laws of most countries are based on cultural attitudes towards business relationships.

Agency law in Brazil almost always favors the Brazilian agent. Once an agent has been hired, it becomes almost impossible to get rid of the agent regardless of performance. A business going into Brazil must move very carefully and cautiously before offering anyone the position as an agent. The same holds in many Islamic countries. In Saudi Arabia, for example, it is also next to impossible to get rid of an agent. Furthermore, agents must be Saudis. A company cannot bring in agents from other countries, even other Arab countries.

Justin Simons was in charge of the international division at Seedlink, an American seed company headquartered in Bloomington, Illinois. As Brazil expanded its soybean production, he saw great potential in selling seed to Brazilian farmers. His company had worked on a type of seed that would be perfect for weather conditions in Brazil. He had been to Brazil once to explore the market. On the last day of the trip he was introduced to Jose Menem, a likable man in his 30s. Menem seemed to know the agricultural market. His English was good, an important point since Justin did not speak any Portuguese. Justin had read somewhere that connections are important in doing business in Brazil, and Menem seemed to know everyone.

Justin did not want to waste any time; he was eager to sell in Brazil well before the competition. Therefore, during his second trip to Brazil, he signed Menem on as agent. A few weeks later, Justin began to wonder what was going on. Menem had been enthusiastic and very optimistic about selling seed, but there were very few orders even though it was the time of year when farmers would buy the seed for the new crop. When he talked to Menem, he only got evasive answers that things were difficult. Justin tried to convince himself that those were typical start-up problems and that things would get better next year. But communication with Menem remained slow. Typically, Justin would wait for several days for a response to his E-mails. When they did talk on the phone, Menem kept assuring Justin that things would get better once conditions improved. Simons never quite understood what this meant. From contacts in Brazil he found out that Menem was spending most of his time promoting products from other foreign companies.

When Justin learned that a major competitor had landed a huge order from Brazil, he decided that it was time to replace Menem. He realized that he had to make sure that neither Menem nor Seedlink would lose face. Menem was well connected, and he could easily damage Seedlink's reputation. After talking to several managers at Seedlink, he decided to contact a lawyer specializing in international business law. He could not believe what the lawyer told him. Unless Menem agreed to a separation, which probably would be rather expensive, Simons would have a hard time getting rid of Menem. In the meantime, the competition would build a substantial advantage in the Brazilian market.

While hiring a local agent presents many advantages, it also poses challenges in intercultural communication. The agent may know the local territory very well but may not be that familiar with the business practices of the country where the firm is headquartered. He may have to struggle with language issues, reporting requirements of headquarters, different attitudes towards planning, establishment of priorities, clients, and suppliers. The foreign manager, on the other hand, may have a limited understanding of the cultural and legal environment of the agent. He may erroneously assume that the agent shares his attitude towards profit and has the same priorities. A firm from the United States may feel that business will improve if it hires two agents in a country so that the agents must compete. The agents, often supported by the laws of their countries, may, however, insist on exclusivity.

It is not enough to hire an agent and then assume that the agent will represent the company and sell the products. The manager and the agent must work together and communicate on an ongoing and regular basis. Ideally, the manager knows the best way to formulate persuasive and negative messages in the agent's culture. The manager must also understand the role of hierarchy and authority in giving directives. If the manager deals with an agent from a culture that values seniority, a younger manager needs to take care when communicating with an agent who is older so as to avoid insulting the dignity of the agent. The agent must be able to translate the goals of the firm he or she represents into actions that go along with the appropriate priorities of the culture. He or she must communicate to the firm the accepted practices in contacting clients, setting prices, requesting payment for goods delivered, and working with government offices.

Trademarks and Intellectual Property

Cultures that emphasize right to private ownership take trademarks very seriously. They assume that a person or group can own something exclusively. Chapter 1, for example, discussed the concept of land ownership among Native Americans. In Native American culture the concept of private ownership does not make sense; no one person can *own* land. Similarly, one cannot own inventions; therefore, Native Americans would traditionally not be concerned about private ownership of trademarks and patents. In cultures where individual recognition and rights are emphasized, trademarks are seen as an important tool in protecting those rights.

Rules relating to trademarks vary from country to country. In the United States, for example, one can only register a trademark if there is a product behind the trademark. One cannot just register a trademark for a product one might develop in the future. The American firm, Babushka Markets, for example, cannot register the trademark, Babushka Cookies, unless it actually has the cookies. The rules are different in Brazil where one can register a trademark without a product. A company or person could take the name of a successful product like Babushka Cookies from the United States and register the trademark in Brazil. If the company from the United States at a later date wanted to sell Babushka Cookies in Brazil, the firm would first have to buy the rights to the trademark.

Trademark regulations have become a major point in international trade negotiations. Businesses see the name of a firm or product and the shape of a product as powerful communication tools. For example Quaker Oats from the United States protects its trademark, the Quaker; Volkswagen protects the trademark *Bug;* and McDonald's protects the arches. Businesspeople must understand the legal background and cultural ramifications and develop an awareness of trademarks as communication emblems that warrant protection.

The Internet has spurred a whole new dispute concerning the registering of names. Some people have developed websites under names that belong to companies or organizations. As a result, a company that was slow in developing a Web presence may have to buy the Web name from the industrious Web entrepreneur. An effective Web name is worth a lot of money. Moldova, for example, recognized that it could use its country designation, *.md,* for financial gain. Physicians in the United States can purchase the right to use the designation *.md* from Moldova for a fee. Moldova then uses the money to develop its Internet system.

Another area for common disputes in international business is the issue of intellectual property rights. Intellectual property includes patents and copyright. With advancing technology, intellectual property has become an important aspect of negotiations. Who has the rights to what, and for how long does anyone hold rights? Under U.S. copyright law, a copyright lasts for 50 years beyond the death of the author. Patent laws are good for 17 years. Concerns about intellectual property rights focus on two areas:

- Countries that either violate copyright and patent agreements or have not signed agreements.
- Individuals who violate laws in the area of intellectual property rights.

An additional problem is that legal regulation of intellectual property is still evolving in many countries. It is difficult to keep the laws current given fast-changing technology and its impact on communication. Concerns about intellectual property have commercial, financial, and cultural roots. A company that has invested its money to develop a new product wants to reap the rewards and not share its new technique with others, at least for a while. The current debate over gene mapping is an example of the issues at hand. Private companies that have mapped genes argue that they should be allowed to sell the gene maps for profit. After all, they have spent a lot of money on this research. Consumers, the government, and potential competitors, on the other hand, may argue that everyone can benefit by sharing new developments and that patents, in this case gene maps, are common property. These are the financial considerations. The cultural attitudes we have already addressed. Some cultures emphasize private property; others don't.

India has not signed agreements on patents. As a result, an Indian firm manufactures pharmaceuticals developed in the United States and sells them under a different name at a much lower price in countries like Russia. Russia desperately needs pharmaceuticals but does not have the hard currency to purchase them from the manufacturer in the United States. One could argue that pharmaceuticals are overpriced, that the Russians need the product, and that it is a humanitarian measure to allow the production in India. The point that the firm in the United States makes, however, is that the Indian firm did not incur any of the research and development costs.

Computer software, videos, and CDs make up another hot area for international legal communication. Frequently developing countries have no laws regulating copyright violations, and if laws exist, often they are not enforced. In Rumania, for example, companies regularly use pirated software. Everyone knows it, but nothing is done about it. Microsoft Office 98 was available in Rumania before it was officially released for sale, and it sold for only a fraction of the price in the United States.

The laws are fairly clear in Western countries: Copying is forbidden. However, it is very difficult to enforce the law. Furthermore, it is very inexpensive to copy software and videos. Even otherwise law-abiding companies have run afoul of copyright laws. A major insurance firm, for example, found that employees had copied software illegally. The problem was solved, and the firm established very strict rules on the use of software, but it takes constant vigilance, education, and enforcement of policies to ensure compliance.

In developing countries with limited access to hard currency, the temptation to violate copyright laws is much greater. Any business firm must be careful to follow the laws of its own country and of the host country as they relate to intellectual property rights.

The issue of intellectual property illustrates very well that all of us bring our cultural priorities and our frame of reference to the negotiation table. Furthermore, the laws of our respective countries tend to reinforce our cultural attitudes. In order to negotiate effectively, we need to know both the laws and the cultural reasons for the laws.

The World Trade Organization (WTO) is attempting to resolve this issue by making compliance with copyright laws a condition of membership. As was discussed earlier under international law, the enforcement of the law could be difficult, however. In 1995 China agreed to improve compliance with intellectual property legislation, but the problem persists. Critics of China's joining the WTO point out that China's past behavior in the area of copyright issues will not change once China is a member of the WTO.

MULTINATIONAL ENTERPRISE AND THE NATIONAL INTEREST

Nations have an interest in regulating businesses within their boundaries. The national interest is to guarantee the continuation of the nation, and business regulation must be seen in that context. A nation is first and foremost interested in business as a promotion of national interests:

- It may be in the national interest to promote trade to improve employment and living standards at home.
- It may be in the national interest to curtail exports of certain items to guarantee that the products are available for domestic consumption.
- It may be in the national interest to curtail the import of certain products to protect domestic industries.

In the 1980s France, for example, very consciously regulated the import of computers. Even though Apple computers had offered to put its computers into schools for free, France rejected the offer. France considered it crucial for the national interest to develop its own computer industry. It was willing to go slower in computerization than other countries if that meant the development of a French computer industry. And to some extent the French were successful in building a French computer industry. In the late 1980s many French households had Minitel, a computer system for shopping, booking plane and train tickets, and researching restaurants and other sites. However, the system was not compatible with the emerging Internet. Since households had access to a variety of information under Minitel, many were reluctant to purchase computers to hook up to the Internet. In many ways the success of the French Minitel slowed the acceptance of the technology that is used worldwide. Even today, France is lagging behind other European countries in computer ownership

The Russians are experimenting with import and export taxes and regulations. Currently the system is changing almost daily. The country has not decided what will ultimately be in its best interest. The result is confusion everywhere. The government does not clearly communicate with its own firms and citizens, let alone with foreign firms. Russia is a good example of how uncertain laws and confusion can affect business communication.

Any nation's government must weigh the short- and long-term interests of the country. If taxes on foreign businesses are too high, then these businesses will not invest in the country and the country may suffer. If Russia puts high export taxes on products, it will hinder the international development of its businesses and endanger the future development of its industries. Currently, the legal uncertainties within the country communicate economic and political uncertainty and instability to other countries and cause serious undervaluation of the currency.

Businesses have different interests from the nation state. In many ways they have outgrown the nation state. They increasingly look at the global picture. They want to produce wherever it is most efficient—they want to move employees around the globe regardless of nationality and country boundaries. They want to do business on a global basis without national restrictions, yet governments try to regulate. The two are clearly at odds in many cases.

Regulations come out of cultural values and concerns. They are meant to protect the national culture, and each country establishes its own laws and rules for competition, taxation, employment, and product quality. The United States has tried in the past to enforce its regulations for foreign subsidiaries of U.S. companies. Foreign countries have resisted this attempt in many ways, arguing, for example, that a Brazilian subsidiary of a U.S. firm is a Brazilian firm subject to Brazilian and not U.S. regulations. This issue has come to the forefront in antitrust legislation, employment, and labor laws. The manager who has been sent from the United States to manage the Brazilian subsidiary must take into consideration

- American culture when communicating with headquarters in New York.
- Brazilian culture when communicating with Brazilians.
- Brazilian laws when dealing in Brazil.
- Brazilian legal aspects of the business in communicating with headquarters.
- U.S. law and its effect on the company's dealings in Brazil.

The national government can also regulate the collection, storing, and dissemination of private information. In the United States, many firms have lists of their customers detailing what products the customer purchased and when. Supermarkets, by using specially coded customer cards, offer lower prices for regular customers, but they also collect information on purchasing patterns. While a number of people in the United States are concerned about this practice, the majority seems to be willing to accept it in return for lower prices at the checkout counter. The governments of the European Union are more concerned about privacy. Under EU regulations, a multinational cannot share its customer list with headquarters without the written permission of the customer. For example, Land's End Europe cannot transfer its customer file from Europe to the computer system at headquarters without the express permission of its individual European customers. From a business viewpoint, this regulation makes it more difficult to develop companywide comprehensive marketing plans.

In many cases national laws protect domestic companies from competition. For example, Germany has very strict legislation on when stores can be open. For many years, German consumers were willing to accept the law. However, as more Germans traveled abroad, they began to question the rules. Nevertheless, the lobby of small store owners was powerful enough to keep the law. And then E-commerce and Wal-Mart arrived. Even if the German government tried to enforce "store hours" on the Internet, it would not work. So companies like Land's End have been able to expand shopping hours for German consumers via the Internet. Wal-Mart had to find another way. The law allows stores to be open between 7 A.M. and 6 P.M., Monday through Friday, and 7 A.M. till 4 P.M. on Saturday. During the last few years stores have been allowed to remain open till 8 P.M. on some days. Most German stores opened about 9 A.M. even though they could have opened earlier. Wal-Mart saw this as an opportunity. When Wal-Mart entered Germany, management decided to open as early and close as late as the law allowed. In addition, Wal-Mart emphasized customer service and a friendly atmosphere. As German stores watch the success of the new arrivals, they are being forced into changing their practices and communication with customers.

LEGAL ISSUES IN LABOR AND MANAGEMENT COMMUNICATION

Labor laws and attitudes towards labor management relations have deep-seated cultural roots and are not easily transplanted. The bargaining process influences the communication patterns between the two parties. Labor–management relations in the United States have been adversarial. Management tries to give as little as possible, and labor asks for as much as possible. The two sides sit down and bargain and negotiate for a settlement. The adversarial process is culturally determined and enforced by bargaining rules (also see Chapter 9).

The British believe that the adversarial process protects the rights of workers and gives companies a competitive edge. The idea of cooperation between management and labor is strange to the class-conscious British. The bargaining process both in the United States and Great Britain emphasizes competition and winning. It is "us" against "them." And the goal typically is to beat "them," whoever "they" are.

The Germans, although also very competitive, have consciously tried to overcome the rift between labor and management and set common goals. As a result, the German system functions very differently. There, labor and management sit down together to determine the future of the company. The so-called *Mitbestimmung* (co-determination) requires that one-half of the members of the *Aufsichtsrat* or Board of Directors are representatives of the employees. The idea is that labor and management are all in the same boat and must therefore work together for the common good.

Also under the German *Mitbestimmung* law, every firm has a *Betriebsrat,* a workers' council. This group is heavily involved in terminating employees and setting work rules and other conditions of employment. Again, management and workers sit down together to review cases. A manager from the United States or Great Britain may find it difficult to adjust to this situation.

Recent court decisions in the United States have held this German-style cooperative approach to be a violation of the law. The unions argue that this cooperation violates the traditional role of the unions and the adversarial relationship. A *Betriebsrat,* they argue, is an illegal company union, which is essentially working for management and does not represent the employees.[2]

Tell that to the Japanese. The Japanese system is entirely different. It emphasizes harmony and the group and avoids open confrontation if at all possible. In Japan, under McArthur's leadership after World War II company unions were established to stabilize the labor market. In a company union both the interest of the workers as well as the interest of the company are represented. Workers are very much aware of the fact that unrealistic demands on their part would threaten the profitability and long-range success of the firm. Management, on the other hand, realizes that it depends on the workers and that good relations will improve the performance of the firm. As a result, they tend to work together.

By Western standards, Japanese unions appear to be docile—not really unions at all. For Japan, they have worked very well in building the country's economy. Company unions have also been able to build on the group orientation of the Japanese. While company unions are fairly new, they have built on old traditional values. With the economic problems Japan is facing, similar to those in other industrialized countries, the bargaining process is changing somewhat. Workers are becoming more outspoken, and companies are reluctant to give in to demands.

Union membership in Japan typically includes everyone up through lower management and supervisory levels. Masataka Ota at Mitsubishi, for example, will be in the company union until he reaches management level. Then he leaves the union. As a result, the gap between union and management, so strong in British, Canadian, and U.S. firms, is smaller in Japanese companies. Managers have all been in the union at one time. In fact, very successful managers often have been union officials. Their success in that position is seen as proof that they can work with people who have different opinions and that they can build consensus and communicate effectively. The Japanese believe that the unions develop the communication skills that are vital for the harmony in Japanese firms. Union membership is a stepping-stone in the hierarchy to get to the top because it develops communication skills.

Any manager working internationally must be familiar with the varying rules governing unions, cooperation, and adversaries. The existing structures, laws, and rules will greatly influence how a manager communicates with workers. Lack of knowledge may at best be disruptive and at its worst will cost the company a great deal of money.

LABOR REGULATIONS

Employment Communication

In day-to-day operations, employment communication may very well be the most important issue. Traditionally, U.S. companies have practiced employment at will for nonunion employees. That means a company can hire and fire an employee at will with or without a cause. Over the past few years, regulations on affirmative action and discrimination based on the Civil Rights Act of 1964 and the Americans with Disabilities Act of 1992 have initiated some change, but compared to Japan and many of the European countries, employment in the United States is a variable cost factor. People are hired when times are good and let go when business is bad. The regulations in other countries are much tighter.

As discussed earlier, large companies in Japan practice lifetime employment, but the system is gradually changing. Under lifetime employment workers are considered a fixed cost, not something that can be changed easily. Regulations in France and Germany are very strict when it comes to terminating employees, and rules and regulations are clearly spelled out. Employees have lengthy written contracts and, after a year's probationary period, are essentially on lifetime employment. A business in the United States wanting to buy a German factory needs to be aware of German labor law. In several cases, U.S. companies have bought a firm under the assumption that the firm would be very profitable if the number of workers could be reduced. They found out after the purchase that any labor force reduction was a complicated and time-consuming process. In legal considerations, the courts of a country tend to be very protective of their jurisdiction in matters of employment. Any foreign subsidiary must comply with the labor laws of the host country, and any contract clause restricting court authority in this area is held to be invalid.

Different legal regulations of the employment process have a definite effect on job search procedures and employment communication in different countries. A student in the United States who has just finished a university degree will put together a résumé and start writing cover letters. The student may even have taken a class about how best to conduct the job search. Many books on the market give advice on how to land the best job. However, rules are very different in different countries, and with increasing foreign investment in the United States, American students cannot limit themselves to the "American way" of finding a job.

The same development is taking place in other countries as well. Job seekers in Great Britain may apply for a job in a United States–based firm. Even though the laws of Great Britain apply, the degree of appropriate assertiveness or follow-up letters and inquiries is nevertheless culturally determined and influenced by the home country, in this case the United States. Also, a firm involved in international business cannot just select employees based on home country employment practices and laws. Any international firm needs to take local employment customs into consideration.

The résumé and the accompanying cover letter are influenced by culture and laws. In the United States, personal information on résumés is discouraged. Yet German firms want personal information. So do the French and the Japanese. Any job applicant in the United States who wants to show sincerity and good business etiquette will laser print the résumé and type the cover letter. In France, either the letter or the résumé should be handwritten so that the firm can conduct a handwriting analysis. In Great Britain, the cover letter may be handwritten. In Japan, the résumé used to be handwritten because nobody owned a typewriter. Any typewriter with *Kanji,* the Chinese-based characters, needed thousands of keys. As a result, typewriters were expensive and cumbersome to use. With the advent of personal computers and word processing, however, today most Japanese résumés are typed. Word-processing programs allow the writer to enter text in *Katakana,* a syllabary. The program can transform the syllabary into *Kanji.*

Even the choice of an envelope can influence an applicant's chance to get the desired job. In the United States, résumé and letter are typically neatly folded and placed in a regular No. 10 business envelope. In Germany all materials are put in a clear plastic cover and then placed in a DINA4 (about 8½" by 11½") envelope, *unfolded.* A folded résumé and cover letter would be unacceptable.

The job interview also varies greatly from country to country. Americans are taught to be assertive. The Japanese, on the other hand, want to show that they are adaptable and fit well into the work group. Managers hiring an employee will intuitively look for the traits that bring success in their own culture. It is natural to feel comfortable with the familiar because it facilitates the interpretation of verbal and nonverbal communication signals. In the process of looking for the familiar, many people who are different and could bring new views and insights to the job may be passed over.

In planning international expansion, managers should be aware of and understand the basic employment issues in the target country. They also need to develop a feel for the role of the manager in the lives of employees. As pointed out in earlier chapters, American managers do not get involved in the personal lives of their employees. There may be a company picnic or company Christmas party, but generally personal life remains outside the office. This is very different from Latin American countries where the manager is not just the manager but also a father figure who takes care of the employees and is involved in their private lives. While this involvement may not be specified by law, it is nevertheless specified by custom, and the international manager needs to act accordingly.

Safety on the Job

All cultures want to keep their workers safe, but they differ in their communication as to how this can be accomplished. Low-context cultures believe that detailed rules and regulations will create a safer work environment. Firms operating in the United States often feel burdened by enormously detailed and complex safety regulations enforced by the Occupational Safety and Health Act (OSHA). OSHA has, in fact, made the workplace safer, but foreigners often think that the rules go too far. The regulations must be seen against the background of the tendency in the United States to believe that all injuries and accidents can be prevented if the regulations are strict enough. That attitude is based on the cultural priority that planning can prevent most problems. Furthermore, there is the assumption that the company must be at fault in the case of an accident and that the remedy is a large lawsuit and additional regulation. In many other countries the rules are less stringent, and common sense is applied more often, in part because going to court is not as profitable and because litigation is not generally practiced.

Safety is considered important in high-context cultures, but people realize that not every accident can be prevented. In Arab countries, for example, people believe that fate will determine to a great extent what will happen, and safety rules can ultimately not interfere with fate. As a result, lawsuits are rare in high-context cultures and if they do occur, settlements tend to be lower.

Every country has its own work rules and attitudes towards what constitutes safety on the job. In the United States, for example, construction workers wear steel-toed work boots to protect their toes from heavy objects. In Japan, construction workers traditionally wear cotton leggings with a very thin and flexible rubber sole. This looks absolutely horrifying to a Westerner. When one of the authors discussed this with Japanese construction workers and pointed out the shortcomings of this flimsy footwear, the Japanese were astounded. How could anybody feel safe on a bamboo scaffolding wearing these inflexible, rigid boots? The Japanese are interested in flexibility and grip, which are better with the Japanese boots. The workers in the United States were more interested in protecting their toes from falling objects.

In U.S. construction companies, alcohol is absolutely forbidden while on the job. Construction workers may drink their beer after the day's work is over but definitely not during the day. In Germany, where beer is often considered a beverage like water rather than alcohol, the consumption of beer during the workday is commonplace; however, during the past few years attitudes have started to change. It would be almost impossible to forbid the consumption of beer; workers might very well walk out. German factory workers might drink a beer during their lunch break; the French might drink wine. They would probably not agree with the argument of people in the United States that even the moderate consumption of alcohol in this environment is a safety issue. Communication about alcohol during the work week is different in different cultures.

Equal Opportunity

In the United States, legal protection for and equal opportunity of women in the workplace have become big issues, and the law says that women should be allowed to work in any field, including construction and mining. There should be no restrictions on women's working night shifts. Women have the same right to any job as men. European countries and Japan look at this rather differently. Women in Japan are not allowed to work night shifts. It is considered bad for their health to work at night. They are also restricted in overtime. France and Germany also have rules protecting women from dangerous or physically taxing work. What is meant as protection often turns out to be reduced opportunities. A well-meaning manager who comes into Japan and wants to provide equal opportunities for women, patterned after the United States, may not only run afoul of the law but also alienate the local workforce. At the same time, foreign businesses coming into the United States often do not take seriously the rules and regulations for equal opportunity. They are surprised that the laws are enforced and that they must abide by them. In their own countries, equal opportunity laws may be on the books, but enforcement may be less vigorous.

Sylvia Drucker recently graduated from a German university with a degree in business. She had had excellent grades, and she was confident that with her academic background and several internships she would have no difficulties in finding a good job. As she studied the job listings, she was glad to see that many companies encouraged women to apply. Some even said that women would receive special consideration.

She had several interviews, and they all went well, but she was still waiting for an offer. The recruiters had been impressed with her credentials, so where was the problem? She noticed that a number of her female friends had similar experiences. Finally, she decided to talk to a family friend who was a manager to get advice. He informed her that both her age, 24, and her family status, recently married, worked against her. The companies looked at her as a young woman in her best childbearing years. If she were to become pregnant, under German law, the company would have to provide paid leave before and after delivery. In case Sylvia wanted to stay home with her baby for two years, the company would have to guarantee that she would get the same job once she returned. In the meantime, the company might have to hire a temporary replacement.

As the companies weighed the options, most decided that hiring her was too great a risk and too much hassle. Legally they could not discriminate against her, but there were no teeth in the law.

In the Middle East, where the role of women is severely restricted in a number of countries, Western firms need to keep local laws and traditions in mind. Any attempts to change the role of women would be seen as outside interference and be rejected in many cases, not just by the men but also by the women. With the growing Islamic fundamentalism, women in countries like Egypt, where they had greater opportunities to study and develop careers in the 1970s and 1980s, are beginning to withdraw more from public life again. In Iran, on the other hand, women are emerging as managers in business after having been marginalized as result of the Iranian revolution at the beginning of the 1980s.

The whole issue of equal opportunity is a sensitive one. For example, many major firms in the United States boast in their codes of conduct that they practice equal rights in all their subsidiaries. However, a look at job application forms of some of the foreign subsidiaries of these firms indicates a different picture. The employment application forms in Germany, for example, comply with German practice and German laws rather than U.S. custom. Many of the forms ask for names and positions of parents and siblings, marital status, number of children, health, and age of the applicant. None of these questions may be asked legally by a firm in the United States. Employment laws are definitely culture bound.

A firm may have the best intentions, but it will also have to deal with the realities of the hiring environment in which the subsidiary operates. The laws of the country will influence how businesspeople communicate with their employees. Some activists in the United States argue that the U.S. government should enforce compliance with equal opportunity regulation in all subsidiaries of U.S. firms. How would those very same people react if the Japanese came in to enforce Japanese employment law in their American subsidiaries?

Managers should be familiar with employment laws and with sensitivities both at home and abroad in relation to these laws. If a company says in its code of conduct that it enforces equal employment throughout the entire company and all foreign subsidiaries, that may be well meant, but it is also unrealistic. Perhaps the communication should point out that it will promote equal opportunity whenever possible while also complying with the local laws and customs. That would be a more honest communication.

LEGAL CONSIDERATIONS IN MARKETING COMMUNICATION

Marketing and advertising are regulated in all countries. Advertising is culture specific and subject to local regulations. Aspects that are typically regulated are the role of children in advertising, claims of superiority, standards of decency, standards relating to claims of performance, and language of the advertisement.

Russia, where advertising did not play a role in the past, is developing government regulations, but the process is slow because Russia has only a limited understanding of the role of advertising and marketing. What counted in the past was production, not distribution. Consumer goods were always in short supply. In addition, choice was limited. As long as only one type of flour or jam was available, the manufacturer did not have to advertise a particular brand. Products in a way sold themselves because of limited supply; as a result, marketing communication did not develop. Today, Russia is experimenting with advertising and marketing legislation. Russians can study what other countries do, but they must also find laws that fit their situation and cultural values.

One of the concerns in Russia is the issue of language in advertising. Driving through Moscow, for example, one can see billboards with Western product names written in the Latin alphabet. The Russian government, fearing to be overrun by Western culture, is beginning to insist that all advertising must also appear in the Cyrillic alphabet. McDonald's is complying with the rule. Signs for McDonald's appear both in the Western and the Cyrillic alphabets in Russia. Like many other countries, Russia also seems to have local content laws when it comes to advertising. There is pressure on foreign firms to produce advertisements intended for Russian television in Russia, but the law is not completely clear.

Increasingly, Poland is insisting on the use of Polish in advertisements by foreign companies. In order to protect the Polish language, for example, Marlboro ads in Poland must give the health warning in Polish.

The French, ever watchful of the preservation of the French language, also have tight rules when it comes to the use of language. They have announced sanctions against the use of terms such as *weekend, sandwich,* and *computer* in advertising. In everyday speech, however, people use these terms anyway, even though officially they are banned. The Japanese, on the other hand, who are so protective of their culture in other ways, do not have any problems with taking on foreign words. Throughout their history, they have imported terms and "Japanized" them in the process to a point where most Japanese children think that *MacuDonaldu* is a Japanese company.

Marketing in the United States involves a lot of *hype.* A product is the latest, newest, best, better than the competition. In Germany, on the other hand, claims to superior performance are strictly regulated. Comparative advertisement is forbidden. The use of a superlative like *best product* is not allowed either, as it is not a probable claim. Japan does not forbid comparative advertisement, but it is hardly ever practiced because it would acknowledge the existence of the competition, which in turn could cause loss of face for the firm.

The national concerns and national regulations of advertising and marketing communication have received a severe challenge over the last decade with the advent of satellites, private TV channels, and the Internet. Some of the laws for regulating marketing and advertising strike us as quaint today.

In the 1970s Luxembourg, which had much more lenient rules on advertising than its European neighbors, threatened to park a satellite right over the country and beam its programs with advertising into other European countries. The regulatory agencies, the media, and businesses in neighboring countries were concerned because this would violate national legislation on advertising and might give an unfair advantage to firms from countries with less stringent regulations. For example, the role of children in advertisement was tightly regulated in most European countries. In some countries children were not allowed to be in commercials, or commercials could not be addressed towards children. In Holland, any advertisement for sweets had to also show a toothbrush to communicate health concerns. By advertising on the Luxembourg channel, firms could circumvent the regulations of their countries.

As the example illustrates, modern technology has rendered much marketing legislation obsolete. Today, no matter what the government regulation of Austria, Holland, Saudi Arabia, New Zealand, or Mexico may be, anyone who gets satellite channels has access to programming and advertising that may violate domestic laws. Governments may regulate advertising on domestic television stations and radio and in the domestic print media, but technology has outrun the power of national governments. This is nowhere more apparent than with the Internet. E-commerce is available to anyone with an Internet hook-up. The German government, for example, may regulate store hours, but on the Internet customers can order goods and browse 24 hours a day. The student from Japan has the same access to Amazon.com as the student in Mexico. China is attempting to block access to the Internet and regulate companies' use of the Internet, but in the long run, this approach is unlikely to work. It seems that the only way to regulate advertising on the Internet is through international treaties and sanctions against countries that do not enforce international agreements. However, as we have discussed earlier in this chapter, this would be very difficult to enforce.

This does not mean anything goes. An advertisement that millions of people can see at the same time all over the globe presents tremendous opportunities but also great challenges. What may be culturally acceptable in one country may be seen as irreverent, insulting, and insensitive somewhere else. For example, a satellite channel that advertises a refrigerator displaying a ham may be good illustrative advertising in Western Europe and North America but offensive in Islamic countries.

The whole advertising regulation presents tremendous challenges for international business communication.

INVESTMENT ATTITUDES AND THE COMMUNICATION OF FINANCIAL INFORMATION

Attitudes towards investment, finance, and accounting have cultural foundations. Each country has rules regulating the collection, interpretation, and communication of this data. International businesspeople regularly communicate financial information to

- Domestic and international operations.
- Governments and regulatory agencies.
- Stockholders.
- Potential investors.

A businessperson who understands the rules and is able to adapt this kind of information to the needs of the various audiences around the globe will be more successful.

How people invest depends greatly on the laws of a country and on cultural attitudes towards risk. A firm that needs to raise capital in a foreign market needs to know how people save and what their attitudes towards risk are. After assessing the attitude towards risk, firms can adapt their communication to the financial community and the people of a culture so that the firm can meet its financial needs. Germans are typically very risk averse. They tend to save their money in the bank rather than invest it in the stock market. The Japanese are known for high savings rates with much of their savings in post office accounts, but the savings rate in Japan is beginning to decline because of growing consumerism. People in Singapore save about 35 percent of their income, but the savings are enforced by the government and are dedicated towards the purchase of apartments and pensions. People in the United States, if they save at all, seem to want a high return on their investment. Knowing how and why people save in a particular culture will help a business in deciding how to communicate its plan to raise money for expansion or to improve operations.

International businesses need to study the various attitudes towards investment by foreigners. People in most countries think it is all right if foreigners buy their products or if they come and spend money as tourists; however, most countries get somewhat nervous if the foreigners start investing in real estate and buying up businesses. Cultural prejudices come out very strongly when it comes to foreign investment.

In the 1980s, for example, many Japanese firms started investing in the United States. Many people in the United States considered this development acceptable as long as the Japanese built factories and created jobs, but when Japan started buying into the entertainment industry and seriously looking into purchasing Sears' Tower in Chicago and the Seattle Mariners baseball team, the cultural defenses went up. The issue became even more charged when the Japanese and other foreigners began buying farmland in the United States. Since then many Japanese firms have sold their American holdings, often at substantial losses. In many cases the Japanese firms had borrowed the purchase money against their real estate holdings in Japan. As the real estate market in Japan collapsed, companies frequently could no longer finance the debt. The ensuing financial crisis brought down several governments and contributed to a general crisis in Asia.

In the panic of the 1970s oil crisis, some Americans feared that Middle Eastern interests would soon own every cornfield in Iowa. These attitudes are definitely not restricted to the United States. In fact, in many ways the United States, as a traditional country of immigration, is much more open to outside investment than other countries. The sentiments do illustrate that anyone negotiating foreign investments needs to take attitudes, feelings, and laws of the host culture into account when encoding messages.

Most countries have rules and tight regulations on foreign investment that specify the level of possible foreign ownership. In India a foreign investor may own over 50 percent only if the majority of the production is exported to earn hard currency. The former communist countries and China have had laws for years that denied foreign ownership altogether. That has changed over the past few years, but the situation regarding foreign ownership is still not settled. In Russia, foreigners may now own parts of a joint venture, but the tax situation is unclear and the repatriation of profits from the joint venture may not be permitted because Russia wants capital reinvested in Russia. A U.S. investor should balance this goal against the perceived climate for investments if the rules get too stringent and hostile. Middle Eastern countries insist on local participation in foreign investment. Their goal is to train and educate local people ultimately to run the businesses and minimize the involvement of foreigners.

The situation in the Middle East is complicated by religious considerations. As discussed earlier in this chapter, Sharia, Islamic law based on the Koran, and the rules regarding usury can hinder foreign investment. Any Western business going into the Middle East should be familiar with the principles of Islam. It is not enough to know the direct religious influences on business transactions. Because Islam influences the daily lives of its followers, managers must also be familiar with the influence of Islam on daily practices and interpersonal relations. Firms from non-Islamic countries need to adapt their communication so that they do not offend Muslims. In Saudi Arabia, for example, all business activities must stop completely during prayer times. This is not an option; it is a must. During Ramadan, the month of fasting, productivity severely declines and the workday is reduced to six hours. A number of Islamic countries, among them Saudi Arabia, Pakistan, and Libya, have instituted Islamic Banking to varying degrees.

Under Islam, charging and earning interest is considered usury and is therefore a violation of the principles of Islam and a violation of the laws. Western business, on the other hand, would totally collapse without the concept of interest. In Islam a savings account will not draw a predetermined amount of interest. Rather, the owner of the account will participate proportionately in the success and failure of the bank. If the bank is doing well, the account shares in the profit. If the bank loses money, then the account will also lose money. This seems to violate the entire Western concept of savings accounts as low return but risk-free investments. Standard Western banking communication with regulatory agencies, businesses, and private citizens concerning interest rates for saving, borrowing, and lending would violate the laws of the Islamic host country.

The picture is further complicated by the fact that Islamic businesspeople tend to accept Western rules when they invest their money abroad. They certainly have no problem with collecting interest on accounts in Western banks for which they have not worked. Muslims sometimes rationalize that different rules apply to dealings with the "infidel" than to dealings with other Muslims. Islamic countries themselves may practice a dual system of banking: Western commercial banking and Islamic Banking. Any foreign investor must, however, be aware that in Saudi Arabia, for example, a foreign businessperson will be subject to the laws of Saudi Arabia. Traditionally Saudi courts tend to favor Saudi businesses over foreign interests. As Western businesspersons negotiate, they must be aware of the religious, national, and cultural influences.

Japan also is known for cultural hurdles to foreign investments. It is interesting to note that Western critics of U.S. business practices, for example, tend to criticize American resistance to Japanese investment as self-centered and imperialistic. When Japan does essentially the same thing and resists foreign investment, those very same critics tend to argue that under international law Japan has a basic right to protect its culture. The Japanese themselves are very fast to point to the uniqueness of their culture that might be threatened by too much foreign investment or immigration. Over the past few years, however, a growing number of people in Japan are in favor of opening Japan to foreign investments.

Still, in Japan many of the hurdles are underground; they are hidden. The official rules do not necessarily discriminate against foreign investment. In the construction industry, for example, the rules did not officially block foreign investment. It just so happened that foreign construction firms were hardly ever given a contract. When foreign firms started to insist on a greater part of the action, the Japanese promised that Western firms would be considered. In practice, little has changed as of today, though individual Japanese may sympathize with Western firms. The arguments are "In order to build in Japan, one must understand Japanese soils, be Japanese," or "Foreigners cannot adapt to Japanese ways." While foreign firms should most certainly do their homework in order to be successful when investing in Japan, all the preparation will be of little use if foreign investment is blocked either officially or unofficially.

The challenges for intercultural communication in the area of investment are daunting as the 1999 demonstrations at the WTO negotiations in Seattle illustrated. Sometimes the implications of investment agreements and national rules are not totally clear until the project is under way.

A German company was building a pharmaceutical plant in the Middle East. In the negotiations, the firm had promised to use local building materials whenever possible and to stimulate and develop the local economy. This sounded easy enough. However, the architectural prints had been developed in Germany. The German architect had, of course, made the plans based on German building materials and German building specifications of the typical pharmaceutical plant. As a result, the building materials had to be imported from Germany. The locals were outraged and charged willful deceit. The Germans, on the other hand, argued that it was impossible to build a modern facility with the local materials.

Clearly, the two sides had negotiated in a vacuum and had not considered the ramifications of their decisions. The whole problem could have been avoided if local conditions and materials had been considered from the very beginning of the planning stages. Neither side acted out of ill will; both sides were simply ignorant of the conditions. If in this case the Middle Eastern country had insisted on local materials, the German investor would probably have given up the project rather than redesign it.

The implications of laws, culture, and local conditions need to be discussed at the beginning to lay the groundwork for fruitful cooperation. As it was, both sides were disillusioned.

Many of the developing countries have a pair of goals that seem to contradict each other. They want foreign investment to provide maximum employment of local workers, but they also want the most up-to-date technology. By definition, the most up-to-date technology employs a minimum number of people. The foreign investor must tread cautiously in this paradoxical state of affairs. Unless foreign investors are very skilled and sensitive, they will easily offend local cultural sensitivities. They need to take into consideration ambivalent cultural attitudes towards technology and change. Some cultures may not want change; others are eager for technical development; more likely they hold both attitudes at once. If the culture wants to change, to suggest something less than state-of-the-art technology (that may employ more people) may be seen as an insult, implying that the industrialized country does not want the developing country to modernize, but instead wants it to continue old colonial and imperialistic practices. The suggestion may have been made with goodwill, seeing the need for employment in the developing country. Or the opposite may occur; the foreign investor may insist on doing "only the best" for the poorer nation.

A European country was building a hospital in an African country. The African country had asked for a "low tech" health care facility that would take local traditions into consideration. Since patients were generally accompanied by their relatives, space had to be provided for them too. Electricity was not reliably

supplied, and it was doubtful whether well-educated doctors would want to spend their careers out in the countryside far away from the city. Therefore, the locals wanted a hospital for basic care with minimum technology. The Western country, on the other hand, had its preconceived notion of a hospital and was not

---

(continued)

going to be accused of building a second-rate facility. It built a modern hospital that could have stood in any Western city. The building was completed; however, even after several years it was not used because the electricity was not sufficient, the air-conditioning could not be used, and doctors refused to go to the rural area.

As the two examples illustrate, engineering, architecture, and medicine have legal as well as cultural aspects that must be taken into account in international negotiations and communication. But there are limits to cultural adaptation. For example, when it comes to aircraft maintenance, objective engineering standards are applied regardless of cultural attitudes.

In addition to expectations of the foreign investor and regulations of foreign investments, countries also have specific rules and regulations on reporting performance, expenses, profit, depreciation, and other accounting information. The basic accounting concepts may be the same, but the way statistics are collected, compiled, and communicated may be rather different from country to country. An Italian branch of a Japanese bank had to explain to headquarters the details of a credit analysis performed on Italian businesses. In the process the Italian branch had to reclassify and respread figures and explain why a certain ratio was good by Italian standards. German companies, for example, are required to consider pension obligations and other social costs required by law under liabilities. This is different in the United States. As a result, a businessperson from the United States may decide that a company from Germany is not doing well enough to invest in because the ratio of assets and liabilities does not lie within the range acceptable in the United States. In fact, the German firm may be doing very well. When businesspeople from different cultures communicate about profitability, assets, liabilities, and depreciation, they need to understand each other's legal and regulatory environment in which financial statements are prepared.

Accounting practices in the United States and Western Europe rely on detailed records that are collected and entered regularly. The SEC (Securities and Exchange Commission) in the United States requires comparative balance sheets and income statements for all U.S. businesses and their subsidiaries. Companies are audited on a regular basis, and penalties for violation are heavy. Ever since the Depression, the financial markets and the communication relating to finances and investments in the United States have been tightly regulated. Investments are regulated by strict disclosure rules as to the source and use of funds.

The financial markets in the former communist countries are only beginning to emerge. Rules and regulations are not very clear yet, and in many ways even businesspeople do not totally understand the concepts of business finance. Since businesses in the past received their money from the government as it was available or as companies needed it, and since they turned over all revenue from sales to the government, the concept of time value of money is underdeveloped. According to that concept, $1,000 today is worth more than $1,000 a year from now. If the money is available today, it can be used and invested; it can earn a return. In the Soviet Union, businesses did not manage money, and they did not have to worry about the cost of money. As a result, the entire area of cost accounting is underdeveloped. The concept of profit is alien.

A businessperson wanting to invest in Russia will face great uncertainties in the financial area, not only because the Russian partner may not want to share information but also because the Russian partner may not understand the information and does not know how to compile it. As a result, communication between a Russian and a Western firm relating to financial matters will be difficult. A foreign firm interested in investing in Russia will improve its chances of success if it can communicate financial considerations clearly. That means the foreign firm needs to

- Understand the Russian environment and attitudes towards finance and investment.
- Explain Western financial concepts.
- Explain the importance of accurate and timely records.
- Evaluate Russian financial reporting based on Russian accounting practices and compare the reporting to Western standards.

Communication in the financial sector is influenced by cultural priorities. Good financial communication is based on an evaluation of a culture's laws, regulations, and attitudes.

CASE

The following case is famous in international business circles. It illustrates the difficulties a company may face if the managers do not communicate clearly. Terms of trade, assumptions as to the meaning of terms, and translation errors add to the problem. The case also illustrates the use of common law. The judge refers several times to previous cases, some of them going back several hundred years. In order to understand the argument and the legal communication issues, the other side clearly needs to be familiar with the legal system and the line of argument that is typically used. After having studied cultural influences on international business communication, you will be able to identify and discuss the problem areas that led to the disaster with the chickens.

Frigaliment Importing Co., Ltd.
Plaintiff
v.
B.N.S. International Sales Corp.,
Defendant
United States District Court
S.D. New York[3]

B.N.S. International Sales Corp. from the United States and Frigaliment Importing Co. from Switzerland had signed a contract under which the B.N.S. would deliver 100,00 pounds of chickens to Frigaliment. The chickens were shipped according to the agreement; however, Frigaliment argued that those were not the chickens that had been ordered and that the American company had promised. Therefore, Frigaliment did not want to pay for the shipment.

Since the two parties could not agree on a solution, Frigaliment went to court. The case was tried in a United States District Court in New York. The judge decided that the Swiss firm could not collect damages but was bound by the contract and had to pay for the chickens. The two issues that are of interest from intercultural issues in legal communication are language and translation issues and the application of common law.

Language issues

The entire case hinges on the definition of the word *chicken.* Is the term used for any chicken, young and old, male and female, or does it mean a particular type of chicken? The Swiss company argued that *chicken* meant young chicken, suitable for broiling and frying. It furthermore argued that stewing chickens are referred to as *fowl*. The Swiss firm in its argument contrasted chicken (broiler) with fowl (Suppenhuhn).

The American company, on the other hand, argued that *chicken* means any chicken. Since the Swiss company had not specified what kind of chicken it wanted, the Swiss should be made to pay for the shipment. At issue are the correct translation of terms as well as the accepted use of terms in the chicken trade.

As we have discussed repeatedly throughout this book, businesspeople must understand the literal meaning of terms and how these terms are used in relevant business situations. Clearly, the two sides in the case did not communicate clearly what they wanted. This is particularly interesting because both sides had experience with international transactions.

Application of common law

In deciding the case, the judge in the United States referred to case law, which he then applied to his particular case.

- Oliver Holmes, a famous judge in the United States, said that "the making of a contract depends not on the agreement of two minds of one intention, but on the agreement of two sets of external signs—not on the parties' having *meant* the same thing but on their having said the *same* thing." [4]
- One of the cases he cites goes back to 1761, *Lord Mansfield* v. *East India Co*. He uses this case to comment on the credibility of witnesses. One of the witnesses testified that to him *chicken* definitely meant broiler. However, the judge argued that this testimony did not support the witness's own practice; the witness in his business always used the word *broiler* if he wanted to make sure that he would get young chickens. The precedent established that no credit should be given to a witness's testimony if the witness was not consistent in usage. [5]

Had this case been tried under code law, the references to old legal cases and opinions of previous judges would have been irrelevant. It would not matter what the judge said about the credibility of a witness in 1761 in London. What would matter is the interpretation of current law today by a legal expert.

SUMMARY

In the course of doing business, international firms must be able to adapt to differing expectations, laws, and regulations. In particular, they need to consider

- *Communication and legal messages.* Laws and legal interpretations are influenced by culture. What is considered legal in one country, may, therefore, be illegal in another.
- *Specific legal systems.* The most common legal systems are code law, Anglo-American common law, and Islamic law. These systems vary in their approach to and judgment of legal situations.
- *Dispute settlement.* Culture influences how managers will approach direct confrontation and arbitration, communication with agents, and trademarks and intellectual property.
- *Multinational enterprise and national interest.* Nations are sovereign entities and as such are intent on protecting their national interests.

- *Legal issues in labor and management communication.* Laws regulate employment communication, safety on the job, and access to career opportunities. This area has major implications for effective intercultural business communication.
- *Legal considerations in marketing communication.* Governments regulate advertising. International managers need to be aware of these regulations in order to avoid inappropriate or illegal messages.
- *Investment attitudes and the communication of financial information.* At first glance, finance appears to be culture-neutral; however, culture plays a major role in people's attitude towards risk management, investment strategies, and evaluation of the financial soundness of a firm.

NOTES

1. R. August, *International Business Law,* (Englewood Cliffs, NJ: Prentice Hall, 1993).
2. Electromation, Inc. 309 NLRB No. 163. 12/16/92.
   E.I. du Pont de Nemour & Co., 311 NLRB No. 88, 5/28/93.
3. *Frigaliment Importing Co., Ltd.* v. *B.N.S. International Sales Corp.*, United States District Court, S.D. New York, 1957.
4. Oliver Wendell Holmes, Jr., "The Path of the Law," in *Collected Legal Papers,* p. 178. New York, 1952.
5. *Walls* v. *Bailey, New York Reports,* vol. 49, p. 464 at pp. 472–473 (Ct. of Appeals, 1872).

CHAPTER ELEVEN

The Influence of Business Structures and Corporate Culture on Intercultural Business Communication

Roberto Ramirez's family has been farming in Brazil for several generations. About 10 years ago the family decided to grow soybeans since the international demand for soybeans was increasing. In the beginning, the Ramirez family simply sold the beans to the closest elevator. They saw themselves as farmers rather than businesspeople. Over the years, however, things began to change. Expenses for fertilizer and seed were going up, and prices were depressed because of oversupply worldwide. Roberto attended several seminars on agricultural marketing and decided to try a new approach. The first step was to grow food-grade soybeans. Rather than selling to the local elevator, he contacted Japanese firms directly to buy his soybeans. The Japanese were interested in the high quality and willing to pay a premium. The new outlet for the crops brought in more cash but otherwise had no great effect on operations. Roberto had to deal with shipping and some paperwork, but he had little regular contact with Japan.

He began to wonder what else he could do to promote his soybeans. After some research, he decided to process the beans before selling them. He contacted Japanese businesses to sell his product. Since he had exported his beans to Japan before, he thought that he was familiar with the process; however, negotiations dragged on. He was confused; in the beginning the Japanese seemed to be very interested, but then things slowed down. He

did not understand why. He had bought the roasting and packaging equipment and hired people to meet production goals, but he was beginning to wonder when he would be able to ship the first container.

Taste tests had indicated that the Japanese preferred a stronger roast; they also wanted smaller packages. The one-pound package he had envisioned was just too big for the Japanese market. As the Japanese venture took more and more of his time, he decided that he needed someone who could work closely with the Japanese, someone who could take care of the day-to-day communication, the negotiation, and the import–export formalities.

Eventually the Japanese market took off and ultimately expanded. Roberto Ramirez decided to enlarge operations and reorganize the business. The one-person international operation had grown to a department of three people. They had daily contact with Japan via fax and E-mail, and several times a year someone went to Japan to discuss issues personally. As a next step, Roberto was contemplating developing his own distribution network in Japan and exploring other Asian markets. He realized that this move would take much more involvement in Japanese business practices and knowledge of international business in general, but he thought chances for success were good. Several times over the years he had attended seminars on Japanese business practices, but he realized that everyone involved in the international operations could benefit from similar training. As he was getting ready for the next phase, he started thinking about how much his family farming business had changed.

So far in this book we have examined the relationship between cultural orientations and business communication. We have looked at values and their influence on the framing and organization of messages, the negotiation process, and the legal framework. We have seen that successful intercultural business communication is based on the understanding of one's own culture and the culture of the partner. But the process does not stop there. Intercultural business communication must also take into consideration the structure of business organizations.

The organizational structure of a firm influences the degree of intercultural understanding necessary for successful business dealings. The type of product a company manufactures and the life-cycle stage of the product also have an impact on the communication process and intercultural communication needs.

CORPORATE CULTURE AND INTERCULTURAL COMMUNICATION

Different cultures prefer different business forms. As Chapter 10 shows, in the United States, for example, there is a tendency to incorporate even small firms to minimize risk. This practice is typical for a low-context culture that attempts to legislate risk and liability. In a culture such as India that believes people are not masters of their own destiny and fate cannot be avoided, businesspeople do not share the belief that one can escape fate by creating a corporation.

At the same time large corporations around the globe, regardless of national origin, have found that certain structures work better for multinational business than others. However, the apparent similarities may cover up different underlying cultural approaches to doing business. As Adler points out,

> Organizations worldwide are growing more similar, while the behavior of people within organizations is maintaining its cultural uniqueness. So organizations in Canada and Germany may look the same from the outside, but Canadians and Germans behave differently within them.[1]

But even within countries organizations are different. They may have similar structures, but they have their own corporate cultures. Intercultural business communication may mean sending and receiving messages from corporate culture to corporate culture.

> Organizations create culture; to be renewed and restructured, they alter it. Culture explains the pattern of assumptions and behavior formulated by human systems in response to their environment, whether it is a nation with its macroculture, a local community with its needs and customs, a market with its consumers and suppliers, or an industry with its colleagues and competitors.[2]

Similar to national cultures, organizational cultures establish rules about how to behave, what attitudes to adopt, and how to rank what is significant. Organizations have their own heroes and symbols, their own vocabulary, and their own histories of events that contain the values, attitudes, beliefs, and behaviors they wish to have employees learn. Rituals and myths also play a part in organizational culture. An organizational culture is

> a shared system of symbols and meanings, performed in speech, that constitutes and reveals a sense of work life; it is a particular way of speaking and meaning, a way of sense-making, that recurs in the oral activities surrounding common tasks.[3]

Each employee's experience is run through the operating environment of the organization. Things that don't fit don't get processed; for purposes of the organization they don't exist. Employees learn correct etiquette for the organization and the customs that indicate relative significance. In other words, they learn the specific priorities of that organization. Every time an employee joins a new organization, he or she has to go through a socialization process that is like growing up in a society. Each employee has to learn all the meanings and behaviors—what is a good achievement, what isn't; whom to address a certain way and when; what to expect in a hundred different work experiences—in short, the corporate culture.

An organizational culture is a particular way of creating meaning. Any workplace is its own little world, with its own inner structure. It is peopled by its own cast of characters. It employs a set of words not known outside the organization, its jargon. It has rules and follows traditional observances.

Think of where you work. What happens in your organization when someone retires? Who is the person to whom you show most respect? Do you and your co-workers have to observe any particular customs about lunch times? Coffee breaks? Is there a department or person everyone has to treat with special care because of his or her reputation as a dragon? Who are the heroes in your organization's history? Now think of what happens when someone joins the organization who is unfamiliar with these things. It is important that the individual learn the culture as soon as possible—important for the individual and important for the culture because members who do not share the culture threaten it. What are the stories people tell the new employee? Who is allowed to tell those stories? Can anyone tell them, or only those who were original participants in the event being retold? What values of the corporation do those stories transmit?

At the heart of each organization are the goals and objectives defined by the organization. They enable the organization to focus human activity; everyone is working with shared aims. The cultural norms enable the organization to manage the flow of information, people, events, and energies that feed it.

The organizational culture also generates the image of the organization to the outside. It determines how the corporation presents itself. The CEO of a corporation identifies its goals in public speeches for customers, shareholders, joint ventures, and the government.

Organizational cultures draw from the culture of their particular industry. The cultures of a particular industry draw from the general business culture for their norms of behavior, values, attitudes, beliefs, and symbols. The business culture, in turn, draws from the larger general culture of a country.[4] As Exhibit 11–1 illustrates, businesspeople are part of all of

EXHIBIT 11–1 The Cultural Environments of Businesspeople

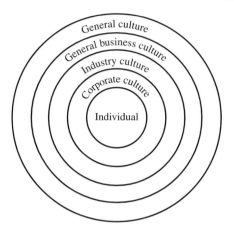

these cultures, and they need to communicate with all of them. That means you may be involved in intercultural communication without ever leaving the country.

A firm that sells strictly in a homogeneous domestic market has less need to be aware of foreign cultures and languages.[5] However, with the growing diversity in the domestic arena that may change considerably. For example, as the number of people from Latin American, Middle Eastern, Korean, Indian, Vietnamese, and African backgrounds in the United States increases and as their purchasing power increases, more and more companies consider it good business practice to cater to the values and wants of these groups. Twenty years ago, American businesses primarily catered to white consumers of European ancestry. Today that is changing.

The same is true for Europe. Germany, for example, has a growing Turkish population; France has many immigrants from Algeria. The Turkish and Algerian immigrants have had a tremendous influence on the way German and French businesses are looking at their workers and customers. Many firms have developed handbooks and instructions in the various languages of the workers. Managers who were used to almost all workers being Christian needed to adapt work rules to employees with different religious backgrounds. For example, Muslims requested time for prayers and food in the company cafeteria that met Islamic dietary restrictions. Even a domestic firm must be able to communicate with a workforce that is increasingly diverse and have some appreciation for different cultural values.

STAGES IN INTERNATIONALIZATION

In the rest of this chapter we will examine intercultural business communication needs in three major forms of international business involvement: the import–export firm, the multinational firm, and the global firm. One form is not better than another. Businesses change their structures if the environment changes and if the old structures do not meet the needs any longer. In reality the lines are often fuzzy. Most firms start out as domestic firms. That is true for businesses all over the world. The exception is the specialized import–export business that often starts with the specific goal of international business. Most major multinational firms started as domestic firms. Examples are McDonald's; Ciba Geigy, the Swiss chemical corporation; BASF (Bayrische Anelin und Soda Fabriken), a German chemical firm; Archer Daniels Midland (ADM), a food company in the Midwest of the United States.

As these companies entered the international arena, their structures changed and their communication changed. They had to develop new communication strategies both for internal and external communication. As we will see, the import–export stage is often a first step in the internationalization of a business.

For our discussion, we distinguish between the multinational and the global firm. The **multinational** firm thinks of itself as a firm that has a nationality; it is a French, Japanese, Chinese, American, or Mexican firm that does business in many nations. Most international firms are multinational firms.

A **global** firm looks at its business as one unit that spans the globe. The true global firm does not think in terms of domestic and international business although the global firm still sees itself as having roots in a given country. Its arena is the globe. Very few firms have reached that stage, and the organization of the world into nations can pose difficulties in the process. Coca-Cola is an example of a global firm.

The globalization of a firm is a process that can take a long time. The particular development will depend on the type of firm, the type of product, the orientation of management, and the political and competitive environment.

International expansion goes hand in hand with the need to deal with different cultures in all aspects of the business. The question that managers must ask is *when* (at what stage) and to *what extent* the international orientation becomes critical and what the communication needs are at each stage.

You may start your career in a domestic company; you may not be particularly interested in doing international business. Yet, over time the firm and you may change. You may see opportunities for selling or even manufacturing your product abroad. A small Illinois firm, for example, is producing scissors and clippers for cutting hair. The founder had no intention of ever going international. But somehow the opportunity came up to export. The owner started exporting the product without any modifications. After some time, he realized that the potential for success would be much greater if he were to study the foreign markets in more detail. He also felt the need to learn at least some Spanish to talk to his customers in Latin America. He also had to look at the cultural attitudes towards cutting hair.

In the United States the product sold to families that wanted to save money by cutting hair at home. In Latin America people do not cut hair at home. After some research and visits to his Latin American market, he started selling the product to barbers and hair salons. In the process, more people in the firm needed to learn about the Latin market and the distribution systems in that market. He also found that the American attitude to "do-it-yourself" had no following in Latin America.

The change to an international business changed the communication in the firm. The firm now had to have people with international expertise and awareness of cultural differences in order to communicate successfully with the new market.

Let us now look at the various stages of international development and the changing communication needs that go with them.

THE IMPORT–EXPORT STAGE

Reasons for Exporting

The first stages of international involvement do not require much international adaptation and involvement in other cultures. For example, most firms start their international experience with exporting through an import–export firm. In that situation they are not directly involved with foreign operations. They often sell abroad because someone abroad wants or needs the product. The attitude tends to be *laissez faire:* "If it works, fine—if it does not work, not much is lost." As sales grow, the firm may adapt the product to some extent. But if the foreign market really wants and needs the product, the adaptation in terms of culture, language, and product may be minimal.

The firm may want to explore new markets either because the domestic market is saturated or because the firm sees growth potential in other markets and opportunities to expand production capacities. In the beginning exporting stage, the firm typically looks at itself as a domestic firm that also sells some of its production overseas. Some firms may look at exporting as the first step of more international involvement; others may have no intention of ever going beyond exporting. In the latter case, the firm will not go through any major changes in its communication.

The typical beginning exporting firm exports its products "as is." The firm may make some surface adaptations, but no major changes. Firms at this stage are not going to spend a lot of money on exporting. The advanced export firm, on the other hand, will adapt its products to specific markets and consider the foreign market as an integral part of its business. Export firms can be at any point of the continuum.

The Internet and E-commerce have provided international markets to small companies that traditionally might not have thought of exporting at all. As soon as a business has a Web page, people from around the globe can view the product line and services. This means that a business can become involved in international business without making a conscious decision to sell internationally. The Internet opens the door for everyone, but it also exposes every business with a Web page to potential blunders and missteps. Most E-business is "B2B" or businesses selling to other businesses. Whether customers are businesses or end-users, however, online communication from a website will have to be constructed with careful attention to cultural priorities in order to succeed with international markets.

Communication in the Import–Export Environment

If a product is exported without adaptations and if it is in demand, the need for adaptations in communication is minimal. A small business may go through an import–export firm or hire an agent. The managers of the firm may have little or no contact with the foreign market. Managers may look at exporting as maximizing production capacities. If the firm directly hires a foreign agent to represent it and distribute its products in foreign markets, the firm must at least be familiar with some of the legal issues involved in hiring, maintaining, and firing agents, but direct contact with the foreign market is not extensive.

A beginning exporting firm will hire translators, go to trade fairs and shows, and advertise its products without adaptation to foreign cultures. The beginning exporting firm will be more interested in technical aspects of exporting such as letters of credit and shipping methods than cultural adaptations. Communication with the foreign market is filtered through the interpreter or agent.

The level of adaptation also depends on the product. Coca-Cola is often cited as proof that global marketing is successful. Indeed, Coca-Cola has a standardized product—all the syrup for Coke is produced in the United States and shipped all over the world; however, the level of sweetness of the syrup is adapted to specific cultural preferences. In addition, it is this particular product that people want. Part of the appeal of Coke is that it is a global product—it looks the same everywhere. People don't think in terms of American Coke, German Coke, Indian Coke, or Mexican Coke—they think of Coke.

What works for Coke may not work for other products and firms. Even though the product itself is standardized, the Coca-Cola company must adapt its communication style and techniques to the various cultures and communication styles of its bottlers around the globe. Even though the product itself is the same everywhere, the packaging, bottle sizes and shapes, for example, vary. In the operations and communication within the worldwide operations, Coca-Cola must adapt to its many varied audiences and take into consideration the expectations and conventions of many cultures.

Home appliances cannot use the same strategy Coke is using. When it comes to home appliances, people want a product that is more adapted to their values, needs, and environment. Washing machines, one can argue, should sell anywhere because they simplify life for everyone, but that does not mean the same machine will be successful everywhere. Germans want front loaders that heat the water in the machine all the way to boiling point. Any German "knows" that top loaders don't get the laundry clean. They also "know" that hot water running into the machine will burn the dirt right into the fabric. The water needs to be gradually heated in the machine to dissolve the dirt. A hookup for running hot water is not necessary. The British, on the other hand, prefer top-loading washing machines and extremely hot water. The French use a mixture. In remote areas of Thailand, the needs may be quite different altogether. Electricity may not be readily available, and running water may be rare also. As a result, the typical American, British, or German washing machine is not feasible even if the culture would not present any hurdles.

In addition, size and price are also factors. If the average wages are $350 per year, very few people will be able to spend $500 on a washing machine or $1,500 on the type of big refrigerator typical in the United States. A Japanese family that has a small apartment in Tokyo of about 500 square feet (50m^2) may have the money but will not want to buy big appliances from the United States. There simply is not enough room for them. Space is too valuable to clutter with huge appliances.

Even if a company has excess capacity and even if a product would make life easier in another culture, the product may not sell unless the firm is willing to research the market in depth, a process that requires a lot of intercultural communication and understanding. A firm would need to research consumer attitudes and preferences, government regulations, and purchasing power of the people. All this data would have to be collected, tabulated, evaluated, organized, and then communicated. Only after the research has been completed can the firm work on product adaptation and marketing. Many firms that see themselves as mostly domestic firms are not willing to expend the energy and money to do that. They may think that adaptation is not cost-effective and that the foreign market is not large enough to justify the effort.

U.S. manufacturers of large appliances typically face that problem. The standard kitchen appliances are big. They fit into American homes but are too large for most European and Japanese homes. Yet manufacturers argue that the number of consumers who would be willing to buy an adapted product is not large enough to justify the cost of consumer attitude surveys and product adaptation. In Spanish, French, and German stores one can see samples of refrigerators, dishwashers, and stoves from the United States, but they are still considered an oddity and curiosity. Since they are also very expensive, very few people consider buying them. The Europeans and the Japanese, on the other hand, have been willing to adapt to the needs of smaller markets, partly because their own domestic markets are comparatively small.

The French firm, SEB, for example, is selling cooking pots in Japan. On the whole, French pots are smaller than American pots but they tend to be larger than Japanese pots. The French studied the Japanese market and packaged sets of smaller pots than they would typically sell in France. The Japanese manager of the French subsidiary said that the quality of the American pots was as good as the French, but the Americans had not been interested in putting together sets of smaller pots to satisfy the Japanese market. This is an example where a firm, in order to export successfully, must adapt its strategy to the foreign conditions and be aware of consumer needs and wants.

As soon as a decision is made to adapt a product to foreign markets, the need for intercultural communication increases. The company must research the market, the competition, and the market potential. This is a complex communication task. Let us assume you are assigned to research the potential market for motorcycles in Spain. You need to find out the Spanish attitude towards motorcycles. You can interview people and you can design questionnaires. This sounds easy enough, but you must find out whether in Spain people are willing to answer questionnaires and whether they are willing to be interviewed. You must determine their attitudes, their preferences, and their needs and wants. All of these areas are influenced by cultural priorities. What may start out as a simple product adaptation or exporting task may grow into an elaborate intercultural communication task (see also Chapter 8 for gathering information).

If international sales increase, a firm may at some point establish an export department to handle demand and distribution. The more the firm gets involved, the greater the need will be to communicate directly with people from different cultural backgrounds. Rather than turning the product over for sale to an agent, the firm at this point will have to have some contact with the foreign market. The extent will vary, however, and much will depend on whether the firm sees international expansion as a way of the future or as an ancillary to domestic operations.

The need of a firm to be aware of intercultural communication practices and conventions depends on the extent of the international involvement of the firm and the cultural diversity within the firm. The needs of the firm for intercultural communication skills increase with the increasing globalization of a firm.

THE MULTINATIONAL CORPORATION

Some multinational firms have national subsidiaries; others have international divisions at headquarters. Each has its own internal and external communication dynamics.

The National Subsidiary

THE STRUCTURE OF THE NATIONAL SUBSIDIARY ORGANIZATION   In the national subsidiary structure, a multinational firm has subsidiaries in various countries (see Exhibit 11–2). These subsidiaries report directly to top management at headquarters without going through regional headquarters or an international division at headquarters. For example, Jesse Hurtado, the president of the subsidiary in Mexico, will direct any concerns or questions directly to top management in Oslo, Norway. He has direct access to top management and knows that he will be heard.

The organization into national subsidiaries takes into consideration the specific needs of the various subsidiaries. It gives importance to local voices and, at least in theory, fosters adaptation to local needs. The top people at the subsidiary can be either home country employees or host country employees. If headquarters sends home country employees, it is in the interest of headquarters to keep these employees at the foreign post for many years so as to ensure continuation of communication and policy implementation. The successful expatriate typically is in the fourth stage of the model for culture shock, the integration stage (see Chapter 1). The expatriate is well adjusted, can relate to the concerns of the host country employees, but also understands the concerns of the home country. The expatriate, who at this stage often speaks at least some of the local language, is an effective communicator and negotiator between the two cultures. The foreign subsidiary structure is characterized by "career expatriates."

EXHIBIT 11–2   National Subsidiary Structure

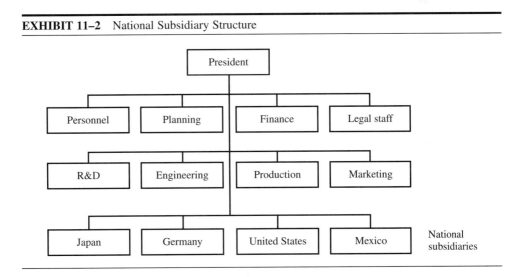

If host country nationals are in the leading positions, then they will, in all likelihood, remain in the country of the subsidiary. Their chances of being promoted to leading positions at headquarters are slim. The argument is that they understand the local culture and can communicate effectively in that environment. As with the career expatriates, their value lies in facilitating between home and host country cultures.

COMMUNICATION IN THE NATIONAL SUBSIDIARY ORGANIZATION The advantage of the subsidiary system is that managers of the subsidiaries have direct access to top managers at headquarters and don't have to go through several layers of management and the accompanying bureaucracy. The difficulty is that the structure can lead to overload at top management. If a firm has many foreign subsidiaries, communication between headquarters and subsidiaries becomes time consuming, and it may be difficult to strike a balance between foreign subsidiaries and concerns at headquarters. Thus managers at the subsidiary may have two choices: follow directions from headquarters that may not be appropriate in the host culture or run the subsidiary as an independent unit and lose the synergy a major corporation can provide.

Top management is responsible for directing concerns of the international subsidiaries to the appropriate departments or sections at headquarters. If managers are overloaded or if managers do not care about the international operations, they could block international involvement and create a bottleneck in international communication. Furthermore, the structure limits communication between subsidiaries. Communication is centralized with headquarters representing the hub of all activity. The subsidiaries function more as autonomous entities that are not effectively linked. In large firms this structure may become dysfunctional because of lack of integration of all entities into one unit. Communication that concentrates on headquarters and subsidiary A, headquarters and subsidiary B, and so on does not encourage the development of multiple networks and linkages.

The International Division

As the international operations expand and as the need for effective international communication grows, firms typically organize their international activities into an international division.

THE STRUCTURE OF THE INTERNATIONAL DIVISION The organization with an international division looks very efficient (see Exhibit 11–3). On the surface, the international division is at the same level as the domestic division. It seems as if international operations are considered as important as domestic operations; however, international is separate, and often it is not very well integrated into the rest of the firm. In many firms the international division is in a different part of the building; sometimes it may even be in an entirely different location. Even though modern communication systems such as fax and E-mail mean that the actual physical location may not be significant, the physical distance tends to create a mental distance. The international structure usually is organized into product divisions.

EXHIBIT 11–3   International Division Structure

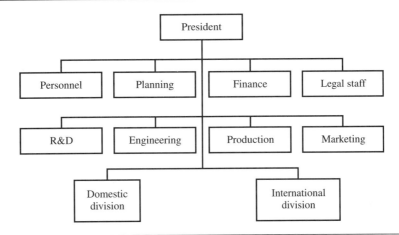

The international division of a firm headquartered in the United States was located at the back of the building. To get there, one had to walk through a huge warehouse. The Japanese subsidiary would send faxes to the international division assuming that the division would share the information with appropriate people in top management who were located at some distance in the front of the building. As far as the Japanese were concerned, all employees at headquarters were in the same location. Every fax coming into the Japanese subsidiary was copied and distributed to all managers. The Japanese erroneously assumed that headquarters in the United States did the same. Since the Japanese did not know about the physical arrangement at headquarters, they had a hard time understanding why communication presented such a hurdle. Matters improved when the entire international division was moved to the front of the building with all the other offices and the domestic division.

What are the results of this international division organization? It easily leads to a duplication of efforts. For example, domestic may have research and development (R&D), and the international division may have its own R&D. Sometimes they may work together, but in many cases they don't. The competition can be constructive or destructive. It depends on the overall culture and on the success of the international division compared to the domestic division. In many cases the domestic and international divisions compete for scarce resources, and each is more intent on expanding its own power than maximizing the return and efficiency of the whole.

Trust can become a major issue in that environment. In cultures where trust is built slowly over a long period of time and where one does business with people one trusts, the competition of domestic and international divisions may be particularly destructive for the climate of the firm.

In many cases the domestic division sees the international division as a drain on resources and may argue, "We would do better domestically if we concentrated on that area rather than running all over the globe." Domestic problems may be attributed to international involvement.

On the other hand, international is seen as a cash cow whose profits can and should be used to improve domestic operations. Profits from international operations are easily considered the property of the domestic market. "After all," according to this viewpoint, "international operations are there to support domestic operations, the real concern of the firm, even though the best expansion opportunities may be abroad." This issue surfaces typically in the area of profit repatriation. The issue is complex because it also involves transfer pricing and fair prices for the transfer between different parts of the company.

A Japanese subsidiary of an American firm had had another record year. Overall, international revenue had almost doubled over the past three years. The Japanese subsidiary wanted to use the profits for extended R&D activities in its respective markets. It also wanted to use the excellent performance to improve its standing and prestige in the Japanese business community. Headquarters should keep in mind the effects of repatriation of profits on morale in the subsidiary when considering what was best for the company.

Headquarters and the domestic division saw the picture quite differently. The subsidiary was expected to repatriate most of its profits to the headquarters in Chicago where the money would be used to support expansion of the domestic division. The repatriation was to happen through transfer of services from headquarters to the Japanese subsidiary. The transfer price would be adjusted so that the book profits of the subsidiary would look much lower than they actually were. The Japanese subsidiary objected in vain, arguing that the weaker performance would weaken its ability to raise money for loans in the Japanese banking community and that the firm would not be as respected in the business community.

This situation illustrates several intercultural communication issues. Headquarters, dominated by managers with mostly domestic backgrounds, used a very patronizing tone: "We know what's best for you and the firm." Headquarters also did not recognize the role profits played in the prestige the subsidiary would gain. The Japanese subsidiary, on the other hand, was not particularly willing to accept a merely supportive role. Managers at the subsidiary had a tendency to look at themselves as an independent unit that simply did everything better than headquarters. Rather than pulling in the same direction, the domestic and international divisions tended to try to outmaneuver each other.

The typical view is that international activity can be turned on and shut off at will. If the international division is not performing very well, the domestic division may argue that international activity should be curtailed. If the international division is doing very well, the domestic division may argue that profits should be at the disposal of domestic operations. While domestic and international divisions may work as a team, the spirit of unhealthy competition is present all too often. In the Japanese example the competition was particularly bad because it was not just restricted to a rivalry between the domestic and international division. It was also present *within* the international division where various subsidiaries competed with each other.

COMMUNICATION IN THE INTERNATIONAL DIVISION ORGANIZATION   The official line of communication goes from the field through the international division to the appropriate areas at headquarters and back. From an operational viewpoint, the channel makes sense; communication seems to be efficient because all international communication goes through the international division. However, that channel may be redundant if the person in the field knows the person at corporate who has the answer or is needed to solve a problem.

This problem has not changed; in fact, with faster and better communications technology it may very well have grown worse. With direct and immediate access to anyone at headquarters or anywhere else in the organization, the temptation to jump channels is great. Why should Pierre from the subsidiary in Seoul waste time contacting the international division if he knows that the manager in Hong Kong can supply him with the answer in five minutes? One could argue that Pierre should at least inform people at the international division. If Pierre writes a letter, then it is easy enough to send a copy to International. If he calls or sends an electronic message, he may forget to inform the international division or not consider it important. After all, he may think that he just had a little chat with Hong Kong, nothing important or earth shaking. So he may feel no need to send copies to half the corporation.

At a practical level there is often confusion about who at headquarters should be contacted outside the international division. People in the subsidiary typically know people in the international division but very few people beyond that. They rely on the international division to take care of them. People in the field can send one memo and expect that people in the international division will talk to all the people that need information or can provide information. Headquarters is far away, so it is tempting to just let them take care of any problems.

The feeling of "us versus them" that is typical in the international division organization can be very destructive to the communication climate. Domestic may be condescending and not inform the international division or subsidiaries of new developments. On the other hand, in a successful international division the feeling of superiority over the domestic division also may create a dysfunctional communication climate. Today, an increasing percentage of revenues of major U.S. companies comes from international activities. The rivalry and competition over who is best can lead to communication problems and a waste of resources. One group may withhold information from another and endanger the profitability of the whole for the benefit of a subgroup.

Language ability is another communication issue. Since the international involvement is restricted to the international division, most firms do not see the need for employees to have a broad international background outside the international division. And even in the international division, the level of intercultural awareness can be low.

The attitude towards intercultural understanding and language competency (also see Chapter 2) is connected with the type of staffing the company practices. Staffing directly affects intercultural communication effectiveness because staffing influences communication networks. A company that wants to improve its intercultural communication should reexamine its staffing patterns and practices.

Firms that have international divisions tend to practice a mixture of ethnocentric and polycentric staffing.[6] In ethnocentric staffing, the management in the host country comes from the home office country. The international communication interface takes place at the subsidiary. As a result, communication has been cleaned up by the time it reaches headquarters, and headquarters may not be directly involved or even aware of cultural and linguistic problems in the field. It is the people at the front who have to cope with intercultural communication and language problems. The success of ethnocentric staffing relies on the linguistic and cultural ability of the expatriates.

Headquarters may be interested in the well-oiled machine rather than open communications. The expatriate may very well be evaluated on how smoothly things run. As a result, the expatriate may play down any problems, and headquarters may not get the full picture until it is too late or problems have become major.

In polycentric staffing, management comes from the host country. Here the culture and communication interface is typically between headquarters and the subsidiary. The international division in this case must deal with intercultural and language issues more directly because there is no expatriate to filter all communication between headquarters and subsidiary.

As long as Bertrand Fowler worked in Delhi, India, he kept headquarters informed of all events and developments at the subsidiary. He had worked in Seattle for a number of years and knew all the major players in the international and domestic divisions at headquarters. He also knew how to package information effectively and channel it to the appropriate person at headquarters.

Raj Kumatar, an Indian with a business degree from an Indian university, has taken his place. Raj does not know anyone at headquarters, and he has not worked with people from the United States before. It will take some time before he can read the people at headquarters and know what they want and how they prefer to be contacted. In this environment the people at headquarters are more directly exposed to the cultural environment of international business. The buffer is gone, and they must now directly communicate with a person who has a different cultural outlook.

In order to minimize the communication problem, firms have a number of options. They can

- Train everyone in the international division in intercultural communication.
- Create specialists for certain regions.
- Have a mixture of host and home country nationals in the subsidiary.
- Hire host country nationals who are familiar with the home country culture.

The first option is expensive, and most firms don't consider that approach practical or necessary. With increasing international competitive pressures, that might change in the future, but currently international expertise is still seen in many firms as nice, but not crucial.

The mixture of ethnocentric and polycentric staffing creates problems in terms of compensation packages and easily creates an atmosphere of home country versus host country personnel. Expatriates tend to get housing allowances, home leave, tuition support for children, and hardship allowances. The host country employees who do the same work right next to the expatriate invariably have inferior compensation packages. As one engineer in a developing country put it, "Why should the expatriate get more money for having blue eyes and blond hair?"

These days expatriates frequently have dual citizenship. Eileen Zhang, for example, is Chinese. She studied in the United States and received her MBA. She then started work at a U.S. multinational corporation. As soon as she was eligible, she became a U.S. citizen. She rotated through several jobs to become familiar with company procedures and practices. Ultimately she was sent to Beijing, the city she originally came from, to head the marketing section in charge of marketing coffee in China. Eileen went to China as an expatriate with an expatriate compensation package. Under these conditions, she was eligible for regular home leave, subsidies for educational expenses for her daughter, Western-style expatriate housing, and a company car with a chauffeur. Chinese employees in the firm who are well educated but have no expatriate status are at times upset that they have no access to the same privileges.

George Blair was sent to Tokyo last year from Canada. He is married and has a small child. His wife did not want to leave her friends in Canada, and they had recently bought a nice house in a very good suburb. Why should the couple give up all of this to go to Japan? As it turned out, the company picked up the rent for a Western-style apartment in Tokyo, over $6,000 per month. And of course, George also received other benefits such as a company-paid home leave every year and an allowance for the cost of living in Tokyo. None of the Japanese employees receive any of these benefits.

One could argue that there is a question of fairness of reward. But more is involved. Will the Japanese employees resent the special expatriate package, and will that undermine George's effectiveness, especially given the fact that George speaks very little Japanese? Special packages may keep the expatriate separate from the Japanese work group and slow down or even hinder integration, and all of this will have an impact on the effectiveness of communication between George and the other Japanese employees and between the subsidiary and headquarters.

On the side of the expatriate the argument is that at home he could afford a big house, his wife could continue her career, and his children could stay in their familiar environments. The extra pay and benefits, supporters of the packages argue, are simply compensation for hardships that he would not have to endure if he stayed at headquarters.

Some firms try to get around the issue by choosing younger, more flexible people to go abroad. These people are not sent as expatriates but are on the payroll of the subsidiary at the same conditions as host country nationals. Accounting firms in the United States are increasingly using that model, and it might work if international experience is deemed essential in career advancement. On the whole, however, many firms in the United States still maintain that it is not worth sending younger employees abroad. They feel an employee must be at least middle management before the firm can profit from the employee's time as an expatriate. The average cost to the company for an expatriate with family who fails to complete an assignment is between $150,000 and $250,000.

The Europeans seem to take a different approach. For example, French firms send many of their younger people abroad. They argue that younger people are less expensive and more flexible in adapting to different cultures. Furthermore, they don't have to worry about schooling for their children. In addition, these employees will bring their international experiences back to their jobs at headquarters and be able to use what they have learned throughout their careers. The French are convinced that early international experience will develop international personalities that are able to communicate more effectively with people from many different cultural backgrounds. They will be able to see the partner's point of view and engage in more productive and creative problem solving. They hope that people with early intercultural work experience will be more flexible and better communicators. For example, the French company Schlumberger hires young engineers and moves them around—from Indonesia to Saudi Arabia to Houston.

U.S. firms have increasingly withdrawn their managers from assignments abroad because of high failure rates, arguing that it is too expensive, that Americans are not good at adapting to different cultures, and that host country nationals educated in the United States are better to fill the void and establish good communication with host country personnel.[7] These arguments are flawed for a variety of reasons. By withdrawing most of their American staff, U.S. firms signal either that Americans are unable to adapt and work successfully in a foreign culture or that firms from the United States can be successful without Americans developing intercultural communication skills. In many ways it means admitting defeat and letting the world know that Americans have given up—they are unable or unwilling to deal with the communication challenge.

The competition—the Japanese, the Germans, the French, the Koreans—generally doesn't share that view. Many firms from these countries expect that their employees can adapt, function, and communicate in many different cultural environments. The whole argument raises a question about the role and function of the expatriate. Is the main task of the expatriate to develop and manage opportunities for the firm, or is the main task to facilitate communication with headquarters so that managers at headquarters don't have to worry about foreign operations? In U.S. firms one sometimes gets the impression that the main task is to make life easy for headquarters rather than to maximize opportunities.

Another assumption is that the foreign manager in a foreign subsidiary who was educated in the country of headquarters will be more successful than a citizen of the headquarters country. Based on this view, for example, an Indian who was educated in Belgium will be more successful in the Indian subsidiary of a Belgian firm than a Belgian manager. But research has shown that the native-born foreign-educated person does not necessarily communicate better with host country employees than a person from the home country. The employees at headquarters may develop a false sense of security thinking that they have taken care of all problems by hiring the Indian-born manager educated in Belgium. They assume that they have someone who is equally at home in both cultures and can communicate with both sides equally well. They may not realize that the Indian may find himself or herself caught in between the native and the culture. How well the Indian will do in this setting will depend on professional status, family background, and degree of adaptation to the culture of Belgium.

Headquarters may select the Indian manager because he can relate so well to the people at headquarters, not realizing that, because of that very same quality, he may have difficulties establishing credibility with Indian businesspeople. What assures the business community in India that the employee has not sold out to the Belgian firm? How can they be certain that he represents the interests of his native culture? In many ways, the better headquarters likes the foreign-born manager, the more his native country may mistrust him. As a result, there may be questions of trust and loyalty. In cultures where loyalty is important, an employee working for a foreign firm may be somewhat suspect and, therefore, decrease his ability to communicate effectively.

In the international division organization, most people agree that

• Cultural sensitivity and language are important.
• Managers must adapt to the culture.
• Technical expertise is not sufficient.[8]

The major disagreements occur over how to reach the goal of being a good intercultural communicator. *One of the biggest stumbling blocks in effective communication is that intercultural sensitivity is considered necessary only for the international division.* The typical attitude in U.S. firms with international divisions is that the people who are actively involved in international affairs on a regular basis should be knowledgeable about the cultural priorities of the people they are dealing with. For the rest of the employees such knowledge is typically not deemed necessary; it does not add to their performance. As a result, the firm remains fragmented into domestic and international divisions. With growing competition, improving global communication systems, and better education, this distinction becomes a hindrance rather than a help.

Businesspeople who have worked abroad often find it challenging when they come back to headquarters. To some extent the reintegration difficulties are related to reverse culture shock, but in many cases the returning expatriate may feel anxious about her future with the firm. Increasingly, firms are carefully planning the return of expatriates to effectively use their international expertise in the operations of the firm.

Tim Brandt, the operations manager of a major U.S. firm, has been in Spain for two years. Before that he set up a joint venture in China and then worked with the subsidiary in Germany for some time. Each time Tim has tried to learn the language so he can at least function in everyday life.

By any definition, Tim has been successful in the international field. At times he is nervous about his career after his foreign assignment, but Tim's firm realizes that he will have developed valuable expertise to play a major role in the international expansion of the firm. Tim will probably stay in Spain for another year, but headquarters is planning his return and has assigned a mentor to Tim to make reentry easier. Tim's international experience, the ability to speak Spanish and some German, his understanding of several other cultures, and his ability to adapt to and work in other cultures will be factors in his advancement at headquarters.

Just a few years ago the path to top management and the presidency in many firms typically led through a major role in the domestic arena. In a number of cases the vice president of the international division was promoted to a similar position in the domestic division. Even though domestic and international divisions carried the same weight on the organizational chart, the reality was somewhat different. As long as the top job in many corporations was reserved for a manager with extensive domestic experience, the upward-moving manager hesitated to spend a great deal of time perfecting communication skills necessary in the international arena.

Things have changed greatly, and during the past few years several major corporations in the United States have promoted people with extensive international experience to the executive suite, thereby clearly signaling that intercultural expertise is important.

The major problem with the international division structure is that international and domestic operations are not integrated. The international division structure gives international operations more visibility, but it also keeps international operations separate. As the importance of international operations grows and as the international competition increases, firms need to reevaluate their view of international operations, and in particular, their view of the importance of intercultural communication. The firms that will be successful are the ones that can adapt to different environments and understand the influence of culture on business behavior, such as negotiation. Several firms are trying to meet that challenge by changing from an international division structure to a global structure.

THE GLOBAL FIRM

The Structure of the Global Firm

The word *global* appears increasingly in the literature in the place of multinational and international, and a number of companies have changed to a global structure. In some cases that change is simply semantic, and there are no significant changes in the organizational structures and communication practices; companies simply refer to themselves as global.

The differences between an international division structure and a global structure are, however, significant. Going global is not something that can be done overnight or just by changing the name or the stationery. In the change from an international division structure to a global structure, the international division disappears and international operations are integrated into the firm.

In a sense the organizational structure has come full circle. The global organization chart resembles the organization chart for a domestic firm, with the difference that the organization encompasses the globe.

The move to a global structure typically begins when international sales are consistently 35 to 50 percent of overall sales. The move to a global structure is an outcome of a company's international success.

Global firms typically use one of three basic structures: a worldwide function format, a worldwide geographic/regional format, or a worldwide product format (see Exhibits 11–4, 11– 5, and 11–6). The structures can be mixed. For example, a firm may combine regional and product structures. A company may also use a matrix structure for its global approach.[9] Which particular global structure a firm chooses will depend on the product, the size of the firm, the extent of global operations, and the philosophy of management.

Regardless of the particular structure, the global firm does not divide operations into domestic and international. Operations are global, and any substructures are an outcome of the needs of the global perspective.

At first glance, the global structure looks very appealing. It does not always work, however, and it is not always the optimal organizational form. If the various international and domestic parts of the firm are at different stages of development, production, and technology, then the global structure may not get the expected results.[10] As pointed out earlier, if the product can be easily standardized and if the world wants that product, then the global structure works fine.

For Shell, Unilever, and Coca-Cola, the global organization is working because of the type of products they manufacture and sell. For other companies the move may be premature or inappropriate because product needs are different in different markets and because cultural adaptations are important. A firm that manufactures and sells sports equipment may find that an international division structure is more advantageous because that structure gives more autonomy to the various subsidiaries and allows subsidiaries to respond to specific market needs and trends more effectively.

For example, golf clubs and tennis rackets in Japan differ in their dimensions, center of gravity, and weight from U.S. dimensions. Just to export equipment from the United States without any modifications does not always work. While some R&D functions may be performed jointly, other operational functions may have different needs and should be developed separately. The products are differentiated enough in various markets to justify different approaches. This is a reality that Coca-Cola does not have to face.

Communication in the Global Organization

What are the implications of a global structure for communication? A shift to a global structure does not make a global person out of a domestic person. The person who in the past exclusively dealt with the domestic market may know Sweden but may not know or care about Hong Kong or Singapore. If the change to a global structure is not prepared carefully, a lot of confusion, bad decisions, and poor communication will result.

Frequently, employees with a domestic background going on their first international trip feel that there is not much to international business, a feeling expressed in the comment, "If you have done one market, you have done them all." These people know the product inside out, but they have no background in the international market, distribution systems, international sensitivities, and intercultural communication issues. They tend to evaluate international procedures using their domestic expertise and their self-reference criterion. They judge everything on the basis of their own backgrounds.

Typically, the instant experts will come back with all sorts of ideas for improvement without thinking through the intercultural implications and ramifications of their suggestions. They may think, "If those people in Nigeria would only adopt the way we do things, then their problems would be solved easily." They do not realize that the way "we" do things is not the way things get done in that culture, and that there may be very valid reasons why "they" do things differently.

Successful communication in a global firm requires a solid and well thought-out structure of the communication process. This structure must be communicated globally. Ramrath, president of GE Plastics Pacific Ltd., points out that in globalization a worldwide communication network is essential. He insists that all employees must develop a global attitude and have a sense of adventure; without it, he warns, the venture will not be successful.[11] The global firm requires coordination, communication, and unity of command.

The worldwide **functional structure** does well at unifying the command (see Exhibit 11–4). Worldwide operations report to the appropriate functional managers, such as marketing, finance, and personnel, at headquarters. The difficulty is that communication can occur along rather narrow and specialized paths. The functional manager may not have the overview of the whole situation because he or she only deals with one functional

EXHIBIT 11–4   Global Functional Structure

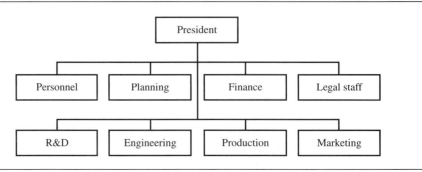

aspect. To be successful in this environment, managers from the various functional areas must keep each other informed on a regular basis. They must communicate with the people in their areas of specialization around the globe, but they also must communicate with managers from other functional areas to coordinate efforts. Many firms spend a great amount of effort on cross-functional training of their management staff to improve operations. The process requires sensitivity and adaptation to different cultural orientations and goals of the various functional areas.

The **geographic structure** coordinates operations within a region but often does not pay enough attention to coordination between regions (see Exhibit 11–5). This structure facilitates adaptation to local and regional conditions. Communication with the various cultural groups within a region improves, but communication between regions may be weak because of different languages and ethnic rivalries. The communication system may be fragmented, and it may be difficult to pull all the regions together to exchange ideas and share resources.

EXHIBIT 11–5   Global Geographic Structure

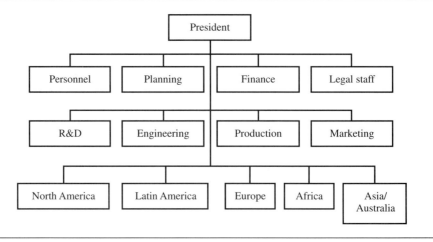

In the worldwide **product structure** (see Exhibit 11–6), global communication relating to one product is efficient, but the communication between various product groups can be weak, and duplication of efforts is common because each product may have its own sales force and marketing channels. As a result, foreign partners may get the impression that the company does not coordinate its efforts very well and that communications are affected negatively by competition and fragmentation.

As the firm becomes a global firm, the changes required for communication will be difficult for personnel at headquarters but even more difficult for people in the field. In the international division structure, foreign subsidiary employees simply had to contact people in the international division; they could expect that the international division would take care of problems. Now employees in the subsidiary must contact a variety of people: product development, production, marketing, finance, sales. In many cases they do not know these people personally. If the company has high turnover in personnel, which is very typical in the United States, the communication problem is exacerbated because the communicator without a background in the company and without intercultural communication skills will have difficulty in structuring the message appropriately and selecting the optimal channel.

An effective global structure requires intercultural communication training of many people, at all levels of the organization, over and over again. When the product development team sits down, members cannot just consider domestic issues; they have to think and plan globally. An advertising campaign cannot be planned with only the domestic market in mind; the team must consider cultural, legal, and regulatory requirements in other markets. While people may carry major responsibility for a particular segment of the advertising campaign, everyone needs to be aware of the overall strategy and know what is going on worldwide. They have to overcome their differences and work as a team.

The communication requirements are even more severe if R&D and production are spread over several locations all over the globe. A number of firms have R&D labs in

EXHIBIT 11–6   Global Product Structure

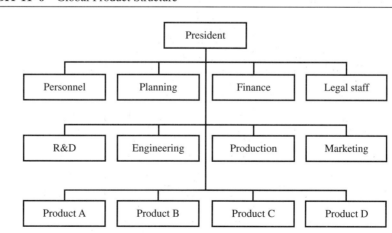

several countries. In the global firm, these labs must coordinate and communicate with each other. This does not mean they cannot adapt to specific markets, but it does mean they must keep each other informed and cooperate rather than compete for resources. Each segment must have in mind the best interest of the firm as a whole.

The global structure can be very beneficial for international operations. In corporations with an international division, advertising tends to emphasize domestic needs and the international advertising budget is smaller than the domestic one in most cases. Global organizations do not distinguish between domestic and international advertising budgets. The voice of the international side of the business is heard together with the domestic voice, and the money is spent where it will do the most good. This requires the managers from around the globe to communicate with each other. They have to understand each other's needs, priorities, and ways of doing things. Without a background in intercultural communication and respect for each other's cultural orientations, this cooperation is not going to happen.

The people involved in finance, marketing, and product development at headquarters must have a global outlook and understand the thought processes, customs, and values of the cultures where the firm does business. A global structure takes a tremendous amount of commitment. It requires regular meetings, frequent communication, and travel. Only so much can be done by E-mail, fax, telephone and teleconference. A global structure costs money, but the improved strategies can increase profits.

A global structure requires effective communication among the employees at headquarters and then full integration of communication strategies on a global basis. The person who gets ahead in this environment is the person who can think and act globally. Staffing in a true global firm is geocentric—the best person gets the job regardless of geographic and national background. The person who gets to the top in that environment needs to have global experience and solid intercultural communication skills. Global experience is no longer an extra, a nice thing to have, but absolutely essential.

Few firms today are truly global. Firms must function under the constraints of visas, work permits, government regulations, and import–export restrictions that can hinder globalization. In many ways the global firm has outgrown the existing political structure, but national laws and different cultural orientations still heavily influence the internal and external communications. NAFTA and the European Community are examples of how national governments are working with each other and with businesses to remove national barriers and create a global business environment.

Which language should the global person speak? Many businesspeople in the United States are fast to point out that English is the business language of the world; therefore, English is sufficient. However, a truly global business strategy requires cultural sensitivity, the ability to understand the other side, and the ability to communicate with people from a variety of backgrounds. Being able to speak the native language of the business partner will help even if the foreign counterpart speaks English.

As the chapter on culture and language pointed out, there is a vast difference between being reasonably functional in a language and being bilingual and bicultural. The person who only speaks English will miss much of the background culture and fine nuances of a conversation. By limiting contacts to people who speak English, a manager will limit her exposure to other opinions that native people hold who do not speak English. The manager may get a very distorted picture of what is actually going on.

The foreign businessperson who appears fluent in English may also present a problem. The surface knowledge, speed of speaking, and a good accent may hide the fact that that person may miss many of the fine points that nevertheless may be important in doing business. An additional problem is the definition of *fluent*. For example, if a businessperson from the United States claims fluency in a language, that can mean anything from very good to just speaking a little. When a businessperson from the Netherlands claims fluency in a foreign language, that typically means excellent use of the language.

The need for language and culture sensitivity is similar in both the international division structure and the global structure. The big difference is that in the global structure many more people need this orientation. In comparison to the international division structure, the need for international knowledge in the global structure is pushed down to lower levels in the organization and encompasses more people.

In summary, to make the switch from international to global is easy on paper. In many cases the switch is probably semantic and nothing changes in the day-to-day operations. Firms that become truly global find that it takes time, training, patience, and detailed attention to communication.

THE EXAMPLE OF LEISURE WHEELS, INC.

Leisure Wheels, Inc., located originally in Dallas, Texas, changed to a global structure in 1991–92. The change came as a result of the growing importance of the international side of the business. It was an attempt to support further growth.

Leisure Wheels, Inc., is a rather informal company. With the restructuring, the firm wanted to keep this culture and therefore consciously avoided a formal organization chart. The feeling was that the overall structure should be loose and flexible. The structure of top management of the firm, however, is more formalized. The chart resembles a wheel with a hub in the center, spokes, and a rim. The center represents the common purpose and goals of the firm. Without it, the operational units would not be able to exist. Just as the rim of the wheel connects the spokes and holds the wheel together, the operational groups are connected to illustrate the emphasis on a team approach.

The lines of communication and functional responsibilities within each operational group have not been formalized on paper. The structure could best be described as a flexible matrix. Each employee has responsibility to his or her boss and to the peers in his or her own team and the other operational groups. This requires coordination. For example, the clothing and the accessories areas must coordinate and pull in the same direction; an isolated approach would not work in achieving the goals of the company as a whole. The operational areas must communicate with each other, and each operational unit must also communicate with its worldwide constituents to reach performance targets.

The firm changed the structure to eliminate the "us versus them" feeling that was prevalent in the international division structure, but a cultural change of this magnitude takes time. Oldtimers from domestic still have a more domestic outlook at this firm.

In the beginning there was mass confusion. People in the field and at headquarters were concerned about where they fit, especially since there was no clear organization chart depicting their particular positions.

The slogan that reverberates throughout the firm is "Think global—act local." This is easier said than done, however. Leisure Wheels, Inc., so far has had some problems with establishing effective lines of communication. People in the field are still confused about whom to contact at headquarters if they have questions and concerns. The problem is exacerbated by the fact that each operations unit has about 40 employees. People from the field simply do not know who the appropriate contact person is.

(continued)

In the reorganization, Leisure Wheels, Inc., split up the international division. Most of the employees went into specific operations areas, and, as a result, the international division was integrated into specific functional areas. Today, employees from the original international division still communicate regularly with each other and keep each other informed; there is still a common bond based on common concerns and experiences.

In the old international division structure, a manager knew exactly who needed to receive copies on what issues. Today, a person in marketing research does not automatically send copies to someone in production, sales, finance, or marketing. Karen, the manager of international operations and analysis, for example, came out of the international division. She regularly and automatically sent copies to people in the international division. Today she sends copies to her boss. It is then up to her boss to inform other people who need and could use the information. But the process is no longer automatic. As a result, information may get lost.

Leisure Wheels, Inc., has found that effective communication lies at the center of an effective global structure. To promote better global communication, each department has regular staff meetings. As a result, communication within operational units has improved; however, there is little formal communication directly to other operational groups. Typically, any concerns raised in a staff meeting are communicated to the next higher level, on the assumption that that level will contact the appropriate unit.

Some managers have begun to sense the need for regular and more systematic communication to improve the efficiency of operations. For example, currently two people from two different units may go to visit the same dealer in Spain within a two-week time frame. They do not know about each other's visit, and they do not know about the purpose of each other's trips. There is no central posting on who is going where for what purpose. It is easy to see that this is not very functional. If a marketing person goes, and a few days later a salesperson goes, and after that perhaps a product development person, the company spends a lot of effort, time, and money, but does not spend resources very effectively and does not communicate with the dealers in Spain effectively. The coordination of trips and communication is a must so that dealers abroad do not get the impression that headquarters is disorganized and does not know what it is doing.

As the change to a global structure occurred, management realized the need for intercultural communication training, but there was some disagreement on what exactly was needed. The company finally decided that all employees needed training in intercultural business communication. In the first phase of the training program the company wanted employees to gain a practical understanding of the work and environment in the various foreign subsidiaries. For example: How are dealers in Spain set up? What are their constraints? Who are their customers? What are their concerns? The company is planning a broader intercultural training program after completion of the first.

The research supports this approach. Daft and Lengel found that employees at lower levels need more technical information and training.[12] After the initial training and information, more detailed intercultural communication training is helpful, but the training should always relate to the context of the specific business.

Currently, it is up to the individual employee going on an international trip to seek out a knowledgeable person to get information about the international dealer. One person suggested the development of a pamphlet describing the nuts and bolts of the organization in the various dealerships abroad.

In summary, the assessment of the change for Leisure Wheels, Inc., overall is positive for the long run. There is a strong conviction that the global structure is absolutely necessary in an increasingly competitive environment. In the short run, the frustrations can be very great. As a manager at Leisure Wheels, Inc., pointed out, communication is the absolute key to the success of the global structure.

IMPLICATIONS OF CULTURAL ASPECTS OF BUSINESS STRUCTURES FOR COMMUNICATION IN THE INTERNATIONAL FIRM

So far in this chapter we have looked at the implications of international expansion and organizational structure for intercultural communication. Some of the communication challenges in this process are universal; a Japanese or a Chilean firm that expands its international operations will face some of the same communication problems.

However, international firms do not just communicate with their own subsidiaries where they still have some control over language, policies, and practices. They also communicate with independent businesses in the countries where their subsidiaries are located. They communicate with third-country businesses. For example, the Taiwanese subsidiary of a firm from the United States may do business with the Taiwanese subsidiary of a French firm. In that case the communication must take into consideration American, Taiwanese, and French concerns. In addition, subsidiaries communicate with the governments of the respective countries. Even if a company has a firm company language policy and practices polycentric staffing, the interface with other cultures is ever present, and the firm must deal with different values, attitudes, and practices, not to mention legal requirements.

Different cultures look at organizational purposes and structures differently. The way they view organizational patterns influences their business structures and their communication policies and practices. Nakane, a Japanese anthropologist, contrasts U.S. and Japanese firms in that context.[13] She argues that U.S. firms emphasize credentials and qualifications, which she calls attributes, whereas Japanese firms emphasize a common context, which she calls frame. In some countries—Middle Eastern countries are an example—the family is the foundation of business organizations. In the former communist countries an authoritarian centralized system still influences the structure and communication of a firm. Let us look at these organizational patterns and their implications for communication.

Communication in the Organization Based on Credentials

People in the United States, Nakane argues, identify themselves by professional attributes such as job qualifications or credentials: They are accountants, salespersons, engineers, carpenters.[14] These job labels give the Americans their professional identity, and they can take these professional credentials with them. A CPA license, for example, is valid in most states in the United States and recognized in several other countries. More and more workers want to have portable credentials. Recently, for example, salespeople have been talking about a sales certificate that would be based on specific educational and work credentials.

Credentials are influenced by cultural priorities, and labels do not necessarily have the same meaning in different cultures. The label *engineer* does not mean the same educational level and expertise in all countries. One credential that is almost universally understood is the MBA. As a result, several universities in a variety of countries have established MBA programs because the MBA is an internationally recognized credential. Everyone knows the MBA is a generalist management degree at the graduate level, and as result, international hiring and evaluation of qualification is made easier. For example, Germany for many years awarded the Staatsexamen as the official degree at the end of one's studies. As long as most business was domestic, this presented no problem. However, with the growth of international business, people from other countries began to wonder what the Staatsexamen was. They did not have any idea how to categorize the qualification. During the last few years, several German universities have added the MBA program to their offerings.

Credentials contribute to the identity of an American businessperson. The identification with the firm for which Americans work is only part of their existence; it is not all encompassing. In the United States, an employee can enter and leave an organization at any level. A person can enter at the beginner level at the bottom or, as has happened in the case of IBM and Kodak, at the level of CEO. What counts is the qualifications the employee has, some of which may be credentials.

People want the job that best corresponds to their qualifications. If that means leaving the firm, that's okay. In fact, most new graduates in the United States will stay with their first companies for only three to four years. Career counselors will tell them that they should reevaluate their employment situation on a regular basis and jump if a better opportunity presents itself. The emphasis is on individual advancement and individual opportunities as discussed in Chapter 3. That, of course, has implications for training. In that environment, training will be job specific and brief. The employer wants to get some work out of the employee before he or she leaves the firm, and the employee wants to develop job attributes that are portable.

The emphasis on portable credentials and individual achievement influences communication within the firm. For example, if the employee is not absolutely loyal to the firm, how much should he or she be involved in sensitive discussions and issues? The tendency will be to concentrate on job-specific information and to limit communication. As a result, it is more difficult to establish teamwork, which requires mutual trust and openness. Firms operating within a low-context culture try to protect their confidential information through contracts. For example, an employee who has access to confidential information and leaves the firm may have to sign a statement that she will not use any of this information. Under these circumstances, the emphasis in communication may be on safeguarding information rather than on long-term education and training and sharing information to reach company goals.

People who come from a cultural environment where sharing is considered very important may not understand why communication does not flow freely and people do not keep each other informed. They will also be puzzled by the constant personnel changes in U.S. firms. If Masataka Hyashi from Nagoya, Japan, talks about the possibilities of a joint venture to Patricia Lesch in Chicago today, there is no guarantee that Patricia Lesch will still be there a few weeks from now. When Masataka Hyashi contacts Chicago again, Patricia Lesch may have left the firm for better opportunities and someone else will have taken that place. The Japanese, for whom the building of personal relationships is a crucial aspect in doing business, find the personnel changes in U.S. firms disorienting.

Communication in the Organization Based on Context

The organization based on context is best exemplified by Japan. Japanese organizations, according to Nakane, are organized on the basis of frame or group belonging, a concept that goes back to the idea of household, *ie*, and emphasizes the importance of the group over the individual.[15] The Japanese male is first and foremost an employee of his firm. He is a Toyota man, a Mitsubishi man, a Komatsu man rather than an engineer or accountant. He identifies with the firm, the corporate household. Credentials are valid within that context but don't mean much outside the context. The lack of portable credentials limits job mobility, but it also provides a certain security.

The employee is part of a family that takes care of its members; in return, the employee supports the goals of the firm. The system is based on reciprocity or *amae* (see Chapter 4). The term *amae* means that a person willingly takes care of another person but is also willing to be taken care of by that person. *Amae* establishes mutual dependency. Nobody can do things alone. As we have discussed in earlier chapters, the Japanese are willing to put personal considerations behind group considerations. Harmony of the group is considered more important. As a result, communication avoids open conflict and confrontation that are common in more individualistic cultures.

Within the frame or context employees know how to act and behave. They know their place; they know what to say, how to address someone, how deep to bow. As soon as that familiar environment changes, the Japanese are at a loss. The culture has not given them the background or the experience to deal with strangers. Japanese are ill at ease in new situations and with strangers. They do not know how to address the other person, and they do not know where they stand in the hierarchy vis-à-vis the other person, all aspects that lead to a certain level of insecurity. The result is incongruous communication behavior.

For example, in his group, Ishido Tanaka is polite, considerate, and nonassertive. When he is confronted with the world outside the group, the familiar norms and guidelines are gone. How does he deal with this environment? In a variety of ways. One is to pretend the other side does not exist, creating psychological space in the middle of crowded conditions. The other is behavior that is at odds with the principles of behavior within the group. The Japanese on subways can be remarkably aggressive and impolite. Pushing with one's elbows, forcing one's way in, using rude language, and spitting are typical signs of behavior that would be unacceptable within the group but are tolerated outside the group.

When it comes to hiring, a company based on group identity will look for someone who will fit into the group, and someone who will bring prestige to the firm. Therefore, many Japanese firms pay more attention to the university attended than the subject studied. A fitting personality is more important than specific skills. After all, technical aspects can be learned; it would be much harder to change or form the personality and character. Even though with economic problems and restructuring of industry the practice of lifetime employment is weakening, the concept is still strong. The Japanese employee is supposed to fit in and take his place. He is part of the firm.

There have always been Japanese who would leave a job and go somewhere else, but the professional move was always downward to a smaller and less prestigious firm. This is just beginning to change. A recent news release announced that a senior official from Toyota had been hired into a leading position by another major Japanese firm. The fact that this move made the headlines indicates how rare such changes are even today. However, mobility is on the rise. Increasingly, Japanese executives insist that Japanese firms need to promote based on merit and encourage young talents if Japan is to be a viable competitive player in the future.

Since one can assume in the Japanese context that people will be in the firm for a long time, it is worth training them in a wide variety of jobs. For example, several Japanese firms regularly send employees to the Thunderbird School of International Management in Glendale, Arizona. During their studies the Japanese employees remain on the payroll of their firms, and their firms pay the tuition. These firms have decided that the investment will pay many returns. The firms are not primarily interested in their employees getting a degree, although that is expected. They are willing to support these employees because they hope that they will learn how Americans think and how they are motivated. In addition, they hope that their employees will build relationships with people who will be in leading positions in the United States in years to come. This kind of investment only makes sense if the employee will remain in the firm.

If employees will stay in the firm for the duration of their careers, it also makes sense to involve them in making decisions and sharing information. After all, they have a stake in the firm. The adversarial labor–management process of American firms is replaced with a more cooperative approach. The feeling is that we are in this together; we must work problems out, and we must cooperate for the benefit of all sides. As we have discussed earlier in this book, building group cohesiveness frequently occurs after hours in bars. Japanese managers have been known for lavish expense accounts to entertain colleagues and partners. Even here, changes are occurring. For example, Japan's biggest brokerage, Nomura Securities and Mitsui Company, halved its entertainment budget between 1992 and 1999. The Bank of Tokyo–Mitsubishi, formed by a merger, spends less on entertainment now than either of the two banks did as separate businesses.

While job mobility in Japan has increased, much of the old sentiment toward employment remains. The Japanese example of a business organization based on group belonging illustrates the connection of culture, organizational structures, and communication. Seniority matters in promotions, and therefore more people tend to reach positions with fairly high titles in the firm. Titles matter; they give face. The differentiation of people is apparent in the job duties rather than the job titles. As a result of the cultural influences on promotions, the organizational chart tends to be broader at the top than in many American firms. Communication emphasizes the well-being of the firm and harmony between employees rather than individual achievement.

Japanese firms going into low-context cultures were initially confused by the adversarial approach of employees and the separation of work time and private or family time. U.S. employees, and Europeans too for that matter, were not willing to sacrifice their evenings and weekends to the betterment of the firm. In Japan, on the other hand, employees are expected to spend time with co-workers after business hours. Typically Japanese expatriates take this practice with them. At a Japanese subsidiary in the U.S. Midwest, for example, the Japanese employees tend to stay at the office long after the American employees have left for the evening.

Communication in the Organization Based on Family Orientation

Business in the Middle East is based on the concept of the family. According to the Koran, the family must take care of its members. A family has a holy obligation towards its members. The family orientation seems to fit the Japanese group structure, but the group in Japan does not necessarily include the blood family. The Middle East looks at the family as all blood relatives.

In contrast to the Japanese firm, which emphasizes the group and consensus building, the firm in the Middle East is ruled by the senior male member of the family. It is much more authoritarian and autocratic than the harmony-based approach of Japan. Even when the senior manager asks for advice, family members understand that the senior member has the cultural right to make decisions. He may listen but does not have to. The Americans hire based on specific qualifications; the Japanese, on character; the Middle Eastern firm must take care of family members first.

A successful businessman may start several new businesses, one for each son, rather than expand the existing business. By doing this he can ensure that after his death each son will be the senior member in his firm. This setup creates clear lines of ownership and communication and avoids squabbles over who is entitled to do what. It can also create a unique communication code that is difficult for outsiders to decipher. In American firms communication codes are more readily transferable. Pezeshkpur states that Middle Easterners function best if the lines of authority and power are clear.[16] The uncertainty connected with negotiating and compromising is culturally more difficult.

Businesspeople in the United States like to toss ideas back and forth and reach a compromise or consensus after arguing. Middle Easterners prefer someone to be in charge and to make final decisions. Their family orientation and emphasis on seniority meet these expectations. In this environment the establishment of authority through appropriate introductions, credentials, and connections is crucial for success.

Communication in the Organization Based on Political Principles

Organizational principles in former communist countries are different altogether. Some people argue that there is no point in discussing the communist system since most of the former communist countries are not communist any longer. However, the influence of the communist system has been so strong and has shaped organizations to such an extent that the results will be there for a long time. People doing business in that part of the world will have to deal with the remnants of communist attitudes. For example, China, a major trading partner of the United States, Europe, Japan, and the Middle East, is still communist even though on the surface economic centralization has given way to a market-oriented economy. In reality much of the old approach is still in place. The party secretary now is a chairman of the board of a so-called "company"—actually a government-run agency. This pattern is common in China because who has better *guanxi* than the party secretary? He simply has changed the English on his business card to say Chairman of the Board rather than Party Secretary—a term that upsets Americans.

In the communist system, the business organization is based on the concept of collective ownership and the absolute right to a job. In the case of China this has been expressed in the concept of the iron rice bowl. While the rewards were minimal, the employee of a firm did not have to worry about unemployment or the basic necessities for life. Furthermore, except for top party people, nobody had much. The business organization was not governed by business principles, but first and foremost by political considerations. The system created a mentality of dependency where people had little motivation and were not willing to take risks. The iron rice bowl is really a thing of the past in China. The biggest practitioners—the huge state-owned enterprises in heavy industry—have been laying off people in huge numbers, and more layoffs are predicted for this and coming years.

Today, the Chinese economy has three parts. One is represented by the risk-oriented entrepreneurs who seize every business opportunity that presents itself. This group is rather small, and all private companies are closely monitored by the government. Another group consists of those who work for foreign firms and joint ventures. Many of these people are well educated, and they aim at an affluent Western lifestyle. The third group consists of those who are still working for the state-owned sector; this remains by far the largest sector of the economy. Increasingly, these people have few economic resources. So far, they have had job security in most cases, but they are falling further and further behind in their standard of living. Communication in these three sectors is very different. In the private companies Chinese managers and employees are beginning to take greater responsibility for their work. They are expected to show initiative and be flexible. The typical top-down communication is giving way to a more open communication style. An outsider who goes to China to do business needs to examine what kind of firm he or she is dealing with and adjust communication to the specific circumstances. At the same time, the Western businessperson needs to realize that even in private companies business practices are strongly influenced by the government.

As the former communist economies become more market oriented, people are eager to reap the profits, but they are not necessarily willing to accept the responsibility for efficiency and take the risk of failure. A number of Western firms that have gone to the former Eastern Block countries and Russia must deal with that attitude. In the case of one firm, the American owner finds that it is very difficult to get information from the employees in Russia—even the most factual and neutral information. Information is power, and to part with it might not be wise, as is discussed in Chapter 8. Employees also fear that information they give to the owner may be used against them.

Since in the past the Soviet government provided raw materials and took care of selling the manufactured products, the accounting and financial systems are underdeveloped. It is not just that the technical systems are weak; more importantly the concepts are not clear. Generally employees understand the term *profit,* but they have a hard time seeing that a profit must be earned, that the production and the sales must be there first before one can enjoy the profits. Some of them ask why the owner cannot just pay them since he is rich and has money. The old structures have partly disappeared, but the new structures have not been formed or they are not fully functioning. Those who are willing to take risk and experiment with new approaches frequently are stifled by political and economic chaos. The problem is exacerbated by the growing influence of organized crime.

DAIMLERCHRYSLER MITSUBISHI MOTORS

At the end of March 2000, DaimlerChrysler took a controlling stake in Mitsubishi Motors for $1.95 billion. Mitsubishi saw the deal as a way to cope with its huge debt; DaimlerChrysler hoped that a stake in Mitsubishi would open up the Asian car market for the parent firm. One more super merger: we could leave it at that. However, this particular conglomeration of firms raises interesting cultural and communication issues. What is the company language? How can different policies be reconciled? Who has the final say in disputes?

The new firm faces issues at the global, national, and company levels. And at each stage cultural priorities play a role as well. When Daimler and Chrysler first merged, many Americans wanted to think that it was a true merger where both parties had equal say. This notion disappeared fairly fast. Daimler made it clear who called the shots. A big concession from the Germans was that the company language would be English. The Americans who would deal with Germany on a regular basis were relieved; no need to learn this difficult language. They had known all along that English would be the official language. When John Craig and Daniel Wilson went to their first meeting in Stuttgart, they were in for a severe shock, however. Yes, during the official meeting everyone spoke English; however, as soon as the meeting was officially over, all the Germans switched to German. John and Daniel did not understand a word and decided that a few German lessons might be useful after all.

The merger required a reconciliation not only of big issues but also of seemingly unimportant points. For example, a committee had to sit down and decide whether a brochure encouraging employees to accept global assignments should have the shape of a globe or a rectangle. The choice of color was another stumbling block. After several months of regular meetings the committee finally decided on the globe shape, but the color was another issue. Ultimately the group agreed on yellow and blue. The Germans immediately thought of Lufthansa, and the Americans, all from the Detroit area, thought of the University of Michigan.

The negotiations for expatriate pay were tough as well. American expatriates are used to lavish compensation packages, much larger than their German counterparts were used to. On the other hand, the Germans are used to long vacations. The proposal that was finally hammered out included the following: Expatriates from Germany and the United States would stay on their home country payroll and would be paid in their home country currency. That means no more special pay packages. The Americans were used to a three-month lump sum at the beginning of an expatriate assignment to cover costs. The Germans wanted none of that. The two sides finally compromised on one month's pay. The company offered to pay for housing in the new location and upkeep of the expatriate's house in his old location including snow removal and lawn care. Expatriates from both countries would be given 25 days of vacation and a plane trip home for themselves and their families once a year. The company offered to help a spouse find employment in the new location. German expatriates in the United States would get Chrysler automobiles at discount rates; the American expatriates in Germany would get Mercedes vehicles at discount rates.

None of these issues dealt with the company product, marketing strategies, or customer relations. At times, the discussions went nowhere. Compromises frequently left both sides disappointed. Less than two years after the Daimler-Chrysler merger, the company bought a controlling share of Mitsubishi. That raised new concerns among employees. Chrysler had had an unsuccessful joint venture with Mitsubishi in 1980 when together they built an automobile assembly plant in

Normal, Illinois. Ultimately, the joint venture was dissolved, to some extent at least because of different approaches to doing business. In the joint venture Chrysler had been the junior partner; Japanese headquarters had the ultimate say on most issues. In the new formation, Chrysler is aligned with the majority partner.

Over the years Mitsubishi has had its share of problems. The parent company accumulated a huge debt, and the subsidiary in the United States was confronted with class action suits over sexual harassment and racial discrimination. When the American subsidiary plant was first built, the company provided training for the American employees to become familiar with Japanese culture and business practices. Japanese expatriates were included in that training. After the first couple of years, however, that type of training was discontinued. Cultural clashes were not immediately apparent, but some were smoldering under the surface. A growing number of employees felt that the Japanese and Americans worked in the same plant but were not on the same team. How will old feelings affect the new arrangement?

Jürgen Schremp is sitting in his office in Stuttgart, Germany, and is contemplating the future of the new company. He will be meeting with executives from Chrysler and Mitsubishi in the next few weeks to discuss product developments and marketing strategies. He knows this will be tough and he will have to tread carefully to get everyone on board.

What advice would you give him to make the new business successful?

SUMMARY

An international firm, no matter what its own organizational structure, must deal with a variety of business structures around the globe. As companies expand internationally, their communication needs change. A domestic firm has very different communication needs from an international firm. An international firm with an international division faces the challenge of competition between domestic and international divisions. A global firm integrates international operations throughout the firm. As a result, the global firm needs people with intercultural communication expertise at all levels.

In addition to adapting communication to the growing internal diversity, international firms must also adapt to the varying communication practices of other firms around the globe.

We have specifically examined the following areas:

- *Corporate culture and intercultural communication.* Companies develop their own unique corporate culture. This culture is embedded in the national culture.
- *Stages in internationalization.* Typically, internationalization starts with an import–export stage, followed by the multinational and global firm. Each stage has its own organizational structure and communication environment.
- *Implications of cultural aspects of business structures for communication* in the international firm. Effective intercultural communication in a firm is influenced by the structure of a firm, which, in turn, is influenced by cultural priorities. Priorities for credentials, context, family, or political considerations will influence how people are hired, trained, and promoted. As a result, communication patterns depend on the specific organizational context.

NOTES

1. Nancy Adler, *International Dimensions of Organizational Behavior,* (Boston: Kent, 1986).
2. Philip R. Harris and Robert T. Moran, *Managing Cultural Differences,* 2nd ed., (Houston: Gulf, 1987), p. 121.
3. Donald Carbaugh, "Cultural Communication and Organizing," in *Communication, Culture, and Organizational Processes,* Intercultural and Intercultural Communication Annual, vol. IX, William B. Gudykunst, Lea P. Stewart, and Stella Ting-Toomey, eds., (Newbury Park, CA: Sage, 1985), p. 37.
4. Vern Terpstra and Kenneth Davis, *The Cultural Environment of International Business,* 2nd ed., (Chicago: Southwestern, 1985).
5. Nancy Adler and F. Ghadar, "International Strategy from the Perspective of People and Culture: the North American Context." in H. Lane & J DiStefano, eds., *International Management Behavior,* (New York: Kent, 1991).
6. H. Lane and J. DiStefano, *International Management Behavior,* (New York: Kent, 1991).
7. S. J. Kobrin, "Expatriate Reduction and Strategic Control in American Multinational Corporations," *Human Resource Management* 27(1), 1988, pp. 63–75.
8. R. L. Tung, "Selection and Training of Personnel for Overseas Assignments," *Columbia Journal of World Business* 16, 1982, pp. 68–78.
9. S. Ronen, *Comparative and Multinational Management,* (New York: Wiley, 1986).
10. Adler and Ghadar, "International Strategy," 1991.
11. H. Ramrath, "Globalization Isn't for Whiners," *The Wall Street Journal,* April 6, 1992.
12. R. Daft and R. Lengel, "Information Richness: A New Approach to Managerial and Organizational Design," In *Research in Organizational Behavior,* (Greenwich, CT: JAI, 1984), pp. 191–233.
13. C. Nakane, *Human Relations in Japan,* (Tokyo, Japan: Ministry of Foreign Affairs, 1972).
14. Ibid.
15. Ibid.
16. C Pezeshkpur, "Challenges to Management in the Arab world," *Business Horizons* 21 (1978), pp. 47–55.

CHAPTER TWELVE

The Effectiveness of Intercultural Business Communication and Business Judgment

In a recent advertisement on television in the United States, an executive enters the board room where all the top managers are sitting around the table. The executive passes out airline tickets to everyone and tells them they must go out and visit their clients to rebuild personal relationships. An important customer of 20 years, the executive explains, just canceled his business with the firm because he felt the firm had lost touch and did not care about him anymore. At issue was not the quality of the product, the payment schedule, or the delivery schedule, but rather the importance of personal relations. Fast electronic communication, telephone calls, faxes, and E-mail were not sufficient. The client wanted the personal touch, the personal attention, and the personal visit. Fortunately, the executive understood the importance of effective interpersonal communication.

So far in this book we have examined the linguistic, cultural, and organizational dimensions of intercultural business communication. While each of these three variables is very important by itself, we also need to focus on how these variables interact in order to communicate effectively.

Effective messages draw upon all dimensions or layers of contexts: verbal and nonverbal codes, the immediate task context of the communication act, the physical channel and the physical environment, the background of the communicators and their positions in the organization, the expected outcomes of the communication, the corporate cultures, the business cultures, and the general cultures of the communicators. Effective communication uses every medium that can help in communicating a message. It synthesizes all aspects of intercultural communication we have discussed so far and helps in transmitting the intended meaning.

As we will see in this chapter, not all communication needs to use all available techniques in order to be effective. Routine organization reports that help in running the firm, for example, updated sales figures for last year, are important, but they require a different mix of communication options than a detailed discussion of the reasons for any changes. The sales figures will help in understanding and shaping the discussion, but the discussion itself will provide insights not contained in the figures. The interpretation of data adds to the understanding of the message.

The right mix of communication options is particularly important in intercultural business communication, when the businessperson is dealing with different languages, communication conventions, cultural priorities, patterns of thinking and organizing messages, means for achieving different outcomes, and legal requirements. The appropriate mix is more complex and difficult to achieve than in a single-culture business.

In the remainder of this chapter we will examine the relationship between the effectiveness of intercultural and international business communication and

- Channel choice.
- Position in the organization.
- Cultural environment of the organization.

THE RELATIONSHIP BETWEEN EFFECTIVENESS AND CHANNEL CHOICE

With the rising cost of travel and the decreasing cost of electronic communication, international businesspeople are becoming particularly aware of the importance of selecting the right mix of communication channels for effective intercultural communication. They regularly evaluate how communication should take place and who should communicate with whom in the foreign subsidiaries, with other foreign partners, and with an increasingly diverse workforce at home.

The effectiveness of a channel—Daft and Lengel refer to this as richness—is influenced by its "potential information-carrying capacity."[1] The channel choice must take into consideration the

- Purpose of the message.
- Availability of technology.
- Concerns for confidentiality.
- Cultural environment.

Purpose of the Message

The channel influences the potential richness of a message, but at the same time the richness requirements and the purpose of the message will influence the channel choice. The two are interrelated. As Exhibit 12–1 illustrates, some channels are richer—they allow more richness in communication than others and carry information more effectively. Generally, the richness of the communication is highest in the face-to-face interchange of ideas. It is lowest in the presentation of tables and numeric data.

A written explanation of statistical information is richer than just the statistical information by itself, but the written explanation is not as rich as an explanation by telephone that adds nonverbal elements, such as hesitation, repetitions, and paraphrasing, to the message. An explanation in a face-to-face discussion would be even richer because the whole range of nonverbal communication aspects can be used to communicate the message.

EXHIBIT 12–1   The Richness of Varying Channels

Information Richness	Channel	Feedback	Language
High	Face-to-Face	Immediate	Verbal and nonverbal
	Videoconference	Immediate	Verbal and most nonverbal. Can be difficult in foreign language.
	Telephone	Fast	Verbal, very little nonverbal. Difficult in foreign language
	Written/E-mail	Fast	Verbal, often casual. Concerns about confidentiality
	Written/fax	Fast	Verbal, concerns with confidentiality
	Written/mail	Slow	Verbal, informal and formal
	Written/formal reports	Slow	Formal
Low	Quantitative/formal Reports/tables	Slow	Numeric

Source: adapted from R. Daft and R. Lengel, "Information Richness: A New Approach to Managerial and Organizational Design," in *Research in Organizational Behavior* (Greenwich, CT: JAI Press, 1984), pp. 191–233.

When communication is rich, we exchange ideas and we receive rapid feedback so we can understand what our partners think and how they see the issues at hand. Both verbal and nonverbal communication add to the richness. Telephone conversations still have some of the personal aspects, but the nonverbal communication is reduced. In addition, telephone conversations in international business are limited because of time differences, language problems, and cultural diversity. For example, telephone calls between Japanese and U.S. partners are not very practical because business hours do not overlap; when offices in the United States are open, offices in Japan are closed. As a result, business-people typically prearrange phone calls by fax or E-mail to ensure that they will reach the partner.

Letters, memos, and formal reports provide important information and establish permanent records, but they take time when it comes to the exchange of ideas and the fruitful discussion of issues and problems. Immediacy, which is a factor in richness, is gone.

The least rich communication is numerical data. Statistics are important, in many ways even crucial, and they often are considered in decision making. But, according to Daft and Lengel, they tend to play a minor role in the discussion and development of ideas.[2]

Over the last decade technology has opened several new channels, such as teleconferencing, Group Decision Support Systems (GDSS), and E-mail, that have affected intercultural business communication. As new technologies are developed, businesspeople need to regularly evaluate and update their choice of channel in intercultural business communication. These channels of communication all have the merit of immediacy; even in a written medium such as E-mail the transmission of information is almost instantaneous.

Complex organizational topics require rich channels. Simple topics, on the other hand, can be communicated through less rich channels. The weekly cafeteria menu can be posted in table format. No translation may be necessary for food items that are often difficult to translate anyway. Most people, even if they do not speak the dominant language, will be able to read the menu. No meeting, lengthy report, or particularly rich communication is necessary. Posting the menu is routine communication through a lean channel.

If the cafeteria decides to make major changes in the menu or price structure, the picture changes. A simple announcement may not be sufficient. This situation may require a meeting between the workers and management. In this case richer communication using a richer channel may be necessary to explain reasons, answer questions, and discuss the decision.

When should a manager meet with a partner, client, or supplier from another culture? When should a manager send an E-mail or a fax, telephone, hold a videoconference, or write a formal letter or report? As we explore these questions, we may realize that channel choice may be limited. Without even considering cultural restrictions, some channels may simply not be available or not affordable.

Availability of Technology

Frequently we take for granted that all channels are easily available anywhere around the world. People everywhere, in the most remote places, seem to have cell-phones and E-mail. In areas where people only a few years ago had no telephone connections, such as China and Indonesia, many now have access to the most modern technology. Yet there may be difficulties in using the technology. For example, videoconferencing will not be an option if the technology is not available or if time differences are too great. In addition, telephone connections for videoconferencing frequently are problematic. In a recent teleconference between a business in the United States and a firm in Helsinki, the technicians just could not establish the connection. It took several days to get the video connection, but problems with the sound persisted. The Finnish side could hear the American side, but the Americans could not hear the Finns. Because of the problems, the pictures were not very clear, and the sides did not get a good "feel" for each other. Ultimately, the two sides reverted to a speaker phone. Given the technical problems, a less rich channel proved more effective.

Even if the technology is working, videoconferencing may not be feasible. An international marketing manager reported that the sales manager in her Silicon Valley computer firm, which sells hardware and software all over the globe, recommended a teleconference of all subsidiaries of the firm to discuss global marketing strategies. The domestic background and experience of the sales manager with teleconferencing led her to consider this approach as feasible and efficient. However, the international realities made the suggestion unworkable. The time differences between Europe, America, and Asia made teleconferencing, with everyone sitting "around the table" at the same time, impractical. Furthermore, the manager assumed that the subsidiary managers in each market could freely purchase satellite time. However, in China access to satellite time was either totally blocked or severely restricted. In addition, the manager had not thought of the language implications. "Sitting around the table" only makes sense if the partners speak a common language. Non-native speakers of English who may be able to manage a conversation in English in a face-to-face situation may panic at the prospect of an intercultural multilingual teleconference. Participants may be worried about losing face or saying the wrong thing. The successful international manager will be aware that in a teleconference the person with the best idea may have the weakest language skills and never be heard. The sales manager's idea of the teleconference had to be abandoned.

Where telephone lines are limited, as in the former Soviet Block countries, faxing may be too cumbersome to be practical. It can take three to four days to send a fax from Russia to the United States because of the limited number of telephone lines. When the fax finally goes through, the quality may be so poor because of the weak lines that the fax is illegible.

E-mail is gaining in popularity because it is more direct, more efficient, and more private. E-mail makes sense, however, only if a majority of employees has access to it. An increasing concern is protection of privacy and company property; in a firm that has major concerns about trade secrets, electronic mail may not be a realistic channel. Therefore, many big firms have established intranets, a computer communication system that connects employees only within the firm as opposed to the Internet, which allows communication with anyone from anywhere. More recent technology allows E-mail delivery and emission without local area networks, and even without computers.

While the technology facilitates communication, it also raises the question of cultural adaptations of messages. For example, how can a firm adapt its message to specific cultural groups if the same Web page is available to anyone? Increasingly, companies design different Web pages for different language versions. A German firm, for example, had different pictures of its CEO for the German and English version of the home page. In the German version, the CEO was formal and serious—after all, business is serious. In the English version, on the other hand, the same CEO was smiling and appeared much more informal and friendly.

Even small businesses have found that the Web has opened the opportunity for international business. Managers in these businesses find themselves communicating worldwide even if they never considered a market outside their own country, with messages that traditionally were geared towards people from their own country and culture. Technology is forcing many of these small firms to become familiar with different communication styles and take the preferences of different cultures into consideration. For example, E-Bay is an American E-commerce company, but anyone can log on. As a result, people who put items for sale on E-Bay have to communicate with potential customers from all over the globe. In any number of cases the sellers have not been particularly user-friendly or interculturally competent. Likewise the buyers brought their own cultural expectations to E-Bay as well.

Concerns for Confidentiality

Where confidentiality is not guaranteed, channel choice may be limited. As a result, the communicator may have to use a channel that reduces the richness of the message. Both faxing and E-mail raise questions of confidentiality and privacy. If Maria Sanchez receives a letter sent by mail from the subsidiary in Singapore, she can control who will see this letter. She may have given her secretary permission to open all her mail and put it on her desk opened. She may, however, have requested that all correspondence addressed to her will come to her desk unopened. Furthermore, if the letter is stamped "confidential," she will be the only one to see it. She then can decide with whom to share the information.

If Maria receives an E-mail message, only she is supposed to have access to her mailbox with her password. However, it is fairly easy to break codes and enter E-mail boxes. E-mail does not guarantee confidentiality. The same is true for faxes. Even if the fax is addressed to Maria Sanchez, others may see the fax before she gets it. The person in charge of taking faxes from the fax machine, for example, will see it. If nobody is in charge of the fax machine, anyone walking by when a fax comes in may see it. The stamp "Confidential" may simply make it more enticing for others to read.

In countries where censorship is widely practiced and government agencies regularly monitor the content of mail, the confidentiality of E-mail and faxes is seldom guaranteed. Government monitoring of communication affects channel choice and impacts on the richness of the message and the channel. China, for example, is attempting to monitor access to and use of the Internet. The government is concerned about encryption technology and is requesting that all companies provide information on the specific encryption technology being used. Firms, of course, are concerned that this move will give the government access to all company information and pose a serious threat to competitive advantages and confidentiality of information.

At this point the legal situation in the United States and most other countries is not totally clear when it comes to the confidentiality and privacy implications of the new technology. To protect themselves and their employees, firms are developing companywide policies on the etiquette and the treatment of faxing.

Some companies make it very clear that E-mail and faxes are not the private property of the recipient but company property. They point out that any communication relating to the company is the property of the company. They may regularly monitor the use of E-mail. One company with which one of the authors consulted made five copies of all faxes coming into the firm and distributed a copy to the top five people. They copied *all* faxes, regardless of the nature. In that environment one is very much aware of the lack of privacy and confidentiality of certain channels. If incoming and outgoing messages are regularly available to other people in the firm, a manager may make channel decisions that influence the richness of the communication.

Cultural Environment of Channel Choice

The ideal channel is also culturally determined. In earlier chapters we pointed out that the Japanese, coming from a high-context culture, don't rank clarity as highly as people from low-context cultures. They have a higher tolerance for ambiguity. As a result, attitudes towards channel choice and richness in a Japanese business environment will be different from attitudes in low-context cultures. Since much of the meaning in Japanese communication is carried by nonverbal communication, often tiny nuances (from a Western viewpoint) in behavior and facial expressions, the Japanese prefer face-to-face communication. The personal contact allows them to get a better idea of true intentions and to establish personal rapport and harmony. Personal contact also provides an immediate context for the message. The non-Japanese businessperson must realize that these cultural elements will impact the channel choice in the Japanese environment even if all the modern technological channels are available.

In a company with a diverse workforce, announcements on bulletin boards may not be effective, particularly if many employees come from high-context cultures. Meetings may be a better channel because they combine verbal and nonverbal communication. Meetings may also fulfill the need for establishing closer personal relations for cooperation.

Language ability will also influence channel choice. Kumi Nakane, a manager from Nagoya, Japan, who speaks very little Arabic, may manage in a face-to-face situation, but she may be unable to communicate in Arabic over the phone and reluctant to say much in a videoconference. As soon as she is supposed to speak Arabic into a camera or into a phone, she freezes and forgets all the Arabic she has ever learned. She avoids these channels if at all possible. The phone and videoconference then are not realistic channels when Kumi Nakane must communicate with her Arabic speaking partners or clients. Yet these channels might provide the richness appropriate in a particular situation.

Managers who supervise a diverse workforce also find that the telephone may not be an appropriate channel. If the employee and the manager speak different languages, they may have to see *and* listen in order to understand. They will need a richer channel than the telephone. Pierre Madec, for example, never calls Mahen Aljanabi on the phone. He goes to his office when he needs to communicate with Mr. Aljanabi because Mr. Aljanabi's French is limited. He has improved very much over the last few months, but for the time being, they need the richer face-to-face communication.

With high-context cultures, the choice of a teleconference may prove less rewarding and less rich as a channel than expected. In teleconferences, only one speaker at a time can speak. For cultures whose members are accustomed to break in on another speaker's words, finish another's sentences, or pause and then resume even when another has begun speaking, the teleconference doesn't work very well.

What is the optimal channel, and what is the optimal packaging of the message? There is no easy answer. The right channel is the channel that will communicate the message most effectively and efficiently by providing the appropriate level of richness, and that changes with new technology.

THE RELATIONSHIP BETWEEN EFFECTIVENESS OF INTERCULTURAL BUSINESS COMMUNICATION AND POSITION IN THE ORGANIZATION

In Chapter 11 we pointed out that in a global organization the need for international and intercultural awareness is pushed down to lower levels in the organization. More people need a basic understanding of intercultural communication principles. Without a commitment to training of its employees, the global endeavor will face difficulties. Language ability and understanding of cultural priorities and values are necessary to function in this environment. The question then becomes, "What do people at various levels of the organization need to know about the international environment?"

The need for information and intercultural communication skills is closely tied to the functions of the various levels in the global or international firm. While the clerks in charge of international orders need an understanding of the procedures and processes the international partner uses, their understanding is of a different nature than the one required of the president of the firm. The president may not know the details of the ordering process, but she must have a broad understanding of the cultural values and legal requirements influencing business decisions and of the customary relationship with suppliers.

Successful international businesses are willing to spend time and effort on developing appropriate intercultural communication skills of their employees. By analyzing the communication needs of employees at various levels of the organization and tying those needs to the mission and goals of the firm, they can develop more effective selection and training processes. Rather than providing generic intercultural training, they assess the specific communication functions. In order to do this, they collect from experienced employees information on what intercultural communication skills are necessary in various jobs. They store and manage this information so that it is available for use when new people enter the intercultural communication arena. Successful international companies manage the knowledge that their expatriates and others in international functions have developed so that it can be used easily. An important result of this knowledge management is the increased retention rate of experienced employees and more effective intercultural communication practices.

Intercultural Business Communication Needs for Upper-Level Managers

Executives and top managers are in charge of setting policies and goals for the organization. They deal with the "big picture" and charter the broad course of the firm. They are typically not involved in the day-to-day running of the operation. Clearly, their communication needs and practices differ from those of the clerks in inventory management. Top management deals with complex problems, and complex problems require a different mix of channels, message organization, and message content. These managers and executives must get a sense of what others think in order to develop policies and explore various options. They will want to raise innovative and controversial ideas, discuss them, and play them back and forth with other managers. For this type of work, meetings are frequently more appropriate than formal reports.

Executives are looking for spontaneous and rapid feedback. They don't just look for what their partners say but how they say it, with what tone, nuances, and hesitation. In many ways, at this level, managers look for the "right feel" or flavor rather than hard data when making decisions.[3] Managers often refer to this as seat-of-the-pants management, which emphasizes intuition over reason.

In spite of all attempts to quantify organizational aspects, organizational reality is not objective. Statistical data pretend to report an objective, one-dimensional reality that does not exist in the mind-set of most managers, who are very well aware of the complexities of reality.[4]

Top managers who set the goals of the organization typically look for qualitative rather than quantitative information. They may concentrate on qualitative information to support existing policies and to develop new policies. They may, however, look at quantitative data, objective data, to overturn a policy or justify the change of existing policies. If that is true, then managers often will use objective information after the fact rather than in the process of arriving at a decision. Upper management scans the environment for anything that will influence the functioning and the goals of the organization. Face-to-face communication provides greater insights than formal reports or letters do because it combines verbal and nonverbal communication.

We are particularly interested in how upper-level managers achieve effective communication in an international environment. International managers jet around the globe on a regular basis. They visit subsidiaries and arrange meetings and conferences to discuss goals for the coming year or years. If they have taken the time to study their international customers, partners, and clients, they may be able to engage in meaningful communication during their visits and engage in fruitful discussions concerning policy issues.

In tight economic times, companies may argue that travel cost is getting out of hand and should be curtailed. They may decide to cut back the travel and have fewer people go abroad, but that may not be a wise decision if the visits facilitate effectiveness of communication that is crucial in keeping the firm efficient and profitable. As we have discussed throughout this book, the new technology has opened up new communication options. Managers can talk to each other in a teleconference. They can use E-mail to set up meetings and discuss issues. They can rely on satellite technology for better and more frequent telephone connections. These new channels can capture many of the nonverbal nuances that a letter or memo might not provide; however, the context of the communication will influence whether the technology is a good substitute for a true face-to-face meeting.

Not all international travel contributes to the effectiveness of communication. In some cases the communication may be less effective than the travel dollars indicate. Studies have shown that managers from Europe and North America are much more inclined to visit a subsidiary in Brazil during the winter months in the northern hemisphere than the summer months. They are much more inclined to go on a business trip to Paris than to Bombay. The schedules seem to indicate that at least part of the travel takes place because of personal preferences rather than strict business needs.

Companies that do not take great care in spending their travel budget often do not set clear goals for the face-to-face visits. Managers may visit a subsidiary without the necessary preparation at the home office, without a good grasp of conditions at the subsidiary, and without adequate intercultural communication skills. Managers who are successful communicators, on the other hand, go well prepared and have a good understanding of what they and the managers at the subsidiary need to discuss. To add to the effectiveness, they will then brief the rest of the management team after they return.

Once the businessperson is at the foreign site, the communication is not always as productive as it could be. For example, the foreign manager may arrange the meeting in a hotel *off-site* so the managers will not be disturbed by the operations in the subsidiary or constantly interrupted by the telephone and the regular office routine while discussing broad goals and strategies. One can make a point that the off-site location encourages better communication; however, the off-site location also removes the discussion from the physical place of activity and therefore at least some of the context for the business interaction. An executive may be abroad for several weeks and meet with many people from inside and outside the company but may not develop a feel for and deeper understanding of the operations in the subsidiaries. As a result, the communication may not be as effective and productive as it could be if the discussions were to take place on-site.

The manager from headquarters and the manager from the subsidiary may be worried about offending each other; therefore, they may not ask necessary questions or provide necessary information that could help them communicate better. In one case the vice president of the international division of a U.S. firm and the president of the Japanese subsidiary met to discuss the goals for the coming year. However, the vice president of the international division later confided that they hardly got beyond the golf game at hand, the weather, and basic business facts because the president of the subsidiary had limited English and the vice president did not speak any Japanese. Since officially the Japanese president spoke English, it would have been an insult to have an interpreter present. The fruitfulness of the discussion was severely limited because of linguistic limitations.

Effective communication at the upper levels in the firm has a positive impact on the functioning of the entire firm. The policies and broad guidelines developed by upper management need to be translated into rules and measurable procedures at the midlevel. That process requires clear communication between upper- and midlevel employees in the organization. In addition, top managers must continue their dialogue with their counterparts at the subsidiaries and keep them informed of how the discussions are translated into specific rules and guidelines. Midlevel managers also coordinate their efforts and keep their counterparts abroad informed. Furthermore, they communicate with lower-level employees. Successful companies are able to establish effective communication links between and within all levels of the organization so that each level can perform its tasks.

Intercultural Business Communication Needs for Middle-Level Managers

At the middle level, policies are fine-tuned and carried out. This requires different types of communication from the top level. The broad discussions at the upper level must now be supplemented with facts and data. Policies must be clarified. While meetings may be necessary, much of the communication can take place through memos, letters, and phone calls. The communication relates to more specific topics and becomes more concrete than at the upper level. It deals with specific issues rather than broad and general goals and policies. Ideas must be translated into rules, guidelines, and production and sales quotas.

Serendipity, a small firm from the United States doing business in Russia, needs regular information on performance of the Russian operation. The president has set the policies for reporting and discussed them with the Russian managers. The Russian managers now must translate the policies and the goal of accurate business and financial reporting into concrete steps. They must see to it that the president of Serendipity in the United States is informed of all events. The Russian managers must also see to it that information is prepared according to government regulations of the United States and Russia. The Russian managers translate the goals of accuracy, efficiency, and legal compliance into specific reports and documents. The lower-level employees at Serendipity then prepare the actual reports. The midlevel managers are the crucial link between the broad goals and the specific tasks.

In the case of Serendipity, the changing political and economic environment of Russia requires particularly effective communication. In the past, Russian firms did not prepare Western-style balance sheets and income statements. The Russian managers of Serendipity did not have the background to supervise the preparation of these documents, and they did not understand the need for this kind of information. The American president repeatedly requested these reports by fax, but the reports were not sent because the Russian managers simply did not understand what he wanted and why he needed that information.

The principles underlying business practices were so different that the Russian managers and the American president had a very hard time communicating effectively. Arguably, they did not engage in a rich enough exchange of communication to clarify ideas and discuss policies and procedures. The fax was not a rich enough channel—personal discussions were

necessary. That channel was difficult because of the cost of travel.

Also, the Russians did not understand the role, authority, and responsibilities of midlevel employees. They continued to function as they had in the past. Information represented power and was to be hoarded rather than shared. The concept of open communication channels was rather alien to them, but effective communication is based on open communication.

For Russian managers to become effective communicators will require more than an understanding of finance and cost accounting; they will need to rethink the goal and purpose of the business organization and its employees and rethink the role of communication. A U.S. manager may wonder and even be shocked at the independence of the Russian subsidiary and argue that his or her company would simply not tolerate such communication behavior. The reality is different. The Russians even today seem to function on the assumption, "Russia is big, and the Czar is far away." As a result, they tend to provide only the information they consider necessary.

In order for midlevel managers to perform efficiently, they need to understand the policies and procedures established at headquarters. It may be necessary for midlevel employees from foreign subsidiaries to travel to headquarters to observe the procedures and gain insight into cultural aspects of operations. As discussed in Chapter 11, international awareness—and with it international travel—has to be integrated throughout the firm in an increasingly international environment.

In companies with a diverse workforce, middle-level managers may need more face-to-face meetings and richer message channels than middle-level managers in a firm with a homogeneous workforce. The written reports and memos that constitute much of the communication at that level may not be sufficient to translate policies into guidelines. Both the managers and the employees may need more personal communication to avoid misunderstandings and to develop trust.

Middle-level managers have a variety of options to communicate effectively, and technology plays an increasingly important part in the process. Rather than sending proposals back and forth, they can discuss the options online in real time. They may use teleconferencing, or they may engage in discussions using a Group Decision Support System (GDSS). With a GDSS, participants can read the comments from everyone in the group, but they don't know who the author of each comment is. By allowing for the anonymous input of opinions and ideas, this technology may be particularly appropriate for multicultural and international groups.

In hierarchical cultures subordinates will seldom feel comfortable criticizing the ideas of a superior. They may also be reluctant to put their name to suggestions and new ideas in fear of being considered egotistic and too individualistic. GDSS can take away those barriers. Studies in Singapore have shown, for example, that GDSS resulted in a more open and productive discussion of problems because middle-level managers felt freer to give their opinions. However, it is also possible that the anonymity can lead to personal criticism and attacks because the commentator knows that he or she is anonymous.[5]

Intercultural Business Communication Needs for Lower-Level Employees

People at this level in the global organization deal with day-to-day operations and very concrete problems. They are concerned with shipping schedules, purchase orders, quality inspections, payment schedules, and financial reports. Much of this information is routine and formulaic. In fact, much of it is accomplished by filling in forms; nevertheless, with the new technology, employees at these levels may have regular contacts with people from around the globe.

A person at this level needs to have the technical vocabulary in his or her native language and preferably in the target language, but typically little abstract and theoretical thinking in the other language is required. In Chapter 11 we pointed out that in a global organization, the need for intercultural training is integrated throughout the organization. People at all levels must have a basic understanding of the intercultural issues; however, the necessary level of understanding differs depending on the position in the organization. As employees rise in the organization, they can build on the skills they acquired at the lower level. The training at the lower level lays the foundation for the more substantive and deeper understanding required at higher levels.

In many cases, employees at the lower levels of the organization appear to be very proficient in speaking a foreign language or dealing with businesspeople from other cultures. The appearance of fluency can be deceptive.

One of the authors purchased some lace in a lace shop in Antwerp. The shop attendant, a woman of about 60, could communicate without any difficulties in English. She appeared to have a large vocabulary when explaining about the different levels of quality and the origin of the lace. Her accent was excellent, and she was very easy to understand. It was only when the conversation went away from lace to other topics that it became apparent that her communication abilities in English were limited. She was fast to point out that she could talk about lace but very little else. She knew that she was good at selling lace, but she did not have the linguistic or cultural background to discuss other issues in English. She was very effective in what she did; she had the personality to deal with people from many different backgrounds in a very limited scope. She is a very good example of the intercultural and language competencies required for employees at lower levels. These people must have concrete knowledge in their area and be able to communicate that expertise to people from other cultural backgrounds.

Lower-level employees typically do not discuss overall company policies with each other or with foreign partners. At this level the how-to approach to cultural understanding may be sufficient as long as the company is aware of the limitations of that approach. As soon as the employee rises in the organization, the need for deeper cultural and broader linguistic understanding will increase to where the employee must not only understand the how-to but also the reasons behind business practices.

Firms in many industrialized countries employ an increasingly diverse workforce. Employees may speak a different language than the manager does, and they may come from a variety of different cultural backgrounds. The success of the business depends on good communication between diverse groups. Several firms offer language training for people who do not speak the country's language. For example, French firms offer French lessons, German firms offer German lessons, and U.S. firms offer English lessons to employees whose native language is different. Depending on the needs of the business, such language instruction for lower-level employees in the beginning concentrates on practical aspects and safety issues. Employees learn the vocabulary to perform the job and communicate about it.

At the same time, U.S., German, or French managers may learn some business vocabulary in the language of the employees to communicate job tasks and performance standards to employees on the factory floor. Basic intercultural communication training may be incorporated into the language training; however, the emphasis is on the improvement of performance rather than intercultural and language training for its own sake.

THE RELATIONSHIP BETWEEN EFFECTIVENESS OF INTERCULTURAL BUSINESS COMMUNICATION AND THE CULTURAL ENVIRONMENT OF THE FIRM

Cultural priorities have a powerful influence on the effectiveness of the message and channel choice. We have discussed the relationship between cultural priorities and communication throughout this book. Here we will summarize some of the major points that influence the effectiveness of the message.

Perceptions of Roles

At times the communication process is complicated because managers from different cultures may perceive their roles differently. They communicate with different perceptions and different self-reference criteria. For example, managers in the United States typically want to be in charge and run the organization. The Japanese may approach their jobs differently. If the two sides cannot agree on what the role of each side should be, they cannot communicate effectively.

The Japanese president of a U.S. subsidiary saw his role in a Japanese context, mostly as a public relations representative rather than leader of the organization. When the Japanese president was first hired, he did not even want to look at the financial performance in detail. He considered that to be the task of the vice president for finance. He saw his role as primarily external communication building relations with government officials, other businesses, and banks so that the Japanese subsidiary would be recognized in the Japanese business community. Headquarters, on the other hand, saw his role quite differently and expected a strong internal and external leader as president.

Linguistic Differences

If the two sides do not speak the same language, they may have to concentrate on basic facts rather than engage in a detailed discussion of issues. But the interpretation of those facts is an important factor in creating effective messages.

In some instances the effectiveness of the message is reduced because one side does not understand the concepts underlying the message. In that culture the concepts may not be well developed or they may not exist at all. A number of Russian managers, for example, speak fairly good English, but often they do not understand the business concepts behind the words. Given their background of collective ownership and a highly centralized economy, they know neither the Russian word, nor the English translation, nor the underlying concept. In a seminar on the principles of cost accounting and finance, the Russian participants had a hard time with the term *owner's equity*. When the translator did not know the term, a lively discussion started among the participants to clarify the concept. It took repeated discussions over several days before the meaning became clear. In this environment, it may be more difficult to achieve effective communication.

Attitudes toward Business

The potential for richness is also affected by the overall attitude towards business. In industrialized countries, business includes production, distribution, and service industries. Businesspeople from these countries take this so much for granted that they do not even point it out. Of course, retailing is business.

Russians look at business very differently. In the 1930s a law was passed that declared that anyone who buys a product from the state and sells it for a higher price is engaged in *speculation*. Speculation is not considered business but immoral profiteering. No wonder the distribution of goods has been such a problem over the years! The definition of distribution as speculation is deeply ingrained. It goes through all age groups and educational levels. There is always something suspicious about the person who makes a living in the distribution channel.

Russian businesses have detailed records of production statistics but nothing on distribution, cost of production, profitability, or marketing. Clearly, a Western businessperson who wants to engage in rich communication with Russian managers must be aware of this background in order to adapt his questions and comments in a discussion on cooperation.

Different Leadership Styles

Often headquarters and subsidiaries of global firms simply assume that they will function according to similar patterns and rules. However, this is seldom the case. As we have seen, the Japanese are consensus oriented; therefore, it is rare for one person to make a decision independently. The person who will get ahead is the one that fits in. The consensus attitude influences the exchange of ideas and has an influence on the richness of the communication.

German managers have great authority over their departments and can run their areas almost independently. They are recognized as the technical experts and specialists.[6] They enjoy great respect, but there are also many checks to their power. For example, they cannot just dismiss a person. Complex legal and work rules limit the power of the department head, and in larger organizations, workers are by law involved in decisions (see also Chapter 10).

In the United States managers have the power to make decisions, but good managers involve subordinates in the process. Managers are responsible for a decision regardless of whether or not they involve workers in the process, but they know subordinates have to carry out the decisions.

The Americans need to get information from others because they are specialists in an area; the Japanese need to get information because they are generalists. The organizational perceptions of the two groups are different; the needs are different; the views of the roles of employees in the organization are different; and consequently the way they communicate is different. People even view the purpose of a business organization very differently. As Charles Handy says, "The Japanese are in business to stay in business; the British [and we might add the Americans] are in business to make a profit."[7] A Japanese manager voiced the same idea by saying, "The business will be here forever." The underlying philosophy of the firm, in this case the view of permanency, influences the communication.

With these differing attitudes, people from different cultures view the need for communication in the functioning of the firm differently. Based on the discussion so far, in organizations in low-context cultures, we would expect many report forms, short memos, and faxes at the lower level, longer reports on setting goals at the middle level, and much face-to-face communication at the upper level. In an organization in a high-context culture, we would expect richer channels, meaning more face-to-face communication at all levels of the organization.

Growing Cultural Diversity in Domestic and International Operations

Businesses in many countries are facing a workforce with increasingly diverse cultural backgrounds, and they find that they need to communicate differently in that environment. Typically, a firm translates guidelines, rules, and handbooks into the native language or languages of employees, but effective communication involves more than the appropriate translation of words. The communication must be adapted to the various cultures of the employees and must take into account the different needs for richness. People from high-context cultures at all levels prefer richer communication channels than people from low-context cultures—they want to establish personal contact and deal with people at a personal level rather than through letters and memos. Employees from Bolivia may be willing to accept orders because of the hierarchical society they come from, but they may prefer to be given the order personally by the boss rather than by memo. When the boss talks to the employees face-to-face, they feel a personal tie that is absent in the written communication. The boss is not just the boss; he is also a father figure who should be there when the employee needs him. Culturally, employees in Bolivia prefer the richer, personal communication. Cultures that value efficiency may consider personal meetings a waste of time if a single memo can communicate the message to everyone.

As diversity in the workforce increases, ideal managers carefully evaluate how they communicate with their employees. They evaluate the content, the wording, and the organization of the message, as well as the channel. Everyone in the firm, from the president on down to the line employees, receives training in intercultural business communication.

It is increasingly difficult to determine the "typical" business behavior in a culture. Globalization has brought many changes, and on the surface many business behaviors appear Westernized. For example, in Japan the old *keiretsu* system is breaking down. *Keiretsu* are groupings of companies into close-knit units. Traditionally, Japan had seven *keiretsu*, among them the Mitsubishi Group and the Mitsui Group. Central to every *keiretsu* was a bank. Whenever possible, companies in a *keiretsu* would do business with each other rather than going outside the *keiretsu*. The *keiretsu* bank tied all of these companies together, and bank managers sat on the board of directors of all the companies in the keiretsu. During the last few years, the *keiretsu* system has started to break down. Increasingly, companies are going outside their *keiretsu* to get supplies for manufacturing. The old sense of *keiretsu* loyalty is fading and being supplemented with greater concern for efficiency and profitability. These changes will have far-reaching effects for communication practices. A few years ago it would have been unthinkable that a foreign firm, such as DaimlerChrysler, would purchase a one-third interest in Mitsubishi Motors, one of the companies in the Mitsubishi *keiretsu*.

The context of business communication in China has changed as well over the last few years (also see Chapter 11). Traditionally, all Chinese companies were state owned. Even though a growing number of Chinese work for private or joint-venture companies today, in reality most people still work for the state. Oil, coal, steel, heavy industry, transportation, banking, much light industry, health, education, agriculture, communications, and many other sectors are government run. One can distinguish between the big state-owned enterprises (SOEs) and the government "companies" run by provinces, counties, townships, and cities. The iron rice bowl was universal in the SOEs. Today that is changing since about three-quarters of the SOEs are unprofitable and many people have been laid off. Many of the former SOEs are now run as "companies" by the province or city or county.

Clearly, the communication context differs between the various types of businesses. A Chinese manager in a joint venture company, such as Caterpillar, will develop different communication behaviors than the employee who works in a state-owned enterprise. The small entrepreneurial firm will have different communication practices than the large international Chinese firm. The manager at Caterpillar may buy into the corporate culture of Caterpillar and adopt a much more Westernized approach to communication, at least on the surface.

When we talk about communication with Chinese managers, we need to take these changes into consideration and adapt our intercultural business communication behavior to the specific circumstances and context. The challenge for the foreign manager is to know exactly who the Chinese managers are and what they represent.

Feelings of Cultural Superiority

Feelings of cultural superiority and ethnocentrism can also influence the effectiveness of communication. After top executives return from visits to subsidiaries, they often issue rules to subsidiaries without further discussion and opportunity for feedback. This indicates lean communication and a lack of cultural awareness and understanding. Typically subsidiaries are helpless to protest, and they resent this approach to corporate communication. Managers at subsidiaries complain that they are given orders to do things differently starting next month without ever being told why they are supposed to do things differently. They may receive requests for information without ever being told why the information is needed. The statement, "The government requires it this way," does not communicate anything other than "Do it this way" because it does not put the message in context. The international business environment requires coordination, sensitivity, and understanding.

In one case, U.S. headquarters requested that, starting immediately, financial reports from the Japanese subsidiary had to be done differently. No reason or explanation was given. Only after repeated inquiries was the subsidiary told that the change was necessary to comply with the legal and financial requirements of the Finnish company that had bought the U.S. parent-firm. The new Finnish owners, the U.S. office, and the Japanese subsidiary all had to meet requirements of their own governments when reporting their performance. However, since the Finns were the new owners, everyone also had to conform to Finnish requirements. Even though executives had traveled the globe after the acquisition, there had not been a meaningful exchange of ideas and discussion of the communication impact of the new setup. People had talked to each other, but clearly the communication had not been very effective at any level.

Volume of Communication

Even though Daft and Lengel argue that upper levels prefer face-to-face communication for discussing policy issues, one would nevertheless expect some correspondence at the upper level about setting policies and the broad issues facing the company.[8] In reality, little of this complex communication seems to take place in written form. And given the language issues and cultural hurdles present in personal meetings, the richness of face-to-face communication also may be limited. Nevertheless, the volume of communication is there. Every manager involved in international business will point out the frequency of reports, the number of international visits and meetings, and the impact of technological developments on the volume of communication. Quantity, however, does not ensure effectiveness.

A number of studies have shown that specifically U.S. companies flood their international subsidiaries with written and oral communication. Part of this practice is related to the U.S. attitude towards time. Everything is pressing and urgent. In many cases U.S. firms stamp *Urgent* on the correspondence or request information *ASAP*. Of course, if everything is urgent, nothing is urgent, and the word loses its meaning. Americans make numerous follow-up phone calls and send second and third reminders that the need for information is crucial and urgent. If anything, technology has increased the flood of communication. Another reason the volume has increased is because the United States is a low-context culture where messages are explicitly encoded in order to avoid ambiguity and promote clarity. In many instances the communication is ineffective, thus ensuring the need for follow-up.

A Japanese firm, over a two-year period, tripled the number of faxes going out and coming into the subsidiary. At the same time the sales volume had doubled, but the increase was handled by the same dealers; the firm had not set up any new dealerships. The increase in correspondence was mostly due to increased communication between headquarters and the Japanese subsidiary and came at a time when faxing became popular.

Most of the communication was at a very low level of richness. Not a single case of the written correspondence addressed policy issues. In many cases faxes simply double-checked information that had been sent or requested earlier. Either the recipient did not understand the correspondence or could not read the writing. In some cases the fax quality was low, and a second request was necessary. Since faxing was so easy, everyone sent faxes without thinking through the purpose and the goal of the communication. In one extreme case, it took 32 faxes to arrange the visit of two Japanese employees at the Chicago office.

A SUMMARY OF THE INTERFACE BETWEEN CHANNEL, POSITION IN THE FIRM, AND CULTURAL ENVIRONMENT

Managers examine the need for communication in the context of the organization. Once managers have evaluated channel choices, determined the communication in view of their position in the corporate structure, and assessed the cultural environment of their own firm and the firm they are working with, they can encode the message to achieve the desired richness.

We can present the three components that influence richness in a model that will help us visualize their interdependence (see Exhibit 12–2). The channel choices are on one axis, the position in the firm on a second axis, and the cultural environment on a third axis. The effectiveness of the message is the dependent variable that is determined by the interaction of the other three variables.

The effectiveness of a message depends on the specific communication context and the interplay of all the variables including the channel, cultural environment, and position in the firm. Lean channels can be as effective as rich channels; the manager has to determine what the communication needs are and what works best in a particular environment. Upper-level managers have different communication needs than lower-level managers. A global firm needs to adapt to many different cultures and change its communication strategy accordingly.

RECOMMENDATIONS FOR SUCCESSFUL INTERCULTURAL BUSINESS COMMUNICATION

Successful intercultural business communication means that a person can encode and decode a message using symbols and signs that are part of the other person's repository or cultural background.[9] It takes time and sensitivity to develop that competence. Based on the discussion of the previous chapters, we can establish some guidelines that all firms can follow to improve their intercultural business communication and performance.

1. Train all employees at all levels in intercultural business communication skills. Training should be appropriate for each level and address the concerns of employees at

EXHIBIT 12–2   Determinants of Effectiveness of Message

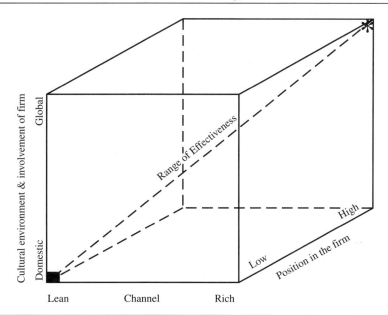

varying levels in the corporation. Currently many consultants provide intercultural train-ing, and companies should evaluate trainers carefully. How much international expertise does the trainer have? What is the cultural, linguistic, and business background of the trainer/consultant?

2. Send more people to foreign subsidiaries and don't restrict travel to top executives. Foreign travel should not be a perk; it should meet specific business goals. It may be more productive for the administrative assistant to visit the foreign subsidiary, if that assistant deals with international partners on a daily basis, than for the supervisory manager to go all the time.

3. Train employees in intercultural communication skills early in their careers. At this point employees are cheaper and more flexible. Furthermore, the company can take advan-tage of the increased intercultural understanding of an employee at an earlier stage. The Europeans provide intercultural training and experience much earlier than U.S. firms. As a result, they have an advantage. Some businesspeople in the United States argue that it is not cost effective to train lower-level employees, that after spending the money on the employee, he or she may leave the company and find employment elsewhere. As a result, the investment is wasted. The employee may indeed leave, but that is part of the cost of doing business. On the other hand, an employee who may think of leaving the firm may stay if given international and intercultural opportunities early in the career.

4. Carefully evaluate employees as they are hired. It is not enough to look for the degree in business, marketing, or finance. Interpersonal skills, language ability, a sense of adven-ture, and an open attitude may be much more important than specific technical skills.

Laura Bozich interviewed for a position marketing electronic telephone equipment. She had a good sense of international affairs, had traveled widely, and had a masters degree in International Management from Thunderbird, but she had no background in technology. During the interview her lack of technical expertise became an issue. Laura took a deep breath and then said: "If you hire me, you will get my expertise, my intercultural background, and my interpersonal communication skills. You can train me in the technology. Or you can hire an engineer who has all the technical background but no understanding of the international environment. You can train the engineer in cross-cultural communication. What do you think is going to be easier?"

Laura got the job, and she has been doing extremely well. The company was able to understand the importance of intercultural communication and flexibility. Clearly, technical expertise is important, but technical expertise alone does not guarantee success.

5. Above all, encourage a climate of excitement, adventure, and open-mindedness. Listen to a multitude of voices and synthesize them to create a unified and effective environment for intercultural business communication.

SUMMARY

In this chapter we have tied together all the variables that determine the effectiveness of intercultural business communication:

- *The relationship between effectiveness and channel choice.* Technology has broadened the channel options. Managers need to evaluate the effectiveness of each channel in order to determine the most appropriate channel for any given context.
- *The relationship between effectiveness of intercultural business communication and position in the organization.* The position in a firm influences the appropriate level of intercultural business communication skills. Upper-level managers have different needs from lower-level managers.
- *The relationship between effectiveness of intercultural business communication and the cultural environment of the firm.* Globalization changes the cultural environment of a firm. As a result, the communication requirements change as well. Rather than looking at Chinese culture, managers of international firms today need to look at Chinese culture in state-owned firms, Chinese culture in privately held firms, and Chinese culture in joint ventures. The context of the particular environment shapes the intercultural business communication practices.
- *Recommendations for successful intercultural business communication.* Companies must carefully select and train their employees for intercultural business communication. They must expose them to the international arena throughout their careers and foster a climate of open-mindedness and adventure.

NOTES

1. R. Daft and R. Lengel, "Information Richness: A New Approach to Managerial and Organizational Design," in B. Straw and L.L. Cummings, eds., *Research in Organizational Behavior,* (Greenwich, CT: JAI Press, 1984), pp. 191–233.

2. Ibid.

3. E. Borganda and R. Nisbett, "The Differential Impact of Abstract versus Concrete Information," *Journal of Applied Social Psychology* 7 (1977), pp. 258–271. C. O'Reilly, "Individual and Information Overload in Organizations: Is More Necessarily Better?" *Academy of Management Journal* 23 (1980), pp. 684–96.

4. J. Martin and M. Powers, "Skepticism and the True Believer: The Effects of Case and/or Baserate Information on Belief and Commitment," paper presented at the Western Psychological Meetings, Honolulu, HI, 1980.

5. M. Neumann, K. Razaki, R. Sarathy, and I.I. Varner, A Framework for the Applicability of Group Support Technology to Multicultural Groups, *Journal of Business and Behavioral Sciences* 1(1), (1995), pp. 44–54.

6. C. Handy, C. Gordon, I. Gow, and C. Randlesome, *Making Managers,* (Avon, Great Britain: Bath Press, 1988).

7. Ibid.

8. Daft and Lengel, "Information Richness."

9. L. Beamer, "Learning Intercultural Communication Competence," *Journal of Business Communication* 29, no. 3, (1992), pp. 285–304.

Index